The Peaceful Path

The Peaceful Path

Building Garden Cities and New Towns

Stephen V. Ward

Hertfordshire Publications
an imprint of
UNIVERSITY OF HERTFORDSHIRE PRESS

First published in Great Britain in 2016 by
Hertfordshire Press
an imprint of
University of Hertfordshire Press
College Lane
Hatfield
Hertfordshire
AL10 9AB

British Library Cataloguing in Publication Data
A catalogue record for this book is available from the British Library

ISBN 978-1-909291-69-0

Design by Arthouse Publishing Solutions Ltd
Printed in Great Britain by Henry Ling Ltd, Dorchester

To Maggie

Contents

Figures

Note on referencing conventions

In the references for each chapter published works are cited in full on first mention, subsequently in abbreviated form. Abbreviations for archival sources are listed below. In the individual references, the class and piece numbers of the files concerned follow the source reference.

Abbreviations

HALS   Hertfordshire Archives and Local Studies, Hertford
LUSCA Liverpool University Special Collections and Archives, Liverpool
NA   The National Archives, Kew, London
RIBA   Royal Institute of British Architects Archives, Victoria and Albert Museum, London

Preface

This book brings together the fruits of many years of work and interest in what can be called the Garden City tradition. As a student in the late 1960s and early 1970s I was fortunate (and I think unique) to be able to study at the University of Birmingham under both Gordon Cherry and Tony Sutcliffe. Between them (though at that stage separately) they spurred my interest in the history of urban planning. In Britain that history was very intimately linked to the development of the Garden City tradition, from which the nascent planning movement drew most of its conceptual basis during the early decades of the twentieth century. Gordon provided the opportunity to produce my first major publication on this theme, an edited book, in 1992, since when it has remained a recurrent element in my work and writings.

Yet, for all the many book chapters, articles, conference papers and consultancy reports, there never seemed to be an opportunity until now to author a substantial book on this subject. So I was pleased to be invited by Jane Housham of the University of Hertfordshire Press to write such a book. I was even more pleased to discover how astonishingly patient she was capable of being while I slowly fulfilled my commitment to write it. I sincerely hope that she, in turn, is pleased with the result.

A working lifetime's worth of debts to others has also been incurred in accumulating what has gone into this book. The names I have mentioned already are, of course, high on that list. So too are all those who have assisted in getting hold of relevant archives, books and other publications. These include Hertfordshire Archives and Local Studies, the First Garden City Heritage Museum in Letchworth, Stevenage Museum and the librarians in charge of local collections in the county's various local libraries. They also include staff at The National Archives at Kew, London, the Town and Country Planning Association, the Bodleian Library in Oxford and the University of Liverpool Special Collections and Archives. Last, but by no means least, are staff at the library of my own institution, Oxford Brookes University, who were always willing to acquire relevant literature even from the most far distant sources.

And then there are the many debts to other scholars who have shared this interest. It may surprise general readers to discover just how many researchers not only in this country but also in many other parts of the world have invested time and effort in uncovering various dimensions of the story that I have to some extent synthesised here. The international planning-history network that was forged by Gordon Cherry and Tony Sutcliffe has devoted a lot of energy to examining how the garden city idea was invented, interpreted and reinvented across the continents. The debt that I owe to many of them will be obvious in the references to each of the chapters and it will be impossible to mention all of them here. However, I particularly thank Mervyn Miller, John Gold, Dennis Hardy, Robert Freestone, Mark Clapson, Dirk Schubert, Mike Hebbert, Helen Meller, Shun-ichi Watanabe, the late Kermit Carlyle Parsons and the late Sir Peter Hall. By their writings and, often, by more specific assistance they have all contributed in some way to the shaping of this book. Naturally, of course, they bear no responsibility for its contents.

Finally, there are the personal debts. I thank all those with whom I have worked happily for so long at Oxford Brookes University (I particularly thank those members of the Faculty Research Committee, whose decisions helped with some travel and other expenses incurred in researching and writing this book). And then last, though certainly not least, there is my deep personal debt to my much-loved wife, Maggie, with whom I have shared my life for many decades. She has cheerfully put up with my research trips (some of which she even accompanied me on), prolonged spells at my desk and general air of distraction for many months. It is, therefore, with my deepest love and as a small token of thanks that I dedicate this book to her.

Grandpont, Oxford
May 2015

CHAPTER ONE

Ebenezer Howard

A peaceful path[1]

Where should this story begin? Perhaps in the memory of a small boy who, years later, still recalled a strange and striking scene near his childhood home in Guessens Road, Welwyn Garden City.[2] Over the last few days of April 1928, outside Number 5, the road's surface was covered with a thick layer of straw. The episode lodged itself in the mind of this boy, Thomas Welwyn Osborn, because it was no common occurrence in his home town. Actually it was very rare indeed anywhere by that date. It was a scene that might have come directly from nineteenth-century London. Gravely ill people, usually figures of some wealth or status, were by this simple means spared something of the noise that daily characterised the streets of what was then the biggest city in the world. This

Figure 1.1 The house in Guessens Road, Welwyn Garden City, where Ebenezer Howard died. (author photograph)

simple practice gave a degree of calm and peace to the final steps on the path leading from life to death. And, because it was an act that took place on a public stage, it was a prelude to the final public ceremony of the funeral itself.

Number 5 (Figure 1.1) was one of the smaller houses in this part of the road, smaller than the one across the road where Tom Osborn himself lived. Inside it Sir Ebenezer Howard, inventor of the garden city and initiator of the two practical experiments at Letchworth and Welwyn Garden City, lay dying. His final days were spent in circumstances that were not exactly deprived but certainly lacking in comfort.[3] Indeed, during the first days of his final illness, he had been obliged to remain day and night on the sofa. Apart from the marital bed, there was no spare in the house until a visiting friend, shocked at seeing the discomfort the old man was forced to endure, had provided another bed that he could use.

Nor was there much real tenderness that might have compensated for this lack of material comfort. Ebenezer's relationship with his second wife, a woman of some mental fragility, was not an easy one. One of Howard's daughters from his first marriage (admittedly not an unbiased observer) reported that she made his home life miserable. Certainly, for several years they had lived separate lives. He had returned a few years before his death because he appears to have taken pity on her (and, very possibly, because his financial means, always slender, were no longer capable of supporting two separate households). But her impatience with the cause to which he had given his life remained. She may have been motivated by a desire to protect him but even his close relatives and associates found it difficult to visit him during his final illness because of her hostility.

Outside the straw strewn in the road displayed a very different public response. It had been put there on the orders of the estates department (headed by young Tom's father, Frederic) of the company responsible for building Welwyn Garden City. We might wonder whether it really did anything to deaden noise. Howard's home was close to the centre of the new garden city but Guessens Road, though it was not far from the company's builders' yard and saw mill, was no busy thoroughfare. The symbolism of the straw was perhaps its most important aspect. Primarily it was a signifier of civil respect – here was a truly great and generous man who had, at much personal cost to himself, made a desire to enhance the public good into his life's work. Now, as he approached his end, a genuinely public display of concern and consideration was a way of trying in a small way to repay his labours.

In a more subtle and unconscious way, it also harked back to the London of Howard's own boyhood, that noisy, teeming city which had variously stimulated and appalled him, and ultimately spurred him to dream of another way of living.

It further served to locate Howard as a figure very much of the nineteenth century. His conception of the big city was one of streets crowded with people, lined with densely occupied buildings and filled with the noisy clatter of horse-drawn traffic on cobbled streets.

Researching Ebenezer's journey

Yet, tracing the exact intellectual and moral journey that Howard made from this hectic life in the heart of London to, in his own term, the 'invention' of the garden city is no easy task. Only a small, confusingly arranged and altogether rather unrewarding Howard archive has survived. In part, this was another result of his second wife's lack of sympathy with his work and anger with his associates in the garden city movement. There are reports that, after his death, she made a bonfire in the garden of most of his papers and notebooks.[4] Under the terms of Howard's will, his son took possession of what remained. The papers subsequently went through several (ostensibly more caring) hands, but almost certainly suffered further fragmentation and losses.

Now, at least, the surviving collection of Howard's papers is being carefully kept in the Hertfordshire County Archives, but the following terse comment in their catalogue in description of one bundle in his Archive speaks volumes about what has happened to the whole collection over the years: 'The torn correspondence … would appear to be the contents of a waste paper basket'.[5] In some different respects, however, there is cause for optimism. Other archives of the garden city movement, particularly the immaculately organised papers of Tom's father, Frederic Osborn, who was a close supporter of Howard, give much more detail about the last 30 years of his life.[6] But the years before 1898, when he finally published his great exposition of the garden city, *To-morrow: a peaceful path to real reform*, remain shadowy.

Both his biographers, Dugald MacFadyen in 1933 and Robert Beevers in 1988, have therefore struggled to provide entirely convincing accounts of this part of his life and thus a key part of the story.[7] MacFadyen's biography was also so coloured by the author's admiration of his subject that it must be regarded as little more than a work of hagiography. However, despite the problems he faced in researching it, the later account by Beevers can be regarded as a scholarly, reliable and insightful work. Osborn, who at one time had hoped to write a full biography, faced the same difficulties in his various shorter insights on Howard's life and work.[8] Finally, we should also note the important contributions of other Howard scholars, particularly Robert Fishman and Stanley Buder as well as, more recently, the insightful work of Peter Hall, Colin Ward and Dennis Hardy.[9]

Early years

What, then, can be said about how Howard spent his life before 1898? The basic facts are easily recounted. He was born at 62 Fore Street in 1850 in the City of London, into a lower-middle-class family. His father, also called Ebenezer, was a confectioner with several small shops, including the one at the junior Ebenezer's birthplace. Extensive wartime bombing, post-war commercial redevelopment and alterations to the street pattern in this part of the City have meant that neither the building nor its site now exists. In 1850, and even up to World War II, the district was a mix of big warehouses and small shops. Today it is occupied by Moor House, a vast iconic office building designed by Foster and Partners.

The young Ebenezer was sent away from London to be educated when he was four and a half. He proved a slow learner initially, but later began to show some promise. At fifteen he left school, with the family intending that he would be a City clerk, like many thousands of other young men from his social background. He largely worked making written copies of business letters. Other than an unusual facility for shorthand writing, which he learnt in his late teenage years, there was nothing remarkable about him. Not unusually, however, he was restless, changing jobs several times in about three years. In 1871 he threw over this rather conventional and tedious pattern of lower-middle-class life to emigrate with two friends to the United States.

He had no very clear idea of what he wanted from this change and seems to have been motivated by romantic notions of the rugged frontier life. In the wake of the 1862 Homestead Act and the increasing pace of railroad construction, this was very much the time when young men were being encouraged to 'go west'. By March 1872 Howard and his friends were homesteading on adjoining 160-acre (65-hectare) quarter sections in the coincidentally named Howard County, Nebraska, some 120 miles due west of Omaha. The land was essentially free on filing title to anyone who was prepared to occupy and improve it (provided they had not fought against the United States).

But the life was hard and it did not suit Howard. City born, with absolutely no farming experience, he soon, like many others, had to accept that he had failed. The romance of the frontier life disappeared as he experienced its realities. Living, very probably, in a typical sod hut on Nebraska's treeless terrain and daily facing gruelling physical labour to clear the land and begin cultivation soon proved too much. The highlight of his brief engagement with frontier life was, improbably enough, an encounter with 'Buffalo Bill' Cody, who began his famous Wild West touring show about the time Howard arrived in the United States.[10] Howard was particularly impressed with Cody's gun, almost certainly the trusted

Springfield rifle used to establish his reputation as a buffalo hunter. Although the encounter is no more than a fascinating footnote in the prehistory of the garden city movement, it was, perhaps, the only moment when the romantic frontier world Howard imagined from teenage readings of *The Boys Own Magazine* even half coincided with reality. Within the year he had moved to the booming city of Chicago and what was, for him, the much more familiar world of shorthand writing, increasingly in a legal context.

He remained in the city for another four years, during which it was still being rebuilt following the great fire of 1871 to become arguably the world's most dynamic and innovative city at that time. Witnessing all the enterprise, energy and technological innovation that were being harnessed in the making of a major city made a deep impression. For the young Howard, then in his mid-twenties, these years were also important in other ways. Prompted by a Quaker colleague and friend he began to read seriously while in Chicago. As a result, he began to move towards – again, in his own words – 'a perfect freedom of thought', unencumbered by religious preconceptions. This gave him, in his own later assessment, 'a fuller and wider outlook on religious and social questions than I think I should have then gained in England'.[11]

Yet this rejection of narrowly doctrinal approaches and the opening of his mind to more rational and scientific ways of thinking did not mean that he ever abandoned religion in any fundamental way. His freethinking came with a growing interest in the connections between the spiritual and the material worlds. The transcendentalist writings of Ralph Waldo Emerson and Henry Thoreau strengthened this interest, characterised as they were by a particular interest in the human relationship to nature.[12] His few months in Nebraska had clearly forced him to confront and try unsuccessfully to tame a far harsher and less forgiving kind of nature than the transcendentalists themselves had experienced, but their themes were now ones that would have made more sense to him. At this stage they were not particularly prominent in his own thinking, but they recurred, of course, in his later formulation of the garden city. Like many Victorians, he was, however, strongly drawn to spiritualism. In his case the interest was sparked by Mrs Cora Richmond, a well-known American spiritualist, who he first heard speak in Chicago in 1876, shortly before his return to England.

Becoming a social reformer

Exactly why he returned permanently to England is, like much else about his early life, unclear. Throughout his subsequent career he maintained contacts with the United States and visited the country on several other occasions. The young man had been changed for life by his years there and retained a definite 'Americanist' strand in his outlook and thinking. But, once back in London, he resumed his stenographic work, increasingly in parliamentary or similar settings. Through this occupation he became a silent witness and faithful recorder of important episodes in public affairs in the last quarter of the nineteenth century. It was a time of rapid urban growth, especially of the big cities, where there were increasing tensions between the needs of capital and the growing aspirations of labour. Many shades of reformist opinion were calling for improvements in social conditions to manage and defuse these conflicting pressures. At the same time he continued the broader intellectual quests he began during his stay in Chicago.

A particularly important year in his life was 1879. It saw his first, and very happy, marriage to Elizabeth (Lizzie).[13] He also joined a freethinking debating group, the Zetetical Society, which was eclectically liberal, radical and Darwinist in its outlook, increasingly rejecting religion in favour of an activist and reformist humanitarianism.[14] Its adherents included many future members of the Fabian Society, a hugely important group of socialist intellectuals founded in 1884. Howard was never strongly drawn to party politics, although at this stage in his life he favoured the Liberal Party. He never joined the Fabians but during the early 1880s the Zetetical Society brought him into contact with many of those who became its key figures. They included the budding socialist playwright George Bernard Shaw (who became an admirer and friend, though never an uncritical one) and future Labour Party intellectual and government minister Sidney Webb. Howard was certainly not a major contributor to Zetetical Society proceedings but in 1880 he presented two papers on spiritualism, indicating that it was continuing interest of his. He also encountered Cora Richmond again and was even more impressed, particularly when she told him he had 'a message to give to the world'.[15]

On their own, such portentous words are rarely sufficient to change the trajectory of a person's life, unless they are giving expression to thoughts and ambitions that are already half-formed in the mind of their subject. During the 1880s Howard certainly appears to have become genuinely personally ambitious for real achievement that would make a positive difference, but for many years much of his inventive energy was concentrated on the development and improvement of mechanical gadgets concerned with the world of shorthand and typing. He never entirely abandoned these interests and, in fact, died with debts incurred trying to perfect a stenographic machine. We know from his letters to the long-suffering Lizzie that in the mid-1880s he strove to make a success of one invention, a proportionate spacing device. To this end, he made two unsuccessful

American visits trying to sell the idea to the major typewriter manufacturers. Although there is no way to be certain, it is tempting to see his more complete concentration on social reform matters from the late 1880s as a compensatory redirection of his inventive energies in the wake of these disappointments.

The sources of Howard's vision

Yet this was a shift in emphasis rather than a complete change of direction, as the roots of his social ideas about cities had clearly begun well before this time. Even before he left for the United States in 1876 he had encountered an English pamphlet written by Dr Benjamin Ward Richardson entitled *Hygeia, or the City of Health*.[16] Richardson advanced an urban vision that was the antithesis of the big cities at the time. Hygeia would be a low-density city, with wide streets, an underground railway and ample parkland. In that sense, it presaged some of the elements that would soon be adopted by Howard, who was, by the late 1880s, taking an ever-growing interest in the flow of reformist literature, much of which was the subject of debate at the Zetetical Society.

An important feature of Howard as an urban visionary was that he saw that it was not enough simply to imagine an ideal; it was necessary also to develop practical means by which it might be realised. In this regard he soon recognised the critical importance of land in determining the nature and quality of urban life.[17] The land taxing ideas of the American land reformer Henry George became widely known in Britain during the 1880s, shortly after the publication of his famous work *Progress and poverty*.[18] Meanwhile, an alternative, more specifically British, approach to the land question was being promoted by Alfred Russel Wallace, who founded the Land Nationalisation Society (LNS) in 1881.[19]

The principal inspiration for the common ownership of land that the LNS sought had come from Herbert Spencer's 1851 book *Social statics*,[20] which challenged the moral legitimacy of private landownership. Although Spencer's later writings took more libertarian and social Darwinist positions, this, his first book, was a seminal work of English socialism, more important in founding British socialist thought than Marx's later work *Capital*, and held in high regard within the Zetetical Society. Yet the LNS programme also went back much further even than Spencer. It revived the arguments of a radical 1775 pamphlet, *Property in land every one's right*, by Thomas Spence, that was given a new timeliness by being re-published (as *The nationalisation of land in 1775 and 1882*) by the socialist H.M. Hyndman in 1882.[21] Spence advocated that all land should be owned collectively by self-governing, democratic parishes, whose inhabitants would then pay their parish a single rent-tax which would be used to provide them with all services and welfare. These were ideas which resonated in Howard's own evolving thinking.

A plethora of other ideas and schemes came to Howard's attention (some by the descriptions of others, rather than in their original form) during the 1880s. From his reading of John Stuart Mill's *Principles of political economy* he discovered Edward Gibbon Wakefield's *The art of colonisation*, published originally in 1849.[22] Despite being a controversial and personally rather dubious figure, Wakefield persuasively outlined what seemed a credible scheme for the free and organised settlement of overseas colonies, especially Australia and New Zealand.[23] Integral to his proposals were consciously planned towns to balance agricultural settlement. Given reality by colonial surveyors in places such as Adelaide, Wellington, Nelson, Christchurch and Dunedin, the towns associated with his projects included town reserves and town belts that were intended to remain (and, to some extent, have remained) free of building development. This systematic approach to territorial colonisation, including planned and spacious urban settlements, certainly helped to shape Howard's evolving reformist ideas.

Another vision of an ideal city, earlier than Richardson's, that came to his attention at this time was that proposed within James Silk Buckingham's *National evils and practical remedies*, also published in 1849.[24] Running to more than 500 pages, Buckingham's rather diffuse arguments included (among very much else) a scheme for a model town called 'Victoria'. Housing some 10,000 people, it was to be spaciously laid out in a geometric fashion on a site one mile square. At its centre there was a very large public square with a tower, from which eight avenues radiated diagonally or at right angles to the edges of the town. The houses and other buildings were arranged concentrically outwards from the central square, with continuous rows between these avenues and corridors of public space separating each line of buildings.

Howard also began to see that the improvement of the conditions of urban life might also be linked to changing economic realities. By the later nineteenth century the circumstances which had favoured factories clustering in big cities were starting to weaken, increasingly facilitating spatial decentralisation of production from the centre of cities to their outskirts. In 1884 the distinguished economist Alfred Marshall advocated harnessing the movement of manufacturing from the big cities to factory villages in rural areas.[25] Such a strategy would also permit real improvements in the housing conditions of the urban poor and offset the marked declines in rural population and agriculture evident at that time. Again, such thinking directly fed Howard's own maturing

Figure 1.2 (Left) Edward Bellamy, the American author of *Looking backward*, which Howard arranged to be published in Britain in 1888. Bellamy envisaged the United States transformed into a technological socialist utopia. His ideas divided socialist opinion and directly stimulated William Morris's *News from nowhere* (1890), which also helped focus Howard's thinking. (author's collection)

Figure 1.3 (Right) Portrait of Ebenezer Howard at about the time that *To-morrow* was published, c.1898. (Garden City Collection, Letchworth Garden City)

ideas. From this and many others of the texts he read, he collected quotations that were to appear in his book.

By the late 1880s there were clear signs that Howard's engagement with radical reformist thought was assuming a progressively more active form. In 1888, for example, it was Howard who actually helped organise the printing in England of an American work which had impressed him. This was *Looking backward*, a visionary novel by an American, Edward Bellamy (Figure 1.2), which tells the story of a young American who falls asleep in 1887, only waking up after 113 years.[26] While he has been sleeping the United States has become a socialist utopia where new technologies have transformed daily life. This scenario provided Bellamy with a platform to criticise contemporary capitalism and promote a socialist alternative involving the nationalisation of all industry. It was a very widely read work, highly regarded by Marxists, which also had a great catalytic influence on Howard's own thinking. Along with other English radical thinkers, however, including William Morris, he had misgivings about Bellamy's evident endorsement of authoritarianism.

Writing *To-morrow*

To judge by the surviving archival material, Howard had begun by about 1890 to synthesise these many influences into a visionary proposal of his own. He was by this time a married man entering his 40s with four children, living what was in most respects a typical lower-middle-class life in a modest suburban home in north London (Figure 1.3). In 1891 he drafted a paper called 'The city of health and how to build it', a reference back to Richardson's *Hygeia* but showing how communal landownership might actually make its realisation possible.[27] At this stage, however, he did not use the term 'garden city'. The archival organisation of his surviving writings is confused, making chronological ordering difficult. It appears, though, that the first name he favoured for his model settlement was 'Unionville'. However, by the spring of 1892, when he drafted a book-length manuscript that was in many important respects similar to that eventually published in October 1898, the preferred name for his ideal settlement had become 'Rurisville'.[28] The first few chapters of his draft were typed up and privately circulated. Crudely drawn prototype versions of his famous diagrams also appeared (along with some others which never made it to the final published book). Howard also began to lecture widely on this topic.

The initial interest in his ideas, such as it was, came largely from the Land Nationalisation Society and, even more so at this early pre-publication stage, the Nationalisation of Labour Society. This body had been formed in 1890 to promote the ideas of Edward Bellamy in Britain. Thanks to Buder's investigations, we know that the Nationalisation of Labour Society provided Howard in early 1893 with his first important public platform to speak about his proposals.[29] We also know that, at about the same time, he became involved in a communitarian project that was promoted mainly by the Nationalisation of Labour Society. The conception and form of the intended project largely reflected Bellamy's ideas, rather than Howard's, envisaging a more collectivist kind of society than Howard ever wished to see. Nothing actually came of the project and Howard made no specific reference to it in his later writings. Through it, however, he did learn of an ambitious but failed model collectivist colony at Topolobampo in Mexico, which did warrant a brief mention in *To-morrow* as it was finally published.[30]

The paucity of documentary evidence means that Howard's early links with the Nationalisation of Labour Society remain rather shadowy. Yet we can perhaps surmise that he was rather chastened by the whole experience of working with an organisation which wanted to make such profound changes to the organisation of society. At any rate, he seems subsequently to have distanced himself from the Society. He continued intermittently to push his own ideas over the next few years, so far as his rather strained financial circumstances would permit. But he had no private income and the needs of his growing family certainly did not allow him to reduce his professional commitments. He also continued to modify and refine his draft book, especially the later chapters.

By 1896 he seems to have finalised the ideas that two years later appeared in print. During that year he submitted a prospective article to the *Contemporary Review*,[31] a leading journal for political discussion which, for example, Alfred Marshall had used to air his own thinking about factory villages. Howard's submitted paper, effectively a summary of his ideas, corresponded very closely indeed with the book which appeared two years later; and, although the article was rejected, it is especially notable in understanding the maturation of Howard's thinking because it marks his first use of the term 'garden city' in preference to 'Rurisville' or 'Unionville'.

Quite where this new term came from is unclear. Some have linked it to the planned settlement of Garden City on Long Island, New York, founded by the millionaire Alexander T. Stewart in 1869.[32] Still more claims have been made for Chicago, which, before the 1871 fire, had been known as the 'city in a garden' (*urbs in horto*).[33] In this connection, much has been made of Riverside, a celebrated railroad garden suburb designed by the famous American park designer Frederick Law Olmsted. This was beginning to be developed when Howard lived in Chicago during the 1870s. Yet Howard denied all such claims and, certainly, there is no mention of Stewart's Garden City, Chicago or Riverside in his book (which has no shortage of references to many other places, ideas and people). Others have argued that the term came from William Morris, who appears to have used it in the 1870s. It does not, however, appear in *News from Nowhere*, Morris's own arcadian and romantic vision of a London transformed (written partly as a riposte to Bellamy), published in 1890.[34]

Yet, whatever his actual source for this key term, it seems likely that, by 1896, Howard had completed the finished book. Not surprisingly, no publisher was prepared to treat it as a commercial proposition without some financial contribution from Howard himself. This was a major obstacle in view of the perpetual fragility of his finances, as he struggled even to maintain his family in some semblance of lower-middle-class respectability. Finally an American friend, George Dickman, the managing director of Kodak in Britain and a fellow admirer of Cora Richmond, gave Howard's wife £50 so that he could bring the book to publication.[35] In October 1898 it was at last published under the title *To-morrow: a peaceful path to real reform* (Figure 1.4).[36] The publishers were Swan

TO-MORROW:

A Peaceful Path to Real Reform

BY

E. HOWARD

" New occasions teach new duties ;
Time makes ancient good uncouth ;
They must upward still, and onward,
Who would keep abreast of Truth.
Lo, before us, gleam her camp-fires !
We ourselves must Pilgrims be,
Launch our Mayflower, and steer boldly
Through the desperate winter sea,
Nor attempt the Future's portal
With the Past's blood-rusted key."
   —" The Present Crisis."—*J. R. Lowell.*

LONDON

SWAN SONNENSCHEIN & CO., Ltd.

PATERNOSTER SQUARE

1898

Figure 1.4 The title page of *To-morrow*. With assistance, Howard underwrote the cost of publication and did not copyright the book. (author's collection)

Sonnenschein, a small London publishing house whose list also included *Capital*, by Karl Marx. Howard did not copyright the book and was paid no royalties.

'A unique combination of proposals'[37]

In the book Howard proposed the creation of a new settlement pattern comprising freestanding garden cities that would ultimately replace the very big concentrated cities (Figure 1.5). Each garden city would normally accommodate 30,000 people, with a further 2,000 living in its surrounding countryside. Occasional slightly larger garden cities (comprising some 58,000 urban and rural

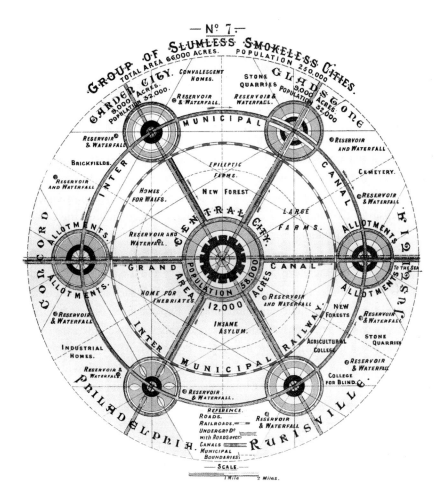

Figure 1.5 The Social City diagram, which gives a sense of both the larger spatial network of garden cities and the extent to which Howard saw it as a way of addressing all the social ills of late Victorian society.

dwellers) might be created as central hubs within this new settlement pattern. Each cluster, based around one of these hub garden cities and together housing 250,000 people, would be known as a 'social city'. The garden cities within these would be distinct places but well connected with the others by various methods of transport. Although he did not go into any detail, this clearly indicates that he did not intend his garden cities to be entirely self-contained and inward-looking. They were to be integral parts of a wider urban region.

Each garden city would, however, be a place where its people could live, work, shop, find the other public and private services that they needed, educate their children and undertake a range of leisure activities. The town was to be laid out spaciously, providing individual gardens, public parks, open space and abundant greenery. Urban growth would be strictly controlled, with an upper limit on the number of inhabitants within each garden city. Around each one there would be a protected rural belt where at least some of the food to be consumed by the garden citizens could be grown. The key to creating this new generous and attractive pattern of living was that the whole of the land needed for the garden city and its rural belt would be acquired cheaply at the outset, at agricultural (i.e. undeveloped) value. It would remain in unified ownership in perpetuity on behalf of the whole community of each garden city. There would be no opportunities for private speculative development and exploitative private landlordism of the kind that occurred in normal cities, forcing up the costs of living for their inhabitants.

This meant that the increase in land value that accompanied urban development could therefore be enjoyed collectively and used to fund the public services and amenities that the garden citizens required (such as public utilities, roads and streets, refuse collection) and chose to have (such as cultural facilities). The theory was quite clear, but how in practice this land value increase was to be harvested, at least in the short term, proved problematic. Howard proposed a system of what he termed 'rate-rent' (a combination of landlord's rent and the local rate, i.e. municipal taxes), the total value of which would rise as the garden city was developed. From this the municipal work of the garden city would be funded without need for additional taxes and any necessary user payments for particular public services would be minimised. Because the speculative profit-seeking associated with private landownership and development in ordinary cities was absent, the 'rent' element of the rate-rent had simply to repay the debt on the purchase of the original estate (which had, of course, been bought at low agricultural value). In theory, this would prevent later migrants to the garden city finding themselves unable to afford to live there. The idea was also that if, as

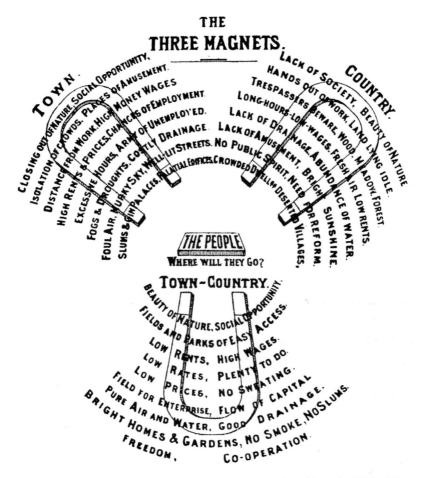

Figure 1.6 The famous 'Three Magnets' diagram, here reproduced from the 1902 edition of Howard's text, was a simple graphic device that shows the social concerns that Howard was trying to address in an easily understandable form. (author's collection)

development proceeded, demand to live in the garden city exceeded the supply of remaining plots, a new garden city would then be established. (To look ahead, we will see in subsequent chapters how Howard's scheme proved unworkable, in turn contributing to the far more serious early problems over financing than he had anticipated.)

'Till we have built Jerusalem in England's green and pleasant land'

A central feature of Howard's conception was that it rested on a 'joyous union' of town and country.[38] To express this, he deployed the first and most resonant of his visual aids, the Three Magnets diagram (Figure 1.6). This was an explanatory device that he had developed by the time he made the earliest handwritten drafts of the book, though it underwent some refinement before finally being published. Howard used the simple analogy of the magnet, capable in equal measure of attracting or repelling a small iron bar, representing the people. He showed how both the town magnet and the country magnet had both desirable and undesirable features, analogous to the positive and negative poles of a magnet. He then proposed his town–country magnet which would combine the positive features of both the other magnets, and more besides. It would thus achieve the physical impossibility of being a magnet with two positive poles, breaking down the analogy but ensuring that the point was even more powerfully made.

In articulating what this conceptual synthesis might mean as a physical reality, Howard opened *To-morrow*'s second chapter by quoting from William Blake's short poem (not yet the well-loved hymn and anthem) known as 'Jerusalem'.[39] It was appropriately inspirational as a prelude, although the chapter which followed was also largely indicative rather than definitive. Howard realised that the uniqueness of each site, the wishes of the leaders and citizens of different garden cities and the need to involve expert professionals would be key variables in shaping each one. As regards their generic socio-economic structure, the book was more emphatic that they would be neither dormitory suburbs nor company towns with just one dominant employer. They were also to be socially mixed places, with different classes of people as citizens of the same garden city. In keeping with the 'joyous union', the social and economic separation of urban and rural dwellers would also be minimised. In their proximity to the town, the rural dwellers could make use of its services and amenities. The town dweller had easy access to the produce of the rural belt and to the countryside itself if the introduction of nature into the town itself was insufficient.

Yet Howard did not provide a planning manual or design code for the garden city. His diagrams relating to the physical layout of the garden city made only very broad suggestions about organising principles. One of the most important was that key land uses, such as factories, housing and central shopping and other services, should be confined to distinct zones. The mixing of activities and land uses typical of the older and poorer parts of existing cities was to be avoided. Beyond that, Howard proposed a few novel ideas, notably a central park and beyond that a 'crystal palace', a glazed shopping arcade, surrounding the park. But there were few specific suggestions about, for example, the design of housing areas. Thus there was no specific guidance on residential densities. In so far as these can be inferred from what he wrote about the range of plot sizes available for houses in the garden city, the net residential density (that is, purely of the residential areas themselves), would have been perhaps 15 or 16 dwellings per acre (37 or 39.5 per hectare). This was a little higher than what within a few years came to be understood as the standard garden city density of 12 dwellings per acre (29.6 per hectare).

In thinking about the physical plan and the design of housing, Howard might perhaps have known the most celebrated of the rustic factory villages which were starting to appear around the time that he wrote his book during the early 1890s. One, Port Sunlight on Merseyside, was created by the soap manufacturer William Hesketh Lever and begun in 1888.[40] Another was at Bournville in suburban Birmingham, which was created from 1894 by the Cadbury family (Figure 1.7) in association with their cocoa and chocolate works (although 24 houses had been built for workers shortly after the factory originally opened in 1879).[41] In fact, Howard did not actually mention either of them in *To-morrow*, although a footnoted reference to 'Bourneville' (sic) does appear in the retitled second edition of 1902.[42] It seems more likely, then, regarding the extent to which they directly shaped his original garden city conception, that it was his subsequent knowledge of them and the men who created them as they became more built up that helped to confirm and refine his thinking.[43]

Figure 1.7 George Cadbury with his wife Elizabeth. The Quaker cocoa manufacturer, his family and associates were key supporters of the Garden City movement. (Bournville Village Trust Archive)

Howard and socialist thought

Viewed as a whole, Howard's garden city vision promised a way of improving people's lives that did not greatly disturb the status quo – it was a peaceful path. He was writing during a severe and prolonged agricultural depression that had brought rapid rural decline. The old order of private landownership in great rural estates already seemed to be weakening. This meant that even his most radical proposal – the buying of tracts of open land in the countryside and then the collective appropriation of the increased land values that accompanied urban development – did not seem quite so threatening. In the early nineteenth century Thomas Spence's advocacy of community landownership as a way of securing freedom from the impost of the landowning classes was seen as seditious. The worst Howard experienced was being patronised (notably by the Fabian Society) as well-intentioned but utopian and impractical.

Where, then, did the Howard of 1898 really stand amid the wider currents of late nineteenth-century English social reformism? The answer is a paradoxical one. He was, undoubtedly, part of the broad evolution of nineteenth-century socialist ideas. Yet an important caveat must immediately be added to this observation, because his thinking was certainly not that of what, by the end of the century, was becoming the socialist mainstream. It has already been noted that he did not make the same personal transition in the 1880s that many fellow members did, from the Zetetical to the Fabian Society. Nor, though he was evidently acquainted with some of the leading figures, did he play any apparent role in the other important bodies which formed that emergent socialist mainstream – the Social Democratic Federation (founded 1883), the Socialist League (founded 1884) or the Independent Labour Party (founded 1893). It was only many years later, in 1917, that his disciple, Frederic Osborn, finally persuaded him to relinquish his membership of the Liberal Party and join the last of these.[44]

Howard was also profoundly suspicious of what by the end of the nineteenth century was becoming the dominant political strategy of English socialists. This involved working gradually through the electoral process to secure representation and ultimately control of the governing institutions of the state. By this means they would promote and eventually use their electoral mandate to implement radical reforms. The approach seemed to be working, so that the first socialist Member of Parliament had been elected in 1892 and the first socialist-controlled local borough council in 1898. The Fabians also wanted a general rise in the quality of administrative competence and expertise within government, whether or not it was directly controlled by the socialists.

This whole approach involved a more direct political engagement with the problems of society. It was distinct from both utopian attempts to create enclaves of a new parallel society, apparent in *To-morrow*'s 'peaceful path', and the unpeaceful path of revolutionary Marxism. Howard's mistrust of approaches based on parliamentary reformism is evident in his concept of the 'Master-Key', mentioned in the first chapter of *To-morrow* and specified in detail in unpublished versions of his text and diagrams.[45] It can be clearly seen in Figure 1.9, where 'Parliamentary Method' is one of the parts he has cut away. Yet he also knew the pitfalls of introspective, communitarian approaches to socialism. Too often such communities turned their backs on the wider world and selfishly focused on the experiences of their few adherents. They were also given to self-regarding preciousness and prone to overbearing codes of behaviour or excessive influence by a few dominating figures. And, not least, they made easy targets for mockery. Yet Howard continued to favour what he called the 'experimental method', trying in a small way to make a fresh start in a new community as a way of demonstrating a different and better way of living.

'Individualistic-Socialism … Freedom not Regimentation'

He was not alone in this, of course, but this does not mean that he had a very central position in advocating non-state, more autonomous forms of socialism. Thus, although he quoted prominent labour union leaders, he had no real connections with the trades unions and was critical of what he saw as their leaders' propensity for friction and negativity. In *To-morrow*, for example, he wrote that,'[i]f labour leaders spent half the energy in co-operative organisation that they now waste in co-operative disorganisation the end of our unjust system would be at hand'.[46]

These words, of course, also show the arena of socialism with which he felt most comfortable – the co-operative movement. He was deeply attracted to the idea of groups of individuals coming together freely to create socialism by practical actions in the way they lived their lives. The word 'Co-operation' appears as one of the attributes of the 'town–country' in his Three Magnets diagram, twinned with 'Freedom'. However, early draft versions from 1891–2 show instead the more cumbersome, but also more revealing, terms 'Individualistic-Socialism' and 'Freedom not Regimentation'.

Yet again, despite his central belief in individualistic, voluntarist socialism, constructed on the basis of non-coercive co-operation, his actual connection to the mainstream of the well-established British co-operative movement, focused on retailing, was not close. Howard wanted the co-operative principle to be extended into other spheres, beyond retailing. When his book appeared in print, however, he still had no very clear idea about how this spirit of co-operative endeavour was to be put into practice. He does not seem yet to have been aware of the nascent co-partnership movement, a variant of co-operation that would soon become a key housing provider for the garden city movement.[47] Co-partnership societies operated for limited profit, drawing finance from a mix of their tenant or worker members, larger private shareholders and lenders and the state in the form of the Public Works Loan Board. Such societies had existed since the 1880s, partly growing out of a rift in the co-operative movement between the principles of consumer co-operation and worker co-operation. (The former sought good quality at low prices, while the latter sought higher producer income through wages and shared profits.) Even by 1898 the co-partnership movement had taken various small initiatives in manufacturing and housing. It differed from 'true' co-operativism, based on all members having equal ownership stakes, principally by allowing different levels of investment by the co-partners, so that in practice it was a mix of co-operative and philanthropic action.

In 1898, however, Howard's approach to the whole principle of co-operation and/or co-partnership was still evolving. After initial enthusiasm, he had decisively rejected Edward Bellamy's overarching approach which pressed all aspects of life into a collective mould, implying thereby a degree of coercion. He was impressed more by the anarchist arguments of Prince Peter Kropotkin. These became known during the early 1890s and were published in collected form, shortly after *To-morrow* appeared, as *Fields, Factories and Workshops*.[48] In his writings, Kropotkin stressed a much freer approach to creating new communities that chimed with Howard's own thinking. Neither Kropotkin nor Howard insisted that those who lived in their communities had to change their behaviour and attitudes, which is one of the key features which differentiates both of them from many other utopian socialists. It is, arguably, one of the main reasons why Howard's ideas had a much greater impact than those of the other Utopians.

Other than an insistence on collective and unified landownership, Howard actually made few other stipulations about how people should live. As he wrote in 1896, 'we must take men pretty much as we find them; and if any attempt is made to impose all sorts of restrictions upon those who are asked to come – they simply will not come'.[49] Thus, on one of the most vexed social questions of the day, alcohol (something he certainly did not wish to promote), he specified only that temperance should be a 'local option'. The citizens of each of his new garden cities should be left to decide for themselves whether they wanted theirs to be a 'dry' town. Nor did he insist on pressing the idea of social enterprise into areas other than landownership. He actively welcomed what he called 'pro-municipal' work (today's 'voluntary sector') to provide goods and services on a not-for-profit or limited profit basis. Philanthropic individuals and co-operative organisations would undertake such work. But he was certainly not insisting on this and fully recognised that many, probably most, employers who came would be organised on ordinary capitalist lines.

'The Master Key'

For all the various individuals, ideas and organisations which had had a bearing, often unknowingly, on helping Howard formulate his vision, his most tangible and active links to existing reformism in 1898 were actually those with the Land Nationalisation Society. This seems to underline the point already stressed, that the collective ownership of land was, in Howard's view, as far as things necessarily needed to go by way of definite reforms. The resultant lower land costs would enable a better quality of housing and life at much lower cost, thus allowing the garden city to benefit a wider social spectrum than would be possible through market processes alone. The worker would be able to enjoy something that hitherto had been the prerogative only of the more affluent. Yet there was a potential problem as to who would really end up as the beneficiary. In earlier drafts of the book Howard worried about whether it might be the capitalist factory owners who moved into his garden cities that ended up as the principal gainers from low rents for worker housing by then being able to keep down the wages they paid to their workers. He hoped this would not happen, but did not manage to demonstrate the assertion convincingly. In the end, he revealed none of these worries in the version finally published.

In this, he appears to have felt that the garden city, the prize to be unlocked by his Master Key, would also be a means to unlock a spirit of altruism. This was one of several points in his argument that was a partial leap of faith rather than an entirely rationally argued step. In turn, it also highlights an important general point, that there remained a significant religious underpinning to all his ideas. Thus both *To-morrow* itself and his unpublished writings include many references to religious motivations. The barrel of the Master-Key, for example, comprised science and religion, encapsulating the material and the spiritual dimensions (Figure 1.8). Similarly, the transcendental relationship of man and nature, representing that between man and God, was central to Howard's concept of town–country. This does not come across as a dominant part of the book's narrative, which Howard had been careful to write in a largely practical and factual manner. Yet, permeating it, there is also a more spiritual language that

Figure 1.8 The Master Key diagram featured in earlier drafts of *To-morrow* but not the published version, although the concept is mentioned. It reveals much about Howard's wider reformist strategy. The metaphor of the key came from the quoted poem by the American James Russell Lowell, which appears on *To-morrow*'s title page (see Figure 1.4). (HALS)

reflects his religious values. More than a century after the book was written such references are less meaningful to readers brought up in a more secular age. But their author belonged to a different age and, for him, they were full of meaning.

In the first chapter of his book, for example, he refers to 'the problem how to restore people to the land – that beautiful land of ours with its canopy of sky, the air that blows upon it, the sun that warms it, the rain and dew that moisten it – the very embodiment of Divine love for man'.[50] A little later on the same page he writes that his garden city will pour a flood of light on many social, political and other problems, 'even the relations of man to the Supreme Power'. The communal ownership of land certainly had its rationalist and even anti-clerical dimensions. Wallace was a well-known atheist, though he was never disrespectful of religious faith in others. This was just as well, since the movement for land nationalisation also appealed to the fundamental Christian notion, especially strongly held within the non-conformist and free churches, that the earth was God's gift to humanity as a whole,[51] and not something to be commodified and exploited by individual landowners as a source of personal profit at the expense of everyone else. Again, we can detect these sentiments in Howard's writings and diagrams, especially the unpublished versions. For example, in the unpublished version of

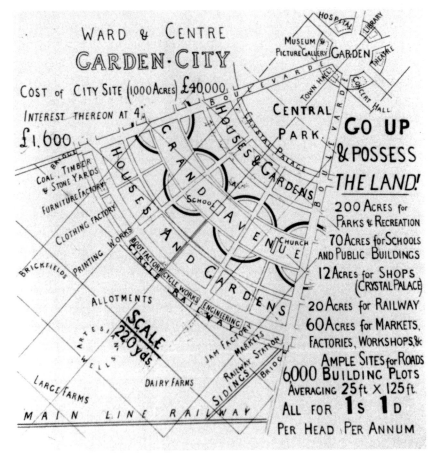

Figure 1.9 A draft diagram that appears in a simpler form in the published work. The words 'Go up and possess the land!' are particularly revealing of the land reformist roots of Howard's ideas and the sources of the earliest support of the movement. (HALS)

his third diagram of Ward and Centre, a sector of the garden city from the centre to the country estate, the slogan 'Go up and possess the land' was added as a heading (Figure 1.9). Its messianic tone underlines these religious foundations for the key reform at the very heart of the garden city idea. It is unclear how and why these changes between early drafts and published work occurred. However, we may surmise that exposure of his evolving ideas allowed him to see how removing some of its more obvious alternative or sectional references would heighten its potential appeal to mainstream opinion. And so it proved.

Creating a garden city movement

When we consider where Howard seemed to be heading – in a markedly different direction to the main currents of social and political thought in the late nineteenth century – it is easy to understand the patronising, though generally sympathetic, tone of early reactions to *To-morrow*. Many mainstream socialists felt he had simply missed the point. Most other commentators saw it simply as an exercise in utopianism: fine on paper but unlikely ever to achieve reality. And, of course, they had a point. There was absolutely no reason to suppose that the garden city as outlined by Howard would not remain, with Victoria or Hygeia, as a romantic and well-meaning prospectus for an unrealisable ideal. The really remarkable thing about *To-morrow* was how much it formed the basis for real achievements.

The first step on the 'peaceful path' was the creation in June 1899 of the Garden City Association to advance the principles contained in *To-morrow*.[52] The new Association's strongest early support came from the Land Nationalisation Society, which provided 6 of the 13 founder members and much of its initial organisational capacity.[53] It even housed the new Association in a corner of its own premises. The other founders included individuals who broadly shared Howard's religious beliefs and interests in a generally co-operative approach to social reform. The contacts and networks of this initial grouping gave a general shape to the early development of the movement. Increasingly, however, figures of greater significance in other walks of life, without a primary allegiance to land nationalisation, came to play more prominent roles.

The Association moved into the mainstream of Edwardian liberal reformism as prominent professionals, industrialists, newspaper proprietors, senior churchmen, politicians of all parties (though chiefly Liberals), landowners and others became involved. Over the next few years the garden city found an important place in the wider repertoire of reformist thought in the early twentieth century. The Association's membership grew steadily from 325 members in 1900 to 530 the following year, 1,800 in 1902 and 2,500 in 1903.[54] The organisation's status and influence were further enhanced by electing many notable public figures as vice-presidents. These posts were essentially honorary, but were a visible way to demonstrate the movement's breadth and influence. Their occupants could also usually be relied upon to make some donation to Association funds on accepting them. By 1902 there were 96 of these, rising to 138 by 1906.

Leading this shift of the garden city movement into the mainstream was a prominent London barrister (later a judge), Ralph Neville.[55] His personal qualities, organisational abilities and great interest in housing reform so impressed Howard that he recruited Neville as chairman of the Association in 1901. He was a pioneer in the co-partnership movement, playing the central role in connecting this with the garden city movement in the years before 1914.[56] This was much the most fruitful of the early elaborations of the original garden city vision, adding much needed organisational precision and practicability within Howard's rather vaguely sketched 'pro-municipal' field.

Co-partnership's main impact was to be in the form of co-partnership societies promoting supposedly affordable housing supply within actual garden city projects. Although there were variations between individual schemes, the essential principle of co-partnership (not always completely achieved in practice) was that the tenants should be members and shareholders in these societies.[57] The rest of the funding would come from a combination of public-spirited investors prepared to accept a dividend of 5 per cent or less and by borrowing from the state in the form of the Public Works Loan Board. In other words, it was a three-way hybrid of philanthropic and co-operative models of voluntaristic provision, assisted by the state.

Yet Neville and the new backers of the Association also brought many other things which certainly would not have come from Howard and his original core supporters. In particular, the movement gained money, organisational and networking skills, social status, public attention and access to power.[58] Quite simply, the social basis of support shifted from broadly lower-middle-class origins similar to those of Howard himself to include those further up the social scale.

The changing composition of the garden city movement

Some of the most important backers were individuals and families who were already building their public reputations as industrial philanthropists with socially progressive views. Many, though by no means all, were active in the Liberal Party. Although somewhat richer than him, many shared with Howard a background in one or other of the non-conformist churches and sensed a need and obligation to do God's work on earth. Thus the Quaker Cadbury family, associated with Bournville, were prominent and loyal supporters. So too was Thomas Purvis Ritzema, the Blackburn-based newspaper proprietor, devout Methodist, social reformer and temperance advocate who managed the progressive *Daily News* newspaper after George Cadbury bought it in 1901.[59]

Another Quaker industrial cocoa and chocolate-making family, the Rowntrees of York, began their own Bournville-like venture to house working families at New Earswick in 1902.[60] Joseph Rowntree, his son Seebohm, who undertook a pioneering study of poverty in York in 1899,[61] and nephew Frederick, a notable Arts and Crafts architect, became active supporters of the Association. Begun before the first actual garden city at Letchworth, the New Earswick garden village was one of the movement's earliest demonstration projects. The soap maker William Hesketh Lever, also briefly a Liberal MP (and, like Howard, a member of the Congregationalist church), was another early supporter, if a more impatient one than most of the others, as his rather brief involvement at Letchworth was to show.[62]

Lever's impatience with the movement was, however, as nothing compared to the extreme animosity he soon felt towards another much more important supporter of the movement.[63] This was Alfred Harmsworth (Lord Northcliffe), proprietor of several popular newspapers, including the *Daily Mail*, which circulated very widely among the aspiring suburban lower middle classes.[64] The target of much public criticism for his journalistic and management methods, Northcliffe instinctively understood something very profound: how much his readers yearned for the type of living environment that the garden city movement was offering. He and his family were generous donors and did much to raise the public profile of the movement by publicising it and giving it free advertising. His brother Cecil, who became a Liberal MP, assisted even more directly in the leadership of the movement.

Other supporters[65] from the business world included Thomas Idris, a chemist and successful manufacturer of mineral waters. A Welsh non-conformist (and ardent nationalist) and local London Progressive (Liberal) politician, Idris served as the first chairman of the new Association from 1899 to 1901. Another was Aneurin Williams, born into a Welsh and Teesside family of ironmasters, who later served as a Liberal MP. Yet there were also notable Conservatives, among them Arthur Balfour and Stanley Baldwin. The Birmingham Unionists, who had much in common with the Liberals, particularly John Nettlefold and his cousin Neville Chamberlain, both Unitarians, were also supporters.[66] For a time, the Birmingham City Housing Committee was a generous institutional member of the Association.

Beyond industry and politics, a wide array of figures in various walks of life was drawn to the movement. As well as Howard's ever critical friend, George Bernard Shaw, supporters from the literary world included the novelist and playwright John Galsworthy. Leading members of the Liberal aristocracy, such as Earl Grey, and even a few Conservative peers, notably Lord Salisbury, lent their patronage. Many churchmen took a close interest, including a few senior figures such as the bishops of London, Winchester and Salford.

Meanwhile, the garden city movement was also attracting more supporters from the design and land professions. Within a few years they were exerting a bigger influence on the movement. Many were architects who subscribed to the ideals and methods of the arts and crafts movement, inspired by John Ruskin and William Morris.[67] Morris himself had died in 1896 and Ruskin was almost at the end of his life when *To-morrow* appeared, so we do not know their personal views of Howard's garden city. It soon became clear, however, that the romantic socialism and pre-industrial vernacular aesthetic of the arts and crafts movement meshed rather neatly with Howard's concept of the garden city.

The most important of these architects, Barry Parker and Raymond Unwin,[68] were not initially the best known. Yet it fell to these two to replace Howard's simple diagrams of the garden city with an aesthetic and physical form of tremendous potency. The pair had already begun to establish a reputation for their Arts and Crafts designs for working-class housing, and Unwin was also beginning to become an influential speaker and writer on this subject. Henceforth it fell to them and those who shared their views to give form to the garden city. In doing so, however, there were some real changes. Typical residential densities, interestingly, were to be roughly a third lower than Howard suggested in *To-morrow*. Yet he never resisted this change and, on the contrary, was well pleased with the outcome.

New emphases and directions

These changes in the movement's composition had important consequences. There were now more figures within the movement who were more accustomed than Howard to the easy exercise of power and influence. They also had specific skills that were more relevant as the first practical steps to realising his garden city vision began to be taken. For his part, Howard remained a compelling speaker and validating moral presence on committees and organising groups as the garden city message spread around the country and across the world. But, in most respects, the dominant view is that he was not a practical man and that others played the main parts in realising his ideas. Even Osborn, Howard's great

Figure 1.10 Title page of the second edition of Howard's book, published as *Garden cities of to-morrow*. Howard's wider social reformist purposes were now more specifically focused on a tangible project. The cover image, designed by the socialist artist Walter Crane, was also used for other publications of the Garden City Association. (author's collection)

admirer, admitted that he, like many others, increasingly saw the older visionary as an 'ineffectual angel'.[69] Nor was his ability to exert an important influence within the movement helped by the traumas of his personal life during the early years of the new century.[70] After some years of growing ill-health, Lizzie, his first and much-loved wife, died in 1904 and he entered upon his disastrous second marriage three years later. Moreover, despite his growing worldwide renown, his financial problems did not diminish. In these circumstances, it is easy to understand why Howard's influence within the movement might have declined.

During this period a subtle rebadging of the garden city project occurred. Perhaps the first sign of this was that *To-morrow* was republished with amendments in 1902 as *Garden Cities of To-morrow* (Figure 1.10).[71] Apart from some new footnotes and changes to diagrams, there were almost no changes to the text. Yet the retitling alone was symptomatic of a subtle shift from Howard's original broad project of social reform towards something that was more about environmental reform and changing the organisation of the city. Howard himself had begun to make some of these changes as he drafted and redrafted the original book. He had, for example, given less emphasis to the concept of the 'Master Key', which had stressed some wider social and political transformation. But this was now going further. The following year the Association began to widen its campaign by seeking to apply garden city principles to existing cities. It set the tone for further widening into what, by 1905, had been given a new name – 'town planning'. The next chapter will show how the first 'true' garden city was begun at Letchworth, but in Chapter 4 we will also illustrate how the focus shifted increasingly to promoting town planning 'on garden city lines'.

This particular turn on the 'peaceful path' had the effect of intensifying certain weaknesses within the alliance of interests that had come together under the garden city banner. Some stemmed from Howard's own rather ambiguous relationship with the mainstream of what would become the Labour Party. The types of organisation that were associated with delivering what the garden city offered before 1914 embodied what many Labour leaders criticised as bourgeois philanthropy and reform. The movement continued to rely on support and investment from industrialists and other big investors. As such, their interests in housing workers could be dismissed as a means of rendering their employees more quiescent. The collective self-help element within co-partnership, of people joining together to create their own housing, seemed largely confined to the middle classes. Howard's real concerns for urban poverty and bad housing were in practice masked by the movement's early emphasis on improving middle-class housing, largely because this was easier to fund. Alongside this, Howard's original radical links with the Land Nationalisation Society seem to have weakened. Prominent individuals remained common to both movements, but in 1913 the LNS Secretary and the man who had actually moved the original motion to create the Garden City Association in June 1899, Joseph Hyder, made not one single reference to the garden city movement in his massive volume *The case for land nationalisation*.[72]

Conclusions

In the next two chapters we will examine Howard's detailed involvement in the two garden cities at Letchworth and Welwyn Garden City. Here the focus has been on how he came to occupy such a central role in the garden city movement, the nature of the ideas he formulated and the 'peaceful path to real reform' that he mapped. Ultimately, perhaps, it is a story of a man of decidedly modest means who was prepared to give a large part of his life to singleminded, even reckless, pursuit of an obsessive interest. His interest in continuing to perfect the stenographic machine continued, but it was the garden city that took over his life. There is evidence that some members of the family viewed the garden city as a kind of affliction.[73] Even associates sometimes felt that he was possessed of a monomania, with only one topic about which he would speak. Despite an underlying sympathy for the movement and admiration of the man, Shaw occasionally referred to him as 'Ebenezer the garden city geyser'.[74]

Those closest to him undoubtedly paid the price for his inventive activities, both mechanical and social. In a letter discussing their debts, written shortly before her death, his first wife, supportive though she always was, revealed how his reformist mission had denied his family a life of reasonable comfort and security. Even in her exasperation with, in this particular case, his willingness to go off on lecture tours without taking any fees, she felt the need to apologise for not quite living up to his standards: 'I may be selfish in this matter, but if I am I fear there are lots of selfish people'.[75]

Her husband was a man who stood apart from the ordinary selfishness of humanity. In the main, his image as the unworldly, even saintly, inventor of the garden city (and, to a large extent, of urban planning) was justified. Yet genius, even gentle genius, has its price. Howard's single-minded pursuit of his own project for changing the world was itself a kind of selfishness, albeit with altruistic outcomes. The costs of the rich conceptual legacy that Howard bequeathed to the garden city movement and to urban planning in general were mainly borne by his family and occasionally by his associates. Removed in time and space from Howard's world, we can see (if perhaps a little too readily) how small was that price compared with what flowed from his obsession and their sacrifices. In a more general sense, though, we can take comfort from the notion that something of Howard's gentle idealism abides still at the conceptual heart of urban planning, an activity that is, too often, riddled with the ordinary selfishness of humanity. His 'peaceful path' may have become overgrown and indistinct. But, should future generations wish to follow it, it is still there.

Notes

1   In parts, this chapter is a slight reworking of my 1998 lecture at Cornell University, published as 'Ebenezer Howard: his life and times', in K.C. Parsons and D. Schuyler (eds), *From garden city to green city: the legacy of Ebenezer Howard* (Baltimore, 2002), pp. 14–37.

2   Witnessed by Thomas Welwyn Osborn, a neighbour of the Howards at Number 16, Guessens Road. See M. de Soissons, *Welwyn Garden City: a town designed for healthy living* (Cambridge, 1988), 70. Dr Osborn also repeated the story in conversation with the author and Geoffrey Howard (Ebenezer's grandson) in October 1998.

3   HALS, Osborn Archive I/35, notes of interview [by F.J. Osborn] with Mrs Berry (Howard's daughter), 21 December 1949.

4   Ibid.

5   Manuscripts, printed books, correspondence and miscellaneous papers of Sir Ebenezer Howard and his personal representatives, 1879–1941, description available at <http://apps.nationalarchives.gov.uk/a2a/records.aspx?cat=046-deho&cid=-1#-1>, accessed 4 September 2014.

6   For Osborn's important role in the history of Garden Cities and New Towns, see especially A. Whittick, *F.J.O. – practical idealist: a biography of Sir Frederic Osborn* (London, 1987); M. Hebbert, 'Frederic Osborn 1885–1978', in G.E. Cherry (ed.), *Pioneers in British planning* (London, 1981), pp. 177–202; M. Hebbert, 'A Hertfordshire solution to London's problems? Sir Frederic Osborn's axioms re-considered', in J. Onslow (ed.), *Garden cities and new towns: five lectures* (Hertford, 1990), pp. 38–47.

7   D. MacFadyen, *Sir Ebenezer Howard and the town planning movement* (Manchester, 1933); R. Beevers, *The garden city utopia: a critical biography of Ebenezer Howard* (Basingstoke, 1988).

8   Particularly F.J. Osborn, 'Preface', in E. Howard, *Garden cities of to-morrow* (London, 1965), pp. 9–28 and F.J. Osborn, 'Sir Ebenezer Howard: the evolution of his ideas', *Town Planning Review*, 21 (1950), pp. 221–35.

9   S. Buder, *Visionaries and planners: the garden city and the modern community* (New York, 1990); R. Fishman, *Urban utopias in the twentieth century: Ebenezer Howard, Frank Lloyd Wright and Le Corbusier* (New York, 1977), pp. 23–88; E. Howard, *To-morrow: a peaceful path to real reform* (London, 2003 [Original 1898 facsimile edition with commentary by P. Hall, D. Hardy and C. Ward]).

10   HALS, Osborn Collection, I/5, typescript notes by F.J. Osborn; G.P. Scholtz, *Ebenezer Howard in Nebraska*, paper delivered to the Association of Collegiate Schools of Planning/Association of European Schools of Planning Joint Congress, Oxford Polytechnic, 8–12 July 1991.

11   HALS, Howard Archive, D/EHo F18/3, 3, typescript by Ebenezer Howard.

12   Beevers, *The garden city utopia*, p. 6.

13   Ibid., p. 13.

14   M. Bevir, *The making of British socialism* (Princeton, 2011), pp. 155, 175–9.

15   HALS, Howard Archive, D/EHo F18, 4.

16   B.W. Richardson, *Hygeia or the city of health* (London, 1876 [reprinted New York, 1985]).

17   F.H.A. Aalen, 'English origins', in S.V. Ward (ed.), *The garden city: past, present, future* (London, 1992), pp. 28–51.

18   H. George, *Progress and poverty: an inquiry into the cause of industrial depressions and of increase of want with increase of wealth – the remedy* (1879; British edn, 1880 [50th anniversary reprint New York, 1949]).

19   A.R. Wallace, *Land nationalisation: its necessity and its aims, being a comparison of the system of landlord and tenant with that of occupying ownership in their influence on the well-being of the people* (London, 1892 [orig. 1882]); J. Yelling, 'Planning and the land question', *Planning History*, 16/1 (1994), pp. 4–9.

20   H. Spencer, *Social statics: or the conditions essential to human happiness specified, and the first of them developed* (London, 1851) (accessed in 2009 facsimile edition, Charleston: BiblioLife).

21   H.M. Hyndman (ed.), *The nationalization of land in 1775 and 1882: being a lecture delivered at Newcastle/Tyne by Thomas Spence 1775* (London, 1882).

22   J.S. Mill, *Principles of political economy with some of their applications to social philosophy* (London, 1909 [orig. 1848]), Vol. 1, 121; E.G. Wakefield, *The art of colonisation* (London, 1849).

23   R. Bunker, 'The early years', in A. Hutchings and R. Bunker (eds), *With conscious purpose: a history of town planning in South Australia* (Adelaide, 1986), pp. 7–20; E. Olssen, 'Mr Wakefield and New Zealand as an experiment in post-enlightenment experimental practice', *New Zealand Journal of History*, 31/2 (1997), pp. 197–218.

24   J.S. Buckingham, *National evils and practical remedies* (London, 1849).

25   A. Marshall, 'The housing of the London poor: where to house them', *Contemporary Review*, 45 (1884), pp. 224–31.

26   E. Bellamy, *Looking backward, 2000–1887* (London, 1888); HALS, Howard Archive, D/EHo F18/6.

27   HALS, Howard Archive, D/EHo F1/5.

28   HALS, Howard Archive, D/EHo F3/8.

29   Buder, *Visionaries and planners*, pp. 57–63.

30   E. Howard, *To-morrow: a peaceful path to real reform* (London, 1898), pp. 98–9.

31   HALS, Howard Archive, *op. cit.*, D/EHo F3/2.

32   C.B. Purdom, *Life over again* (London, 1951), p. 46. R.A.M. Stern, D. Fishman and J. Tilove, *Paradise planned: the garden suburb and the modern city* (New York, 2013), pp. 241–4.

33   Pro-Chicago opinions on the origins of Howard's use of the term 'garden city' can be found in Osborn, 'Preface', p. 26 (who also mentions Howard's denial) and P. Hall, *Cities of tomorrow: an intellectual history of planning and urban design in the twentieth century* (Oxford, 1988), p. 89. For arguments in favour of a Riverside connection, see A. Garvin, *The American city: what works, what doesn't* (New York, 1996), p. 315 and Stern et al., *Paradise planned*, pp. 122–7 and 212. On this last page, these authors suggest why Howard might have concealed the connection.

34   W. Morris, *News from nowhere* (1890), reproduced in A. Briggs (ed.), *William Morris: selected writings and designs* (Harmondsworth, 1962), pp. 83–301. The case for William Morris as inventor of the term 'garden city' is given by M. Naslas, *The concept of the town in the writings of William Morris*, paper presented at the History of Planning Group Meeting, University of Birmingham, March 1977.

35   HALS, Howard Archive, D/EHo F18/8.

36   Howard, *To-morrow*.

37   Ibid., p. 102.

38   Ibid., p. 10. The Three Magnets diagram appears between pages 8 and 9.

39   Ibid., p. 12. The chapter is actually labelled as Chapter 1 but follows an introductory chapter.

40   E. Hubbard and M. Shippobottom, *A guide to Port Sunlight Village* (Liverpool, 1988).

41   M. Harrison, *Bournville: model village to garden suburb* (Chichester, 1999).

42   E. Howard, *Garden cities of tomorrow* (London, 1902), p. 85.

43   HALS, Howard Archive, D/EHo F18, 10.

44   Beevers, *The garden city utopia*, 150.

45   Howard, *To-morrow*, 5.

46   Ibid., p. 86.

47   J. Birchall, 'Co-partnership housing and the garden city movement', *Planning Perspectives*, 10/4 (1995), pp. 329–58.

48   P. Kropotkin, *Fields, factories and workshops* (London, 1974 [orig. 1899]). An acknowledgement of Kropotkin's book appeared as a footnote in the 1902 edition of Howard's book (page 31).

49   HALS, Howard Archive, D/EHo F3/2/10.

50   Howard, *To-morrow*, 5.

51   Aalen, 'English origins', especially pp. 42–51.

52   D. Hardy, *From garden cities to new towns: campaigning for town and country planning, 1899–1946* (London, 1991), pp. 16–35.

53   Macfadyen, *Sir Ebenezer Howard*, pp. 25–6, 40; Hardy, *Garden cities to new towns*, pp. 16–19.

54   Hardy, *Garden cities to new towns*, pp. 36–113.

55   MacFadyen, *Sir Ebenezer Howard*, pp. 44–8.

56   K.J. Skilleter, 'The role of public utility societies in early British town planning and housing reform, 1901–36', *Planning Perspectives*, 8/2 (1993), pp. 125–65; Birchall, 'Co-partnership housing'.

57   LLEC (Liberal Land Enquiry Committee), 1914, pp. 104–8.

58   E.G. Culpin, *The garden city movement up-to-date* (London, 1913), pp. 57–63, gives a list of donors to the Association at that time. This is used freely in the paragraphs which follow, in addition to specifically cited sources.

59   J. Bradshaw, 'Newspaper tycoon', *Journal of the Northumberland and Durham Family History Society*, 15/3 (1990), pp. 72–3.

60   L. Waddilove, *One man's vision* (London, 1954).

61   B.S. Rowntree, *Poverty: a study of town life* (London, 1901).

62   C.B. Purdom, *The Letchworth achievement* (London, 1963), pp. 21–2.

63   This was because of the repeated libelling in 1906 by the *Daily Mail* of Lever's business methods, which led to a successful legal action against the newspaper the following year. Lever used the proceeds to endow, *inter alia*, the Department of Civic Design (the first British planning school) at the University of Liverpool. Richard Davenport-Hines, 'Lever, William Hesketh, first Viscount Leverhulme (1851–1925)', *Oxford dictionary of national biography* (Oxford, 2004); online edn January 2011 <http://www.oxforddnb.com.oxfordbrookes.idm.oclc.org/view/article/34506>, accessed 24 September 2014.

64   Hardy, *Garden cities to new towns*, especially p. 80; D. Read, *Edwardian England 1901–15: society and politics* (London, 1972), pp. 57–61.

65   Hardy, *Garden cities to new towns*, pp. 19, 47; Culpin, *The garden city movement*, pp. 57–63.

66   G.E. Cherry, *Birmingham: a study in geography, history and planning* (Chichester, 1994), pp. 102–9; G.E. Cherry, 'The place of Neville Chamberlain in British town planning', in G.E. Cherry (ed.), *Shaping an urban world* (London, 1980), pp. 161–79; M. James, 'John Sutton Nettlefold, Liberalism and the early town planning movement', *Journal of Liberal History*, 75 (2012), pp. 30–37, <http://www.liberalhistory.org.uk/wp-content/uploads/2014/10/75_James_Nettlefold_Liberalism_and_Town_Planning.pdf>, accessed 1 September 2015.

67   M. Swenarton, *Artisans and architects: the Ruskinian tradition in architectural thought* (London, 1988).

68   M. Miller, *Letchworth: the first garden city*, 2nd edn (Chichester, 2002); M. Miller, *Raymond Unwin: garden cities and town planning* (Leicester, 1992).

69   HALS, Osborn Archive, File I /1, 8, Osborn's Afterthoughts on E.H.

70   Beevers, *The garden city utopia*, pp. 104–6.

71   Howard, *Garden cities*.

72   J. Hyder, *The case for land nationalisation* (London, 1913).

73   E.g. Beevers, *The garden city utopia*, p. 122.

74   Ibid., p. 70.

75   HALS, Osborn Archive, File I/1, Letter Elizabeth–Ebenezer Howard 8 October 1904 (typescript copy).

CHAPTER TWO

Letchworth Garden City

'... an insignificant little man'

It could so easily have been Staffordshire rather than Hertfordshire where the first attempt to give tangible expression to Ebenezer Howard's peaceful path was played out. In June 1902 the Garden City Association launched a Pioneer Garden City Company, tasked with seeking a site on which the garden city might be built.[1] Ralph Neville was its Chairman and other prominent Board members were Thomas Idris and Edward Cadbury. Most Board members were also the main investors, the other principal funders being Lever, George Cadbury and Alfred Harmsworth. Howard became Managing Director, a role which quickly showed the limits of his abilities to those around him.[2]

In one sense the Company's task was an easy one. By then, agriculture had recovered a little from its very depressed state in the late nineteenth century, but the multiple effects of cheap food imports, successive bad harvests and animal diseases had taken their toll, and many landowners were eager to divest themselves of farmland giving little return. The result was that a large amount of rural land throughout England was either actively available for sale or certainly up for offers. After discreetly approaching land agents and solicitors around the country, the site sub-committee of the Company found itself sifting through a bewildering number of possibilities.[3]

The Company wanted a freehold block of rural land of between 4,000 and 6,000 acres (1,619 and 2,429 hectares), with a mainline railway through or adjacent to it. Ideally there would also be means of moving goods by river or canal. The chosen site would have to be capable of being economically drained and must have a good supply of potable water. Finally, it should be near to London or some other large centre of labour. Many sites brought to the sub-committee's attention were simply too small, but, by October 1902, an 8,000-acre (3,239-hectare) estate at Chartley, a few miles north-east of Stafford, had emerged as the front runner.[4] Mainly used for dairying and sporting purposes, it contained several villages, the owning family's mansion and a ruined castle.

Otherwise it comprised gently undulating countryside. And, very importantly, its aristocratic owner was badly in debt and eager for a sale.

In almost all respects it was the perfect site, with most expert opinions sought by the Company being favourable. Yet the location, remote from the nearest big industrial centres of Birmingham, the Black Country or the Potteries, was risky. Stafford was around eight miles from the centre of the estate but was still only a modest country town, though one beginning to attract new industries. There was also some dispute about the site itself, with one expert report doubting that it had a suitable area for a town centre. Despite this, however, Howard continued serious negotiations during spring 1903 and provisional agreement about buying Chartley seemed close.

But by July it was all off, as the Company had another site, Letchworth Manor in Hertfordshire. It had not been an early front runner because, at only 1,014 acres (410 hectares), it was too small. Yet it was very well placed: 35 miles north of Kings Cross on the Cambridge branch of the Great Northern Railway, very close to the mainline connection at Hitchin and on the Great North Road. Howard mentioned the idea to Reginald Hine, then a young solicitor's clerk who became a prominent local figure in Hitchin. Hine thought him an 'insignificant little man', patently lacking the personal wealth and standing to bring off such an ambitious project.[5]

The site was, however, sufficiently tempting to encourage the Board to explore whether further land might be available,[6] and it did not have to rely on Howard to make it happen. The Company's own solicitor, Herbert Warren, had from the start championed this location. His country practice was in this area and he and his colleagues had excellent local knowledge. Within a few weeks they had successfully approached 15 owners and managed to assemble a potential consolidated site that, at 3,818 acres (1,546 hectares), was just about the right size. After several months of muddling through, all had now fallen into place and the purchases occurred in quick succession (Figure 2.1). Most were undertaken in the names of nominees, disguising the Company's involvement and the true purpose of these ostensibly quite separate transactions.

First Garden City Ltd

The average cost per acre of about £42 (£105 per hectare) was more costly, acre for acre, than Chartley would have been (although, because the whole estate was smaller, the total cost was lower). Edward Cadbury still felt that they were paying too much and that the site was too close to Hitchin to be a true test of Howard's vision.[7] But, against this, the likelihood of attracting industry was rated very

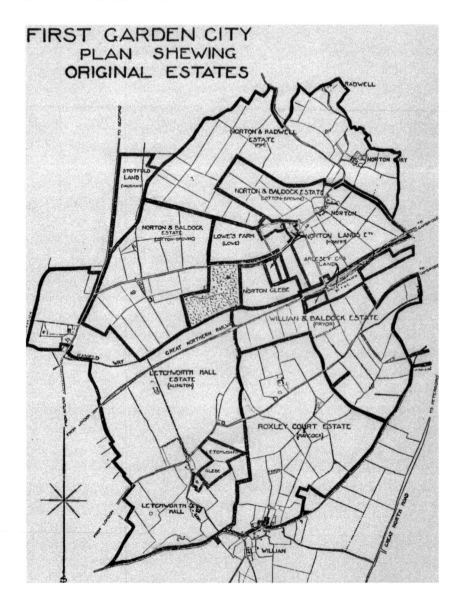

Figure 2.1 The original land holdings bought through nominees by the Pioneer Company. Without compulsory purchase powers, complete secrecy was necessary to prevent the price rising excessively. (author's collection)

high. Manufacturing firms were starting to shift both from provincial Britain to sites nearer the London market and from London to more spacious sites out of the capital. There were also a few foreign firms looking for new industrial sites, and their number was growing. At any rate, the Board was confident that their new venture would soon be able to offer the space and modern serviced layouts that industrialists were increasingly seeking.

The purchased land included Letchworth Hall and associated buildings, several farms and the existing village of Norton. It was immediately adjoined to the east by the small town of Baldock. The site would be enlarged to the south in 1912, adding a further 748 acres (303 hectares) that included the village of Willian and its surroundings.[8] This supplementary acquisition was made by a different and more enduring company, First Garden City Limited. It was registered in September 1903 to develop a garden city for about 30,000 people. Its Board was similar to the Pioneer Company's, though Lever, already a major backer, was a new addition (a very short-term one, as it turned out). The secretary of the Garden City Association (a role he quickly relinquished), Thomas Adams, became secretary of the Company and was soon its estate manager. Howard had not distinguished himself as a managing director and was not reappointed, but he remained a director with a more constrained role, limited largely to promotional activity and overseeing decisions about planning and design. Yet, in a real sense, he had triumphed. Within five years of *To-morrow* appearing, his garden city project was on the brink of practical expression and was a symbol (and to some extent a focus) of the reformist hopes of the early Edwardian years.

'We … hoped that the dawn might soon come and shatter all their dreams'

However, as happened on many subsequent steps on the peaceful path, the prospect of a new settlement and a new population appearing in a predominantly rural area with nearby small towns was not welcomed. With only one significant exception the few inhabitants – tenant farmers and labourers – within the purchased area were hostile.[9] Only Herbert Hailey, the tenant of the largest farm and a substantial farmer in the wider area, was welcoming and helpful to the Company. Yet even in his tolerance and goodwill he regarded the whole venture with amusement. This attitude was typical of the wider area, though often tinged with rather greater ill-will. Hitchin was a historic town of great charm and beauty (though also squalor, for some of its poorest residents) and its inhabitants were on the whole rather prosperous and set in their ways, enjoying the town's common characterisation as 'Sleepy Hollow'.[10]

Reginald Hine, who had been so dismissive of Howard on first meeting, was himself a recent arrival in Hitchin, just two years before Howard and his followers came. He described it as then being very much under the 'beneficent autocracy' of Quakers and not disposed to embrace new outside thinking.[11] Hine soon became a prominent and eloquent local historian and commentator with a witty and sometimes cruel tongue and pen. He was able to view both old Hitchin and the new upstart with a degree of sardonic detachment (even though his sympathies remained predominantly with 'Sleepy Hollow'). Not without some added melodrama, he described the first phase of relations between old and new as 'primitive and brutal'; 'we hated one another like poison'.[12] This quickly gave way to a more one-sided hostility from Hitchin's inhabitants during the 'crucially testing years of the Garden City', which lasted until around 1914. Yet, in hindsight, he at least was later honest enough to concede that 'we were jealous of these pioneers. They might increase and we might decrease. We called them dreamers and hoped that the dawn might soon come and shatter all their dreams.'[13]

Early crises
It nearly did, though not because of the animosity of the inhabitants of 'Sleepy Hollow'. The problem was rather that having a site and a Company was all well and good but did not translate into the funding necessary to allow the garden city to take shape at more than a snail's pace.[14] The Company's articles of association limited the maximum dividend payable to 5 per cent and imposed even stricter conditions on the procedure if the Company were wound up. Any surplus remaining beyond a 10 per cent terminal bonus had to be used for the benefit of the local inhabitants. The result was that the normal incentives for stockholders – that they had a real stake in the equity of the Company and that dividends would be unlimited – were absent. Unless they were investing purely out of sympathy with the cause, anyone taking serious financial advice shunned the share issue. In the event, no dividends at all were paid for ten years and the 5 per cent ceiling was not reached until 1923. The original share issue was not fully subscribed until 1935.

The Company therefore lacked the capital even to meet its liabilities in the early years. Practically nothing was available to provide the infrastructure and road works needed to foster building development. Moreover, Howard's novel scheme of 'rate-rent' as a way of regularly harvesting land value uplift as development proceeded was judged a deterrent to would-be developers. Instead, a more conventional system of leasehold sales of development sites was adopted, initially with decennial ground rent reviews. Yet developers were also wary of this and the practice of granting leases of 99 years at fixed rents or 999 years with 99-year revisions (except for factories, where a ground rent was fixed for the whole period) soon became usual. The advantage for developers was that future cost uncertainties were minimised, even though land values rose so slowly in the earliest years that the other arrangements would almost certainly have been cheaper.

Another consequence was that the Company itself ran on a shoestring. Of the directors, only Howard (with no other source of income) was paid a salary. As to a permanent professional staff, the Company's establishment was also lean. Consultants were hired temporarily to undertake major tasks. Talented and hardworking though he was, Adams effectively became overall manager without having the skills to take on such a role.[15] He was given some specialist assistance to deal with specific aspects. But the Company in its early months lacked a clear sense of direction.

By the end of 1903 matters were coming to a head. With no sign of building or significant preparatory work, Lever was pressing for development sites to be disposed of freehold to speed things up and boost funding. But, for Neville and the rest of the Board, this was a step too far, something which would have destroyed the unity of the estate and a cornerstone of the whole project. The result was that Lever, the most powerful industrialist directly associated with the venture, resigned in frustration in February 1904.[16]

Making the plan

Meanwhile, the master plan for the garden city was under consideration.[17] Following various consultations and unsuccessful approaches to a few very prominent architects of the period, the Company organised a limited competition in October 1903. Three pairs of architects were asked to prepare plans for the garden city. The first pair, Raymond Unwin and Barry Parker, had already been involved, advising on the potential of possible sites for the Pioneer Company. However, the Company certainly gave no sense that this made them an automatic choice. Yet they had experience designing housing for workers and had already written influentially on this subject. Their socialist sympathies also made them interested in the garden city from an ideological perspective. Howard had been impressed by Unwin's talk at the 1901 Garden City Association conference in Bournville about how the garden city might be designed. By 1903 Parker and Unwin were actively working on the design of Rowntree's garden village at New Earswick near York for workers at its chocolate factory.

The second pair was W.R. (William Richard) Lethaby and Halsey Ricardo.[18] The former was a prominent theorist (though less so an architect) of the Arts and Crafts movement. Ricardo was known as an architect of several notable Arts and Crafts houses and, his largest commission, the great Howrah Railway Station in Calcutta. Finally, a Hitchin architect, Geoffry Lucas, who had worked extensively in the local area, along with Sidney White Cranfield, also participated, although whether on their own initiative or by subsequent invitation is unclear.

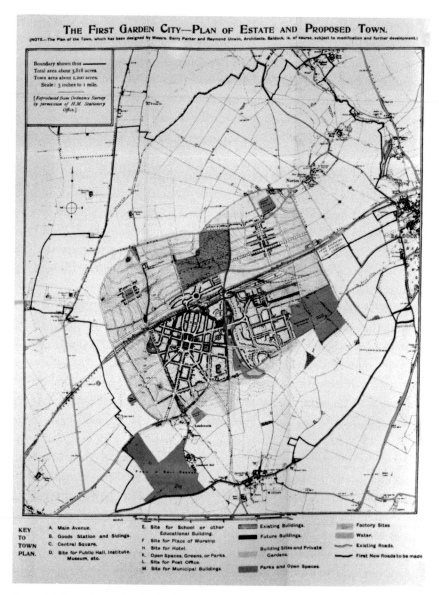

Figure 2.2 The original plan for the first garden city. Largely the work of Raymond Unwin, it had functional advantages, was well related to the site and combined central formality with more informal residential areas. (First Garden City Heritage Museum, Letchworth)

The Parker–Unwin plan was the most carefully thought through (Figure 2.2). It was a rather formal modified grid yet also closely attuned to site topography and existing natural features. Their plan was the most spacious, covering the biggest proportion of the site, and the layout of residential areas became less formal further from the centre. At a time when there was almost no town planning theory or practice to work from, the plan showed clear functional zoning, with a well-considered factory estate on the eastern side. The positioning of the railway station, main roads and rail crossing points effectively incorporated the advice of a consulting engineer who had already reported for the Company.

The other two plans were weaker in these functional aspects, although were perhaps more in keeping with contemporary architectural thinking. Both were much more formal, the Lucas–Cranfield effort especially so. They were also more compact. The elegant Lethaby–Ricardo plan won some support, especially from Thomas Adams. It was much more sophisticated than the Lucas–Cranfield Plan, combining a grid with key radial diagonals and curved avenues that followed contours. Yet the industrial area was poorly located to the north-west of the town and generally less considered in its layout. The main through-roads only partly followed engineering advice and the plan's overall relationship to topography and natural features was less sensitive than that of the Parker–Unwin entry.

The Board favoured the Parker–Unwin plan, though not without some misgivings. After some modifications to reflect railway company advice, it was accepted as the Company's provisional plan. Some slight changes were also made to mitigate the grid effect, with modest curves introduced to some central road lines. The pair was retained as consulting architects until 1914, when their partnership was dissolved, after which Parker alone held the role until 1939. As will shortly be shown, however, this continuing involvement with overseeing design control did not work as well as they, especially Unwin, had hoped.

Becoming Letchworth (Garden City)

Another fundamental matter was decided in 1904 – the name of the garden city.[19] Actually there was little external pressure to do this, because 'garden city' was itself then a unique name. It was the only one, in Britain at least, though it was often being linked in the press with neighbouring Hitchin or Baldock, associations which the Company wanted to avoid. There was also the strong intention that this would be merely the first step, with many others to follow. To add a distinctive aspect to the first one, a specific name was needed. Many names were duly proposed and a shortlist drawn up comprising: 'Garden City', 'Letchworth', 'Letchworth (Garden City)', 'Wellworth', 'Homesworth' and 'Alseopolis'. Wellworth was an amalgam of the names of local parishes and the last proposal combined the Greek words for garden and city. The names were put to a ballot of shareholders in August 1904 and the name Letchworth (Garden City) chosen. Given the balance of shortlisted names, this choice was hardly a surprise.

Over time, however, the generic words in brackets were dropped from the official postal address and in 1937 from the railway station name.[20] This was something that the Company itself welcomed, so that the town might soon be seen as a normal place, not just an experiment. In recent decades, however, this loss of the original name was regretted. It was also a source of jealousy because the supplementary words always remained (despite, as will be seen in Chapters 3 and 6, recurrent hopes to the contrary) an integral part of the official name of Howard's second foundation, Welwyn Garden City. Eventually this spurred moves during the later 1990s to reinstate it (without the brackets) for the first garden city. This was achieved for the town's railway station in 1999 and the official name was also changed to Letchworth Garden City by the Post Office in 2003 to coincide with the town's centenary.[21] Despite this, however, it is still widely referred to simply as 'Letchworth'.

The Cheap Cottages Exhibition

A few weeks before the original name was decided, the first resident of the garden city, Miss Elizabeth Revill, had already moved in to her speculatively built home at Alpha Cottages on Baldock Road.[22] The estate's existing roads provided the first development sites and it was not until that summer that the first new roads, the waterworks and the first stage of the sewerage scheme were constructed to facilitate more completely new development. By the end of the year there were 36 new buildings and the population had grown to an estimated 450, from 400 the previous year. The first houses were for affluent professional and business people, rather than working-class families. Many of the first residents were directly associated with the Company. However, commuting from Letchworth was possible from the outset using the stations at Hitchin or Baldock (for those who could get there). A crude railway halt opened at the garden city site in 1903 and a regular passenger service began in Spring 1905, offering 12 London trains a day in each direction by the following year.[23]

Nevertheless, progress implementing the plan remained slow. Despite Adams's persuasive gifts, developer interest was not great and the absence of a critical mass of houses affordable to workers inhibited employment growth. Industrialists were reluctant to move to a place where workers could not be attracted. The effect on Letchworth's development as a whole was serious, but the weakness of the Company's financial resources prevented any early or significant moves to rectify this.

At this point, though, Adams had a brainwave.[24] In October 1904 the *County Gentleman* newspaper had published a piece by John St Loe Strachey, the editor and proprietor of the *Spectator* magazine. Strachey argued that a method must be found to build rural cottages for no more than £150. His point was that they should be capable of being affordable to agricultural labourers whose wages had been driven down by the agricultural depression. Only in this way could rural depopulation be stemmed. To this end he called for a competition that would encourage new construction techniques to reduce housing costs. Although agricultural housing was never going to be a significant concern for the Company, cheaper housing was. Adams saw the article and opportunistically decided that having such an exhibition in Letchworth would both increase the garden city's supply of low-cost housing and generate a huge amount of publicity. In November he convinced the Board to offer a site at a peppercorn rent to host a Cheap Cottages Exhibition where the entrants could build their cottages.

The exhibition was opened in late July 1905 by the duke of Devonshire. A total of 121 cottages was built as competition entries on two separate sites, necessary because of the limited amount of land with services which was then available. One was just north of the railway station, the other further away, across Norton Common. The *County Gentleman* and the *Spectator* gave much exposure in their pages and around 60,000 visitors (80,000 according to some) came during the three months the exhibition was open.

The impact of the exhibition

In terms of publicity, the impact for Letchworth was immense, though much reporting was not positive and opinions differed as to the overall balance of benefits and costs. Many journalists portrayed Letchworth simply as a place where an urbanite might find a cheap country cottage.[25] Visitors also saw at first hand the desultory nature of the garden city at that time, with odd groups of houses set here and there surrounded by fields, a few as yet unmade-up roads and mud, lots of it. (As later chapters confirm, the peaceful path was often a muddy one.) Yet almost all the cottages showed ingenuity and some genuine innovation in their construction that has increased their interest over time (Figure 2.3). It was debatable, though, how relevant their headline £150 costing was, since serviced land costs, professional fees, builders' profits, fencing and other normal charges were excluded.

The cottages themselves attracted criticism from an aesthetic standpoint, including from Unwin. He and Parker had already run into difficulties trying to assert any design control over what was being built. Such was the pressure to get building underway that the Company was already acceding to developers who rejected Parker and Unwin's guidance. The 1905 exhibition was an even

Figure 2.3 The most remarkable of the 1905 Cheap Cottage Exhibits, this concrete 'cottage' was built by a prefabricated technique with the potential for mass production (never realised). It was designed by John A. Brodie, the City Engineer of Liverpool. (author photograph)

more acute symptom of this early dilution of standards, something which made it difficult for the Company ever to regain any authority in this aspect.[26] There was also a broader related debate about making housing affordable for the labouring masses. Even though Letchworth did not yet have a resident industrial working population, this was already a real local problem. Some of its building workers had to come from surrounding districts, many being obliged to leave their homes at 5.00 a.m. to walk from Hitchin or Baldock before doing their day's work.[27] Others were unemployed labourers from the capital, temporarily housed in wooden huts built by the London Central Unemployed Fund Committee.[28]

Many reformers asserted that the answer to the housing question did not lie in technological innovations to cheapen construction. Instead they variously argued that land speculation should be eliminated (a key part of the mission of the garden city movement); that municipal councils should build housing with public subsidies; and, most radical of all, that wages should be raised. These opinions often coincided with the view that the standard of working-class housing needed to be raised. This became a key theme of a second Urban Cottages Exhibition on a site just south of the town centre, in 1907, this time under the auspices of the National Housing Reform Council.[29] The quality was indeed much higher and much closer to what Unwin and Parker wanted. As an event, however, it failed to stir much popular interest.

Industrialising the garden city

Although the 1905 Exhibition produced a sudden burst of activity it could not change the Company's early under-capitalisation. There were, however, some cautious infrastructural investments that allowed the Company to supply water and gas from 1905 and electricity from 1907.[30] These utility services were easier to finance because sales would quite soon generate the revenue to repay any borrowing to build the water and gas works, the power station and the distribution systems.

The effects of a sound plan and fundamentally good locational conditions for factory development, together with these cautious investments in infrastructure, quickened the pace of development. From 450 in 1904, Letchworth's population rose to 1,500 in 1905, 4,300 in 1907 and 9,000 in 1914.[31] A key change was that expansion was now being fuelled by employment growth, as the first factories opened. In 1905 Heatly-Gresham Engineering and the Garden City Press became the first two industrial firms in Letchworth.[32] Heatly-Gresham moved to Letchworth from Bassingbourn in Cambridgeshire to expand its business in the motor industry. The Press was a new firm, formed by a group of Leicester printers as a co-partnership venture, in keeping with Howard's general hopes for the garden city.

These two sectors were also strongly represented in the industries which followed.[33] Most important of the early factories was J.M. Dent and Sons, printers and publishers, who moved from cramped premises in the East End of London. Dent himself was a socially concerned industrialist attracted by the reformist spirit of Letchworth as well as its lower rentals.[34] W.H. Smith's bookbinding works and the firm's subsidiary, Arden Press, were also early recruits (though they did not long survive wartime disruption before returning to London). On the engineering side, Lacre and Phoenix were two early motor companies that moved from London.

Within a few years other types of industry also appeared. Spirella, an American corset company, began manufacturing in 1910, expanding rapidly to open what was ultimately a large and imposing factory in 1912–20 (Figure 2.4).[35] Unusually for this period, the firm's proprietor William Kincaid preferred married women workers. It was part of a wider strategy to project a company image of great respectability in an industry that produced such intimate garments

Figure 2.4 'Castle Corset', the Spirella factory building. This American corset company was an early industrial arrival and its enlightened employer built this prominent factory with an attractive garden for his workers. It has been recently been beautifully conserved and regenerated as prestige business premises. (author photograph)

for women. In pursuit of this, Kincaid deliberately located his new factory away from the industrial estate on the north-west edge of the town centre, abutting instead a completely residential area. Widely known as 'Castle Corset', the factory was a model of enlightened management and industrial welfare, with a factory garden added in the 1930s. Many workers lived close to the factory, something Kincaid encouraged. It ensured that there was no risk of Spirella ladies having to run a gauntlet of coarse comments from men on the industrial estate.

Other significant new firms included the Marmet pram factory, which opened in 1913 and grew rapidly between the wars.[36] Then, as Letchworth's path, like everywhere else's, became very unpeaceful with the outbreak of the Great War, a large metal works was established by Belgian refugees Kryn and Lahy in 1915 and became a major munitions works. At its wartime peak it employed 3,000 workers, many of them Belgians who temporarily swelled Letchworth's population, who made shells, tank parts and portable bridges. After 1919 job numbers fell, but it remained the largest local employer, with 1,000 workers in 1924. An important new arrival in 1920 was the British Tabulating Machine Company, marking the beginnings of a long-term Letchworth connection with information technology.[37] Shortly after, in 1922, another company of long-term importance, Shelvoke and Drewry, appeared as a spin-off from the Lacre company. It soon achieved a strong position in the specialist market for public cleansing vehicles. A further important interwar arrival was the Irving Air Chute company, the British subsidiary of an American firm, which opened in 1926.

Overall Letchworth showed a trend of steady industrial growth. By 1930 the town provided 6,900 jobs, compared with a total population of about 14,500 in the following year.[38] In 1937 the Company estimated that some 10,000 insured workers were employed in Letchworth (though not all of them living in the town).[39] Research in the early 1940s showed that 22 per cent of its firms were transfers or branches of firms from elsewhere in the UK, 18 per cent were foreign firms and 48 per cent were new firms.[40] The Company had made strenuous efforts to promote industrial development, especially between 1903 and 1917 under successive estate managers Thomas Adams (to 1905) and Walter H. Gaunt (1905–17). Adams had some important industrial successes, but had too many other duties. The Company wanted to prioritise industrial promotion and brought Gaunt in from the pioneering industrial estate developed (on normal commercial lines) at Trafford Park in Manchester.[41] He was derided by some garden city purists as a northern philistine, yet he both made an important contribution to Letchworth's industrial diversification and played a significant role in the subsequent history of the peaceful path.

'The best location in England for manufacturers is ...'

Industrialists did not consider Letchworth merely because of the reformist potential of Howard's ideas. Even those who were interested, such as Dent or Kincaid, based their decisions on more hard-headed calculations. Accordingly, it made sense to market Letchworth in this way. Gaunt brought the industrial promotion expertise of Trafford Park and would have known of the pioneering and highly successful new industries programme adopted at nearby Luton from 1899.[42] That town's links with the garden city movement were especially strong from 1910 to 1918, when the chairman of the national Garden Cities and Town Planning Association, Cecil Harmsworth, was also Luton's MP.[43] Other nearby towns, such as Watford, were also adopting similar new industry campaigns around this time.[44]

Gaunt used a range of promotional tactics (Figure 2.5). Letchworth became one of the first British settlements to make extensive use of boosterist advertising on the American pattern to proclaim the advantages and attractions of places.[45] Deployed originally to help open up the American West, it was also used to boost the continent's newly established towns and cities.[46] By the early twentieth century it was already being used by British holiday resorts, and Letchworth became one of the first places to use it to attract industrial investors. Simultaneously, the

Why Manufacturers

move to . . .

11 FACTORIES
ALREADY . . .
WORKING. . .

Letchworth (Garden City)

6,000
Inhabitants

INTERIOR—W. H. SMITH & SON'S BOCKBINDING WORKS, GARDEN CITY.

CHEAP GAS AND WATER.
GOOD COTTAGES.   LOW RATES.
CHEAP ELECTRIC POWER.
UP-TO-DATE FACILITIES.
BRACING AIR.
AMPLE & EFFICIENT LABOUR.

Figure 2.5 An early example of the industrial promotional work of Walter Gaunt. A practical and down-to-earth man, he played down the social reformist aspirations of Letchworth and stressed straightforward business advantages. (author's collection)

increased use of electric power for industrial purposes was allowing flexibility in the location of industry within Britain. There was also a growing interest from foreign firms in establishing British factories. This was further stimulated by the 1907 Patent Act, which effectively meant that foreign firms needed a presence in Britain to ensure their patents would be respected within the country.[47] Building on all these new opportunities, Letchworth publicity circulated in Germany, France and the USA, as well as in Britain. One of Gaunt's earliest efforts began by asserting that '[t]he best location in England for manufacturers is the new industrial town of Letchworth (Garden City)'.[48] It was hardly snappy, but was notable in portraying Letchworth as an industrial town. Gaunt was determined to stop it being seen only as a rather eccentric residential town.

Important among the advertised advantages were low land costs. Dent, for example, had leased five acres for £2550, as against £17,500 for a similar central London site.[49] Because the First Garden City Company took responsibility for many municipal functions, local taxes were very low. Much was made of the Company's investments in utility services and the low prices which could be offered. Other advertised advantages included good rail links (with sidings serving the industrial area), good cottage housing and the healthy environment of Letchworth, including its 'bracing air'. A more dubious claim was the presence of an ample and efficient labour force.

The Company regularly considered building standard factories for rent, potentially a huge advantage to firms short of capital. Yet the Company itself was also short of capital, which delayed action. In one case, though, a housing society provided a factory for leasing to a particular firm. Finally, in 1914 the Company itself provided a tenement factory with nine 'nursery' units for rent.[50] It also gave financial assistance to several firms to build. Some directors personally took a financial stake in certain firms to persuade them to come to Letchworth.

For their part, industrialists were attracted by Letchworth's low land costs, good environment and increasing supply of decent worker housing. Thus the Spirella company commented in the 1920s on Letchworth's advantages:

> The stamina of the employee at Letchworth is greater than in an overcrowded industrial area, and in a self-contained community such as we have closer individual touch with the worker is obtainable, with the result that the estrangement between employer and employee is less marked than in the larger towns.[51]

Yet many employers also complained in these early years about high railway freight rates and problems of getting sufficient skilled workers in such a small place. Many wanted more rapid growth to the originally envisaged 30,000 population. There were also complaints about relatively high electricity costs and some shortages of homes.

'A decent home and garden for every family that come here'

The lack of sufficient housing in the early decades of the twentieth century was not peculiar to Letchworth, but was compounded there because the town lacked the diverse existing housing stock of an older-established town. The Cheap Cottages Exhibition began to address the problem. Already, however, other means of building more affordable new houses (at least for better-off workers) were appearing in the form of limited profit co-partnership societies, which used a combination of tenant, private and state funding. As shown in the last chapter, the connection between co-partnership and garden city movements was close. Ralph Neville, chairman of the Garden City Association and (until 1906) the First Garden City Company Ltd was himself a pioneer of the co-partnership movement and Howard soon became a keen supporter.

The first housing co-partnership society associated with the garden city movement, Ealing Tenants Ltd, founded in 1901, was an entrant for the 1905 Exhibition. Yet already, in January 1905, Garden City Tenants, the first of Letchworth's own housing societies, was established on a limited dividend basis. It began as an offshoot of the Garden City Press (itself an industrial co-partnership) and initially provided houses for its workers. By 1914 it had built over 300 houses, though there were criticisms that its first efforts were still too expensive for lower-paid workers. In response, Unwin argued strongly against reducing standards and asserted that the garden city should mean 'a decent home and garden for every family'.[52] Nevertheless, it was a criticism that struck home and affected subsequent housing development.

Several other housing societies soon followed.[53] Letchworth Cottages and Buildings, a subsidiary of the First Garden City Company, appeared in 1907, its first houses being successful entrants in the Urban Cottages Exhibition of that year. Two further societies, the Howard Cottage Society and the Letchworth Housing Society, were formed in 1911. Howard became closely associated with the society bearing his name, which soon became the most active. It took over schemes already initiated by Letchworth Cottages and Buildings. All these limited-dividend bodies were eligible for government loans at low interest rates, which became more favourable for housing societies after 1909. This combination of local needs and national housing policy shifts brought more economical housing developments let at noticeably cheaper rents that were more affordable by lower-paid workers. By 1914 Letchworth's housing societies had together built or were building 1,060 dwellings.

Municipal and private house-building

In contrast, the local authority, the Hitchin Rural District Council, had built only four dwellings in Letchworth. However, the wartime population influx exacerbated an existing shortage of cheaper housing. At a time of general price inflation, rents charged by private landlords rose and there was a local rent strike in 1915, similar to those then occurring around industrial Britain.[54] The national problem was so serious as to require government action, resulting in the 1915 Rent and Mortgage Interest (Wartime Restrictions) Act, which pegged all rents at August 1914 levels. Locally these various changes also prompted the Council to greater activity and it built just over 100 dwellings during the war years.

In 1919 the newly formed Letchworth Urban District Council, bolstered by a national policy which gave generous Treasury subsidies for housing, proved much more active.[55] By 1924 there were 865 council dwellings, making up 28 per cent of the total housing stock. The housing societies, though initially less active after 1919, accounted for 1,086 homes (35 per cent), with the remainder built by private developers, mainly on a small scale for sale, rent or, in a few cases, self-occupation. A small number had been built by some employers, notably Dent's, for some key employees. Yet, although most factory owners wanted housing for their workers, direct employer provision was uncommon.

Opportunities for true speculative housing development were limited in Letchworth because the Company monopolised land supply and kept freehold ownership, with leasehold control over what was built. A large proportion of private dwellings were built to order for individuals by local builders, though some builders began to provide a few ready-built houses when market conditions seemed favourable. The main pioneer was the local entrepreneur J.F. Bentley, who began building his £170 'Palace Gem' bungalows extensively before 1914, continuing in the 1920s.[56] Others followed, especially in the 1930s, when private developers building for owner occupation dominated housing output.[57] Even then, however, the scale of individual developments remained very modest. There were no big private housing estates because the Company's retention of the freehold of the entire Letchworth estate was incompatible with the packaged speculative development process operated by the major 1930s private house-builders.[58]

Nor did the council have a major role in house-building during the 1930s. The national shift of housing subsidies after 1933 towards slum clearance and relief of overcrowding had little relevance for a town with a dwelling stock less than 30 years old. By 1939 1,353 dwellings, or 27 per cent of the total stock, were council-owned, though the proportion had, a few years earlier, risen to around a third.[59] There were 1,950 privately owned dwellings (almost 39 per cent of the total), of which about four-fifths were owner occupied (including those still mortgaged).[60] Housing society activity revived from the mid-1930s and by 1939 1,708 dwellings (just over 34 per cent) were owned by the societies.[61] The Howard Cottage Society was by then much the most important of these. By 1947 it held 689 homes of the total 1,705 owned by all Letchworth's housing societies and the Company itself.[62]

'Where town and country meet'

At their best, the residential environments of Letchworth helped shape national thinking about housing design. Parker and Unwin's master plan had envisaged maximum net residential densities of 12 dwellings per acre (almost 30 per hectare), even for the most modest cottages, an intention that was largely fulfilled. This was much lower than prevailing densities of housing for equivalent inhabitants in existing urban areas under local authority bylaws, which were typically 25 houses per acre (approximately 62 per hectare) or more. As hinted in the last chapter, actual densities achieved at Letchworth were even lower than those envisaged in *To-morrow*. The smallest residential plots (2,000 square feet) proposed by Howard suggested densities of perhaps 18 dwellings per acre (roughly 45 per hectare).[63]

This density allowed much larger individual gardens than were hitherto usual in working-class homes. The architecture was also influential in both general and specific senses. At the broader level it gave unprecedented emphasis to working-class housing design. In the more specific sense, the mainly Arts and Crafts architecture of Parker and Unwin, and those following their lead, articulated a new architectural form for Howard's conceptual ideal of 'Town–Country'.[64] It brought closeness to nature and the vernacular aesthetics of the country cottage into an urban industrial setting. Inspiration came from John Ruskin and William Morris, with materials used honestly and simply, without embellishment.

The first schemes for the Garden City Tenants co-partnership society at Westholm Green and Birds Hill (1906–7) arranged the housing in small groups, typically of four or six dwellings, with wider frontages than were found in bylaw housing (Figure 2.6).[65] Avoiding the long narrow terraced houses of the old type meant that more natural light could now enter all rooms. Externally, the grouping of different sizes of dwellings within the housing groups was combined

Figure 2.6 A 1906–7 housing development by Garden City Tenants Ltd at Westholm Green, grouped informally around a green space, based on earlier ideas by Raymond Unwin. The houses, however, proved beyond the means of most working-class families. (author photograph)

with the use of gables and dormer windows to give design interest to the façades. The concern with grouping also moved housing design from a focus on the individual dwelling to one on the wider design conception of the whole housing group, including the relationship of buildings with the street and public space.

Even before Letchworth, Unwin had been thinking about how small dwellings might be grouped around informal greens, and his work with Parker at New Earswick had seen some moves in this direction. But Westholm Green was an almost exact realisation of site-planning ideas that he had developed in 1899. Birds Hill also made use of greens, placing some housing groups back from streets. Cul-de-sacs also began to be used, with narrower paved roadways, thus reducing development costs. This was a form of development that could not then have been achieved in larger towns and cities because the local building bylaws still required developers to provide much wider streets.

Larger housing groups with more emphasis on affordability and integral community facilities soon followed. The largest development by Garden City Tenants Ltd (164 dwellings developed off Pixmore Avenue in 1907–9) also went farthest in the pursuit of economy. Its site plan by Unwin included several small greens, but he provided only a very narrow access road (Pix Road), lacking even a footpath, through the site to serve about half the houses on the site. This economy greatly reduced development costs but, with only 18 feet between the front gardens, has brought serious car parking problems in more recent years.

The later housing societies went further in their attempts to combine economy and affordability without seriously compromising what had become garden city ideals. Letchworth Cottages and Buildings Ltd developed about 200 cottages between 1907 and 1911. Some cost no more than £120 to build, allowing them to be offered at the lowest rents then available in Letchworth. Mainly located in the North Avenue/Common View area north of the railway, they included simple designs by Barry Parker and another important Letchworth architect, Courtenay Crickmer.[66] In the general quest for cheap but attractive houses, the Howard Cottage Society's Rushby Mead development of 1911 was an important landmark (Figure 2.7). The site layout by Unwin featured cul-de-sacs and standardised groupings of cottages. Crickmer, Parker and Unwin and another important local architectural office, Robert Bennett and Benjamin W. Bidwell, designed the actual housing.[67] This scheme has often been regarded as the most successful of the early low-cost housing estates.

Over just a few years, housing designs had become far more standardised than those of Garden City Tenants Ltd. Other low-cost schemes followed during World War I in response to the sudden influx of industrial workers. Yet, through all these important changes to widen social access to living in Letchworth, the social unit which was designed for was the individual nuclear family. There were,

Figure 2.7 The Howard Cottage Society more directly addressed the needs of those with lower incomes. This is part of the Rushby Mead development (1911–12), with small but extremely attractive housing built in small groups: the epitome of early garden city housing architecture. (author photograph)

Figure 2.8 Housing in Ridge Avenue for the Howard Cottage Society (1912). The architects were Bennett and Bidwell. This housing shows real continuities with that produced by local authorities with government subsidies after 1919. (Jane Housham)

however, two schemes that offered a much more co-operative form of living. Howard had a keen personal interest in the first of these, at Homesgarth, a co-operative housekeeping enterprise with shared kitchen and dining facilities, that was developed in 1909.[68] A similar scheme at Meadow Way followed in 1915, developed by the Howard Cottage Society.

Although these two developments revealed the spirit of social experiment in early Letchworth, they were much less significant for the subsequent development of wider housing policy and design than were the first garden city's other pre-war housing schemes. After the war, the Urban District Council's housing schemes showed direct continuity with these pre-war housing-society schemes (Figure 2.8). Some of the same architects were involved, notably Bennett and Bidwell, who designed the Jackman's Place scheme of 1919–21. In addition, a larger story lay behind the similarity, in that the low-cost pre-1914 housing that was evolved by Letchworth architects became one of the principal templates for the housing standards adopted for subsidised local authority housing across Britain after 1919.[69] Letchworth's architects, principally Raymond Unwin with Crickmer, played a direct and crucial early role in pressing design standards pioneered in the first garden city on the new Ministry of Health. As will be shown in Chapter 4, however, the continuity did not extend to Howard's overall conception of creating entirely new settlements.

The town centre

The town centre plan was one of the most elaborated and formal aspects of the Parker and Unwin plan of 1904.[70] At its heart was the major formal axis which extended north/north-east–south/south-west through Letchworth. In the centre it stretched along Broadway from the railway station, bisecting the town square, which was conceived as the civic centre, with public and religious buildings for the first garden city. In practice, however, the plan's intentions were never realised. There were several reasons for this, the most basic being that the amount of space needed for the civic centre and related buildings was simply over-estimated.

Yet there had been early criticisms of the lack of proper civic design at Letchworth, especially when compared with Sir Edwin Lutyens's grand central area of Hampstead Garden Suburb. In Letchworth the Company charged Parker and Unwin in 1912 with planning a very grandiose preliminary scheme. Sketched out by F.J. Watson Hart, it showed Town Square as an imagined complex of civic buildings in the manner of what Lutyens referred to as 'Wrennaissance' architecture. The square's perimeter was shown lined with colonnaded buildings of a similar scale.

But the Company, though feeling a little more robust financially, soon began to worry about how to implement such a plan. The original proposals were scaled back a little and the square was planted in anticipation of the realisation of the buildings, the outline of the central civic complex being marked out with Lombardy poplars as a prelude to the actual construction. However, the doubts of Letchworth's estate manager Walter Gaunt about the wisdom of such grandiosity and the outbreak of war in 1914 discouraged any immediate action. The inaction turned out to be permanent. The original poplars remained until Letchworth celebrated its centenary, when they were replaced by a new planting scheme and a more general embellishment of the area, including the fountain (Figure 2.9). No buildings have ever encroached on the Town Square itself (now called Broadway Gardens).

Retailing ideals and realities

The initial factor in developing the centre was not a need for civic buildings but a steadily growing demand for shops and related commercial facilities, which eventually had their main impact in a different part of the centre. This was because the concentration of early housing and industrial development on the northern and eastern sides of the town had the effect of skewing shopping and related provision to the north-eastern side of Letchworth's centre. By contrast,

Figure 2.9 Town Square (Broadway Gardens), looking south-west. The original plan was far too ambitious as regards the size of the centre. The grand civic complex proposed in 1912 for Town Square was never realised and the square has remained a formal open space. The fountain is a recent addition. St Michael's Church, visible on the right, was built in the late 1960s. (author photograph)

Broadway, the Square and the western side of the centre remained rather undeveloped for many years.

In *To-morrow* Howard had proposed that retailing should be provided in a manner similar to the public market halls which existed for food and other everyday products in most cities and large towns. Thus there would be a common, collectively provided, glazed retailing space which he called the Crystal Palace.[71] The environment this provided would be sheltered, convenient and attractive, offering a diverse and interesting place for customers and thereby concentrating their purchasing power. It was essentially an elaboration of the retail arcades that already existed as commercial ventures in bigger urban centres and anticipated the more recent notion of the enclosed shopping mall.[72] Howard also hoped that, in retailing just as in other facets of the garden city development, co-operative enterprise would come to play a large role in providing for the needs of garden citizens.

In the event, neither of his initial intentions for retailing was fulfilled in the way that Howard had hoped. Most retailing was provided in conventional shop units that fronted onto Station Road, Leys Avenue and, later, Eastcheap.[73] The idea of a Crystal Palace was not seriously pursued (although in 1922 a short shopping arcade was built between Leys Avenue and Station Road). The Company began by itself giving a cautious lead, but a commercial shop development company was formed in 1914 to build shops and attract retailers.

Figure 2.10 Leys Avenue. The end of the earliest shopping group (1905–7) is visible on the left, with the 1920s group and the arcade visible beyond. The recent pedestrianisation scheme allows the street to be seen at its best. (author photograph)

Figure 2.11 The former Urban District Council's offices and the Broadway Cinema beyond were important 1930s buildings facing the northern side of Town Square, adding to the sense of Letchworth as a more mature town. (Jane Housham)

Initially many garden city promoters had shared Howard's view that priority should be given from the outset to the co-operative movement, which they hoped would occupy a central place in Letchworth's life and growth. Yet their overtures were ignored by the Co-operative Wholesale Society, perhaps because the risks that the garden city experiment would not succeed were so high. It was, in fact, through local initiative that a new co-operative society was formed. In 1905 the manager of the Garden City Press established the Garden City Co-operators, opening for trading first in an estate cottage. In 1907, however, a proper store was built in conjunction with Garden City Tenants Ltd in Leys Avenue. By 1913 the first stage of what eventually became a much larger Co-operative Store had opened in Eastcheap.

Shopping development

The architectural form of the shops and other commercial buildings reflected the rather incremental process of central development.[74] Although a favouring of neo-Georgian gradually emerged, development began with no very strong unifying style. This was something which attracted criticism but also, over time, gave Letchworth's centre the look of a town that had developed organically, rather than being a consciously planned new settlement. The first significant group of shops (with offices and flats above), designed by local architects Bennett and Bidwell, was developed in 1906–7 along the south side of Leys Avenue. The permanent railway station opened in 1913 and at about this time development also began along Broadway. Thus the main Post Office, designed by Bennett and Bidwell, and the First Garden City Company's offices, designed in neo-Georgian style by Parker and Unwin, appeared on adjoining sites in 1913–14. A little further along Broadway, on Town Square, the Letchworth Museum, designed by Parker and Unwin, was built in 1914.

After a wartime hiatus, an important central development was promoted by the shop development company in 1922–3 on the triangular site between Station Road and Leys Avenue (Figure 2.10). Designed in neo-Georgian style by Bennett and Bidwell, it comprised the Midland Bank (now HSBC) and adjoining shops (including the already mentioned arcade). In the 1930s more central buildings were added to Broadway and the Town Square. Notable buildings were the Letchworth Grammar School (1931), designed by Barry Parker; and Letchworth Garden City Urban District Council Offices (1935) and the Broadway Cinema (1936–7), both designed by Bennett and Bidwell (Figure 2.11). The Public Library, designed by Crickmer, had also just recently been built next to the Museum at the adjoining corner of the Town Square.

As all this implies, it was some time before Letchworth gave any real sense of having a coherent and filled-in town centre. In the early years, many gaps and open sites remained. Not until the later 1930s was this lack of coherence substantially diminished, giving a more 'urban' feel to the town centre. Even so, however, a few large undeveloped sites remained until after 1945, most notably along Eastcheap and around Town Square. The original lack of balance between the eastern and western sides of the centre, though now diminished, is still noticeable.

An improving financial position

Despite these outward signs of unfulfilled promise in the town centre, the underlying financial position of the Company was, by the later 1930s, fulfilling the original hopes.[75] Even when physical development was still quite desultory, before 1914 the Company's finances had begun to look healthier. After the very disappointing response to the original share issue the Company decided in 1906 to raise further capital by the private sale of debentures for a fixed term and the paying of a specified interest rate of 4 per cent each year. This was more immediately attractive to investors; there was a further issue in 1915 and, specifically against the asset of the gas works, in 1920 (though at the higher interest rate of 7 per cent, reflecting prevailing market conditions).

Ordinary mortgages were also used to top up ongoing borrowing needs in the interwar decades. By this stage, however, the Company's finances were becoming much more soundly based. In 1913 the first dividend (of just 1 per cent) on the shares was paid. These dividends were suspended during the war but resumed in 1918 and succeeding years, with progressively higher dividends. In 1923 dividends reached the permitted upper limit of 5 per cent, a level which was then maintained. A further sign of financial confidence came in 1937, when arrears started to be paid on dividends for those years when either no dividend had been paid or the rate had been below 5 per cent. The 5 per cent dividend level was finally achieved in the early post-war years, after which the intention was that surpluses would go to the wider community. As we will see, this and other important changes of the early post-war years eventually created a crisis for the Company and the town.

A community emerges

The strongest aspect of the young garden city was the strength of its community, which, even from the very early days, was exceptional and very lively. The mix of human ingredients was fascinating. The people directly associated with the Company gave much social leadership in the early days.[76] Thomas Adams held the record. He was soon president of the local Free Church, vice-president of the Liberal and Radical Association, president of the Letchworth Debating Society, treasurer of the Horticultural Society, a keen local tennis player and an instigator of the Letchworth Golf Club. Other figures, such as directors Ralph Neville and Howard Pearsall and Company solicitor Herbert Warren, were almost as active. Raymond Unwin was soon a leading light in the educational life of Letchworth, teaching its citizens about the works of Ruskin, Morris and others. Wives were equally active, with Caroline Adams president of the Women's Liberal Association, Free Church stalwart, pianist and unofficial social worker for the nascent community.

Yet this was to be no top-down paternalism in the manner of a single employer company town. From its very early years Letchworth attracted many radical and freethinking spirits, broadly socialist in their thinking, seeing all as equal. In unpublished drafts of his famous 'Three Magnets' diagram, Howard had originally used the term 'individualistic socialism', a phase which encapsulated much of the early spirit of the place. Theirs was not primarily the socialism of industrial workers seeking higher wages and better conditions through trades unionism or seeking to gain Parliamentary representation. Much as Howard had imagined his peaceful path, the formation of the community of Letchworth was first and foremost social and cultural rather than overtly political. It was about finding a new, freer, simpler and more natural way to live within an urban and industrial society.

An integral part of this was the making of new choices about basic aspects of day-to-day existence, on matters such as marriage, spirituality, diet, dress and child-rearing. Not everyone associated with Letchworth went in exactly the same direction in these choices. But there was a more generalised desire for a simpler life than could be lived in existing towns and cities. This was mirrored in the nascent town's remarkably wide religious sentiments. Although established and Catholic churches were present, nonconformity and freethinking sentiments were the stronger elements. The Free Church, in 1905 the first new church building to appear in Letchworth, was perhaps most representative of the town's early religious life. But agnosticism appears to have been relatively strong, as were less dogmatic forms of spiritual faith that did not fit neatly into denominational categories.

There were also many other indicators of the distinctive tenor of Letchworth's social and cultural life. From a very early stage it generated a remarkable number of associations covering a bewildering range of subjects. That sardonic observer of the local scene, Reginald Hine, reported the observation by a local journalist that before Letchworth was four years old it had one committee for

Figure 2.12 Design for a tapestry made by Edmund Hunter c.1909 and paraded on local public occasions such as the 1911 Coronation celebrations. Its aesthetic expresses the mix of natural and medieval references that typified the Arts and Crafts movement. (author's collection)

each inhabitant.[77] Its artistic and creative life was always very rich for such a small place, tending to follow in the wake of John Ruskin and William Morris (Figure 2.12). Another, not unrelated, enthusiasm was revealed by its unusual concentration of Esperanto speakers.[78] This relatively new artificial language was a vehicle for strong internationalist sentiments and was used to help spread the garden city idea to new lands. It hinted at a significant though certainly not overwhelming strand of pacifism which was present in Letchworth. For this section of Letchworth's population, the peaceful path really did mean peaceful. As a result, despite many local young men joining the armed forces to fight and the opening of an important munitions factory at Kryn and Lahy, there was

Figure 2.13 This 1909 cartoon expresses how the early garden citizens felt themselves to be portrayed by outsiders, especially in popular newspapers. Specific figures associated with the Company portrayed at the bottom of the cartoon are (left to right) Walter Gaunt, with the dark beard; Raymond Unwin, seated at the drawing board; and Howard Pearsall, with spade. There is no evidence that any of them ever dressed in smocks. (First Garden City Heritage Museum)

also a strong local movement against the war.[79] Some Letchworth conscientious objectors were imprisoned for their beliefs, while others were allowed to work on the land as an alternative (among them a future minister in Labour governments, Herbert Morrison).

'What some people think of us'

Particularly salient as an indicator of the nature of Letchworth was the notable (though never universal) popularity of vegetarianism and food reform within the emergent new community.[80] Today the search for more natural and wholesome forms of food and the avoidance of meat have become quite common. During the early Edwardian years, however, such an outlook was widely viewed as the prerogative only of cranks. A cartoon captioned '[w]hat some people think of us' published in Letchworth in 1909 satirised this perception (Figure 2.13).[81] It showed a rather conventional family viewing the garden city as a sort of zoo, its inmates feeding on nuts, raisins and rice.

The cartoon also depicted the parallel currency of rational clothing ideas in early Letchworth, at least among some early residents. The dress-reform movement was driven by a desire for looser and more natural forms of clothing that did not constrain the body and allowed the wearer greater freedom and contact with fresh air and sunshine. Its most adventurous advocates (always few in number) favoured rustic loose smocks and open sandals. Fed by reports of sightings of such eccentricity, journalists were dispatched to Letchworth to find particularly outlandish examples, although a *Daily Mail* reporter in 1910 found only one man in sandals and a Roman toga.[82] More common was a tendency to dispense with everyday articles of clothing such as hats, ties, gloves, socks, ordinary shoes or boots. Shorts were also more commonly seen than elsewhere. Few in number though its purist advocates always were, they had a disproportionate and enduring impact on wider perceptions of Letchworth.

In fact, the enthusiasm for rational clothing was a symptom of a wider interest in personal freedoms. These early years saw a wider rise in political and social concern for women's rights, a subject on which Letchworth's citizens tended to have advanced views. Ironically, given the later importance of Spirella in the town's economic and social life, it was not a place where laced-up conceptions of femininity predominated. Women were encouraged to adopt, and many adopted, a more active, sporting lifestyle. The town's experiments in co-operative living at Homesgarth reflected something of this concern for women's freedoms, providing an alternative to the bourgeois ideal of the family and female domesticity.[83] Rather than being seen and not heard, young children

Figure 2.14 Howard Park, laid out 1904–11, remains a focal point for the community. What was originally a paddling pool, opened in 1929, has recently become a larger splash pool, immensely popular with Letchworth's children. Here they continue to enjoy the fresh air, sunshine and freedom that Howard imagined for them in 1898. (author photograph)

were also encouraged to freer behaviour, enjoying the many parks and green spaces of the garden city barefoot and sometimes entirely naked.[84] Despite all the contemporary anxieties which we project onto our children today, it is pleasing to see that something of this spirit lives on in the town today (Figure 2.14).

'Local option – temperance reform'[85]

If dress and food reform were more marginal interests, temperance was a subject of major concern in late Victorian and Edwardian Britain, during which time there was almost no national regulation. On the one hand, the beer and liquor trade was deeply entrenched politically (in the Tory interest). On the other, there were wide views on the Liberal side of politics and within the church, especially the nonconformist churches, favouring varying degrees of control of the drink trade. Howard and his followers were very much in the latter category. In *To-morrow* he had posed the question of whether the garden city ought to be dry, with no public houses, concluding that that should instead be a local option on which garden citizens could vote. In Letchworth the first such ballot occurred in 1907, conducted on the basis of all adults, men and women, having the vote.[86] Women's votes were reckoned to have been key in rejecting any licensed premises. Despite national changes during World War I which brought real controls over the drink trade, successive local ballots for the next half century went repeatedly in favour of temperance.

The result was that, until 1957, when a local vote finally went the opposite way, Letchworth was an almost completely dry town. 'Almost', because there were actually two existing inns in the outlying villages of Willian and Norton. However, one resident later recalled that Letchworth 'always appeared to be a town of secret drinkers'.[87] There was nothing to stop its people buying from off-licences in Hitchin or elsewhere, with some helpfully offering delivery services, which many households used. A few private clubs in Letchworth received private licences and the Letchworth Hall Hotel (in the rural belt) gained a meals licence. Otherwise, in Letchworth proper there was from 1907 the Skittles Inn, the pub with no beer, which gave opportunities for the social fellowship of a traditional hostelry.[88] Attractively designed by Parker and Unwin, it was well used until the 1920s, when a building in the town centre replaced it. The former Skittles building continued as The Settlement, an adult education centre, where various events (and idiosyncrasies) of Letchworth's social and cultural life have continued to unfold.

The emergence of local political life

Temperance was far from being the only topic of concern to the local community. There had been earlier signs of a more widely questioning and challenging approach to all sources of authority in Letchworth, including the Company itself. Criticisms were often given cultural expression in satirical theatrical productions, writing or cartoons. But it was not long before these sentiments began to take a more overtly political form. Yet, as in any new settlement, there is an early period when no formal electoral mechanisms exist for articulating the viewpoints of newcomers. This was particularly so in both the garden cities because they were both sprung upon quite unsuspecting local areas. The later New Towns did at least arise from a more formal process of prior consideration and consultation, so that political representation had at least been considered.

The First Garden City estate was split between three parishes within the Hitchin Rural District. This meant that there was no obvious setting within which the interests of the new garden city could be discussed or advanced. In the material sense this was less important, because the Company expected little from the Rural District Council to support the development. Yet, despite Howard's hopes, a development company, however well-intentioned, could not be a substitute for a representative form of local government. At the very simplest level, residents had no way of registering their opinions unless they owned shares, which few did.

A Letchworth Residents Union was formed in July 1905 with a committee elected on full adult suffrage, a forward-looking initiative at a time when relatively few women could vote in local government elections.[89] The Union defined its role as looking out for the interests of the residents during the development of the estate. It was very active in its first years, acting as a sounding board for community views and a means of organising and finding potential leaders within the new community. In 1908, however, a 15-member parish council was formed with a few minor responsibilities, including street lighting, which it took over from the Company. Its first chairman was a progressive Conservative and former minister, Sir John E. Gorst, who had recently moved to Letchworth.[90] Meanwhile, the growing town's representation on the Rural District Council was increased to six councillors in 1909.

The Urban District Council

It was not long, however, before the idea surfaced of forming an urban district council solely for the garden city.[91] This was not immediately pursued because the Company had a quasi-municipal role, but, although this kept local taxes lower, it came at the price of a 'democratic deficit'. This was something which could not go on indefinitely, especially so in such an opinionated community as Letchworth. Eventually the Rural District, the Parish and the Company all agreed and Letchworth Urban District Council came into being in 1919. We have already seen how it soon became a second active force shaping the town.

As was true throughout local government at that time, party politics began to play some part in Letchworth's affairs. Yet, as in many smaller towns, other party loyalties were not yet overtly declared, with the majority of council members identifying themselves as 'All-Party' or Independent. This tended to moderate the actions of the Council but, even so, it was soon a potential challenge to the dominance of the Company in shaping the town's destiny. The first signs of this came in 1923 when the Council, aware that the Company could now pay the full permitted dividend to shareholders, asked why the estate should not pass into its care. Howard's intention in *To-morrow* was that, ultimately, each garden city would become the property of its citizens, whose interests the Council saw itself as representing. Their view was also that the Council now seemed to be providing all the lower-cost housing and that, in other respects, the town seemed to be progressing much more under its own momentum. Two years were spent investigating this matter, but it was eventually dropped because no financial basis for achieving the transfer could be found.[92]

After this initial challenge, the Council managed to co-exist reasonably successfully with the Company until the 1940s. A pattern of quarterly meetings of representatives of the two bodies was established in which issues of common concern could be discussed in an 'off-the-record' way. This meant that each body came to have a good understanding of the other's perspective and intentions. Yet it meant that the Council ceded some of the roles that were increasingly being fulfilled by similar councils in 'normal' towns. Town planning, for example, was a subject of growing local authority importance by the 1930s, but one on which the Letchworth Council took no action until 1938.[93] In that year the Council hired a planning consultant who advised them that they should seriously consider preparing a statutory town planning scheme themselves. No action was taken on this until after 1945, although, in the interim, the role of local planning authority was unequivocally passed to the Council under the wider terms of the 1943 Town and Country Planning Act.

A changing population

This tendency to passivity in accepting the Company's local hegemony was to some extent reflective of a wider shift that had occurred in the local community. By 1939 Letchworth's population had grown significantly, to about 18,200. The town certainly had retained some of its former cultural eccentricity and intensity, but such tendencies were being diluted and to some extent submerged in the public sphere. Although temperance continued to hold sway in the town, the wider sense of being part of a great social experiment to find new ways of living diminished. Some observers have seen the hand of Walter Gaunt, the Company's second estate manager after Adams, in this change. It was part of the Company's drive to establish Letchworth as a 'normal' town, attractive for business investors. As Charles Purdom later commented, 'The nonsense of the idealists was to be squashed. That was Gaunt's aim.'[94] The supposed result was profound, as the leaders of what might have remained an 'alternative' community departed or learned to keep their heads down. Again from Purdom: 'Unwin had already run away, so others followed; many threw up public interests and retired into their shells or personal cliques, others took comfort in the arts or the churches … but local affairs were too much for them.'[95] Although some of these changes happened, it would be wrong to see one man as wholly responsible. We might also doubt how viable Letchworth would have been had it stayed absolutely true to its original identity. It would certainly have remained a smaller town.

Industrialisation and local employment growth definitely brought a new social dynamic. Personal histories of individuals point to people moving from London, from the wider region and from other regions to fill these jobs.[96] In some cases such moves were related to movement of firms themselves, with employees, from previous locations to Letchworth. This played an important part in bringing skilled workers into the town. Movement of workers from regions with higher unemployment in search of work were also important. Some of these were actively orchestrated by government policies in the 1930s. In 1930 a factory on the industrial estate occupied by a firm which had just gone out of business was reopened as a Ministry of Labour Training Centre.[97] It was geared towards receiving the unemployed (including the never employed) from other regions and equipping them with new skills to work in new trades. By 1935 (i.e. over five years) some 3,000 youths from the mining districts (many from south Wales) had been sent to Letchworth to be trained in this way. Not all stayed to become a permanent part of Letchworth's workforce, but certainly some of the local demand for juvenile and semi-skilled workers was met in this way.

Even as the supply of housing in the town grew, the early pattern of workers coming daily from outside Letchworth to work there continued. In 1935 it was reported that between 30 and 40 per cent of Letchworth jobs were being filled by workers from outside the town, including many young people and women.[98] In 1938 the Company thought that 40 per cent (4,000 workers) was probably an overestimate, but could not offer a precise alternative figure, so that the proportion might well have been around a third.[99] However, the amount of out-commuting of workers living in Letchworth to other areas, particularly London, was thought by the Company to be small, perhaps only 200.

A life more ordinary
Letchworth, begun as the first step on Howard's peaceful path, had become one of the new industrial towns of the interwar years. Although wages for many of the new jobs, those not requiring high skills, were certainly not high, it was, in relative terms, a prosperous town. Unemployment was very low compared with the depressed coalfield areas. Although some of its new workers and residents came from older industrial areas, where trades unionism was strong, industrial relations were generally calm. The air of confrontation which characterised many of the older industries during the 1920s barely touched Letchworth's factories. Just after World War II, for example, the manager of one well-established company reported that 'the labour available is of a good type, and steady'. He also mentioned 'the benefit of a small town outlook, with the knowledge that people have of each other and their willingness to co-operate'.[100]

Much of the growth after 1914 had introduced many more 'ordinary' people, less pre-occupied with actively developing a new way of living. As millions of new houses with generous gardens were built between the wars in suburban locations throughout Britain, the novelty of the garden city as a place to live and as an ideal diminished. It was a pleasant place to live rather than somewhere where a new way of living was being invented. The Company had long been embarrassed by the town's social exceptionalism, so welcomed this onset of normality. Interwar Letchworth could still attract radical elements, but was less a place where social mores were being actively challenged.

A revealing example was the Taylor family, new arrivals in the town in 1923. James, the notional head of the household, was a skilled engineer who later became an instructor at the Government Training Centre.[101] His wife was Annie Kenney, formerly the key working-class figure in the Women's Social and Political Union, a close ally and friend of Christabel Pankhurst in her militant struggle to gain votes for women before 1918. Yet now, worn out by the personal impact of her brave struggles and the punitive consequences which followed, she lived a quiet life with her small family in Letchworth.

Even so, the town could still be a minor rallying point for that particular strand of socialism and radicalism which rebelled against the social conventionality of the mainstream. Those who lived in the town in these years remember the eccentricities of some residents. The Independent Labour Party was increasingly the spiritual home for such sentiments by the interwar years and Letchworth periodically hosted gatherings of its (by the 1930s) rapidly dwindling membership. The socialist writer George Orwell, living in nearby Wallington during this period, wrote about an incident he witnessed on a Letchworth bus in about 1936 while one such event was occurring. Although he was making a general observation about how socialism was perceived, he gives an insight into how the town's social mood had shifted since in its early days:

> …two dreadful-looking old men got on [the bus] … They were both about sixty, very short, pink and chubby, and both hatless. One of them was obscenely bald, the other had long grey hair bobbed in the Lloyd George style. They were dressed in pistachio-coloured shirts and khaki shorts into which their huge bottoms were crammed so tightly you could see every dimple. Their appearance created a mild stir of horror on top of the bus. The man next to me, a commercial traveller I should say, looked at me, at them, and back again at me, and murmured 'Socialists…'.[102]

The first garden city, in other words, might still be a rallying point for eccentric and unconventional proponents of socialism, but such people now tended to be seen by Letchworth's people as something *distinct* from them rather than being, as was the case in the early years, an intrinsic part of the place. Whether or not the shift was down to Gaunt or simply the growth of the town as an industrial centre, the social life of Letchworth had changed. It had become more 'normal'.

Post-war strains

In 1945, however, it was the mainstream, far more conventional Labour Party that, reflecting a national political change, took control of Letchworth's Council. The town had seen a similar wartime boost to industry to that which occurred during World War I. Far more visible as war ended, however, were familiar problems of serious local housing shortages as more people had come to the town (reaching an estimated wartime peak of over 23,000 in 1944[103]), while house-building largely ceased. Yet at least there was no significant physical destruction. The new Letchworth Council had no wish to go back to its former deference to the Company. As well as existing local needs for housing, the Greater London Plan of 1944, led by Patrick Abercrombie, now laid new obligations on the town. In effect, Letchworth was to roughly double in size, mainly reflecting a planned movement of people from inner London, taking the population to roughly 35,000.[104]

Nationally the New Towns Bill was an early sign in 1946 from the new Attlee Labour government that there would soon be a different way to follow the peaceful path (see Chapter 4). Letchworth councillors noted that New Towns would ultimately be handed over to the local authorities for their areas, which emboldened them in their dealings with the Company. In early 1948, when it became clear that Welwyn Garden City was to be made a New Town, Letchworth Council urged the minister of town and country planning, Lewis Silkin, to do the same for Letchworth.[105] However, as we will see in Chapters 3 and 6, the circumstances of the two garden cities were not the same. The Letchworth Company, though seen by Silkin as 'rather moribund', had so far stayed true to its original ideals of limited profit. Nor, unlike in Welwyn Garden City, did the government have plans for the town that differed from those of the Company. It must also have helped that there was more genuine affection within the government for Letchworth, especially so from the deputy prime minister, Herbert Morrison, a former Independent Labour Party member who knew the town in its early days.[106] The result was that the Letchworth Company, which also agreed to full cooperation with both the government and the Council, was allowed to remain. And there, for the moment at least, the matter rested.

Planning for housing

Already, in early 1946, the Council and the Company had fallen out over the more immediately pressing matter of local housing needs, seen as a serious problem by many local people and employers. The Council wanted to buy the freehold of almost 238 acres (96 hectares) of Company land north of Wilbury Road. Freehold purchase went beyond the leasehold-only sales of pre-war

Figure 2.15 The neighbourhood centre on the post-1945 Grange estate. Largely developed by the local council, the dispute over buying the land was a sign of growing tension with the Company. The estate helped to meet post-war housing needs but shows how the distinctive 'sense of place' was diminishing. (author photograph)

years and the Company refused, whereupon the Council made a Compulsory Purchase Order.[107] A shocked and indignant Company, supported by local manufacturers, claimed that this would herald the end of proper planning. Yet the Council actually had more recent experience of planning affordable housing development than did the Company. Moreover, since the Council would (so it was thought) eventually take over the entire Letchworth estate, it was argued that this was merely a way of beginning that process.

The threat of compulsion was enough. A freehold conveyance was agreed, though only for the 178 acres (72 hectares) for the Council's housing and related functions. Other land for housing association (as they were now called) and private housing development was excluded. The Grange estate, as it was called, had been begun in a small way before 1939 by the Howard Cottage Society, but was now planned as a residential neighbourhood by Geoffrey Jellicoe (who later prepared the controversial original master plan for Hemel Hempstead New Town). By the early 1960s over 1,400 dwellings had been built (Figure 2.15).

In July 1955 the Council and Company agreed to house Londoners in the town under the Town Development Act of 1952 (about which more in Chapter 7). It involved building around 1,500 dwellings on the Jackmans estate for families seeking council housing in London.[108] The advantage for Letchworth was that it got more financial assistance than for its own council housing because of London weighting and funding for infrastructure and because local jobs would be available for the new workers. The implementation of this heralded another argument between Council and Company. As earlier, the Company was now prepared to part with freehold land for council housing, but baulked at selling industrial land. This time, however, a Compulsory Purchase Order was enforced.

Land values and the Company

This land was bought on what turned out to have been particularly favourable terms for the Council. Shortly afterwards the law changed, so that public authorities would have to pay a price based on full market value. This change and other legislation since 1947 had dramatic consequences.[109] In the main, the changes were in planning law, which affected land values. However, the nationalisations of electricity and gas supply and distribution in 1947–8 removed two profitable public utility businesses from Company ownership. This increased its reliance on its land assets, which became complete in 1961 when the Letchworth water undertaking was sold.

The 1947 Town and Country Planning Act as originally enacted determined that future land-value increases consequent on planning permissions would be taxed at 100 per cent under what was called a development charge. As far as Letchworth was concerned, 'planning permission' was no longer something that the Company effectively gave itself, as it had been until the 1940s. It was henceforth a permit to allow development granted by the local planning authority, now Hertfordshire County Council. The development charge was intended to prevent the granting of planning permissions that changed land uses or allowed building to cause rising land values. The brave intention was to make land a neutral platform for urban development, where decisions could be based on considerations other than the changing commodity value of land. In practice, however, the charge proved very unpopular in the property industry and was consequently unworkable. The development charge was abolished in 1953, which certainly stimulated development but, along with it, rising land prices. An anomaly existed until 1959 because there was a dual land market, with acquisitions for public sector development continuing to be at existing use value. (It was this which allowed the Jackmans estate to be bought on favourable terms.)

But there was a wider significance. The financing principle for Howard's peaceful path rested on capturing the uplift in land values for wider community benefit. The development charge under the original provisions of the 1947 Act threatened the ability of the Company to do that. The extent of this threat was debatable because Letchworth's development was already well established, so that much of the increase would come from rental-value increases on existing development. In other words, it did not rely on future planning permissions. Nevertheless, the Company sought an exemption and, failing to get it, abolished the limited dividend rule in September 1949, still maintaining the principle that it, the Company, existed for the common benefit of the people of Letchworth. The Council was unhappy at this change, which meant that dividends to shareholders that were above 5 per cent might henceforth be awarded. However, the Company established a Letchworth Common Good Fund in 1950 as a way of transferring some funds to voluntary organisations in the town. It also reiterated the ultimate intention to transfer the Letchworth estate to a public body to be managed on behalf of the community. On this basis the Council became reconciled to this important change.

'No sentimental Ebenezer miasma'

However, matters did not rest there for very long. The changes of 1949, 1953 and 1959 removed the obstacles to the Company being able to keep future increases in the value of the Estate. As property values generally began to rise, the change was noticed by investors looking for land assets that represented previously unrealised value. The value of Company shares began to rise and it became vulnerable to a takeover bid and a more radical change in Company policy.

Matters began to come to a head in September 1960, when one property group with a big shareholding in the Company called for it to pursue 'a more vigorous and realistic policy in the interests of shareholders'.[110] A takeover bid for further shares sufficient to take control of the Company was launched in November, prompting a rather more subtle counter-bid from another property group, Hotel York, headed by the formidable Amy Rose. She claimed that she would maintain the unity of the Letchworth estate and the principles on which the town was founded, but few took this statement at face value. The York company's record was not particularly public spirited. In early 1961 Mrs Rose became managing director of the First Garden City Company and her son joined the Board. At an ill-tempered meeting with the Council in October 1961 the Company's new intentions became clear: 'There is no sentimental Ebenezer miasma – we are a commercial company.'[111]

The Council had a Labour majority but on this matter had unanimous support from all political groups. Its members had been very worried for some time and in July 1961 announced that a private parliamentary bill would be promoted to protect the town.[112] A public trust would take over the

Company's assets and manage them for the benefit of the town's people. The local Conservative MP, Martin Madden, fully supported this move throughout, facilitating its passage. Meanwhile, the flurry of activity had alerted both local people and a wide and influential group nationally, with much parliamentary support from all sides. A 'Save Letchworth Garden City' campaign was mobilised locally, winning widespread support. The government was also sympathetic to the idea of replacing the Company, provided that the cost would not be an excessive burden on local ratepayers. Hertfordshire County Council, though sympathetic in principle, was not prepared to give financial assistance.

Letchworth Garden City Corporation

Despite these worries, a Bill was framed to create a public corporation similar to the development corporations used to develop individual New Towns. The main difference was that the acquisition of its land assets would be funded by the local authority and would in time be passed on to the locality. As a public corporation, it avoided the risks of future takeovers. There was great parliamentary support and the Letchworth Garden City Corporation Act became law in 1962.[113] The Corporation took over from the Company in January 1963, with the exact price to be paid for the Company remaining the subject of legal determination until 1966, when it was finally settled at just over £3 million.[114] This avoided the rapid property inflation that began from the later part of the decade. All things considered, it was a bargain.

Thus was Letchworth Garden City saved. Yet it had been saved by making the body responsible for its development and management into a public corporation. In view of Howard's perpetual mistrust of the state, this was scarcely following the peaceful path. At least the key principle of unified ownership of its land for the benefit of the town's people remained intact. Or had it? No sooner had the ink dried on the financial settlement than the 1967 Leasehold Reform Act gave leaseholders the right to buy the freeholds of their homes.[115] Potentially this struck at the heart of privately planned ventures such as Letchworth (Welwyn Garden City, Bournville and others were similarly affected). However, the Act allowed a scheme of management to maintain the estate's relatively tight planning under leasehold controls.[116] (Far more controversial locally were the high valuations for freehold acquisition placed on the shorter 99-year leases as they came closer to expiry.[117])

By 1968 the financial position of the Corporation allowed it to make regular and increasingly substantial payments to fund community projects and, over the next 20 years, some £7 million was disbursed. It was a sign that, under Corporation stewardship, Letchworth had at last come to maturity.[118] Population growth caused by net in-migration to the town came to an end during the 1960s. From around 25,000 in 1961, Letchworth's population rose to 31,000 in 1971, close to the level proposed by Howard in *To-morrow*. The figure then stabilised, so that by 2011 it had grown only slightly, to just over 33,000. For much of its life, therefore, the Corporation was responsible for completing developments already initiated and managing a substantially developed estate. Yet, despite the slight population growth, smaller family sizes still meant demand for new private housing during the 1970s and 1980s. There was also an attempt to modernise the centre to attract a major supermarket. The only partially successful result was a purpose-built pedestrianised shopping precinct developed in the early–middle 1970s.

By the 1980s and 1990s economic changes and the passage of time were taking their toll on the town. Long-established main manufacturing industries shrank, went out of business or left, creating a growing need for regeneration both to reuse vacant sites and to create new employment. In its final years the Corporation was largely pre-occupied with developing a new business park on vacant industrial land east of the original industrial estate. The park fed to some extent on the boom in high technology and knowledge-based industries in nearby Cambridge, as well as on Letchworth's own well-established business advantages.

Discovering the garden city as heritage

Looking at the way the town changed over the post-war decades, both before and after the Corporation was created, the dispassionate observer could reasonably wonder whether in the visual and design sense it really had been saved in 1962. Much of what was developed in the post-war decades, especially from the 1960s – the Grange and Jackmans estates, the private housing development, the town centre shopping precinct or the business park – might in truth have been built anywhere in southern Britain at that time. Moreover, what had been distinctive in the earliest parts of Letchworth was at real risk of being eroded. The ill-considered reconditioning and extending of older housing and the accommodation of cars were inexorably nibbling away at the distinctive qualities of the first garden city.

During the early 1970s attitudes began to change. North Hertfordshire District Council incorporated Letchworth with the adjoining areas of Hitchin, Royston and Baldock. Of these, Letchworth was the only one without conservation areas (although some buildings were listed as being of historic or architectural interest). One of the new Council's first actions in 1974 was to create a large conservation area covering the town centre, the early residential

Figure 2.16 Lytton Avenue, 1907 Urban Cottages Exhibition housing. From the 1970s the early garden city environment of Letchworth was increasingly cherished by owners, occupiers and local policy. (author photograph)

areas and old Letchworth.[119] This did not give the measure of protection that could be achieved by the listing of individual buildings, but it brought an added degree of planning protection to a wider area and, importantly, was a clear public signal of the town's historic value (Figure 2.16).

The public mood was certainly ready for this and protection of the unique qualities of the first garden city has subsequently become an enduring theme in planning the town. It added to the sense that Letchworth had reached its natural size and should grow no further, an idea which those of the town's residents resisting further development have invariably drawn on ever since. However, conservation was never intended to be synonymous with preservation and its challenge has often been to accommodate necessary change in a way that cherishes and honours heritage. The economic changes which affected Letchworth during the 1980s and 1990s fully exemplified this challenge, especially so in the town centre.

The Letchworth Garden City Heritage Foundation

From 1995 the management of this challenge fell to a new body, the Letchworth Garden City Heritage Foundation.[120] During the 1980s and 1990s Conservative governments accelerated the wind-up of the entire New Town programme, abolishing the remaining Development Corporations. Though not identical to those bodies, Letchworth Garden City Corporation had enough similarities to be tarred with the same brush. Fortunately, because it was not subject to New Towns legislation, there was no obvious exit strategy (normally, undeveloped New Town land and commercial property went to the Commission for the New Towns and housing and non-commercial assets to the local authority).

Therefore, an exit strategy and successor body had to be invented. The result was unveiled in 1992: a not-for-profit agency run by a Board of Management and governors with a preponderance of local interests, both elected and appointed. This was an attempt finally to overcome long-running complaints of remoteness from local concerns and interests that had dogged both the Company and the Corporation throughout their existence. The objectives of the new body were essentially to protect and enhance the vitality and the existing qualities of the garden city and to assist in any activities for the good of the people of Letchworth. After some parliamentary delays, the Foundation was finally created in 1995.[121] Its fixed assets – essentially the garden city estate – were valued at £57.5 million. It represented the Howard legacy and, quite simply, was an endowment to die for.

For most of its life, until 2010, the Foundation had one director general, Stuart Kenny, subject to decision-making by the governors and a smaller Board

Figure 2.17 Broadway, looking from Town Square/Broadway Gardens towards the railway station. North Hertfordshire College (left foreground) was redeveloped thanks to the arrival of Morrisons supermarket (beyond the college) in 1999. This brought much trade into the town centre and began to shift the commercial impetus to the undeveloped west side of Broadway. (author photograph)

of Management. Kenny, an economist and former civil servant, was a dynamic figure who celebrated the Foundation's creation with a bungee jump in Town Square that launched festivities throughout the town.[122] He brought property and regeneration experience from work on the Merseyside Taskforce in the 1980s and latterly as the deputy chief executive of Leeds Development Corporation.

Regeneration and conservation

Much use was made of this experience, especially in the exemplary regeneration and conservation of the Spirella factory as prime business and office premises.[123] The town centre was also a major problem. By the 1990s Letchworth residents did most of their shopping outside the town, particularly after the supermarket that had briefly occupied the shopping precinct moved elsewhere. In 1999, however, a much larger Morrisons superstore was built fronting Broadway on a large site formerly occupied by the further education college, which was rebuilt on an adjacent site on the corner of Town Square (Figure 2.17). The retail chain's head, Ken Morrison, was known to Stuart Kenny from his time in Leeds and throughout there was close co-operation over the project's development and design.[124] Like most large superstores, this one was set in a large car park, but it was not allowed to dominate the face that the development presented to the town and the Foundation ensured that the town centre as a whole would benefit

Figure 2.18 View from Station Place down Leys Avenue. This shows the extensive and recently completed improvements to the pedestrian environment of the town centre. The first shopping parade can be seen on the right and the 1920s parade on the left. Compare with Figure 2.10. (author photograph)

from access to this parking. The store's design and that of the rebuilt college (the latter effectively paid for by the development) were highly sensitive to the setting, particularly in scale and materials.

The result did much to regenerate the centre, bringing more customers in and finally achieving the elusive major retail development west of Broadway, thus encouraging further improvement. A scheme to improve the pedestrian environment and reduce traffic flow on the existing central streets of Eastcheap and Leys Avenue had long been under consideration. Its implementation was well underway when Kenny left and it was seen through to completion by his successor John Lewis. The finished result adds greatly to the attractiveness of the town centre (Figure 2.18). Overall the Foundation's work has made a major positive contribution to the town in these and other ways. By 2012 some £4 million was being donated annually for the benefit of the community, including towards running a free day hospital, the local cinema, a local transport network to take residents to and from their social clubs, a museum and a farm attraction.[125] Grants were also provided to individuals, groups and organisations in support of a wide variety of activities that bring depth and interest to the town.

Yet, in doing all this, it has still not entirely overcome the historic problem of how to find a way of melding real local accountability with effective estate

Figure 2.19 There is a strong feeling in Letchworth that, having reached its planned size, it should grow no further. Any sign that the Heritage Foundation or the North Hertfordshire District Council might be inclined otherwise prompts strong opposition, as here in early 2015. (Harry Hubbard/*The Comet*)

management and development. Any development proposal associated with the Foundation might easily trigger opposition.[126] The curious episode of Letchworth Garden City Town Council, which existed briefly from 2005 to 2013, also owes something to disenchantment with the Foundation and what some residents have seen as its unholy alliance with North Hertfordshire District Council (Figure 2.19). The erstwhile council's supposed raison d'être was to represent the town more effectively than was possible when so much of its destiny was in the hands of a larger local authority and the only semi-accountable Foundation. However, it soon became far more disliked for doing little that justified its existence or expense and was, after only a few years, abolished.[127] If nothing else, it demonstrates that Letchworth remains a place of strong loyalties and opinions.

Conclusion: *To-morrow* slowly came

In Letchworth, then, the promise of *To-morrow* slowly came into being. Here the peaceful path led not quite to the destination that Howard had imagined but somewhere close – a thriving small town with a very pleasant environment and, most importantly, a rich endowment to the local community that does not rely on local tax revenue. As we will see, other towns offered environments which delivered on the physical promise of the garden city or updated versions of it.

Almost without exception, they grew much faster and to a greater extent, yet nowhere else managed to realise Howard's central principle. Of the garden cities and new towns, Letchworth was the only one in which its citizens have secured continuing, collective and generally increasing financial benefits from the increased land value associated with their town's development. In that sense, Letchworth remains an active garden city after over 110 years. This is why this chapter has been particularly lengthy, as it relates a story that was only really fulfilled after the town's prolonged period of growth had finished. To understand how Howard's legacy was delivered it has been necessary to tell the story of Letchworth in its entirety.

Yet, despite this central difference, there are many aspects of Letchworth's story that would recur elsewhere. Thus the slow pace of early development reflecting a shortage of capital was also a feature of the second garden city, as we will see in the next chapter. Even when funding was more secure, in the New Towns, the inherent problems of starting from scratch inevitably meant a delay before the town began to appear. Tension with the existing inhabitants of the area in which the new settlements were built was another universal theme. Even though Letchworth (Garden City) was clearly home to a community like no other, the friction that arose between the new garden citizens and the body responsible for developing and managing the town, successively the Company, the Corporation and the Foundation, had obvious echoes in most other new settlements. The same applies to the problems in the early decades of balancing the supply of suitable housing with the attraction of employers. In turn, this had consequences for how far the town could be self-contained in employment terms or the extent to which it was a residential town for those who commuted out to a place of employment or business elsewhere or a workplace for those who commuted into the town. All these themes, and others, will appear in the chapters which follow.

Notes

1   C.B. Purdom, *The garden city: a study in the development of a modern town* (London, 1913), pp. 27–9.
2   Beevers, *The garden city utopia*, pp. 79–91.
3   M. Simpson, *Thomas Adams and the modern town planning movement: Britain, Canada and the United States, 1900–1940* (London, 1985), 14–16; Miller, *Letchworth*, 2nd edn, pp. 22–4.
4   Miller, *Letchworth*, 2nd edn, p. 21.
5   R.L. Hine, *Relics of an un-common attorney* (London, 1951), p. 45.
6   Purdom, *The garden city*, pp. 29–31.
7   Miller, *Letchworth*, 2nd edn, pp. 23–4.
8   Purdom, *The garden city*, p. 187.

9   C.B. Purdom, *The building of satellite towns*, 2nd edn (London, 1949), pp. 58–9.

10   Miller, *Letchworth*, 2nd edn, p. 22.

11   R.L. Hine, quoted in MacFadyen, *Sir Ebenezer Howard*, p. 58.

12   R.L. Hine in ibid., pp. 51–2.

13   R.L. Hine in ibid., p. 53.

14   Purdom, *Satellite towns*, 2nd edn, pp. 147–72.

15   Simpson, *Thomas Adams*, p. 17.

16   Beevers, *The garden city utopia*, pp. 93–4.

17   Miller, *Raymond Unwin*, pp. 49–77.

18   Miller, *Letchworth*, 2nd edn, pp. 43–7.

19   Purdom, *The garden city*, pp. 44–5.

20   R.V.J. Butt, *The directory of railway stations* (Yeovil, 1995), p. 142.

21   Miller, *Letchworth*, 2nd edn, p. 36 and information supplied by the First Garden City Archives.

22   Purdom, *Satellite towns*, 2nd edn, p. 59; Miller, *Letchworth*, 2nd edn, p. 53.

23   First Garden City Ltd, *Guide to garden city* (London, 1906), p. 60

24   Purdom, *The garden city*, pp. 49–51; Simpson, *Thomas Adams*, pp. 55–9.

25   Purdom, *Life over again*, pp. 47–8.

26   Purdom, *The garden city*, pp. 50–51.

27   Simpson, *Thomas Adams*, pp. 27–9.

28   First Garden City Ltd, *Guide*, p. 58.

29   First Garden City Ltd, *Where shall I live? Guide to Letchworth (Garden City) and catalogue of urban cottages and rural homesteads exhibition* (Letchworth, 1907).

30   Purdom, *Satellite towns*, 2nd edn, pp. 135–8.

31   Purdom, *Satellite towns*, 2nd edn, p. 83.

32   First Garden City Ltd, *Guide*, pp. 49–54; Purdom, *Satellite towns*, 2nd edn, pp. 111–12; Miller, *Letchworth*, 2nd edn, pp. 100–108.

33   First Garden City Ltd, *The best location in England for manufacturers is the new industrial town of Letchworth (Garden City)* (Letchworth, c.1908); First Garden City Ltd, *Letchworth as a manufacturing centre* (Letchworth, 1908); First Garden City Ltd, *First garden city estate – why manufacturers move to garden city* (Letchworth, c.1909).

34   J.M. Dent, *The memoirs of J.M. Dent* (London, 1928).

35   Miller, *Letchworth*, 2nd edn, pp. 106–8.

36   Purdom, *Satellite towns*, 2nd edn, p. 118.

37   See Grace's Guide, 'British Tabulating Machine Co' <http://www.gracesguide.co.uk/British_Tabulating_Machine_Co>, accessed 15 March 2015.

38   Miller, *Letchworth*, 2nd edn, p. 132.

39   Royal Commission on the Geographical Distribution of the Industrial Population, 1938 *Minutes of evidence taken before the Royal Commission on the Geographical Distribution of the Industrial Population: twentieth day*, Thursday 5 May 1938, Memorandum of Evidence Submitted by First Garden City of Letchworth, pp. 637; 643.

40   P. Scott, *The triumph of the south: a regional economic history of early twentieth century Britain* (Aldershot, 2007), p. 164.

41   Purdom, *Life over again*, pp. 52–6.

42   Luton New Industries Committee, *Luton as an industrial centre* (Luton, 1900); Luton New Industries Committee, *Luton as an industrial centre* (Luton, 1905); S.V. Ward, *Selling places: the marketing and promotion of towns and cities 1850–2000* (London, 1998), pp. 150–56.

43   Hardy, *From garden cities to new towns*, pp. 80, 117.

44   W.F. Goodrich, *Watford: its advantages as an industrial and residential centre* (Watford, c.1908).

45   First Garden City Ltd, *The best location*; First Garden City Ltd, *Letchworth as a manufacturing*

centre; First Garden City Ltd, *First Garden City Estate*.

46 Ward, *Selling places*, passim.

47 G. Jones, 'Foreign multi-nationals and British industry before 1945', *Economic History Review*, 2nd series, 41/3 (1988), pp. 429–53.

48 First Garden City Ltd, *The best location*.

49 C.B. Purdom, *The building of satellite towns* (London, 1925), pp. 112–13.

50 Purdom, *Satellite towns*, 2nd edn, pp. 112–13.

51 Purdom, *Satellite towns*, pp. 112–13.

52 1906, cited in Miller, *Raymond Unwin*, 72.

53 H.D. Pearsall, 'The building of workmen's cottages in garden city', in Purdom, *The garden city*, pp. 261–71.

54 J. Payne, *Co-operation and conflict in the garden city: the Letchworth rent strike of 1915* (Hitchin, 1982).

55 Miller, *Letchworth*, 2nd edn, 119.

56 M. Miller, *Letchworth: the first garden city* (Chichester, 1989), p. 83.

57 First Garden City Ltd, *Letchworth – a town in the country: a description of its advantages* (Letchworth, *c.*1929); First Garden City Ltd, *Letchworth: where town and country meet* (Letchworth, 1934).

58 A.A. Jackson, *Semi-detached London: suburban development, life and transport* (2nd edn, Didcot, 1991), pp. 61–81.

59 E. Bonham-Carter, 'Planning and development of Letchworth Garden City', *Town Planning Review*, 21/4 (1951), pp. 362–76, especially p. 373.

60 Purdom, *Satellite towns*, 2nd edn, p. 61.

61 Bonham-Carter, 'Letchworth Garden City', p. 373.

62 Purdom, *Satellite towns*, 2nd edn, p. 67.

63 Howard, *To-morrow*, p. 15.

64 See Miller, *Raymond Unwin*, and M.G. Day, 'The contribution of Sir Raymond Unwin (1863–1940) and R. Barry Parker (1867–1947) to the development of site planning theory and practice, c1890–1918', in A. Sutcliffe (ed.), *British town planning: the formative years* (Leicester, 1981), pp. 156–99.

65 Miller, *Letchworth*, 2nd edn, 59–62.

66 M. Miller, *C.M. Crickmer 1879–1971* (Letchworth, 1999).

67 M. Miller, *Robert Bennett 1878–1956 and Benjamin Wilson Bidwell, 1877–1944* (Letchworth, 1999).

68 L. Pearson, *The architectural and social history of co-operative living* (London, 1988).

69 Miller, *Raymond Unwin*, pp. 161–88.

70 Miller, *Raymond Unwin*, pp. 60–66.

71 Howard, *To-morrow*, pp. 72–7.

72 M. MacKeith, *The history and conservation of shopping arcades* (London, 1986).

73 Purdom, *Satellite towns*, 2nd edn, pp. 104–9.

74 Miller, *Robert Bennett*; Miller, *Crickmer*.

75 Purdom, *Satellite towns*, 2nd edn, pp. 148–61.

76 Purdom, *Satellite towns*, 2nd edn, pp. 59–60; Purdom, *Life over again*, pp. 49–56; M. Simpson, 'Thomas Adams 1971–1940', in G.E. Cherry (ed.), *Pioneers in British planning* (London, 1981), pp. 32–4; Miller, *Letchworth*, 2nd edn, pp. 76–99.

77 R.L. Hine quoted in Macfadyen, *Sir Ebenezer Howard*, p. 58.

78 Elliott and Sanderson, *Letchworth recollections*, pp. 56–7.

79 Ibid., pp. 42, 76.

80 Aalen, 'English origins'; Elliott and Sanderson, *Letchworth recollections*, p. 43.

81 Reproduced in Miller, *Letchworth*, 2nd edn, p. 79.

82   R.L. Hine quoted in Macfadyen, *Sir Ebenezer Howard*, p. 56.

83   M. Aldridge, 'Only demi-paradise? Women in garden cities and new towns', *Planning Perspectives*, 11/1 (1996), pp. 23–39.

84   Elliott and Sanderson, *Letchworth recollections*, pp. 42–4.

85   Howard, *To-morrow*, pp. 72; 79–81.

86   Purdom, *Satellite towns*, 2nd edn, pp. 77–80; Miller, *Letchworth*, pp. 80–81; 161.

87   Elliott and Sanderson, *Letchworth recollections*, p. 58.

88   Purdom, *Satellite towns*, 2nd edn, pp. 79–80.

89   Miller, *Letchworth*, 2nd edn, pp. 113–16; Purdom, *Satellite towns*, 2nd edn, pp. 70–71.

90   A. Hunter, *A life of Sir John Eldon Gorst: Disraeli's awkward disciple* (London, 2001), pp. 269–70.

91   Miller, *Letchworth*, 2nd edn, pp. 117–18.

92   Purdom, *The Letchworth Achievement*, p. 33.

93   Purdom, *Satellite towns*, 2nd edn, p. 99.

94   Purdom, *Life over again*, p. 52.

95   Ibid., p. 55.

96   Elliott and Sanderson, *Letchworth recollections*, pp. 17–19.

97   Letchworth Museum, author unknown, 1935, *Letchworth – some economic and industrial aspects*, typescript, cited in Scott, *Triumph of the south*, p. 218; Elliott and Sanderson, *Letchworth recollections*, p. 93.

98   Scott, *Triumph of the south*, p. 199.

99   Royal Commission on the Geographical Distribution of the Industrial Population, *Minutes*, p. 643.

100 Purdom, *Satellite towns*, 2nd edn, p. 123.

101 D. Sharp, *The Kenney papers: a guide*, typescript (Norwich, 2004) <https://www.uea.ac.uk/polopoly_fs/1.76986!the%20kenney%20papers.pdf>, accessed 24 February 2015, pp. 5–6.

102 G. Orwell, *The road to Wigan pier* (Harmondsworth, 1962 [orig. 1937]), pp. 152–3.

103 Purdom, *Satellite towns*, 2nd edn, p. 83.

104 P. Abercrombie, *Greater London Plan 1944* (London, 1945), pp. 140–41, 198.

105 H. Plinston, *A tale of one city: the story of Letchworth's fight for independence* (Letchworth, 1981), pp. 16–18; J.B. Cullingworth, *Environmental planning 1939-1969: vol. III new towns policy* (London, 1979), p. 84.

106 Miller, *Letchworth*, 2nd edn, p. 98.

107 Plinston, *One city*, pp. 12–16.

108 Ibid., pp. 35–8; Miller, *Letchworth*, 2nd edn, pp. 159–60

109 The national dimension of these complex but fundamental changes is briefly but ably summarised in D.H. McKay and A.W. Cox, *The politics of urban change* (Beckenham, 1979), pp. 77–82. A very full account is J.B. Cullingworth, *Environmental planning 1939-1969: vol. IV land values, compensation and betterment* (London, 1980). The local implications are examined in Plinston, *One city*, and Purdom, *The Letchworth achievement*.

110 Cited Plinston, *One city*, p. 38.

111 Cited Plinston, *One city*, p. 94.

112 Purdom, *The Letchworth achievement*; Miller, *Letchworth*, 2nd edn, pp. 166–75.

113 Reproduced in Purdom, *The Letchworth achievement*, pp. 115–43.

114 Plinston, *One city*, pp. 213–16.

115 Plinston, *One city*, pp. 217–18; Miller, *Letchworth*, 2nd edn, pp. 175; 180.

116 Letchworth Garden City Heritage Foundation, *Scheme of Management*, 2004 <http://www.letchworth.com/sites/default/files/attachments/scheme_of_management.pdf>, accessed 3 March 2015. This remains the same as that originally adopted by the Letchworth Garden City Corporation.

117 Miller, *Letchworth*, 2nd edn, pp. 186–7.

118   Miller, *Letchworth*, 2nd edn, pp. 180–92.
119   North Hertfordshire District Council, *Letchworth Conservation Area, Letchworth Garden City: North Hertfordshire District Council*, 2001 <http://www.north-herts.gov.uk/letchworth_ conservation_area_appraisal.pdf>, accessed 4 March 2015.
120   Miller, *Letchworth*, 2nd edn, pp. 193–224.
121   The founding Act is available at legislation.gov.uk, 'Letchworth Garden City Heritage Foundation Act 1995' <http://www.legislation.gov.uk/ukla/1995/2/enacted>, accessed 18 March 2015.
122   Miller, *Letchworth*, 2nd edn, p. 194.
123   Heritage Foundation, Letchworth Garden City <http://www.letchworth.com/heritage-foundation>, accessed 18 March 2015.
124   From information supplied by Stuart Kenny.
125   J. Lewis and D. Ames, 'A model for investment and governance', *Town and Country Planning*, 81/9 (2012), pp. 389–92; Heritage Foundation, Letchworth Garden City, 'Our Charitable Commitments' <http://www.letchworth.com/heritage-foundation/our-charitable-commitments>, accessed 17 August 2015.
126   R. Day, 'GALLERY: campaigners rally at Letchworth march to save world's first garden city', *The Comet*, 2 November 2015.
127   H. Gill, 'End in sight for town council as Letchworth votes for abolition', *The Comet*, 2 November 2012.

CHAPTER THREE

Welwyn Garden City

'… more agitated than I have ever seen an Englishman …'

The second garden city, Welwyn Garden City, was a more extraordinary product of Ebenezer Howard's quixotic imagination and capacity for singular action even than Letchworth had been. This is not to deny that other individuals played critical roles in realising the project, but it would never have happened at all without Howard's willingness to be, even in old age, a man of destiny, risking everything to achieve something that he wanted but which had not been agreed with those around him.

During the last years of peace before 1914, most leaders of the Garden Cities and Town Planning Association (GCTPA), as it was now called, had come to think that repeating the Letchworth formula was impractical. The growth of the first garden city had been painful and slow, a consequence of trying to establish a totally new town in a long-settled country on a limited-profit, privately financed basis. As we will see in the next chapter, garden suburbs appeared a much more practicable approach. This was largely the position adopted by the movement as the wartime debate about the acute housing shortage and housing standards moved decisively towards wholesale government intervention.

But, by 1917, Howard and some of his younger followers, particularly Charles B. Purdom and Frederic J. Osborn, had come to a different view: that the movement had strayed too far from its true path. To this end, they launched the National Garden Cities Committee to press government to instigate and fund a post-war programme of garden cities.[1] The following year, Purdom, Osborn, Howard and W.G. Taylor, a director of the Letchworth-based publisher Dent, published *New towns after the war* under the collective nom de plume of the 'New Townsmen'.[2] Largely written by Osborn, it was a short manifesto for the new Committee's policy. The aim was also partly to shame the GCTPA out of its complacency. In that they quickly succeeded. Sure enough, within a few months, in March 1918, the Association began to draw the National Garden Cities Committee back into the fold.[3] Soon afterwards, Purdom became the new

GCTPA Secretary and, henceforth, the promotion of new garden cities again became a key part of the Association's campaign. Yet there was one crucially important difference from Howard's original formulation, namely a new reliance on the initiative, power and finance of the state.

Despite ostensibly signing up to this new approach, however, Howard retained his profound mistrust of the state as a force for positive change. On the contrary, he continued to think that a second garden city could be developed on much the same lines as Letchworth. Though they knew he held such views, his associates never thought he could or would do anything to put them into practice. Towards the end of 1918 he took Purdom and Osborn on a long walk through what was then a very rural part of Hertfordshire which sat astride the Great Northern Railway (GNR) main line north of Hatfield, remarking that it would make a good site for a garden city.[4] Believing this to be an incidental observation, his companions agreed that it was, at most, a potential site that could be used for illustrative purposes in their arguments to ministers.

For Howard, it was much more than this. At the time he believed it to be part of Lord Salisbury's huge Hatfield estate. In April 1919, entirely on his own initiative, he approached Salisbury with a proposal that the site should made available for a second garden city. Salisbury, then president of the GCTPA, had huge respect for Howard but doubted whether he could manage to launch another garden city without a proper organisation behind him. In any case, most of the site in which Howard was interested was owned not by him but by Lord Desborough. Coincidentally, however, Desborough put this very same land up for auction at the end of May 1919. On learning this, Howard was beside himself with excitement. In a tea shop near King's Cross station he shared his vision with Richard Reiss, GCTPA chairman, and a few influential friends much richer than himself. A Norwegian journalist friend of Howard's recorded that the old man was 'more agitated than I have ever seen an Englishman'.[5] Together Reiss and his friends helped raise a deposit that proved almost enough to put down on the required land at the auction.

'One step further in the uglification of England ...'

On the day itself, Howard secured 1,458 acres (590 hectares) of land for £51,000, meeting the deposit only as a result of a last-minute £200 donation by his agent at the auction, Norman Savill. Realising that he had taken an irrevocable step, Howard began to tremble uncontrollably and broke into a cold sweat. But he soon regained his composure sufficiently to recruit Osborn and Purdom (who, until then, had played no part in this adventure) to help him realise the project.

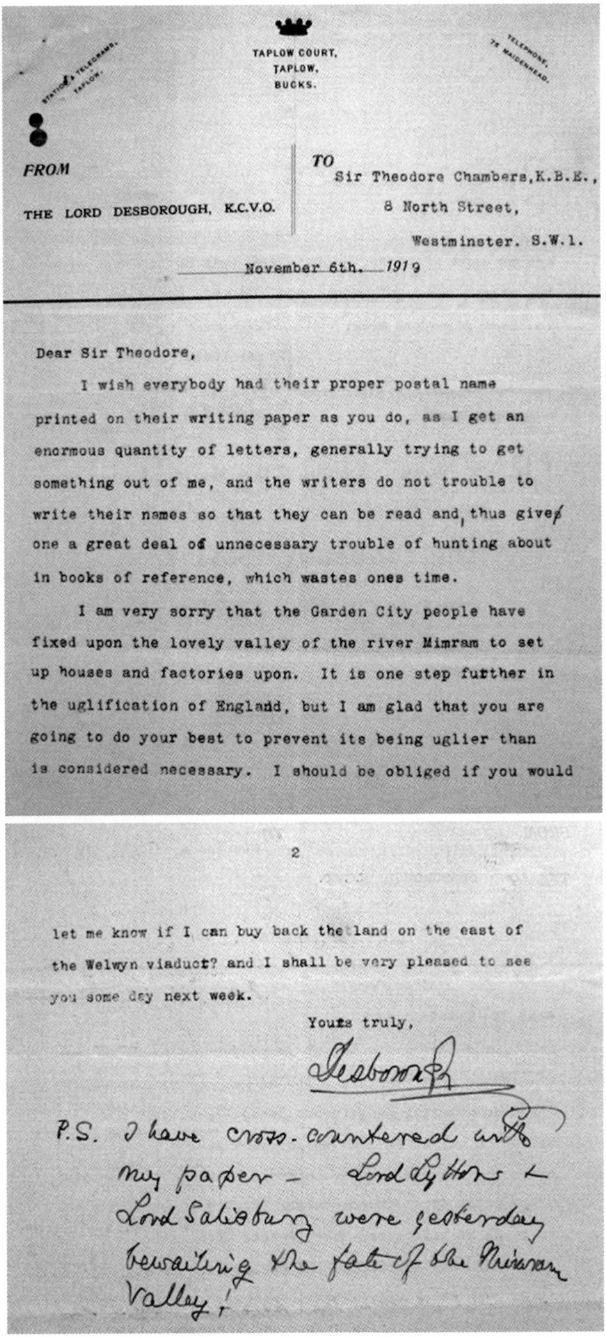

TAPLOW COURT,
TAPLOW,
BUCKS.

FROM

THE LORD DESBOROUGH, K.C.V.O.

TO
Sir Theodore Chambers, K.B.E.,
8 North Street,
Westminster. S.W.1.

November 6th. 1919

Dear Sir Theodore,

I wish everybody had their proper postal name printed on their writing paper as you do, as I get an enormous quantity of letters, generally trying to get something out of me, and the writers do not trouble to write their names so that they can be read and, thus give one a great deal of unnecessary trouble of hunting about in books of reference, which wastes ones time.

I am very sorry that the Garden City people have fixed upon the lovely valley of the river Mimram to set up houses and factories upon. It is one step further in the uglification of England, but I am glad that you are going to do your best to prevent its being uglier than is considered necessary. I should be obliged if you would

2

let me know if I can buy back the land on the east of the Welwyn viaduct? and I shall be very pleased to see you some day next week.

Yours truly,

Desborough

P.S. I have cross-countered with my paper — Lord Lytton & Lord Salisbury were yesterday bewailing the fate of the Mimram Valley!

Figure 3.1 Letter from Lord Desborough to Sir Theodore Chambers very courteously bemoaning the fact that his former land was to become a garden city. The handwritten P.S. refers to the concerns of other Hertfordshire grandees. (HALS)

Both were deeply shocked at what Howard had done, yet saw no choice but to back him.[6] To do otherwise would probably have meant the failure of the venture. Howard would have been humiliated and probably bankrupted; the entire movement would have been deeply discredited. But they quickly decided it could not be another Letchworth, developed on a very pragmatic, amateurish basis. It needed to be a fully professional operation, presented from the outset as a model of good planning for the future.

For his part Desborough was deeply mortified to discover what was planned for this beautiful site (which in 1919 contained almost no buildings), writing that it was 'one step further in the uglification of England...' (Figure 3.1).[7] Resigned to its fate, however, he agreed to sell a further 230 acres (92 hectares) at Sherrards Wood to make a more coherent estate. Yet this land remained insufficient for a garden city of the desired size (in the event, a population of over 40,000). Howard and the other promoters still needed land to the south of the former Desborough properties, on Lord Salisbury's estate. Realising that the circumstances had changed dramatically, they wanted to reconsider how they should now approach Salisbury. They also stressed the need, for the moment, to keep silent about their true purpose.

Again, Howard ignored what his associates thought had been agreed.[8] Addressing the Letchworth Theosophical Society a few days after the auction, Howard made an impassioned speech revealing this second garden city project and how he would get further land from Salisbury. The story appeared in the London newspapers, infuriating Salisbury, who refused to have any further dealings with Howard and his madcap scheme. It was only after the formation of Second Garden City Limited in October 1919 and further lengthy negotiations that sufficient land was secured from Salisbury to create an estate of 2,378 acres (951 hectares). This was nothing like as much as they had hoped for, but was enough to be able to press ahead with a viable garden city. Over time more land was bought, including 700 acres (280 hectares) north of the river Mimram in 1936.[9] By 1948 the Company owned some 4,500 acres (1,800 hectares).

Digswell Garden City?

As it stood in early 1920, the Company's name palpably gave no indication of what the new garden city was actually going to be called. Although many other matters demanded attention, this one had quickly to be decided in February 1920.[10] Most of the initial public discussion referred to it as the new garden city near Welwyn, an existing village immediately north of the Company's site. It had a small railway station and gave its name to the Rural District Council responsible for most of the area (part of it was initially in the Hatfield Rural District but it was soon decided by the Ministry of Health to make just one district authority responsible for the new area). Thus the association between 'Welwyn' and 'Garden City' was already being established in the public mind.

Yet the selection of the name 'Welwyn Garden City' was by no means a foregone conclusion. (Although Letchworth had originally been known as 'Letchworth (Garden City)' for a long period the permanent postal address did not include the bracketed words.) Several names that included a Welwyn reference were considered, including, as well as the name finally chosen, 'New Welwyn' and 'South Welwyn'. Also suggested were 'Handside', 'Hatfield Hyde', 'Sherrards Park' (which Chambers preferred but Reiss thought sounded too much like a name that might be given to a suburb) and 'Digswell', which were local names of parts of the area for the garden city. The option of continuing to call it 'Second Garden City' was also considered.

On 4 February, the Board's Development Committee resolved to recommend the name 'Digswell', which had deep historical associations. But the decision came at the end of their meeting and immediately afterwards several members began to have second thoughts. At the full Board on 10 February the name 'Welwyn Garden City' was instead reluctantly selected. Only one Board member actually voted against this, but the rest of the Board certainly thought it much too cumbersome. However, it was confirmed following a meeting of inhabitants called by the parish council in 1924.[11] Some influential figures, particularly Osborn, hoped that, in time, they would be able to usurp the name 'Welwyn', so that the pre-existing village would then become 'old' Welwyn. By 1935 Osborn was confident that the time was ripe for this to be made official through the intermediate stage of bracketing the words 'Garden City' Letchworth-style.[12] Yet the inhabitants of both Welwyn and Welwyn Garden City had got used to things as they were, and by this time the name and status of the local district council had changed to use what had become the recognised name of the new settlement. Against the odds, therefore, the original name, without brackets, has persisted. (The issue resurfaced in 1948, albeit in a slightly different form, as we see in Chapter 6.)

Creating an organisation

The more professional organisation that Purdom and Osborn wanted was also being created in these early months.[13] Second Garden City Ltd functioned solely as a pioneer company, undertaking the organisational groundwork. In April 1920 it was succeeded by Welwyn Garden City Ltd (WGC Ltd) as the recently named new settlement's principal development agency. The central figure in both Companies was the chairman, Sir Theodore G. Chambers, who was appointed in October 1919. Suggested by Norman Savill, Chambers was a prominent surveyor and Freemason who had been controller of the War Savings Committee. He had very wide contacts in finance, business, the professions and politics. His Conservative political sympathies were useful as an antidote to the prevailing impression of the socialistic nature of the garden city idea, but this did not imply any lack of understanding or sympathy for the movement. On the contrary, he was unusual in having a real practical grasp of the land economics that underpinned the garden city. He remained chairman until the Company was superseded by the New Town Development Corporation in 1948.

As well as Howard, Reiss and Purdom, the Board of Directors initially included J.R. Farquharson, the philanthropic businessman and director of the Howard Cottage Society in Letchworth, who had been the main funder of Howard's deposit for the auction sale. Another Welwyn Garden City director was the consulting medical officer of health for Hertfordshire (soon to be Conservative MP for St Albans), Francis Fremantle. There was also a director of First Garden City Ltd, Bolton Smart, and a distinguished (Liberal) economist, Walter Layton. The successful Lancashire house-builder Samuel Smethurst and Sir John Mann, a well-known accountant, also were early members. The Liberal peer, major Hertfordshire landowner and great friend of the garden city movement the earl of Lytton was briefly a member before joining Lloyd George's government as secretary for India.

There were many subsequent changes, but this first Board shows how much there was a conscious desire for a balance of interests. Yet this did not simply mean attracting figures who would help raise finance and offset the image that this was a venture motivated only by radical and unworldly Utopianism. Thus unsuccessful attempts were made to recruit a leading Labour politician: first Ramsay MacDonald, who refused, citing the controversy that memory of his wartime pacifist views would inevitably attract (not that this was a problem for Howard or Osborn); then J.R. Clynes, a leading Lancashire trade unionist and future minister in the first two Labour governments, who accepted the offer, only to be denied permission by his trade union.

Alongside these moves to create a credible and sympathetic Board, Chambers, Osborn and Purdom were making professional appointments of people to perform the detailed work of the Company. For several years, however, the latter two 'amateurs' were exceptions, serving in essentially professional roles though without formal training in the relevant skills. Osborn initially served as company secretary, but then took on the role of estates manager until 1936. Purdom's tenure as director of finance (effectively the chief officer) proved shorter. His 1928 'resignation' (effectively a dismissal) followed complaints from other officers about his overbearing and interfering style of management.[14] His departure was indicative of a growing shift from the 'amateur believer' in the garden city (and it is relevant that Howard himself died very soon after) to those who saw it in disinterestedly professional terms. As will be shown, the trend went further in the following decade.

After Purdom went, a professional finance manager, John Eccles, was appointed. In 1936 he became general manager, anticipating the pattern in the development corporations of the post-war New Towns. Professional posts covering other responsibilities had been created at an earlier stage; the most notable officers from the outset were William James, a devout Christian, who became the Company's long-serving engineer, and C.W. Care, the Company's first accountant. The most important professional in the long-term development of Welwyn Garden City was Louis de Soissons, the young man who became chief architect and planner in April 1920. His work will be discussed in more detail below.

'... reasonable backing to try'

Despite this growing emphasis on being a professionally run development company, however, secure financing remained a problem. Once the initial deposit for the land had been paid, the Company had to rely on its bank, initially Barclays, to keep it afloat with overdrafts until longer-term finance was secured. In May 1920 the Company launched an ordinary share issue of £250,000.[15] In line with the general philosophy of the movement as a venture intended for public benefit rather than private profit, the dividend payable on shares was limited to 7 per cent. Profits beyond that level were to be used for the benefit of the garden city. This permitted dividend was higher than the 5 per cent favoured for Victorian and Edwardian philanthropic ventures that had been adopted at Letchworth, because prevailing interest rates were then higher than pre-war rates. But this did not prevent the share issue failing miserably. Only £40,000 was raised initially, creeping up to £90,000 by the end of the year and edging only slightly upwards to just over £124,000 by 1930.

This failure reflected an aversion on the part of stock-market investors to limited-dividend share issues, especially in the early 1920s, when interest rates were very high and the economic optimism of the early post-war months was being replaced by gloomier expectations. The failure had various consequences. In the short term most of the directors were asked to buy up some of the unsubscribed shares. As a show of their confidence in the venture this was impressive, but it did not solve the problem. Less public forms of fixed-interest borrowing had to be adopted from 1921, in the form of debentures and development bonds.

The failure of the public share issue also pushed the Company towards a partial reliance on state loans via the Treasury and the Public Works Loan Board (PWLB). This became possible only under the 1921 Housing Act, which allowed advances of public funds to be made to 'authorised associations' to develop garden cities. This power reflected lobbying from the Company and the wider garden city movement.[16] Yet public loans were certainly not a long-term answer. The Treasury and the PWLB did not make matters easy, giving loans only reluctantly, well after the relevant expenditure had occurred and on onerous terms.[17] A major problem was that these loans used the entire estate, both developed and undeveloped, and the water undertaking as collateral. This made it very difficult to raise other loans secured against specific revenues.[18] Nor was this state assistance comparable to that which went to the New Towns. The total amount received (£313,577 by 1932) was too small to promote rapid development. Moreover, as prevailing interest rates fell, even these loans proved costly to service and brought unhelpful interference in the detailed plans to develop the town.

These various difficulties meant the Company had to rely on bank overdrafts. Even before the 1920 share issue money was urgently needed simply to complete the purchase of the land. Barclays, who were originally approached, wanted too many conditions for any overdraft, but Chambers tried one of his many contacts, Reginald McKenna of the Midland Bank, in the hope that he would be more flexible.[19] McKenna visited the town but was by no means optimistic about its future, remarking that 'If you succeed in getting 200 people to come and live here, the future will be assured – but I doubt that you will succeed in getting the first 200.' Yet, for all this, he then added that '...we will give you reasonable backing to try.' More than McKenna appreciated at the time, these overdraft facilities from the Midland later proved crucial for the Company's survival. As Eccles commented much later, the bank was '... bullied, cajoled and wheedled into lending almost continuously much more than they really liked ...', sometimes up to three-quarters of a million pounds.

This sense of managing a continuing financial crisis persisted well into the 1930s. The Company eventually moved on, but the difficulties of the early years should not be underestimated. They slowed the very development process that eventually would generate sufficient revenue to put the Company's finances on a sound footing.

The role of the subsidiary companies

A key part of the strategy to achieve financial security as soon as possible was the assumption by the Company of direct control of many aspects of the Welwyn Garden City economy.[20] This differed somewhat from Howard's original theory of frequent harvesting of the uplift in land value that resulted from urban development. By this means, it would soon repay shareholders and other investors while allowing the creation of a high quality of life for its inhabitants. Yet to do this quickly it would have been necessary to increase the ground rents on sites leased to developers at frequent intervals. As at Letchworth, it was soon recognised that frequent rent reviews would be impractical, since no one would want to develop sites saddled with so much uncertainty about future costs.[21] The system adopted – selling land on 999-year leases at fixed ground rents – avoided this problem. As the town became established, more could certainly be charged for later leasehold sales, which were valued at prevailing market rates, but this would take time. At Welwyn Garden City, therefore, the Company tried to capture that increasing value by other means which, it was hoped, would also accelerate development. Thus it was that, unlike in the cases of the post-1946 New Towns and to a much greater extent than at Letchworth, the Company spawned an astonishing array of subsidiary companies involving all aspects of the town's development and life.[22]

The first to be formed, in 1921, was Welwyn Restaurants Ltd, which took over the two existing public houses on the Company estate and built a temporary restaurant, the Cherry Tree, on Bridge Street.[23] (The Company, though hardly pro-drink, did not want the second garden city to become a dry town like its older sister.) Many other subsidiary companies soon followed. At their peak they also dealt with building services, brickmaking, sand and gravel extraction, electricity distribution, water supply and sewerage, retailing, industrial and commercial buildings, housing, transport, plant nurseries, cinema and theatre, newspaper publication, agricultural activities and laundry services.[24] In due course they grew to be an important element of revenues. Excluding water services, the subsidiaries had an annual income of over £21,000 by 1930, compared with just over £14,000 from rents.[25] However, these receipts were much more vulnerable than were rents to economic recession.

Over time there were some significant changes to the subsidiaries. In particular, the water and sewerage undertaking was sold to the district council in 1932.[26] The money received was an important stage in allowing the Company finally to free itself of PWLB funding. A few of the other undertakings changed ownership, being taken over by independent private businesses. The Company also sold its interest in its restaurant and pubs to the Whitbread brewery, which immediately rebuilt the by then decaying Cherry Tree (its replacement now being the Waitrose supermarket).

There is no doubt that this general policy of having subsidiaries gave the Company more control over the town's development. This had advantages: better retailing, cultural and restaurant provision emerged much earlier than if normal competition had been allowed. The income from them was also useful, though not decisive in making the Company financially secure. As time went on, however, Company thinking about its portfolio of subsidiaries changed. In 1922, for example, potential investors were told how important the subsidiaries would be in the town's achieving early profitability.[27] A decade on, however, the message (in their evidence to a government study) was noticeably more nuanced. Some activities were not essential and it was recognised that their growth might stifle diversity.[28]

The truth was that, explicitly or otherwise, the Company was granting monopolies or at least highly privileged positions to its subsidiaries. This prompted many complaints, such as those about the Welwyn Theatre cinema (opened in 1927) which, not being part of the national chains, did not always offer the latest releases.[29] Welwyn Restaurants also had a local monopoly of alcohol sales (which Whitbread took over in 1932). The Company's *Welwyn Garden City News* newspaper, started in 1921, gave very much its own slant on local news.[30] A rival newspaper, the *Pilot*, began at the same time, but its critical approach irritated the Company so much that it was bought up in 1928 and amalgamated with the *News* to form the *Welwyn Times*, which continued to give an official version of local affairs.

The *Pilot* fell foul of the Company primarily in its reporting of its retail subsidiary, Welwyn Stores Ltd, the most controversial example of its local monopolies.[31] The business was established in 1921, after Howard had unsuccessfully approached both Gordon Selfridge and the local Co-operative Society. Its first and main store was a single-storey building at the corner of Parkway and Bridge Street (the site of the present Rosanne House). It was not until the later 1930s, by which time the Stores subsidiary was well established, that other seriously competing retailers were permitted.[32] Yet it was debatable whether the town was yet big enough (at just under 15,000 in 1939) to sustain many competing shops. A captive market allowed the Stores alone, its defenders claimed, to sell a wider range of goods than in a 'normal' town of similar size. The proof for those who took this view was the grand new department store of Welwyn Stores (replacing the original store) which opened in mid-1939 (Figure 3.2).[33]

Figure 3.2 The flagship department store of Welwyn Stores Ltd, designed by Louis de Soissons, opened in 1939. Now a John Lewis store, it was an important milestone in the maturing of the second garden city. Nevertheless, residents in the working-class east resented the Stores' near monopoly of retailing, yearning for the lower prices of a Woolworths. (author photograph)

'... a young superman ...'

Two decades earlier, a prize such as this flagship department store would have been a pipedream in the then non-existent new settlement. At that stage, the broad ideas about how the new garden city might be laid out were only just being drawn up, by Osborn, to guide thinking about just how much land additional to the Desborough property would be needed.[34] After the site was secured, it was surveyed and its drainage considered. The scheme of development was considered in more detail[35] and in January 1920 the Company hired Courtenay M. Crickmer, who was a significant Letchworth architect (referred to in Chapter 2), to give these initial ideas a more formal expression. He produced a plan which specified the broad land-use zones that were finally adopted.[36] However, the intention that the new garden city would be a model of planning implied a continuing and not just a one-off process, involving the long-term appointment of an architect–planner. Seeking a suitable candidate, Chambers consulted the president of the Royal Institute of British Architects, who recommended Louis de Soissons.[37] Not yet 30 years old, he had been born in Montreal and educated and trained in the office of J.H. Eastwood and at the Royal Academy in London, the British Academy School in Rome and the École des Beaux Arts in Paris.

Figure 3.3 The 1920 de Soissons plan for Welwyn Garden City. Combined with much tighter development control than occurred at Letchworth, it largely shaped the town's character. The plan also became a widely reproduced icon of the Welwyn Garden City 'brand', a marketing device later used by most New Towns. (author's collection)

This glittering early career promised much for the future and de Soissons certainly did not disappoint. He combined his professional skill with a strong and persuasive personality and soon gained the respect of other architects who worked on individual buildings within the garden city. At Letchworth the original plan was almost immediately compromised in order to secure development. In sharp contrast, de Soissons used the Company's freehold ownership of the entire garden city (except, as will be shown, the railway land) to exert tight development control via the site leases granted to developers. To do this he had tactfully to resist special pleading on behalf of individual developers and pressures from Ministry of Health officials for more economical development (reflecting the financial need to use government funds).

Chambers was supportive of this firm stance and everyone eventually saw it as one of the most positive planning lessons of the second garden city. Yet this view was in hindsight; other directors certainly had moments of doubt at the outset. An early, undated letter from Reiss to Chambers reveals this: 'I cannot consent to have de Soissons acting as a dictator on matters of taste ... he has delayed building and caused a large amount of friction ... if a young superman is to come and impose his will on us and stop work I for one shall have to resign ....'[38] However, neither he nor any other members of the Company resigned and de Soissons's strong line was soon vindicated. The overall planning concept also contrasted with the very English Arts and Crafts cottage vernacular of Letchworth (which he disliked). As a Francophile, de Soissons favoured a more formal and classically influenced approach to urban design. He felt that the British architectural engagement with such formality, most evident in the Georgian period, had been disrupted by gothic and later styles.[39] At Welwyn Garden City he consciously returned to this tradition of urban formality, using an updated version of the domestic Georgian architecture found in Hertfordshire towns such as Welwyn, Hertford, old Hatfield and St Albans. This was skilfully combined with the much lower residential densities associated with the garden-city tradition, here at residential densities of 12 or fewer dwellings per acre (30 per hectare).[40]

The plan for Welwyn Garden City, presented in June 1920, was for a town with an ultimate population of about 40,000, a little larger than Letchworth.[41] As in the Letchworth plan, de Soissons had a rigid land use and density zoning scheme and a containing agricultural belt (Figure 3.3). A compact town centre was planned, close to the garden city's geographical centre, with a civic centre immediately to the north. Far more so than in the first garden city, however, the railways were a dominating consideration in planning. The site of the garden city was bisected by the main line of the Great Northern Railway and further divided

Figure 3.4 A key focal point of the de Soissons plan at the intersection of Parkway and Howardsgate, looking down the latter towards the rather prosaic 1980s Howard Centre, which now conceals the railway station. In other respects the view epitomises the outstanding visual qualities of Welwyn Garden City's neo-Georgian elegance. The fountain was added in 1953. (author photograph)

into unequal quadrants by branch lines to the west and east. Much of the basic alignment of roads and streets in the plan was accordingly determined by the bridging points of the railways. This was particularly important along the six-track mainline, where the GNR refused permission for extra bridges.

The GNR also pressed WGC Ltd into a hard bargain in return for co-operating with plans for a new central station, which opened in 1926. The Company was obliged to sell, at very modest price, the freehold of a wide corridor of land some 1,300 yards (1.19 kilometres) long amounting to almost 70 acres (28 hectares) along the route of the main line through the garden city.[42] This corridor, together with the new town centre to the west and the single large industrial zone on the level land to the east, meant that the first two main residential zones were very widely separated. There was further annoyance when the London and North Eastern Railway (LNER, the successor to the GNR) allowed some uncongenial businesses, including dog kennels and a poultry farm, into this highly visible part of the garden city.

The Company was all the more irritated because this eyesore was rather close to the town's central area and the most striking feature of de Soissons' plan,

Figure 3.5 Promotional advertisement of 1920 which perfectly expresses the planning rationale for garden cities and echoes Howard's 1898 book title. From the very outset Welwyn Garden City adopted a conscious place-marketing strategy that became increasingly segmented for both potential residents and industrial investors. (author's collection)

Parkway. This was a formal dual avenue landscaped road axis that ran to the west of and parallel to the LNER main line. Originally planned as the main southern approach to the centre from the Great North Road, it was handled in a grand landscaped manner that was rare in Britain, being graced by the planting of long stands of trees. A later enhancement was the centrepiece fountain created at Parkway's intersection with the main retail axis to commemorate the coronation of Queen Elizabeth II in 1953 (Figure 3.4). Overall, Parkway epitomises the thinking which guided the entire plan and is the clearest expression of de Soissons' admiration of the formality of Beaux Arts and American City Beautiful planning.

From planning to building

Following Howard's theory, the basic conception of Welwyn Garden City was that it should be a town where people lived and worked, rather than simply a commuter settlement (Figure 3.5). Yet, as experience in Letchworth (and later in the post-war New Towns) showed, it was extraordinarily difficult to co-ordinate the growth of both housing and employment so that they kept pace with each other. Moreover, the agricultural nature of the area meant that in 1920 there was virtually no suitable employment already available. The formation of the Garden City Company and the first building operations began to create more local jobs, but it took time for industrialists to feel sufficiently confident that either their existing workers who moved to work in the town would be able to find local housing or they would be able to recruit a new workforce locally. Responding to these fears meant that, in practice, worker housing had to be built first, before employers would come.

As at Letchworth, the Company's ability to do this itself was greatly handicapped by its financial problems. Yet the acceptance by the state of a great financial responsibility for housing during World War I and its aftermath opened up more possibilities than had been available to the First Garden City. The first houses were built by what were then called 'public utility societies' (effectively housing associations).[43] Some of these societies were wholly owned subsidiary organisations of WGC Ltd. Others were independent, even though there was often some connection (for example, through common Board members) with the main Company. Since before 1914 societies of this type, which often operated on a co-partnership basis that required tenants to own a share in their society, had been able to secure some of their funding from the PWLB in return for operating on a limited-profit basis. Now, however, the Housing and Town Planning Etc. Act and the Housing (Additional Powers) Act of 1919 gave them enhanced PWLB funding and, if they were building housing for local workers, actual government subsidies, paid via the local authorities.

These concessions (especially those under the second Act) were secured only after pressure in which the desperately underfunded Welwyn Garden City Company played a significant part. Even so, these subsidies still did not squarely address the new garden city's real housing needs: to house not an already present population but one that was hopefully on the point of moving there to newly created employment. The Company itself was providing some jobs and the first 50 houses were developed by a subsidiary society of the main Company, Handside Houses Ltd, for the Company's own workmen and staff,[44] but many of those who worked in the emergent new settlement had to put up with less comfortable living conditions. Thus the contractor for much of the early construction work in Welwyn Garden City, Trollope and Colls, built a temporary camp on the site of the present Campus. Managed by WGC Ltd, it housed 200 building workers and provided sleeping accommodation, canteen and club room.

This area was also the hub of the temporary two-foot-gauge light railway system created to distribute building materials to building sites around the whole estate from Horn's Siding on the Luton branch line of the GNR/LNER.[45]

It also linked the two brickworks and various sand and gravel excavations on the Company's estate. This method of moving goods around such a large site seems to have derived from military experience and the first locomotives were war surplus acquisitions (one of these reputedly never recovered from an early high-speed trial by Chambers' son, however). Light railways were not unusual on very large construction sites at this time, as at the gigantic London County Council housing estate at Becontree, built 1920–34, where there had also been few existing roads. The light railway at Welwyn Garden City was most significant in the early–mid 1920s, when it was occasionally used even to move early residents into their new homes.[46] It also fascinated the young children of the town and many details of its operation appear in oral history accounts of the interwar years.[47] Over time, however, better roads began to be built and the main sidings for building-material deliveries from other areas shifted to the LNER mainline, close to the new station. It was entirely closed in 1936, though some sections of the track remained until the 1950s.

In 1920 the Company established its own works department providing construction and building services. The following year this became Welwyn Builders Ltd, a subsidiary of the Company which henceforth did virtually all Company's building work and that of its burgeoning subsidiaries. This particular subsidiary firm also operated as building contractors on a competitive tender basis. As a result, Welwyn Builders constructed a very large proportion of the houses (including many of those for owner occupation), shops, offices, public buildings, cultural facilities and factories in the growing town. Employment peaked at around 1,500 workers. Along with unified land ownership, tight planning and architectural control and the ubiquity of locally produced bricks, Welwyn Builders Ltd helped to foster the extraordinary visual unity which characterises much of early Welwyn Garden City (Figure 3.6).

'For town joys in the country live in Welwyn Garden City'

For several years the Company struggled with the big question of how to finance the building of permanent working-class housing that in turn could begin to attract significant factory employment. At the outset, any real demand to live in the as yet unbuilt town was slight. A middle-class visitor recalled visiting the 'promised land' in May 1920, shortly after national advertisements had appeared in the magazine *Punch*. Years later she described what she found:

There was not a soul to be seen, but having come so far, I thought I had better try to see somebody. I had, of course, expected to find crowds of *Punch* readers besieging

Figure 3.6 Very early (c.1921) three-bedroomed houses (Type XVI) designed by de Soissons and built for sale in Handside. The sales material stressed their charming situation and bright sunny rooms, and the fact that they were within five minutes' walk of the station. (Sarah Elvins)

the office for information. I plucked up my courage and knocked at the door [of the site office], and out came Mr Rawlinson, one of the very early landmarks. He looked as if he had seen a ghost, and I realised that instead of one of hundreds of eager applicants I must be an isolated phenomenon.[48]

Yet this did not put her off and she and her husband became very early residents, living at the western edge of Handside.

An obvious temptation for the Company was to adopt more spectacular tactics to speed up development. In Letchworth the 1905 Cheap Cottages Exhibition had helped focus attention on lower-cost housing while also effectively publicising the first garden city. But there was always less enthusiasm for this tactic at Welwyn Garden City, probably because it had almost immediately begun to compromise the Letchworth plan. There was, however, one very early housing scheme with some similarities, which also proved a mixed blessing. Lord Northcliffe, the proprietor of the *Daily Mail*, and his family were important early supporters of the garden city movement, seeing within it a lifestyle for which many of his readers yearned. This led him in 1921 to promote an 'ideal village' at Meadow Green in Handside which, though never fully completed, comprised 43 dwellings. Unlike the 1905 Letchworth Exhibition, it had an architectural unity that broadly reflected what de Soissons wanted. It certainly also provided publicity, even if it benefited the *Daily Mail* rather more than Welwyn Garden City. But it was not the breakthrough in providing working-class housing that the Company wanted.

In fact, it proved much easier in the early years to build housing for a quite different need. Other public-utility societies created during the 1920s, notably Labour Saving Homes Ltd and Welwyn Homes Ltd, began to provide middle-class housing. Other societies created a little later included Moatwood Houses Ltd, Country Homes Ltd and Sherrards Wood Properties Ltd. Financing their schemes was much easier because the tenants (some of whom later bought their homes) had more funds behind them than typical factory workers and did not need state subsidies.

Another early scheme of unsubsidised housing was developed by the New Town Trust, a Quaker public-utility society (though, like most of the others, it later became a subsidiary of the Company) at Guessens Court. This comprised 41 flats mainly for single people though with some larger apartments for families or groups of friends, operated on a co-operative-housekeeping basis. Small numbers of houses began to be built by the Company for individuals who wanted a home for their own occupation or by a few speculative developers, also catering for middle-class occupiers. However, it is clear that, even in some of the more opulent roads of Handside, some middle-class houses intended for sale were actually being rented out during the 1920s when sales were slow.[49]

Yet many of those living in this unsubsidised housing were more likely than factory workers to be commuters, travelling elsewhere to work. This ostensibly undermined one of the Company's main objectives for the town. Pragmatically, however, the Company recognised the importance of attracting this group to Welwyn Garden City. Throughout the 1920s and 1930s advertising designed to attract wealthier commuters appeared in the press and on posters displayed in railway stations, especially King's Cross. Their messages were aimed directly at commuters, with slogans such as 'For Town Joys in the Country live in Welwyn Garden City' (*c.*1928) or 'Welwyn Garden City, A Greatly Improved Train Service to King's Cross' (1930s).

Generally, though, LNER season-ticket sales at the Welwyn Garden City station, the best available indicator of the extent of commuting, had peaked by the end of the 1920s. Between 1930 and 1937 the numbers remained static[50] and further population growth was by then underpinned by local employment. Moreover, the numbers of dwellings built privately or by the more middle-class of the housing societies were not very large (Labour Saving Homes Ltd built just

Figure 3.7 Later 1920s housing on Parkway, showing the more formal architectural treatment on this principal axis of the town. (author photograph)

90, for example). Yet their inhabitants together helped boost demand for local services, which, in turn, sustained local employment. Most of this early middle-class housing was built in Handside, just west of the future town centre, where many of the local services would be provided (Figure 3.7). Thus the presence of affluent commuters also helped to give a tangible physical substance to Welwyn Garden City, transforming it from being just a hypothetical planning proposition.

The shortage of working-class housing

Useful though they were in building up the town as a physical entity, none of these various schemes addressed the principal housing need for affordable working-class housing.[51] The Company had rather naively hoped that Welwyn Rural District Council (WRDC), which was enlarged to include all the future new settlement, would voluntarily play a key role in meeting this need. In fact it did so only with great reluctance. This was partly because the subsidy system operated by the Ministry of Health explicitly encouraged local authorities to build only for existing local need as manifest on a waiting list where length of residence in the district was invariably an important criterion of eligibility. The Ministry did not wish council housing itself to become a factor that could attract a new population to an area. This thinking also coloured the district council's attitude to the subsidies it passed on to public utility societies under the 1923 Housing Act.

Nor were many members of the RDC sympathetic to the Company, an organisation that had arrived uninvited to, as they saw it, upset the balance of life in a quiet rural backwater. However, the creation at an early stage of a parish covering Welwyn Garden City allowed a separation of the financial liabilities on local rate (i.e. tax) payers that might arise from the housing account. But in general the WRDC moved only slowly and tentatively. In Handside 50 council houses were built in 1921–2 at Elm Gardens and a further 93 went up on Guessens Road in 1923–4 and Longcroft Lane in 1924–5. Its last and biggest scheme, of 200 dwellings, was at Peartree, east of the railway, which was developed in 1926–7.

By 1924, however, the Company had already decided itself to force the pace on providing working-class housing (and therefore industrial development).[52] Using the more generous terms of the 1924 Housing Act, the Welwyn Public Utility Society was formed. This body eventually absorbed several existing societies to become the Company's housing arm. Yet it began by developing its own estate at Peartree, the largest yet built in the town. The Moatwood Society also began to build nearby and some 500 houses were complete in Peartree by 1927, all built using a non-traditional construction technology (Figure 3.8). Its solid walls were constructed by pouring concrete into formwork, which kept costs and rents down owing to savings in time, materials and skilled labour. It was a bold experiment and the houses themselves did not lack some architectural charm, though in the long term they experienced serious condensation and

Figure 3.8 The Peartree estate was built in the 1920s as part of a push to attract industry. The rents were more affordable for factory workers but their cheap concrete construction caused long-term problems, leading to demolition and redevelopment in the 1980s. (Photograph by J.P. Steele from F.J. Osborn, *Green-Belt Cities. The British Contribution* (London, 1946))

structural problems. As a result, they were demolished during the 1980s and the site has been redeveloped. In the short term, however, the boost they gave to investor confidence and major factory building at a critical period was crucial to the economic success of Welwyn Garden City.

Also in 1927, with the population approaching 7,000, a new Welwyn Garden City Urban District Council (WGCUDC) was formed, covering the same area as the Company's estate at the time. This body, initially at least, had much more in common with the new settlement than its predecessor council, which had covered a rather wider area that was still less than sympathetic to the new settlement. Initially it used the Company's officers as its professional staff in addition to their main roles, and Company members also became councillors. The hope was that the new Council would be more active in building working-class housing than its predecessor. Yet in six years the new body built only 365 dwellings. Moreover, at this point, in 1933, the government ended its so-called 'general needs' housing subsidy under the 1924 Act, which had come closest to addressing Welwyn Garden City's housing needs.

From 1933 until the new wartime and post-war housing programmes were adopted, the only government subsidies available to build housing were for those displaced by slum clearance or living in overcrowded conditions. Neither applied in Welwyn Garden City, so the UDC could build only a further 234 dwellings by 1939. For these there were no central subsidies, but some compensation existed in the form of a greater flexibility in their allocation, which meant that they could more easily be let, for example, to recently arrived key workers and without the usual limitations in setting rents. Yet clear frustration remained and in 1938 the Council, asserting a growing sense of independence from the Company, explored the idea of an ambitious scheme for expansion in the east.[53] Although the Company actively disliked this proposal, it would have provided a very large amount of housing, but the outbreak of war meant that the proposal was dropped. Just over 200 dwellings were actually completed by the Council during the war and 173 afterwards, until Welwyn Garden City was designated as a New Town in 1948.

The absence of mass private house-building

Other rapidly growing 'conventional' towns of the interwar period, such as Luton, Coventry, Oxford and Slough, had quite similar housing pressures. They needed a supply of relatively low-cost housing for populations only recently arrived to work in new industries. Admittedly some of these places had significant slum housing, which meant that they could draw on national housing subsidies in the

1930s. But the key difference between them and Welwyn Garden City as regards the housing of newcomers lay in the role of the new mass speculative house-builders that emerged during the later 1920s and 1930s. In most rapidly growing towns these mass builders, building both for sale and (to a lesser extent) for rent, filled an important gap, accommodating many workers in the new growth industries of the interwar years. Yet Welwyn Garden City's very tight planning and land-availability regime discouraged large-scale speculative building.

From 1920 to 1941 just under 988 new dwellings had been developed by the private (i.e. for-profit) sector, less than a quarter of total new housing construction.[54] Local authority housing stood at just under 30 per cent (1,250 dwellings), while that provided by the Welwyn Public Utility Society and other housing societies amounted to not quite half (2,027 dwellings). This was a very unusual pattern of local housing supply, with over three-quarters of the town's housing stock rented and the proportion of owner occupation low compared with other high-growth towns. Yet it was a tenure mix conducive to rapid growth because renting, especially weekly renting, was more inherently flexible for a mobile workforce than buying a home on a mortgage. Since building Peartree the Company's housing society had exploited this flexibility to the full. It did much to ensure employers' needs to house their workers were met. Over time the council had also become more prepared to allocate its own housing to those recent arrivals with jobs in the new industries.

Where Welwyn Garden City also gained was in the generally high quality (with a few exceptions) of the residential environments. As Handside and Peartree became more built up by the early 1930s, new areas were beginning to become established. The building of the White Bridge over the Luton branch railway north of the Campus in 1925 allowed development to begin in the north-west section, off Digswell Road. Relatively little building occurred until the 1930s, when the Sherrards Wood area started to take shape.[55] A big local political issue was how much of the wood should be retained, leading to one of the Company's first serious disputes with the Council in 1936 (which also resurfaced after 1945).[56] Adjoining the wood Sherrards Park grew up: this was an attractive high-class residential area of fine detached houses, largely individual in design but reflecting the principles of overall design unity and architectural good manners that characterised the whole town (Figure 3.9). There were a few nods towards the emergent design thinking of international modernism, with occasional flat-roofed houses, but the overall effect was unadventurous. The vulgarity of much of interwar private suburbia recognised by architectural critics such as Osbert Lancaster might have been avoided, but so too was any real design boldness.

Figure 3.9 Sherrards Park, in the north-west of the town, grew up as a high-class residential area largely of detached houses during the 1930s. (author photograph)

This pattern of growth in the north-west 'quarter' contrasted somewhat with that in the Woodhall area, east of the LNER mainline and south of Peartree. Development began here in the later 1930s with a mixture of weekly and monthly rented housing built as short terraces, with some semi-detached housing. The housing was of reasonable quality and certainly did not have the construction defects of the concrete houses on the Peartree estate of a few years earlier, but there were growing concerns by 1935 that the Company's development planning for the whole south-east sector would intensify the emerging working-class character of the eastern side of the LNER mainline. This was a further issue on which the UDC actively questioned Company intentions. The Council argued that it would create an undesirable east–west social divide, raising an issue which remained another bone of contention through to the post-war years.[57]

'… one of the most important and virile communities in the Home Counties'

The main justification for the situation of this lower-rent housing development on the eastern side was that this was where the new factory jobs were located. The first three industries came in 1923, but, as already hinted, it took a little longer for major factory development to begin.[58] In 1924 the first larger employers, Dawnay construction engineers and Shredded Wheat breakfast cereals, decided to move from London. Like Spirella in Letchworth, both were British subsidiaries of American companies seeking suitable locations for major expansion. Dawnay was the smaller of the two, but was soon employing about 150 workers. The

Shredded Wheat factory, which began operations in late 1925, was conceived as an altogether bigger operation. Although there were initially only around 100 workers, numbers soon grew as the factory expanded and production grew, peaking at around 1,000 employees. 'The Wheat' stood on a very prominent seven-acre (2.8-hectare) site alongside the LNER mainline railway. In contrast to the town's neo-Georgian domestic and civic architecture, its tall white concrete grain silos epitomized modern industrial design (Figure 3.10).[59] In both material and symbolic senses, Shredded Wheat established Welwyn Garden City as a modern industrial location.

Some other firms grew in even more spectacular fashion. The Company recognised the need to build advance factory space for rent, rather than relying simply on providing sites. In 1927 it opened its first sectional (nursery) factories, which could be configured flexibly to create units of varying sizes, allowing scope for firms to grow without major initial capital outlay. It was an approach well suited to firms in the growth industries with an initially uncertain market. Thus Frank Murphy established his radio business on an experimental basis in a garage in 1928 before renting a sectional factory with just six employees in the following year.[60] Thereafter the firm expanded very rapidly in the 1930s and by

Figure 3.10 The Shredded Wheat factory, with its modernist grain silos, was the first major industry in the town. Its prominent location alongside the main railway line from London to the North was extremely important in emphasising Welwyn Garden City's reputation as a modern industrial town. (author photograph)

1937 was employing 800 workers, growing to be even more important during the war years.[61]

Although the business did not grow quite as spectacularly as Murphy's, Barcley Foundations (later Barcley Corsets), another American company, also began in a small way in the town in 1927. Originally occupying a small building adjoining the sectional factories, it soon prospered. In 1939 the firm moved into a much larger and very distinctive purpose-built factory. Its striking central glazed rotunda containing the entrance foyer and staircases was typical of the modernistic commercial architecture of this emergent decade of the age of mass consumption. In a different way, the arrival of British Instructional Films, with their large new state-of-the-art film studios, in 1928 was another sign of the times. Widely used for the making of documentary and instructional films, its studios were also used for feature films through to the early post-war years. Like the arrival of Shredded Wheat, this opening, with its hint of silver-screen glamour, attracted national publicity to Welwyn Garden City.

Particularly important in diversifying and consolidating the local economic base was Norton Grinding Wheel Ltd, the British subsidiary of an American firm which made abrasives. The firm occupied a large factory, purpose-built by Welwyn Builders, which opened in 1931, and was soon employing more than 1,000 workers. The beginning of production at almost the worst point of the depression was striking confirmation of what Bank of England director Sir Basil Blackett had said when inaugurating the Welwyn Chamber of Commerce in 1929: the town was 'one of the most important and virile communities in the Home Counties'.[62]

More new firms came in the 1930s, several also of foreign ownership though now mainly European rather than American. The costs of serving the distant British market from the USA had been a key factor in encouraging American companies to establish branch factories in Britain. Now, however, protectionist trade policies introduced in the early 1930s made it more costly to sell imported goods even from much closer countries. Welwyn Garden City was thus able to attract companies from several European countries. One of the most notable was Biersdorf, a Hamburg firm which arrived in 1931 to manufacture Nivea cream and medical plasters. In 1939 it was anglicised as Herts Pharmaceutical. In the same broad sector and even more important for the long-term development of the town was the Swiss pharmaceutical company Roche Products Ltd, which opened in 1938, initially employing 240 workers. Another successful foreign company, though in a completely different industry, was the Norwegian company Skarsten, which arrived in 1934, manufacturing scraping tools and various door fittings.

By 1939 there were also very many other businesses of various types, and other new firms came in the 1940s. Of the others, the most important individual firm not so far mentioned was the ICI Plastics Group, which brought its large headquarters and research and manufacturing divisions to the town in 1938. But, buttressing this and the other larger firms, there were also many smaller firms, largely in the broad sectors already identified – food processing, clothing and textiles, metal working, engineering, chemicals and pharmaceuticals. Together, they gave Welwyn Garden City a diverse industrial base with many successful firms in growth industries. Yet this positive picture was not matched by the occupational structure that resulted. This typified the situation in many growing industrial towns of the period, with the creation of predominantly semi-skilled jobs, with relatively few opportunities for higher-paid skilled work. Nevertheless, for a place with no industrial employment 16 years earlier, it was an extraordinary transformation.

Factors in industrial success

But why, exactly, had the town been so successful in attracting industry? Some of the reasons were related to the national and regional economies.[63] Thus the new industries of the time were largely based on mass consumption and, not needing coal, heavy raw materials or particular labour skills, tended to grow in regions where their markets were strongest. Such areas also benefited in having no legacy of the older, more troubled and declining industries to restrain their growth possibilities. These were not, of course, advantages peculiar to Welwyn Garden City. In this respect the town benefited from natural and pre-existing locational advantages. The large area of flat land available immediately alongside the railways was important, and was skilfully exploited in the industrial zoning in the town plan. It gave, for example, a full two miles of rail frontage that allowed straightforward siding accommodation without the need to disrupt other parts of the site by train movements. The mainline and branch lines also gave easy connections to London, the Midlands, the North and Scotland. Moreover, as road traffic became more important, it was useful to have one of the major national trunk routes, the Great North Road, flanking the west of the town.

The development policies of the Company built on these advantages. The fact that the town was internationally recognised as a model of good town planning was itself an attraction to many of the bigger companies, especially those that were foreign-owned.[64] The latter tended to use scientific methods for site selection, typically producing comparative rankings of sites/locations by numeric values according to their predicted impact on key factors of production

Figure 3.11 The Company adopted a very professional approach to industrial promotion and development. The industrial estate was large and well planned, with extensive railway frontages. Incoming firms could either build their own premises or rent from the Company, which provided a variety of smaller units, as shown here. (author photograph)

and distribution. But many more specific Company policies also had an impact. Many industrialists were attracted to the high-quality industrial space and the flexible way it was provided, as sites or modern buildings, in various sizes and for sale or rent (Figure 3.11). The Company also undertook an active marketing policy that included general promotional brochures,[65] advertising in the trade press and carefully tailored approaches to specific firms.[66] By the 1930s it had become one of the leaders in this form of place marketing and promotion.[67] As more industries were attracted and prospered, their presence further validated Welwyn Garden City's claims to be a successful location.

With so many growing industries arriving, however, there were potential problems of labour shortage and consequent rising wages. These were eased partly by the industries' requirements for largely semi- and unskilled labour, a sizeable proportion of which was provided by women and young people (aged 14–21), who were paid less than adult men. Yet the way in which the Company overcame the early shortages of housing was also important. With good-quality moderately priced housing available in addition to jobs, many migrants came to the town, further easing the labour supply.

Such voluntary movement was also augmented by the government's industrial transference scheme, which, from 1928, encouraged migration from the most depressed areas and offered some training for new jobs.[68] The scale of this longer-distance migration, both voluntary and that encouraged through official transference policies, can be gauged from a 1939 social survey of Welwyn Garden City. This suggested that a third of working-class households in Welwyn

Garden City had moved from the north, Wales and Scotland, compared to 30 per cent from Greater London and a fifth from Hertfordshire.[69] Yet, wherever they came from, the overall effect of this in-migration was that, despite low local unemployment, average wages in Welwyn Garden City remained a little below the national average, something which clearly suited employers.

It also appears to have been tolerated (if grudgingly) by the new workers themselves. This reflected relatively weak unionisation among less skilled workers, especially women and young people, and fears about the national scale of unemployment. In some boom towns, such as Oxford, there was some agitation among recent-migrant workforces about housing costs and employment conditions. In Welwyn Garden City the availability of what was, considering its good quality, moderately priced rented housing and the possibility of exceptionally short journeys to work (often 15 minutes or less walking times) helped keep living costs down for some working-class families. Along with the social-welfare policies adopted by some employers (particularly Shredded Wheat), such factors probably helped foster Welwyn Garden City's relatively quiescent labour relations. The town also appealed to the managers and salaried staff of new industries because it had sizeable areas of good-quality, more expensive housing with an already established and diverse middle-class community. The town's proximity to London was important to this group for both business and leisure reasons.

Overall, therefore, there was a dramatic change in the character of Welwyn Garden City. In 1926 over half of its resident workers had commuted out to work, but by 1930 around four-fifths were locally employed, and this proportion remained fairly constant through the 1930s and 1940s. Of those who commuted outwards, it was no longer just to London, as it had overwhelmingly been in the early days. Thus the town soon proved an attractive location for better-paid employees of the de Havilland aircraft works at nearby Hatfield, which had opened in 1934. Yet this outflow was offset by a significant daily inflow of workers from surrounding areas – around 750 each day by 1937.[70]

The improving financial position

As this growth occurred, so the financial position of the Company strengthened, its various income flows improving during the 1920s. Rental incomes and proceeds from sales of leasehold sites gradually increased. Supplemented by the trading surpluses from the subsidiary companies, the overall operating surplus of the Company (before repayment of interest charges on loans), though small, grew fairly steadily except in the worst years of the depression. However, the costs of servicing the Company's debt, much of it accumulated on rather unfavourable terms during periods when high interest rates prevailed, remained onerous. Once these repayment costs were included, the Company's position looked very much bleaker.

The reality of this began to be recognised by the Directors and effectively tackled only from the later 1920s. Attempts were made to reconstruct the Company's finances and debt in 1928, 1932 and, finally, in 1934.[71] As noted, a key concern was to minimise and eventually eliminate debts to the PWLB, in which the sale of the water undertaking played an important part. However, it was the sustained and very low interest rates which began during 1932 and remained in place for the rest of the decade that gave the major opportunity for substantial reconstruction. It was this restructuring, authorised by the High Court in 1934, that finally freed the Company from its weak financial position.

Even so, the process was a complex and potentially very contentious one. The debenture holders who had given loans on fixed terms in the 1920s received new shares in the Company equivalent to their previous investments. Investors in the housing bonds which had been used to finance the Welwyn Public Utility Society received shares in the Company worth about half the value of their bonds. The main losers were the original shareholders in the Company, who lost much of their original investment. They included the original directors, particularly if they had taken up some of the unsold first share issue in the early days. Investors in the originally independent New Towns Trust, which undertook agricultural and other activities (including a specialist housing role) on the estate, had been taken over by the Company when its own financial position became hopeless. But the Company gave little or nothing to the Trust's investors, who lost even more on the face value of their shares. Overall it was a solution that was hardest on those who had shown early faith in the Company, had borne its travails during the harsh deflationary climate of the 1920s and had received no financial returns on their investments.

Another thing that was lost was the principle of limited dividend. Henceforth, the 1934 shares would pay any dividends in full to the shareholders. The commitment that, beyond 7 per cent, dividends would be used for the common good of the town was abandoned. So too was the principle of civic directors appointed by the UDC. Henceforth the Board would be smaller and more rigorously run on strictly business lines, as befitted what had now, in many respects, become an ordinary joint stock company. The new directors who came in at this time were soon pressing Chambers that the Company had too many highly paid staff, tended 'to subordinate business to sentiment' and lacked 'drive and vitality'.[72] This strengthened emphasis on enhancing shareholder value appears to have been a key factor in Osborn's otherwise inexplicable 'resignation' in early 1936.[73] This was the final act in replacing those motivated primarily by adherence to garden-city ideals by other, more disinterested, servants of what was now a fully commercial business.

The promise within all this, to investors if not the community, was that the Company would now, at last, be able to proceed vigorously. In doing this it would soon be possible to repay in annual dividends something of what had been lost on the face value of previous share and bond issues. Sure enough, in 1936 a dividend of 2 per cent was paid, in 1937 one of 3 per cent, in 1938 4 per cent and in 1939 5 per cent. This compared well with a bank rate of 2 per cent at this time. No dividend was paid in the early war years, but from 1942 an annual dividend of 2.5 per cent was paid for several years, rising to 4 per cent in 1947 and 5 per cent in the Company's last year of existence, 1949.

At an early stage in the history of the movement, George Bernard Shaw had argued that, whatever the stated intentions, the ordinary profit-seeking motivations of market capitalism would, sooner or later, assume dominance.[74] This did not happen until the early 1960s at Letchworth, but the 1934 financial reconstruction saw that moment arrive sooner in the second garden city. At the time, it seemed to the new Board that it was a price well worth paying. Yet the change began to open up more divisions of interest with the local community, the local council and, most fatefully of all, a future national government.

Garden citizens

These shifts also had important social implications. In the early years the Company had played a key part in the initial social development of the town. As the area had been so completely rural, with just 400 existing inhabitants, there was little by way of an existing social fabric. Despite Lord Desborough's record as a major sportsman and important public figure who had chaired the committee which had organised the 1908 London Olympic Games, he quickly washed his hands of Welwyn Garden City. Salisbury played occasional, largely ceremonial roles (such as opening the Shredded Wheat factory). But the leaders of rural Hertfordshire society were certainly not active forces in the formation of the new settlement's social life.

A lingering resentment of Welwyn Garden City remained in the surrounding area. Once the estate was purchased the tenant farmers began to pay their rents to the Company and were eventually displaced when building on their farms began. When that time came, most resentfully accepted their fate and moved on.[75] One continued to live on the site but remained aloof, with a 'buffer zone' between his former farmhouse and the growing town. The only conspicuous exception was W.C. Horn, who had farmed land in the western side of the town (and whose farm rail sidings became the hub of the early building operations). The Horn family displayed an unusual generosity of spirit in the face of the loss of their livelihood and participated very fully in the life of the growing town. As Horn's son (who was soon playing an active role in the young garden city's local theatre and sports activities) recalled many years later:

> We all welcomed this as a family. Welcomed this in many ways, this new coming, new interest, new individuals. I gather since that some people have been rather surprised at our attitude, thinking that we would resent the coming of the new town. I don't think that we ever did really. My father threw himself into the public work of the place ...[76]

Horn was one of Welwyn Garden City's first non-Company civic leaders and became first chairman of the UDC in 1927.

As in many other aspects of the town, the Company's directors and senior staff played important and direct personal roles in establishing or promoting many of its voluntary social and cultural activities.[77] Reiss, for example, established the boys' club, became a central figure in the local Education and Health Associations and established many sporting activities, particularly cricket, in the town.[78] Chambers and his wife were keen members of the tennis club and hosted the chess club at their home, and Sir Theodore was a founder of the Mimram Lodge of the Freemasons. Purdom and Osborn were both active in promoting the flourishing of local theatre and much other cultural activity. The Cherry Tree restaurant, for example, was opened in early 1921 with a grand concert, with Osborn duetting with another early resident as the first performance.[79] The Company's engineer, William James, was a founder of town's Free Church and also pioneered its citizens' meetings as an early outlet for public opinion.[80]

They were enthusiastically joined in their activities by many of the new middle-class residents. Although there was certainly a more 'rough and ready'[81] element among the early population, the social tone of the nascent community, with artistic events and performances, was largely set by the more culturally minded of the middle class. An extract from a letter one early resident, a Swiss Quaker with an English husband, wrote to her sister in the autumn of 1922 gives a sense of how this new community began to form: 'There is a charming woman here who I visited yesterday, she spins and weaves wool she dyes herself. She ...

welcomed us with open arms ... The social last night was nice. Fred and I sang quite well I think.'[82] Like many communities associated with the garden city movement, it attracted a strong Quaker presence and, with this, a continuing commitment to supporting good causes such as relief and reconstruction work after World War I and a mass feeding project in Germany during 1920–22.[83] The Quaker influence was also important in promoting a widespread belief in temperance (though it was not, of course, actively promoted by the Company). The result was that by 1939 there were only two public houses in the town, which some people still thought too many.

Yet the second garden city did not attract 'alternative' groups promoting radical lifestyles in the way that Letchworth had done, although it became home to a remarkable array of individuals. Local cultural efforts were supported by people who were, or became, national figures, such as the actors Flora Robson (who began as Shredded Wheat's welfare officer) and Dinah Sheridan,[84] who were active in the town's amateur and professional theatrical scenes. The renowned playwright George Bernard Shaw also lived in a nearby village. A friend and admirer of Howard (though not above sometimes poking fun at him) and shareholder in the Company, he was an inspirational if occasional presence.

And it is not difficult to find other examples of residents, principally of Handside or Sherrards Park, who were in various ways remarkable. Rather oddly, perhaps, the author of the most outstanding piece of Scottish twentieth-century literature, *The Scots Quair* trilogy, Lewis Grassic Gibbon (a nom de plume of James Leslie Mitchell), wrote it largely while resident in Welwyn Garden City.[85] Even more exotic were various emigrés, principally those escaping Nazi anti-Semitism, who settled after 1933, actively encouraged by the efforts of local Quakers and other liberal-minded residents.[86] A young man who came from Leipzig thanks to a mission by local Quakers to bring 18 or 20 young people to the town recalled his impressions on his arrival at Welwyn Garden City in 1939: 'That was heaven ... if that is not heaven I must have woken up next door to it ... People in Welwyn Garden City are terrific. Invitations right left and centre.'[87] He stayed at the Quaker hostel and the Quakers also helped him to find unpaid garden work at Digswell Nursery.

Another German Jew who came in quite different circumstances was the architect–planner Eugen Kaufmann (later known as Eugene Kent).[88] He had worked with the German modernist garden-city planner Ernst May (whose significance will be examined in Chapter 4) on Frankfurt's renowned social-housing programme of the late 1920s (which he had shown to a visiting Louis de Soissons). On leaving Frankfurt in 1931 he had worked again with May in the Soviet Union, in Kharkov and Moscow. Unwilling and unable to return to Germany, he settled in Welwyn Garden City (despite what he saw as its conservative architecture), where he worked with Paul Mauger to design the few modernist flat-roofed houses (one of them his own family home) in Sherrards Park.

And, of course, there were many who came from destinations nearer home. In a town like Welwyn Garden City almost everyone was from somewhere else, be it Frankfurt, Leipzig, London or Huddersfield.[89] These various examples, however, give a small insight into that part of the town that shaped external perceptions of its dominant social character. It was, at once, decent, well-meaning, liberal-minded, socialist-leaning, earnestly creative and outward-looking, while also capable at times of being paternalistic, conservative and self-centred. But it was the former characteristics which predominated. It would surely have been difficult in the late 1930s to say about it what Orwell wrote about much of London's suburbia at that time, that it was '… sleeping the deep, deep sleep of England'.[90] Yet, even within the town itself, there was a surprising slowness to understand the new and quite different society that was emerging on the other side of the tracks.

The new working class
By 1939, however, something of an awakening to all this was underway. Spurred by the local Labour Party, a range of local organisations, including the Chamber of Commerce, Trades Council, local church congregations and the Company itself, came together to commission a social survey undertaken in the last springtime of peace.[91] The Labour Party had the previous year taken control of the UDC.[92] It saw itself as spanning the two worlds of Welwyn Garden City, appealing to both socially progressive middle-class residents and the new working families. But it did not push its new strength too far. Once it had facilitated initial contacts for the survey, it stepped back to avoid the result carrying any taint of political influence. What emerged was a revealing picture of the new industrial society, highlighting striking differences of income, living conditions, lifestyle and attitudes to Welwyn Garden City compared with the town's affluent side.

Though it would have been less remarkable in a 'normal' town, the very fact that there was such a social division belied the self-image of what a garden city was supposed to be. The active and cohesive social relations that had quickly emerged among the early affluent garden citizens did not readily extend to the somewhat less affluent industrial population that grew up from the late 1920s. This was not simply because of differences in class outlook and income level; these were important, but this new working class was itself rather diverse, and did not immediately cohere within itself, let alone with the 'older' Welwyn Garden City.

The town was conceived as a demonstration project for a planning strategy to move people out of congested London, anticipating the post-war New Towns, but had achieved this intention only to a small extent by 1939. The survey suggested that around 70 per cent of its working-class population actually came from parts of Britain other than London. In some cases, unemployed workers from depressed regions were paid their travel and removal expenses to take jobs in expanding towns such as Welwyn Garden City. If they had families, they would be most likely to live on the eastern side of the town, as did the one man who moved as a teenager with his family from Sunderland to live in Woodhall.[93] Before long he and his brothers had also found work locally. Other families came from other north-eastern towns, such as South Shields,[94] or from the depressed south Wales coalfield.

Yet some of the moves from these regions and especially from other parts of Britain were not motivated by unemployment. One family moved to Peartree from Manchester during the second half of the 1920s while the father remained employed by the same Manchester-based firm.[95] Despite finding Peartree very friendly for several years, with its village-like community, the family moved in 1938 to the west side of the railway with a strong sense that this was the '... good side, as it were. Nobody liked to live on the other side.' A problem that was apparent on the eastern side by the late 1930s was that many people, apart perhaps from those who came from Hertfordshire itself, lacked the immediate common ground of having moved from a similar point of origin. There were noticeable differences identified in the 1939 survey between those who came from depressed older industrial areas with a stronger tradition of challenging authority and those of more local origins.

As in many other rapidly growing industrial towns at this time, there was some animosity towards in-migrants from more distant regions. At least some working people who had settled earlier from closer points of origin resented the later rapid influx of people from the depressed areas, especially south Wales. They believed this had made it 'more difficult for local men to get good jobs, and had also altered the social tone ... to spoil our place.'[96] Such perceptions were partly reinforced by some marked differences within the demographic structure of the new population. For example, the town's largest families tended to be among the recent arrivals from the North and south Wales. And in a place that had many young people a significant proportion of them were without local family ties, arriving under government transference schemes from the depressed areas. The

Figure 3.12 Houses built in 1938 in the Woodhall area on the east side of the railway. Much of the housing built in this period was less affordable for families on lower incomes than that of the 1920s because government subsidies favoured the rehousing of families from cleared slum areas, which the town did not have. (author photograph)

latter, especially, triggered many concerns about bored and rootless young people. Many appeared to have what were 'blind alley' jobs with few long-term prospects and, outside work, few were drawn into the town's uplifting sporting and cultural activities.

There were other common issues of social concern across the whole working-class population. The high quality of the housing was widely acknowledged, but it was less affordable for many working-class families than the Company and industrialists imagined. It was a housing stock that would have better suited a skilled workforce receiving higher wages than were typical in the town (Figure 3.12). The lack of older housing, usually available at lower rents in 'normal' towns, was significant here, but so too were the Company housing society's and the local council's policies of building mainly larger, three-bedroom houses. Those who could afford to live there certainly appreciated the housing. One woman, remembering arriving in 1939 as a young girl with her family from London to live in a house in Peartree, said how much she

loved Welwyn Garden City, because we had a lavatory indoors and we had running water – I should say that my mother enjoyed it more – I didn't really appreciate the difference – but in London we had no running water and we had gas light and we had a lavatory out on the landing which we shared with the next door neighbour –

amazing – Mum paid more rent for that flat in London than she did when she was allocated a house in Welwyn Garden City.[97]

Yet high rents produced the paradoxical situation that many of the least-skilled and lowest-paid workers actually had to commute daily into the town, usually by cycling. For some, the taking-in of lodgers from among the town's single industrial working population was a way of meeting the town's higher rents. But by the late 1930s there was recognition by the Company of a need to build a larger proportion of smaller houses that were cheaper to rent and run.

The generally high cost of living in Welwyn Garden City compounded specific concerns about high rents. The great majority of working-class families felt that the town was not well served by the Company's subsidiary Welwyn Stores Ltd because its prices for many essentials and other items were too high. As was the case with housing, the Stores' retail offerings in its shops prioritised quality above cheapness. Opportunistic mobile street traders found a ready market, especially on the eastern side. Many housewives were members of shopping clubs that organised visits to St Albans and Hertford, where there was more choice and prices were cheaper at chain stores such as Woolworths and Marks & Spencers. Admittedly, many of these complaints were being voiced before Welwyn Stores Ltd's new department store opened, but it seems doubtful whether this development really addressed them. Such concerns also became more muted as wartime rationing was introduced and issues of price, choice and quality became less active factors in retailing.

A major problem for the largely working-class eastern half of the town was the sheer distance to shops and other amenities (especially the cinema), involving a long trek over the railway bridge to the town centre. A wonderfully vivid account of this trek has been given by a man who was a small boy in the 1930s.[98] His family lived in one of the few rural cottages that made up Lower Hatfield Hyde, beyond the eastern edge of the built-up area at that time. The effort required on the part of his mother to supervise him and his younger brother in a pushchair is easy to imagine. As well as highlighting just how long it took to get to the town centre, even after they reached the streets of Peartree, he comments on many other aspects of what it was actually like to live in this more industrial half of the town. He remembered the aromas of the area's various industries, particularly the 'metallic smell emanating from the British Lead Mills. I later wondered how anyone could stand living on that part of Peartree Lane.' Proximity and prevailing winds ensured that these fumes and diverse smells from the Welwyn Foundry, the Shredded Wheat factory, the Welwyn Bakeries

Figure 3.13 A new centre for the east side of Welwyn Garden City began to be built in the late 1930s, with this large shopping parade at Woodhall (1938) the first main stage. The war delayed other elements, some of which never materialised. It did not eliminate the sense that residents on the less affluent east side were only second-class garden citizens. (author photograph)

and other factories lingered in the adjacent eastern residential areas far more than on the other side of the railway.

The Company made some efforts to improve matters regarding the length of the trek to shops for those in the east, firstly by opening a small Peartree branch of Welwyn Stores Ltd in 1925. In 1938 a new local shopping parade with, eventually, around 30 shops was opened as the core of a local centre (Figure 3.13). However, its other facilities appeared only slowly over subsequent decades and the promised cinema never materialised. Despite growing efforts by the Company to offset it,[99] the sense of unevenness persisted and perpetuated itself in many different aspects of the town's life, lingering in the memories of people who experienced it. It also had a major impact on what happened to the Company and town in the following decade.

The final act

No sooner had the 1939 social survey been completed than it was overtaken by events. There were no accurate counts of wartime population to record the very substantial temporary increase to at least 20,000 residents that occurred as a result of official and voluntary evacuation from London. There were also some more international refugees, including, anecdotal evidence suggests, more German and other Jews and various others, including at least some Italians. Increased production at its own and neighbouring Hatfield's factories also brought many new war workers. There was some but certainly not enough new housing construction to cope with the growth during these years, and many households were swelled by the arrival of lodgers. Yet, although a few houses and a factory were destroyed by German bombs, the town escaped relatively unscathed, apparently supporting pre-war arguments that planned decentralisation made sense in national defence terms.

The Greater London Plan of 1944 confirmed the Company's own intentions that the planned expansion of the town would continue. In this spirit the Company embarked on planning its post-war growth, buying further land mainly north of the river Mimram. In June 1947 the Company published a major revision of its 1920 plan that would expand the town to some 50,000 inhabitants, with three entirely new neighbourhoods.[100] It showed the virtual disappearance of the green buffer that had separated the town from Welwyn and Digswell. There were many objections, not least from those places, at this proposed surge to the north. Yet this was to be one of the Company's last acts. As will be shown in Chapter 6, the new minister of Town and Country Planning by then wanted to incorporate the town directly into his New Towns programme. He sanctioned neither the plan nor the continuance of the Company.

Conclusion

During the 29 years of its existence, the Company (and its pioneer predecessor) attempted to find a practical way of following Howard's 'peaceful path'. In doing this, it completed the transition of the garden city from an experiment in social reform to a demonstration project in town planning. De Soissons' 1920 plan became a widely known icon of the town-planning movement, in Britain and elsewhere. The realisation of his plan through far more careful controls than were exercised in the first garden city produced something that jarred with the new modernist *zeitgeist*. But over time it has proved to have enduring qualities that have conveyed a true and distinctive sense of place.

In many other respects, however, it represented significant modifications and compromises of the garden-city ideal. As at Letchworth, its directors soon recognised that Howard's original desire for regular ground-rent reviews to secure quick returns on land-value uplift was not feasible. As such, the Company struggled with early financial problems, with the added handicap here of operating during an exceptionally uncertain period in which investors and lenders showed extreme caution. Major funding from the state was not an option, unlike in the cases of the New Towns that followed. The attempt in

Welwyn Garden City to create and exploit local monopolies through subsidiary companies was unique as a way to try to capture the accumulating monetary value of the growing town. As shown, however, this proved a mixed blessing. While some of the subsidiaries yielded significant returns, others did not. They also made the second garden city far more of a 'company town' than either Letchworth or the New Towns.

As such, the Company was subjected to complaints of being an overbearing presence in the town's life and an inflator of the local cost of living. The local council, which had begun as the Company's compliant and subordinate partner, became increasingly suspicious and assertive at an earlier stage in the town's life than had been the case at Letchworth. This tension was further fuelled by the glaring social divide which was created between the west and east, challenging Howardian ideals of social harmony. It grew further as the contradictions inherent in creating an entirely new settlement on a limited-dividend basis caused the Company to reconstruct itself so that future profits could henceforth be translated into unlimited shareholder dividends. This was scarcely what Howard had in mind when he set out on the peaceful path. Only its traditions as a garden city founded by Ebenezer Howard and the more tangible perpetuation of unified freehold ownership thereafter distinguished the Company from a fully commercialised development company. As we will see in Chapter 6, these matters were ultimately to have a bearing on what happened in 1948 and the way the town was developed subsequently.

Notes

1   S.V. Ward, 'Introduction', in E.G. Culpin, *The garden city movement up-to-date* (London, 2015 [reprint edition of 1914 original]).
2   The 'New Townsmen' [E. Howard, F.J. Osborn, C.B. Purdom, W.G. Taylor], *New towns after the war, an argument for garden cities* (London, 1918).
3   Hardy, *Garden cities to new towns*, pp. 126–9.
4   Purdom, *Life over again*, pp. 4–8; F.J. Osborn, *Genesis of Welwyn Garden City: some Jubilee memories* (London, 1970), pp. 8–12.
5   Cited in Beevers, *The garden city utopia*, p. 163.
6   Purdom, *Life over again*, p. 66; Osborn, *Genesis*, p. 10.
7   HALS, D/EES B51, Desborough–T. Chambers, 6.11.1919.
8   Purdom, *Life over again*, p. 67.
9   T. Rook, *Welwyn Garden City past* (Chichester, 2001), p. 111.
10   HALS, D/EES B60, Name of Town, Copies of Second Garden City Ltd, Board and Development Committee Papers, 2, 4, 8, 10.2.1920.
11   Purdom, *Satellite towns*, 2nd edn, p. 225.
12   HALS, D/EES B64, Letter F.J. Osborn–T.G. Chambers, 18.5.1935.
13   Purdom, *Satellite towns*, 2nd edn, pp. 186–8; Purdom, *Life over again*, pp. 68–70; Osborn, *Genesis*, pp. 12–26.

14   Purdom, *Life over again*, pp. 80–83; de Soissons, *Welwyn Garden City*, pp. 70–72.

15   Purdom, *Satellite towns*, 2nd edn, pp. 318–39.

16   Hardy, *Garden cities to new towns*, pp. 146–7.

17   E.g. HALS, D/EES B60, Memo. re Treasury Loans, undated, *c*.3.12.1921.

18   Purdom, *Satellite towns*, 2nd edn, pp. 322–3; p. 330.

19   HALS, D/EES B64, Note for T.G.C.[hambers] by J.F.E.[ccles], 1946.

20   Purdom, *Life over again*, pp. 76–80.

21   Purdom, *Satellite towns*, 2nd edn, 334–7.

22   Purdom, *Life over again*, pp. 94–115.

23   Purdom, *Satellite towns*, 2nd edn, pp. 222–3.

24   HALS, CNT/WH/13/1/4/23. WGC Ltd, *An account of Welwyn Garden City, being the Evidence submitted in November 1932 to the Departmental Committee on Garden Cities*, 1932, pp. 5–10; 31–3.

25   Purdom, *Satellite towns*, 2nd edn, p. 327.

26   HALS, D/EES B64, Welwyn Garden City Ltd, estimated effect of transfer of sewage disposal works and water undertaking to the Urban District Council; Purdom, *Satellite towns*, 2nd edn, p. 330.

27   HALS, D/EES B66, Memorandum on the subject of the revenues of the garden city company, 10.2.1922.

28   HALS, CNT/WH/13/1/4/23. WGC Ltd, *An account of Welwyn Garden City, being the evidence submitted in November 1932 to the Departmental Committee on Garden Cities*, 1932, p. 33.

29   J. Tyrwhitt, *Life and work in Welwyn Garden City* (1939) <http://cashewnut.me.uk/WGCbooks/>, accessed 26 August 2014.

30   Purdom, *Satellite towns*, 2nd edn, p. 224

31   HALS, D/EES B63, Original note on shops policy in Welwyn Garden City prepared by Sir Theodore Chambers 7.12.1920; Purdom, *Satellite towns*, 2nd edn, pp. 256–74.

32   HALS, D/EES B64, F.J. Osborn, Welwyn Garden City Limited, notes on shop policy and the present position, 11.2.1935.

33   R. Filler, *A history of Welwyn Garden City* (Chichester, 1986), pp. 122–3.

34   Osborn, *Genesis*, p. 10; Rook, *Welwyn Garden City*, p. 71.

35   HALS, D/EES B60, Development Committee, notes on town plan: first building sites, paper by F.J. Osborn, 30.12.1919.

36   Purdom, *Life over again*, p. 69; Osborn, *Genesis*, p. 15.

37   W.A. Allen, 2004 'Soissons, Louis Emmanuel Jean Guy de (1890–1962)', rev. Andrew Saint, *Oxford dictionary of national biography* (Oxford, 2004) <http://www.oxforddnb.com.oxfordbrookes.idm.oclc.org/view/article/32792>, accessed 14 August 2014.

38   HALS, D/EES B55, Letter R.L. Reiss–T.G. Chambers, undated.

39   De Soissons, *Welwyn Garden City*, p. 48.

40   L. de Soissons, C.B. Purdom and A.W. Kenyon, *Site planning in practice at Welwyn Garden City* (London, 1927).

41   Purdom, *Satellite towns*, 2nd edn, pp. 227–55.

42   HALS, D/EES B64, Memorandum on land sold to L.&N.E.R., 31.10.1927.

43   Skilleter, 'The role of public utility societies', pp. 125–65.

44   HALS, D/EES B63, 14 July: 9–10, Welwyn Garden City Ltd, General Information about Welwyn Garden City, 1925.

45   A.M. Clarke, 'The Welwyn Garden City Light Railway', *Industrial Railway Record*, 62/October (1975) <www.welwyngarden-heritage.org/archive/>, accessed 18 August 2014.

46   HALS, CNT/WH/13/1/4/23. WGC Ltd, *An account of Welwyn Garden City, being the Evidence submitted in November 1932 to the Departmental Committee on Garden Cities*, 1932, p. 8.

47   M. Angwin, 'Memories of Welwyn Garden City 1930s and 1940s' <http://www.ourwelwyngardencity.org.uk/page_id__515.aspx?path=0p3p>, accessed 20 August 2015; P.

Cochrane, 'Cochrane family memories: As it was in the 30s – thro young eyes' <http://www.ourwelwyngardencity.org.uk/page_id__443.aspx?path=0p3p>, accessed 20 August 2015.

48   M. Jennings, 'Molly Jennings Part 1: Welwyn Garden City's first resident (reminiscences written down by R. Filler 1969–76)' <http://www.ourwelwyngardencity.org.uk/page_id__90.aspx?path=0p3p62p>, accessed 20 August 2015.

49   V. Godfrey, 'A family arrives in 1924' <http://www.ourwelwyngardencity.org.uk/page_id__417.aspx?path=0p162p137p>, accessed 20 August 2015.

50   Royal Commission on the Geographical Distribution of the Industrial Population, *Minutes*, p. 654.

51   Purdom, *Satellite towns*, 2nd edn, pp. 200–203.

52   De Soissons, *Welwyn Garden City*, pp. 62–5.

53   Purdom, *Satellite towns*, 2nd edn, p. 252.

54   De Soissons, *Welwyn Garden City*, pp. 236–7.

55   Welwyn Garden City Ltd, *A selection of admirable detached houses to let and for sale in Sherrards Park, Welwyn Garden City* (Welwyn Garden City, n.d. *c.*1937).

56   HALS, D/EES B44, WGC Ltd Board 11.12.1935, Paper by General Manager, Sherrardspark Wood Development and appended papers.

57   HALS, D/EES B44, WGC Ltd Board 11.12.1935, Copy of Letter, Deamer, B.H. (WGCUDC)–Page, F.M. (WGC Ltd) 4.12.1935.

58   Filler, *Welwyn Garden City*, pp. 127–39.

59   R.J. Butterfield, 'The Shredded Wheat factory at Welwyn Garden City', abridged version reproduced in D. Goodman (ed.), *The European cities and technology reader* (London, 1999), pp. 125–38.

60   Filler, *Welwyn Garden City*, p. 133.

61   Royal Commission on the Geographical Distribution of the Industrial Population, *Minutes*, p. 650.

62   Inauguration of the Welwyn Chamber of Commerce (1929) <www.ourwelwyngardencity.org.uk/page_id__230_path__0p82p.aspx>, accessed 21 August 2014.

63   Scott, *Triumph of the south*.

64   Royal Commission on the Geographical Distribution of the Industrial Population, *Minutes*, p. 653.

65   E.g. Welwyn Garden City Ltd *The book of Welwyn* (Welwyn Garden City, n.d. *c.*1937).

66   HALS, D/EES B118, Industrial Development Department, preliminary notes on general policy, 12.2.1936.

67   M.P. Fogarty, *Plan your own industries: a study of local and regional development organizations* (Oxford, 1947).

68   A.D.K. Owen, 'The social consequences of industrial transference', *Sociological Review*, 29 (1937), pp. 331–54; D.E. Pitfield, 'The quest for an effective regional policy, 1934–37', *Regional Studies*, 12 (1978), pp. 429–43.

69   Tyrwhitt, *Life and work*.

70   Royal Commission on the Geographical Distribution of the Industrial Population, *Minutes*, p. 648.

71   HALS, D/EES B5, Articles of Association of Welwyn Garden City Ltd, adopted by Special Resolution passed on 23.4.1934; Purdom, *Satellite towns*, 2nd edn, pp. 300–332; De Soissons, *Welwyn Garden City*, p. 81.

72   HALS, D/EES B118, Copy of T.G. Chambers Diary 17.1.1935

73   HALS, D/EES B118, Letter F.J. Osborn–T.G. Chambers, 21.1.1936; De Soissons, *Welwyn Garden City*, pp. 83–4.

74   Beevers, *The garden city utopia*, pp. 70–71.

75   Osborn, *Genesis*, pp. 18–20.

76   B. Horn, 'Memories of Bill Horn, Part Three – reminiscences of Welwyn Garden and area'

(recorded 1976 by R. Filler) <http://www.ourwelwyngardencity.org.uk/page_id__143.aspx?path=0p4p29p>, accessed 20 August 2015.

77   Osborn, *Genesis*, pp. 26–7. Whittick, *F.J.O. – practical idealist*, pp. 35–7.

78   C. Reiss, *R.L. Reiss: a memoir by Celia Reiss* (privately published, 1966), pp. 23–9.

79   M. Jennings, 'Molly Jennings Part 4: Welwyn Garden City's first resident' (recorded 1969 by R. Filler) <http://www.ourwelwyngardencity.org.uk/page_id__93.aspx?path=0p3p62p>, accessed 20 August 2015.

80   De Soissons, *Welwyn Garden City*, p. 42; Filler, *Welwyn Garden City*, p. 75.

81   R. Page, 'Expectations of a new home, Letter dated October 5th 1922' <http://www.ourwelwyngardencity.org.uk/page_id__218.aspx?path=0p3p109p>, accessed 20 August 2015.

82   Ibid.

83   R. Page, 'Quaker social night: preparing refreshments – 16th December 1923' <http://www.ourwelwyngardencity.org.uk/page_id__229.aspx?path=0p3p109p>, accessed 20 August 2015.

84   R. Filler, 'Dinah Sheridan' <http://www.ourwelwyngardencity.org.uk/page_id__490.aspx?path=0p3p>, accessed 29 September 2014.

85   D.F. Young, 'Mitchell, (James) Leslie (1901–1935)', *Oxford dictionary of national biography* (Oxford, 2004); online edn May 2008 <http://www.oxforddnb.com.oxfordbrookes.idm.oclc.org/view/article/38328>, accessed 29 September 2014.

86   De Soissons, *Welwyn Garden City*, p. 92; E.F.H. Strauss, 'Some 1940s memories of Welwyn Garden City' <http://www.ourwelwyngardencity.org.uk/page/some_1940s_memories_of_welwyn_garden_city?path=0p3p>, accessed 20 August 2015.

87   V. Godfrey, 'A difficult journey to WGC in 1939 from Leipzig with help from WGC Quakers' <http://www.ourwelwyngardencity.org.uk/page_id__391.aspx?path=0p162p137p>, accessed 20 August 2015.

88   RIBA Archives, *Memoirs of Eugene Kent* (typescript, *c.*1978) KeE/1, pp. 224–32.

89   V. Godfrey, 'First impressions of the town in 1931' <http://www.ourwelwyngardencity.org.uk/page_id__420.aspx?path=0p162p137p>, accessed 20 August 2015.

90   G. Orwell, *Homage to Catalonia* (Harmondsworth, 1962 [orig. 1938]), p. 221.

91   Tyrwhitt, *Life and work*. This source is used extensively in this section, in addition to other sources cited.

92   Filler, *Welwyn Garden City*, p. 77

93   V. Godfrey, 'A move from Sunderland' <http://www.ourwelwyngardencity.org.uk/page_id__433.aspx>, accessed 20 August 2015.

94   V. Godfrey, 'From South Shields to WGC' <http://www.ourwelwyngardencity.org.uk/page_id__409.aspx?path=0p162p137p>, accessed 20 August 2015.

95   V. Godfrey, 'East-side and West-side' <http://www.ourwelwyngardencity.org.uk/page_id__392.aspx?path=0p162p137p>, accessed 20 August 2015.

96   Tyrwhitt, *Life and work*, section 7.

97   V. Godfrey, 'A 1940s Eastside Memory' <http://www.ourwelwyngardencity.org.uk/page_id__347.aspx?path=0p162p137p>, accessed 20 August 2015.

98   Cochrane, 'Cochrane family memories'.

99   Purdom, *Satellite towns*, 2nd edn, pp. 256–71.

100   Ibid., pp. 249–51; De Soissons, *Welwyn Garden City*, pp. 113–15.

CHAPTER FOUR

Finding other paths

The 'true' path?

For many years the dominant historical narrative of the garden city movement in Britain took what can be called a 'purist' perspective. Essentially, this 'inside' story was told as if there was a 'true' path to real reform, leading from Howard's *To-morrow* through Letchworth and Welwyn Garden City to the New Towns. At times, adherents of the movement had wandered from this path, finding contentment in options that were easier to realise. Yet, ultimately, these proved less satisfactory than what might have been achieved if only they had kept the 'true' faith. (And it is a narrative with a quasi-biblical sub-text boasting a rich cast of prophets, disciples, missionaries, high priests, unbelievers and apostates.) The culmination of this narrative was Britain's celebrated post-war New Towns programme, under which 32 New Towns were created during the half century from 1946. This was essentially the perspective promoted by Frederic Osborn and, to a large extent, Charles Purdom. Its heyday was during the period when the New Towns were in the ascendant, were, as one commentator put it, 'the brightest stars in the firmament of British planning.'[1] Few subsequent historians have been fully able to escape from it.

Yet it is a perspective with obvious weaknesses. As shown in the previous chapters, neither Letchworth nor Welwyn Garden City was an exact realisation of what Howard had originally wanted. Instead of being a wide-ranging social reform, the garden city became a means to achieve the physical reform of the city. The key principle of unified ownership of the garden city estate was certainly respected in both ventures, but a truly *community* ownership that ensured land value increases were used to benefit the garden citizens was compromised at Letchworth and effectively abandoned at Welwyn Garden City. And, as will be shown, many more compromises were to follow. Not least, Howard's dislike of the involvement of the state had to be compromised to some extent in both garden cities. The 'New Townsmen', in their 1918 book,[2] had already argued that the state should become the primary driver of the development, an argument that was to carry increasing weight. Even adherents of the movement had been happy to jettison the original 'garden city' label in favour of the new, more modern label of 'new town'.

A further weakness in the argument showed itself much later, at the other end of this path, as the government's New Towns programme began to wane from the 1970s, leading eventually to its demise. Yet the extinction of what had come since 1945 to be seen as the Howardian quest, being fulfilled via the New Towns, patently signified no ending of the history of the garden city movement. Over time, the public, politicians and professionals became aware of the limitations of the New Towns (arguably, in many cases, exaggerating those weaknesses). From the 1970s, in a more environmentally conscious age that was growing more suspicious of the state, Howard's original utopian radicalism began to be tentatively revisited.

There is now a greater willingness to acknowledge that several paths emanated from Howard's work. As we shall see, what were once supposed to be 'false' paths often actually led to arguably greater gains in human welfare than did the 'true' path. Moreover, these historical paths did not bifurcate irrevocably to reach completely different destinations. In many cases they productively reconnected at various points over time and joined other paths which had not originated in *To-morrow*. This growing plurality of concerns within the garden city movement forms the subject of this chapter. To understand it, however, we need to step back in time, to the very earliest years after Howard's book was published.

Industrial garden villages

It was scarcely surprising that the focus of the movement soon shifted from the 'true' path. The Garden City Association was founded in 1899 with the prime aim of establishing a garden city, yet it was several years before Letchworth was able to function as a showpiece. In the interim, however, there were other early exemplar schemes to which the movement could refer. These were the attractive garden village settlements being developed by a few progressively minded industrialists close to their own factories. They differed sharply from Howard's ideal by relying on just one source of investment capital and had many of the attributes of company towns. We have seen that Howard may well have been aware of these examples from their earliest stages while he was writing *To-morrow*. What is absolutely clear is that, after the book was published, two of these model factory villages became the immediate physical templates for the movement. One, Bournville, was associated with the Quaker Cadbury Brothers cocoa and chocolate factory in suburban Birmingham (although it was also home to many non-Cadbury employees) (Figure 4.1).[3] The other was Port Sunlight, the company town serving the Lever Brothers soap works on the suburban Wirral peninsula, close to Birkenhead and Liverpool (Figure 4.2).[4]

A further Bournville-like venture launched in 1902, the Rowntree family's New Earswick, on the edge of York, also preceded Letchworth, if only by a small margin.[5] Yet it too played an early part in perfecting the physical and architectural character of the garden city because its architect–planners, Barry Parker and Raymond Unwin, became involved shortly before their appointment at Letchworth.[6] Even so, it was the more developed conditions of Bournville and Port Sunlight that gave these settlements the bigger role, particularly since they hosted important early Garden City Association conferences in 1901 and 1902. Attended by several hundred and well over a thousand delegates respectively, the conferences embedded these two places into the consciousness of the early garden city movement.[7]

As never before, such places showed that it was realistic for urban working-class people (except the very poor) to want to live in the kinds of arcadian living environments that previously had been confined to urban elites.[8] The houses in these innovative model settlements might be inspired more by the country cottage than the country house of the rural elite that had been the model in the more exclusive areas, yet densities were low compared to similarly priced housing in nearby lower-middle-class suburban areas – typically around 12 dwellings per acre (30 per hectare) compared with around 25 per acre (62 per hectare) upwards in comparably priced suburbs.[9]

In contrast to the long terraces and narrow-fronted houses being built by private speculators under local authority building bylaws to let at broadly similar rents, these exemplar projects had dwellings grouped in short terraced or even semi-detached formations (Figure 4.3). House frontages could be wider, allowing each household to enjoy more light, air and greenery. There were individual gardens front and rear (especially so in Bournville and New Earswick) and ample public open space. Street layouts were freer than the often gridiron layouts found in urban bylaw housing estates and thus better able to make use of topography, aspect and existing natural features. Significant public buildings were deliberately placed and grouped to close street vistas, emphasise centrality and generally use physical design to convey a clear sense of place identity. Combined with rather cottage-like domestic architecture, the overall effect was rustic and village-like, albeit more romanticised and carefully manicured than the real thing. Overall they were places which promised a more attractive and healthy setting for urban lower-middle-class and upper-working-class life than was currently available.

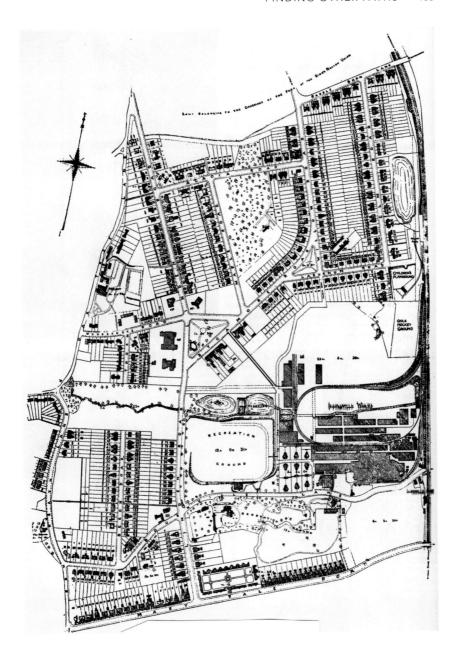

Figure 4.1 Bournville Village in 1901. Though not just a company village, it was created in association with the Cadbury factory mainly from the late 1890s (though the first few houses date from 1879). It embodied many social and physical qualities sought by the Garden City movement. (author's collection)

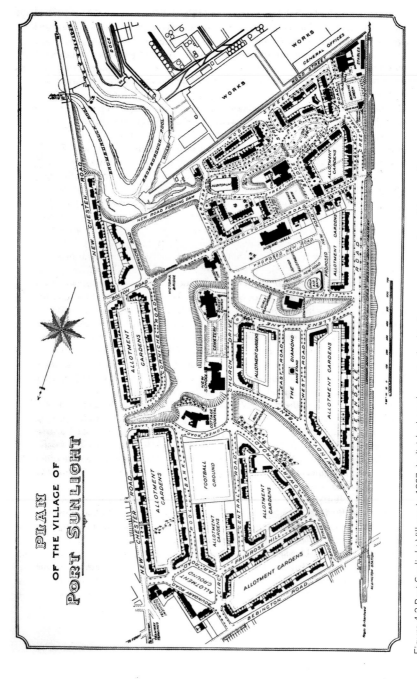

Figure 4.2 Port Sunlight Village in 1907. Individual gardens attached to houses were smaller, with open fronts and allotment gardens behind. In 1910 the plan was significantly modified to create a much more formal axial layout in the village centre. The Diamond became a much longer north–south axis. (author's collection)

Figure 4.3 Early housing on Sycamore Road, Bournville, showing why it was an obvious location in 1901 for the Garden City Association's first conference. A mix of housing was provided, all subject to leasehold control by the Bournville Village Trust (founded 1900). (author photograph)

The emergence of the garden suburb

The critical problem was how to fund this new ideal so that it could be realised on anything but a very small scale. There were some, but only a few, developers with the deep pockets and philanthropic inclinations of Lever, Cadbury or Rowntree (Figure 4.4). Moreover, though the land on which they were built was bought very cheaply, both the garden cities suffered, as we have seen, from serious undercapitalisation during their early years. In part this was because investors did not like limited-dividend companies. This was compounded by the inherent problems of building a new town from scratch, because so much early investment was needed in infrastructure, such as water supply, sewerage and roads, before house building could even start.

It was, quite simply, much easier to provide the most appealing parts of the garden city's offering in settings on the fringes of existing towns and cities. Here 'front-end' development costs and time could be reduced by using existing drainage, public utilities, services and social amenities. There was also easier access to existing sources of employment nearer the centre or in the newer factories then being established by major industries in suburban areas. The problem was, however, that the unit costs of providing such good-quality, spacious housing would certainly be higher in these more urban locations than in a freestanding, entirely new, garden city. The only way to offset this was to

Figure 4.4 William Lever, the founder of a major global soap company, was a great philanthropist; he is seen here with children from his company garden village, Port Sunlight. He was another early supporter of the Garden City movement, though certainly not an uncritical one. (author's collection)

find some way of reducing the price of land, the costs of development and/or the profits of developers and landlords. Yet, if governmental regulation of land and housing markets to achieve this result became too drastic, investors in new house building would be deterred.

Though none was entirely satisfactory, several potential options presented themselves in the Edwardian period. There were still occasional philanthropic industrialists prepared and able to follow the path of Lever, Cadbury and Rowntree. Other individuals or families who were not employers might also act as philanthropists by endowing trusts or creating limited-dividend companies. This was similar to the pattern of much Victorian philanthropy in housing which, particularly in London, had provided for a few of the 'deserving poor', mainly in model tenement flats.[10] The same mechanisms might also be used by larger groups of the 'great and the good', raising contributions through their social networks. Leadership normally came from a 'philanthropic catalyst', a persuasive individual of public standing and probity. Although the individual investors did not need to put in a large stake, this option still needed enough people with the means and inclination to forgo normal profits on their investments.

Apart from those already mentioned, there were other prominent philanthropic spirits who were willing to engage with the latest thinking about housing and planning reform. In the classic industrial philanthropist mould was James Reckitt, the Hull manufacturer of starch, drugs and household chemicals.[11] Like the Cadburys and Rowntrees, Reckitt was a Quaker with a similar desire to do God's work on earth. Among other benevolent acts, in 1907 Reckitt set up a 3 per cent-dividend company (about two-thirds directly owned by him) to develop and manage a 'garden village' in suburban Hull. It was less innovative in design than Port Sunlight, Bournville and New Earswick, but had some of the same features. Developed close by his factories, roughly half the estate (planned for up to 700 dwellings) housed Reckitt's workers.

Hampstead Garden Suburb

Much better known, however, was Dame Henrietta Barnett, who was the extraordinary 'philanthropic catalyst' responsible for Hampstead Garden Suburb. This scheme was of seminal importance in shifting prevailing thinking from the freestanding garden city to the garden suburb.[12] Barnett and her husband, Samuel, were already widely known for their good works with the poor in London. Henrietta saw the garden city as a model that could be applied to a large unbuilt-up area being opened up by the new underground tube railway to Golders Green (which finally opened in 1907) (Figure 4.5). Henrietta campaigned for it to become, rather than a speculatively developed suburb for the relatively affluent, a socially mixed area developed along garden city lines. Here the poor would be exposed to the 'contagion of refinement' and the well-to-do would be inspired by 'knowledge of strenuous lives and patient endurance'.[13]

The size (by 1914 1,550 dwellings[14] had been built) and metropolitan location of Hampstead Garden Suburb immediately gave it a high profile in reformist thinking. Yet Henrietta Barnett did several other things which further embedded the idea that the garden suburb would henceforth be *the* principal contemporary expression of the garden city. Not least, her promotional abilities unlocked philanthropic impulses to attract investment, ensuring that its finance was on a sound footing. At an early stage, in 1904, she also hired the architect and planner of New Earswick and Letchworth, Raymond Unwin, to design her new venture.[15] In doing this she underlined the design credentials of the project as a genuine and innovative development 'on garden city lines'. Finally she secured the passing of a private Act of Parliament, the Hampstead Garden Suburb Act 1906. This suspended local building bylaws to allow a more flexible garden city-style layout with narrower road widths in low-density residential areas. Rigid local bylaws

Figure 4.5 Dame Henrietta Barnett's new Hampstead Garden Suburb was made possible by the extension of the Underground to Golders Green. It was the 'place of delightful prospects' referred to in this delightful 1909 poster. (© TfL from the London Transport Museum collection).

that stipulated unnecessarily wide streets had been a handicap in early garden villages and suburbs in semi-urban locations, such as Bournville and Hull Garden Village. Although he was not the first to grasp the problem, Unwin most clearly showed (in his famous 1912 pamphlet, *Nothing gained by overcrowding!*) that reducing road space was an important way of cutting development costs.[16]

The success of Hampstead Garden Suburb ensured that it was soon seen as the new showpiece of the garden city movement. However, the basis on which its first phase was built – that is, by a trust reliant on raising philanthropic private capital – was being superseded. In earlier chapters we showed how Howard made early links with the emergent co-partnership movement and how housing societies operating on this basis played a significant role in the two garden cities. In fact, however, the contribution of co-partnership was to be greatest in building the garden suburbs of the pre-1914 period.[17] Even more than in Letchworth and Welwyn Garden City, it seemed for a time that co-partnership societies would be able to bridge the funding gap to allow the garden suburbs to become a reality on a larger scale.

Co-partnership garden suburbs

The specific idea of co-partnership in housing was first attempted, not entirely successfully, in 1888, when Tenant Co-operators Ltd was formed in London with the intention of building houses for its members, who were largely skilled workers.[18] The second housing venture was initiated in 1890 by Henry Vivian, a London carpenter and trade unionist, as a co-partnership building company to provide homes for its workers. Both were based on each co-partner tenant owning a £1 share in the society, with other investors or income from the building side of the second company providing the rest of the loan finance. Related problems of maintaining both commercial viability and the co-partnership principle were, however, experienced by both. In practice, the co-partnership model had to evolve into something that was a mix of co-operation, philanthropy and state funding before it could begin to seem a viable mechanism to address housing needs. However, many social reformers were attracted to the idea that tenants might, albeit with some external assistance, collectively provide for their own housing needs.

A further problem, albeit a less intractable one than the others, was that none of the houses built by the pioneering co-partnership ventures showed any noticeable improvement in design quality on what was being produced at the time in speculative developments around the capital. This was not surprising, as this was not part of their original remit. However, as we saw in Chapter 2, there was an increasing coming together of the garden city and the co-partnership movements at the very beginning of the twentieth century. The first really successful application of the co-partnership principle in housing from the point of view of the garden city movement came at Brentham in Ealing. In 1901 Vivian and some fellow builders set up Ealing Tenants Ltd, a housing co-partnership society, to develop houses for themselves. Initially, as with earlier schemes, the houses were similar to those being built on better-quality contemporary speculative estates around London. The area being developed, however, changed into a garden suburb in the generally understood sense during subsequent phases of building after Raymond Unwin produced a new plan for the Brentham estate in 1906–7.

In the meantime co-partnership had appeared at Letchworth (1905), but all the other new societies formed were to build what were, increasingly, garden suburbs. Notable early examples were at Sevenoaks (1903), Bournville, Burnage in Manchester, Oldham (all 1906), Fallings Park in Wolverhampton, Harborne in Birmingham, Hampstead Garden Suburb and Humberstone in Leicester (all 1907).[19] Thereafter the proliferation of co-partnership garden suburbs became even more rapid. A 1914 study estimated that there were around 50 co-partnership housing societies, almost all of them developing garden suburbs.[20] As was first the case in Letchworth and Bournville, the model was adopted to develop the later sections of settlements that had begun in other ways. At Hampstead Garden Suburb there were several co-partnership societies,[21] while further societies were created at Bournville.[22] Though some of their external funders might be common, these various societies had different tenant memberships, built on different sites and often housed different groups of people. In some cases some of these societies merged. In the years before 1914 the co-partnership garden suburb became a very promising path to urban reform. It was seen as a way of improving both the quality and quantity of housing while avoiding or at least reducing the need for direct state intervention.

Town planning on garden city lines
This widening acceptance that garden city principles could be achieved in developments that were not parts of actual garden cities was mirrored in the changing objectives (which were to a large extent further reflected in the actions) of the Garden City Association.[23] In 1902, for example, Bournville and Port Sunlight were specifically commended as successful experiments. The following year the Association began to encourage manufacturers more broadly to move to rural districts, co-operating with them and the public authorities to ensure

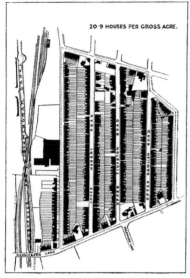
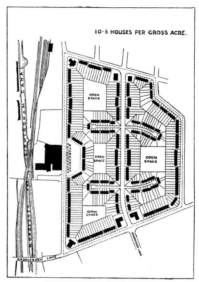

Figure 4.6 Alternative site layouts by George Cadbury Jnr, rehearsing the argument (first made by Unwin) that, despite cheap land, high road and infrastructure costs under local bylaws led to unnecessarily dense, narrow-fronted housing layouts. Lower densities meant lower development costs, making sense commercially and socially. (author's collection)

the creation of healthy housing for their workers. In addition, the Association stated that it would press for legislation to enable public authorities to deal with the housing problem and improve communications. It would also stimulate the scientific development of urban areas to avoid haphazard growth and promote the erection of healthy and beautiful dwellings with gardens and recreation space (Figure 4.6). The objectives remained secondary to promoting freestanding garden cities, but this would not last for long.

By 1906 the objectives explicitly referred to creating garden cities, garden suburbs and garden villages, now with no distinction as to which should take precedence. There was also reference to seeking the improvement of existing towns and villages on garden city principles. In this, the Association was moving towards more general support for what had by then been labelled as 'town planning' (though this still-new term was not yet being used by the Association). In February 1908, however, the name of the Association's journal was changed from *The Garden City* to *Garden Cities and Town Planning*. Even so, the first editorial under the new title made clear that ensuring the success of Letchworth remained dearest to its heart. The widening of the Association's scope was completed in 1909, when the promotion of what was now being explicitly termed 'town planning' became part of the Association's objectives. It was also formally renamed as the Garden Cities and Town Planning Association (GCTPA).

These last changes reflected the arrival of statutory town planning under the 1909 Housing, Town Planning Etc. Act.[24] This measure introduced the town planning scheme, a detailed local plan that could be prepared on land liable to be used for building development on the fringes of towns and cities (adoption was voluntary). A planning scheme specified land use and density zones and reserved major future road lines. This planning instrument derived largely from the well-established German concept of town-extension (*Stadterweiterungen*) planning, which successive visitors to Germany had been admiring since the Manchester reformer, Thomas C. Horsfall, drew it to British attention in 1904.[25]

John S. Nettlefold and the Birmingham model

Rather than developing these extensions with the higher density apartment housing typical of most German town extensions, the concept was instead replaced by the British notion of the garden suburb. The central figure in achieving this hybrid was a Birmingham Unionist councillor, John Sutton Nettlefold, a member of a powerful Unitarian manufacturing dynasty in the city who played a central part in its progressive municipal policies.[26] He was a nephew of that city's great reforming Mayor, Joseph Chamberlain, and cousin of Neville Chamberlain. Nettlefold, as chairman of the city's Housing Committee, visited Germany in 1905, returning convinced that planning outward growth pointed the way for British cities, especially Birmingham, to tackle their housing problems.[27] Suburban railways and municipal tramway extensions could be exploited to expand the living area of the city. Proper extension planning would avoid repeating past mistakes, gradually allowing overcrowded areas in inner parts of the city to be decongested and renewed. In the autumn of 1905 Nettlefold and the Birmingham medical officer of health, John S. Robertson, coined the neologism 'town planning' to describe this new approach.[28]

In all this, Nettlefold (a member of the GCTPA's Council) showed important similarities with Howard's reasoning, but, instead of replacing the big concentrated city, this reforming councillor would expand it peripherally on planned garden city lines.[29] Just as Howard thought that London in time might be emptied out and redeveloped as a network of garden cities, Nettlefold's strategy would eventually permit Birmingham's densely populated inner areas to be redeveloped on more spacious lines. But this was an ultimate goal. In the interim he began partial demolition, rehabilitation and improved sanitary provision in the courts of back-to-back housing which typified Birmingham's inner areas. This policy of gradual improvement to 'open up' the courts was much cheaper than the wholesale slum clearance and redevelopment with municipal flats then being pursued in London and Liverpool.

For Nettlefold, the long-term answer was to widen social access to the new garden suburbs. Cost was, of course, the critical consideration and the price of development land was the key element. Like Howard, he wanted as much development land as possible (unless it was owned by public-spirited landowners such as the Bournville Village Trust) to be in public ownership. Unlike Howard, however, he saw the municipality as the proper body to do this. The city rehearsed this policy on a small suburban site in Bordesley Green in 1908,[30] but it remained a rare instance both in Birmingham and elsewhere; Nettlefold did not manage to embed municipal ownership of development land within the conception of planning that he introduced in Birmingham, and nor was it a part of the 1909 Act.

This was perhaps surprising because, working through the Association of Municipal Corporations, Nettlefold was the principal author of the town planning powers passed into law in 1909.[31] The trouble was that many compromises with landed interests were necessary to get the measure enacted. In practice, therefore, the Act rested on the over-optimistic assumption that density zoning in approved town planning scheme areas, aided by rather tentative provisions for compensation and betterment (which involved offsetting any fall or taxing any increase in land values that was attributable to planning), would be sufficient to moderate the private land market. Denied the much stronger control that came with public land ownership, Nettlefold also favoured co-partnership societies. Their mutual structure meant that they would be likely to resist 'sweating' land assets – that is, deliberately holding back land from development to force up land prices, thereby often pushing up housing costs when there was private speculative development of suburban areas. He was already actively involved in the co-partnership movement as chairman of Harborne Tenants Ltd in the eponymous west Birmingham suburb.[32] There the society developed a pleasant garden suburb of almost 500 dwellings that soon became a key component of Birmingham's Quinton, Harborne and Edgbaston town planning scheme (Figure 4.7).[33]

This was the very first statutory scheme in the country to be approved, in 1913, and was intended to ensure that the whole of this outer sector of west Birmingham would develop along the same broad lines as Harborne. Soon similar town planning schemes were in hand for the whole of the city's suburban fringe. Combined with the Bournville Village Trust estate in the south of the city,

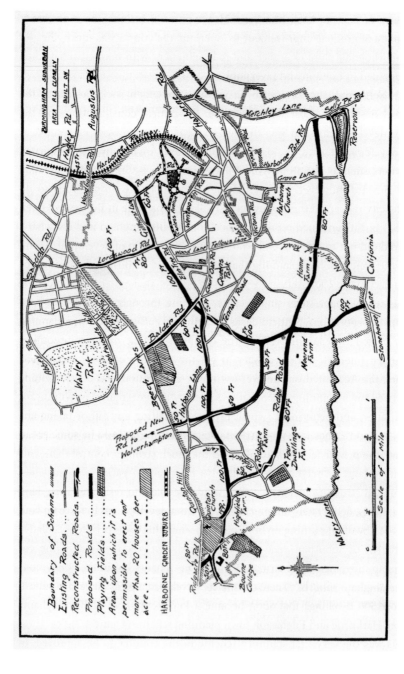

Figure 4.7 Birmingham's Quinton, Harborne and Edgbaston town planning scheme. This was the first statutory town planning scheme to be approved under the 1909 Act. It embodied the ideas of Nettlefold and the Cadburys that town planning should be undertaken 'on garden city lines'. (author's collection)

Nettlefold's vision promised the most complete realisation anywhere in Britain of the planned extension of a great city 'on garden city lines'. Other cities seemed poised to follow suit. Here, many thought, was a viable alternative to the lonely and frustratingly slow-growing splendour of Letchworth.

The leadership of the GCTPA was also thinking the same way. In 1913 and 1914 the Association published two editions of a short book called *The garden city movement up-to-date*, compiled by the secretary of the Association, Ewart G. Culpin.[34] This effectively confirmed that the way forward was now to promote garden suburbs within a wider campaign for town planning.[35] The Birmingham flowering of co-partnership garden suburbia and enlightened municipal town-extension planning seemed confirmation of this strategy, a harbinger of a golden age to come.

The growth of state involvement

Yet although this revisionist path might have seemed a more practical route than holding out for more 'true' garden cities, it too proved unequal to the scale of the problem. Already by 1914 the housing shortage was worsening as the pace of housing construction fell sharply in the last years of peace.[36] There was also a massive problem of housing obsolescence in all the bigger cities. Even in Birmingham the city's policies and enlightened private actions had brought few improvements. A Special Housing Enquiry by Birmingham City Council in 1913 found about 50,000 back-to-back houses, many overcrowded, needing early replacement.[37] Though still shying away from large-scale municipal house building, the Enquiry's recommendations wanted a more aggressive strategy with more direct municipal intervention in land supply, town planning, slum clearance and redevelopment.

War deepened the housing problem in all big cities and industrial areas, as house building dried up and more workers came to factories working at full stretch. Reluctantly, central government accepted the inevitability of more direct intervention at national level, initially to control rents but then to subsidise housing provision on a large scale.[38] The 1919 Housing, Town Planning Etc. Act for the first time subsidised the provision of housing on a large scale by local authorities.[39] These initial terms were extraordinarily generous, limiting any municipal loss incurred between the rental income and loan repayment charges to the product of a one-old-penny increase on the rate (i.e. the local tax). The 1919 Housing (Additional Powers) Act gave less generous subsidies to the private builders, including housing societies. The main 1919 subsidies were soon dropped because of their cost, but fixed subsidies per dwelling were reintroduced under the 1923 and 1924 Housing Acts. The former favoured private builders, though the latter, available only to local authorities, was the more generous and its subsidy available for longer, until 1934. The 1930 and 1935 Housing Acts introduced subsidies to provide housing for families rehoused from slum clearance areas or formerly living in overcrowded conditions.

Although co-partnership housing societies benefited to some extent, subsidies were generally available to them on less favourable terms than to local authorities.[40] Perhaps unsurprisingly, therefore, their role in interwar housing supply was small.[41] Subsidised private building – that is, by ordinary private builders and housing societies together – accounted for under 11 per cent of the 4.31 million dwellings built in Britain between 1919 and 1939. Much the biggest provider of subsidised housing was the municipal sector, which accounted for nearly 1.33 million dwellings (about 31 per cent of all new housing). The remaining 58 per cent was unsubsidised, sharply contrasting with the pre-war pattern, when it had been over 90 per cent. In total, this amounted to a dramatic change in the way housing was supplied. Before 1914 council housing for rent had grown in importance but remained a very small tenure sector, amounting to perhaps only around 22,000 dwellings nationally. The main municipal providers were in London and Liverpool.[42] Like Birmingham, most local authorities did not want to take on the commitments represented by large-scale housing programmes. They risked having to fund deficits on their housing revenue accounts from local tax income.

Municipal garden suburbs

Moreover, pre-1914 municipal housing had been almost completely synonymous with tenement flats. Although cottage-style municipal housing was beginning to appear, especially in London, this was not yet of garden city standards. This also changed after 1918, as government accepted that housing standards had to be raised. Here the pre-war garden suburbs and planning on garden city lines certainly became the model for what followed. This was thanks largely to the official government committee which was established to define appropriate standards for subsidised housing.[43] It was chaired by a Liberal MP and architect, Sir John Tudor-Walters, but its most influential member was Raymond Unwin, who drew on everything he had learned at New Earswick, Letchworth and Hampstead Garden Suburb and the work he had done during the war designing housing for munitions workers. The Tudor-Walters report formed the basis of the 1919 *Housing Manual*, the new handbook for local authorities and other agencies building subsidised housing.

Figure 4.8 The Allen's Cross council estate in Birmingham, built in the late 1920s, embodied the housing standards and site layout principles pioneered by the pre-war garden cities, suburbs and villages, albeit on a much bigger scale. With more than 2,000 dwellings, it was several times larger than most pre-war garden suburbs. (author's collection)

The result was that the many council-house estates that began to appear throughout Britain in the interwar years were, in many respects, municipal garden suburbs. Not only were they built at what had become the garden city density of 12 houses per acre but their designers used the Arts and Crafts or neo-Georgian architectural styles of the pre-war garden suburbs and ensured that houses had individual private gardens. Familiar also were estate layouts, use of aspect, architectural treatment of street corners and the grouping of houses (Figure 4.8). There was liberal use of green space in the streets and generous provision of parkland and playing fields was also common. Yet their size and number inevitably gave a formulaic quality to them. The scale of individual estates could be vast. For example, between 1920 and 1934 the London County Council built a giant cottage estate with over 25,000 dwellings at Becontree in the eastern suburbs, accommodating an estimated 117,890 people in 1934.[44] By any standards (it was the biggest municipal scheme anywhere in the world at the time) it was an extraordinary achievement, greater in population size than most existing towns and some cities in Britain. Only a few of the post-war New Towns were larger. It was also significantly larger than the 1939 population of both garden cities and all the pre-1914 garden suburbs combined.

Although no other municipal estates approached Becontree in size, by the later 1930s estates of several thousand dwellings existed around all the big cities. The London County Council had other very big estates, notably at St Helier in the south-western suburbs (9,070 dwellings) and Downham in the south-eastern suburbs (6,070 dwellings).[45] In Liverpool the Norris Green estate had about 7,700 dwellings and the Dovecot estate just over 3,000.[46] Birmingham, which had long resisted municipal housing, now became the most active builder among the big provincial cities.[47] Its Kingstanding estate had 4,800 dwellings and, immediately adjoined by three other estates, was claimed as the largest area of council housing outside London. Elsewhere, Glasgow's Knightswood estate had over 6,700 dwellings and Bristol's estate at Knowle and Bedminster over 5,400 municipal dwellings, while the Gipton estate in Leeds had almost 3,500.[48] There were also many other small and medium-sized estates in most towns and smaller cities. Some villages also had smaller groups of council housing.

This programme was on a scale of which the Edwardian reformers could have only dreamt. Moreover, these municipal garden suburbs were occupied increasingly by genuinely working-class people, rather than the lower-middle-class groups who were typical residents of the pre-1914 co-partnership garden suburbs. Even former slum dwellers, long the subject of reformist hopes, were beginning to be housed in such settings by the later 1930s. While there had been some compromises to reduce rent levels, the housing on these cottage estates compared reasonably well with that which had been pioneered in the industrial garden villages, at Letchworth and in the Edwardian garden suburbs. Most was traditionally built, mainly in brick or rendered brick, and unpretentious in its architecture, with decent-sized individual gardens. In themselves, the scale of these estates meant that they made an important quantitative and qualitative contribution to planning on garden city lines.

Social imbalances on the new estates

Yet, although many of their residents clearly enjoyed many of the aspects of living in these large new municipal estates, this phenomenon became the subject of growing criticism. There were several notable social inquiries into the estates, which played an important part in shaping future thinking about how large new communities could be better planned. A common criticism was that they were too homogenous in their social composition. The dwelling mix was overwhelmingly three-bedroom houses, favouring a particular kind of family structure, typically families with children.[49] There were fewer older people or young people wishing to live collectively in service-hostel accommodation or small flats than was typical in bigger cities. The effect was to put acute pressure on particular kinds of services, especially schools, where there was an initial struggle to provide places for many young children which then was reproduced in classes for older pupils as the children grew up. The results could easily produce overprovision after the initial surge had passed.

Social-class homogeneity was also seen as a problem. Henrietta Barnett's quaint words in favour of social mix,[50] noted earlier, were echoed in the later words of sociologists. A 1934 study of Becontree noted some of the problems of social polarisation, so that '... each income group ceases to learn how members of another income group live'.[51] If at least some social mix could be achieved, however, '[e]ven if there is antipathy, there is a certain amount of understanding'. Its absence created specific difficulties in raising money for voluntary social and religious activities because those able to afford to contribute lived too far away to identify with the places and people concerned. This led some, such as Purdom in 1949, also writing about Becontree and with the two garden cities in mind as comparators, to believe that it had 'nothing worth calling social life at all'.[52] Yet social polarisation also gave these big estates their character as places. Thus a 1963 study concluded that Becontree, despite being more spacious, was really just 'the East End reborn',[53] with all the characteristic social networks of a working-class area.

At least some of those who had planned these bigger new estates had wanted a greater social mix. The initial 1919 plans for Becontree had proposed that a quarter of the housing would be for better-off families, though these hopes failed to materialise.[54] The priority was overwhelmingly housing the working classes, and it would have been difficult to justify devoting resources to those better able to house themselves. Some dwellings were added at the last stage of building, though by then the dominant character of the estate had become fixed in popular perceptions and there was some reluctance on the part of better-off families to live there. There was also resistance from better-off areas to any mixing. In Oxford the City Council sold half of its land at Cutteslowe, in the north of the city, for private development. However, the private developer who bought the site took great exception to his house buyers having to live in such close proximity to municipal tenants (including a handful from slum clearance areas). In 1934 he constructed walls across linking roads to completely segregate the two areas.[55] Despite several attempts to remove them by both legal and direct action, they survived until 1959. Nor were these walls the first. At the London County Council estate of Downham, a similar wall, also built by a private developer, had existed since 1926 and survived until 1950.[56]

Weaknesses in social provision

Many of these areas also had problems similar to those of other new communities, including the garden cities and New Towns. These were typically associated with the inadequate or tardy provision of local services and social amenities. This happened everywhere, but tended to be worse where the estates lay outside the limits of the city. The usual consequence, at least for the big cities, was that county authorities were responsible for schools and other public services, even though the actual housing had been built by the cities. A dearth of shops, by contrast, often resulted in informal retailing by enterprising householders, even though this breached tenancy agreements and could lead to eviction.[57] Even when the proper facilities appeared, their planned arrangement could also cause problems, with, for example, shopping being inconveniently located.[58] Efforts by the churches and voluntary organisations were often important in the early social provision of facilities such as community centres.[59] In Birmingham, for example, the city council itself did not provide its first one until 1936, long after the estate in question was finished.

By the later 1930s central government advice acknowledged the social value of public houses and recommended that they should be provided on council estates. The question was a vexed one, with some authorities (notably Liverpool and Glasgow) prohibiting them on its housing estates.[60] The result was that pubs were often built just beyond estate boundaries, so that sobriety was not necessarily enhanced. In Glasgow, the 'dry' policy was also linked to disturbances on late-night public transport as drinkers returned to the estate.[61] The London County Council revealed similar though less extreme temperance sentiments in its provision of what it called 'licensed refreshment houses'.[62] These large and rather soulless places sold alcohol but also tried to offer a more diverse and family-friendly ambience, with non-alcoholic drinks and food. They also provided spaces for social events, dancing and entertainment.

Distance to employment was frequently an important issue. In most cities workers on these large new housing estates had to travel further and spend more time and money on travelling to their workplaces than workers in older areas nearer the centre of the city.[63] In some cases, local employment was already available or grew up nearby, most notably when the Ford car factory moved to Dagenham, adjoining the Becontree estate. Yet the estate (which lay outside the London County area) was intended to house only those who had originally lived within the County.[64] The rather odd result was that Ford workers, many who had moved from Manchester, were not initially eligible to live on the estate.

Many of these various problems had the effect of increasing the cost of living for residents of these estates.[65] The shops were not as cheap as shops and markets in the older parts of cities, for example. Public transport fares were higher and homes that were larger than former accommodation invariably cost more to furnish and keep warm. The welfare consequences, especially as more former slum dwellers began to move into suburban council estates, could be significant. Some local authorities introduced rent-relief schemes based on assessments of household needs, and by 1938 around 100 authorities had adopted schemes of this type.[66] Municipal furniture-hire-purchase schemes were also used to assist families with furnishing their council houses. Yet, despite such initiatives, surveys in several cities during the 1930s found evidence of poverty on these new estates. Some investigators claimed that this led to poorer nutrition and worse health than in former environments.[67] Considering that housing reformers had been drawn to garden city residential design to raise standards of public health and welfare, this was a very disappointing finding.

The private housing boom

Although it lay a little off the 'true' path, interwar municipal cottage housing certainly had its authentic connections to the garden city. However, the privately developed suburbs of the same period went much more their own way, their developers often claiming a link but to the satisfaction of few serious commentators. In their favour, however, was their massive quantitative contribution to interwar housing output. Thus private for-profit developers completed some 2.51 million unsubsidised dwellings in Britain during the period 1919–39, efforts more spectacular even than those of the municipal sector.[68] In the 1920s private developers also accounted for the lion's share of the 473,000 subsidised non-municipal dwelling completions (which also included housing societies).

Virtually all this privately developed housing was built in the suburbs, much of it for sale, but during the 1930s some estates were also being built for rent by private landlords. As in the municipal sector, housing densities were much lower than had been common before 1914. The long terraces of narrow-fronted bylaw houses were superseded by more open layouts, even for cheaper housing. The new pattern was predominantly of semi-detached houses, giving residents more light and space, and set in substantial private gardens. Grass verges, sometimes with trees, were provided between road and pavement on residential streets (Figure 4.9).

The extent to which this new privately developed suburbia owed allegiance to garden city ideology can certainly be disputed. The architecture rarely

The Best Tonic !

SPRING IS HERE

Time for a Tonic. And the best Tonics are fresh air and a change of surroundings.

You will get both at EDGWARE.

Edgware is in London's north-west countryside—a healthy spot—300 feet above sea-level. It is now linked up with London by the Underground, and in consequence is developing rapidly as a new and pleasant garden suburb. You will have brighter outlooks and daily doses of fresh air if you

Live at
EDGWARE
on the

E3'30/26

Figure 4.9 From the later 1920s there was a private house-building boom in the suburbs. Developers, building societies and transport providers all promoted this boom, as here in this 1926 Underground advertisement to live in 'the new and pleasant garden suburb' of Edgware. (© TfL from the London Transport Museum collection)

showed the rustic Arts and Crafts simplicity or neo-Georgian good manners that characterised pre-1914 garden suburbs and the best of the new municipal estates. Similarly, premeditated developer efforts to create physically integrated settings for community life were often totally lacking (rather than merely inadequate or late, as they more usually were in the bigger municipal estates). Arguably, perhaps, such planned efforts were less needed. The generally better-off inhabitants of these estates more easily stimulated nearby private service provision such as shops or doctor's practices or themselves had more inclination and capacity to organise voluntary efforts such as sports and leisure clubs. Yet, whatever the shortfalls of these areas – and there were many – they were still a mass realisation of an essential feature of the garden city residential 'offer': relatively low-density houses with individual gardens.

Overall, looking at the qualitative housing improvements which occurred between the wars and the huge numbers of people who benefited, it would be churlish not to give some credit to the garden suburb revisionist arguments developed before 1914. Yet they alone were not responsible for the huge outward growth of towns and cities, which resulted in the extension of the built-up area of Britain by some 40 per cent. Other factors were certainly involved.[69] Improvements in urban public transport as railways were electrified and reliable, regular motor-bus services were introduced greatly extended the potentially developable area around cities. The depressed state of agriculture encouraged many sales of even good-quality farming land on the urban fringe. This ensured very low land costs per dwelling, particularly since there were no planning restraints stopping peripheral residential development. Interest rates were also very low and private-housing finance underwent important changes, widening social access to home ownership. But the pre-1914 advocates of the garden suburb had essentially authored the ideal that was now being so extensively realised, albeit by quite different mechanisms to those that Unwin, Culpin, Nettlefold and their fellow revisionists had imagined.

Criticisms and new problems

Not everyone was impressed by the garden city movement in either its pure or its revisionist forms. In 1932 Thomas Sharp, a young town planner completely disconnected from the mainstream circles of planning thinking in London and the South East, stunned the entire movement with an eloquent but unrelentingly savage diatribe: 'Howard's new hope, new life, new civilisation, Town–Country, is a hermaphrodite; sterile, imbecile, a monster; abhorrent and loathsome to the Nature which he worships.'[70] His objection was that the low-density garden city and all its imitators in the building boom that was then underway were destroying both the urbanity of the town and the rurality of the country. Others had occasionally gone part of the way with this argument before him. As early as 1913, Trystan Edwards had also criticised the garden city-inspired move to lower-density, less compact cities – 'monotonous diffuseness' in his words.[71] This was a critique that Sharp absorbed directly into his own polemic, citing Edwards's seminal book *Good and bad manners in architecture* with (for Sharp) a rare approval.[72]

But in 1932 the garden city was still the only show in town as far as British planning as a whole was concerned. It had undeniably been the direct inspiration for post-war housing standards and those promoted by statutory town planning. For its part, the garden city movement could share some of Sharp's criticisms of continuous suburban development around the bigger cities, particularly once the new mass private house-builders became dominant. But they saw the answer not in rejecting lower densities but in creating new alternative centres for development away from the big cities. There might only be two extant examples, at Letchworth and Welwyn Garden City, yet they could be rationalised as necessary experiments to demonstrate wider lessons that, one day, surely, would be more boldly applied.

Against this sense of achievement, Sharp's unexpected and savage words were damaging in a way that no previous criticisms had been. Importantly, though, garden city movement supporters noticed that Sharp's actual gripe was with open development, not the principle of creating new towns. But his assault was so brutal and frontal that it demanded and got a strong response from the Association: 'He ignores the harassing difficulties, forgets the world war, never mentions finance, and goes all over the world with his muck-rake to collect mistakes which other people have made and to label them as "garden cities".'[73] In a deeper sense that garden city supporters did not fully articulate in public, they also saw Sharp as an unconscious apologist for country-house elitism: 'small-minded people living in large houses', as MacFadyen, Howard's first biographer and one of the most ardent defenders of his legacy, put it in his response to Sharp in 1933.[74]

In this, his critics were entirely mistaken. Actually Sharp was a socialist with a commitment to better urban housing and other progressive causes, particularly regional development policies, that was at least equal to and in some respects more radical than their own.[75] Yet his palpable love for the countryside and the form of traditional villages caused garden city supporters to fear that Sharp was feeding the arguments of those wanting to protect the existing privileges and lifestyle of a rural, landowning elite. This conservative preservationist viewpoint held that the countryside could be protected only by forcing most people to live at much higher urban housing densities, which would be inconsistent with satisfactory living conditions. The seriousness with which the garden city movement took this fear can be gauged by Osborn's later, private reflection in 1945 about the 'countryhouse following' of those who sympathised with Sharp.[76] Looking back on the 1930s, he felt that Sharp's ideas had been a bigger threat to the success of garden city principles than the radical modernist ideas of the Swiss–French architect Le Corbusier, who, before 1939, had had only a limited appeal for a few British architects and planners. But, in the early post-war years, Osborn was already having to revise his assessments of both of them.

The truth was that Sharp had thrown open the planning debate in 1932. His temerity in suggesting that the garden city might be flawed created a new space for other thinking. More importantly for the longer-term trajectory of British planning, it also forced the garden city movement itself to update and rethink its vision. Not for the last time, one generation's planning solution was becoming the next generation's planning problem. Such was the immense scale of the outward expansion of cities during this period, largely on account of housing development, that new concerns appeared.[77] Not least was the loss of rural land, making 'real' countryside ever more distant from city dwellers, destroying natural amenities and threatening home food production at a time of growing international insecurity. The sheer size of cities also began to be seen as a problem. New suburban transport investments came to be seen as a 'zero-sum game' where gains in the income from fares in the outer areas were being offset by declines in inner areas. The time and expense of long journeys to work for individual travellers and the inefficiencies of having rolling stock and vehicles that were fully used only during peak hours were other costs of excessive suburbanisation.

Although the costs to individual families of suburban living had been reduced by the 1930s, it remained a way of life that lay beyond the reach of many who lived in the poorer inner city areas. This was not just a matter of housing and transport costs. For example, suburban shops were more expensive than inner-city street markets and the persistence of casual employment allocated several times a day in the biggest, especially the port, cities discouraged living on a distant estate in the suburbs. The 1930s saw a big shift in housing subsidies towards slum clearance and redevelopment of inner sites. However, in contrast to the pre-war hopes of Howard and Nettlefold, this demolition and replanning did not allow residential and population densities to reduce to garden city standards. In the biggest cities especially, high-density blocks of flats set what would become the new pattern.

The regional unevenness of development was also identified as a major problem.[78] The decline of older industries in the coalfield areas stood in stark contrast to what was increasingly seen as the overgrowth of the big cities, particularly the biggest. The private building boom did not reach the less buoyant regions until the latter half of the 1930s and left the most depressed towns, such as those of county Durham (places very dear to the heart of Thomas Sharp, who was from Bishop Auckland) or the south Wales valleys, largely untouched. Substantial interregional migration was occurring, leaving these unfortunate places increasingly locked into a vicious circle of decline. The skilled, the ambitious and the able-bodied were the typical migrants. They left behind a more dependent population and local authorities with shrinking local tax bases that were increasingly unable to provide the welfare services required.

Beyond the urban fringe the more remote countryside was also facing economic and social problems as agriculture and traditional rural craft industries declined.[79] The significance of the traditional land-owning custodians who had managed the rural landscapes declined with them. Alongside this, the increased leisure use of motor vehicles, especially buses and cars, began to have a noticeable impact on coastal areas and other places of high scenic value. Pressure grew for tourism-related development such as cafes, petrol stations and cheap accommodation, often in beauty spots. Increasingly the countryside was seen as under threat, something which Sharp and others had warned about.

A new variant – the satellite town

There were attempts to seek new planning solutions, producing further variants of the garden city tradition. One of the most favoured between the wars was the satellite town. This was seen as an alternative to the continuously built-up suburb but more readily achievable than a 'pure' garden city. Yet the concept was only loosely defined and used by different commentators in different ways. The essential idea was that it would be a way of extending cities in a more articulated fashion than occurred with peripheral suburbanisation. Satellites would be distinct 'towns', with greater social balance than in the more polarised suburbs and some (but certainly not complete) social self-containment, with a good level of local shopping and other local service provision. There would also be some local employment, a clear design identity and real physical separation from the parent city. The idea had an obvious connection with Howard's concept of the social city. There was, however, the important difference that the satellite town was no longer part of a regional settlement pattern that would ultimately replace the big concentrated city. It was now a means to achieve metropolitan decentralisation rather than to challenge the big city's very existence.

The spatial concept of the satellite had been introduced by Raymond Unwin in his 1912 booklet *Nothing gained by overcrowding!* He saw it as a way of articulating and giving form to suburban growth around larger urban centres. As he wrote:

> instead of being a huge aggregation of units ever spreading further and further away from the original centre and losing all touch with that centre, [the town] should consist of a federation of groups constantly clustering around new subsidiary centres, each group limited to a size that can effectively keep in touch with and be controlled from the subsidiary centre, and through that centre have connection with the original and main centre of the federated area.[80]

The term 'satellite' was not yet being used, but Unwin had defined something which, via Germany, soon acquired this label.

The most important early applications of the notion of the satellite town actually came in Weimar Germany. Even before 1914 there had been keen German interest in Howard's book. A translated version appeared in 1902 and a German Garden City society (*Deutsche Gartenstadtgesellschaft*) the same year. Actually ideas with some similarities to Howard's were already circulating in Germany, notably those of the extreme nationalist Theodor Fritsch.[81] The physical, moral and racial purity of the life in smaller rural towns and the idea of avoiding the perceived pernicious effects of the big city chimed in ultra-conservative *Volkisch* thinking. Yet Howard's more liberal approach appealed more to the German urban reformers, who attended several garden city conferences. The early British schemes were closely studied. Soon there were some fine pre-1914 German interpretations of the garden city, notably Hellerau in Dresden and Margarethenhöhe in Essen (Figure 4.10).[82] The former showed many affinities with the co-operative community principles that Howard had sought and that were present to some extent at Letchworth. Margarethenhöhe, one of several garden settlements built in the Ruhr at this time, was created by the famous Krupp industrial dynasty to fulfil a similar role to Bournville – part company town, part lower-middle-class garden suburb.

Among the pre-war German visitors to Britain was a young architect and planner, Ernst May. During 1910–12 May was apprenticed to Unwin's design office, then working on Hampstead Garden Suburb. The young German left

Figure 4.10 Margarethenhöhe in Essen, Germany, was developed from 1908 by the Krupp industrial dynasty for its workers and other residents. The design echoes the feel of a small medieval walled German town, surrounded by a wooded belt and approached through an archway. (author photograph)

Britain convinced that Unwin's as yet untitled satellites pointed the way forward for urban growth. Possibly echoing an earlier use of the term in Germany (by Alfred Abendroth in 1905), May later began to use the German word 'Trabanten' to describe them; literally, 'satellites'.[83] After the war May worked designing rural housing schemes around Breslau (the present Wrocław in Poland). In 1921–2 there was a competition to plan the wider city region, for which May and his associate, Herbert Böhm, proposed a scheme based on the satellite principle. May especially elaborated these ideas further over the next few years in Breslau (Figure 4.11).[84] From 1925, however, he was able to realise his thinking in Frankfurt-am-Main after being put in charge of the city's social housing programme.[85] Combining the satellite principle and modernist housing designs, the 'New Frankfurt' that was created in the second half of the 1920s became one of the most influential experiments in planned social housing provision anywhere at that time.

Satellite towns in Britain

Competing definitions of the satellite town were, however, appearing in Britain. In 1925 Charles Purdom adopted it in the title of his book *The building of satellite towns*, largely describing the growth of Letchworth and Welwyn Garden City.[86] He,

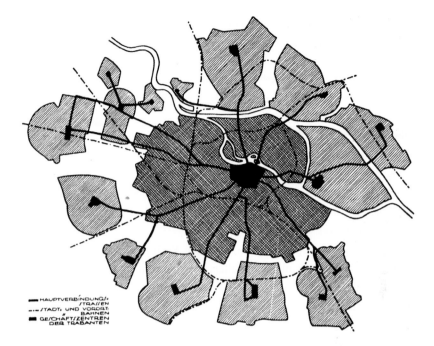

Figure 4.11 Ernst May drew on Unwin's ideas to propose a planning scheme in 1921–2 based on the principle of Trabanten (satellites) for the then German city of Breslau (Wrocław). He implemented these ideas in Frankfurt later in the decade. (author's collection)

however, used the term 'satellite town' interchangeably with 'garden city'. Purdom, representing the 'purists', felt that Unwin, with other leaders of the pre-war movement such as Culpin, had strayed from the 'true' path by advocating mass suburbanisation 'on garden city lines' and thus fatally compromised the clarity of the holistic garden city vision as the creation of new, freestanding settlements.[87]

In such 'purist' eyes Unwin was soon to redeem himself through his work from 1927 for the Greater London Regional Planning Committee. He authored two seminal reports published in 1929 and 1933.[88] The first championed the idea of a 'green girdle' – an idea again heavily influenced by a German example, in this case Fritz Schumacher and Konrad Adenauer's scheme to create a double 'Grüngürtel' for Cologne. Applied to London, it marked the origins of the present metropolitan green belt, that term being adopted when the London County Council started tentatively to implement Unwin's policy in 1935. The second report focused on how to achieve planned decentralisation as a way of decongesting the inner and central parts of London.[89] Unwin proposed a combination of planned suburbs, satellite towns and garden cities. Garden cities would be located between 12 and 35 miles from the centre of the 'parent' city and be the most self-contained in terms of employment and services. Satellite towns would be located up to 12 miles from the centre and have spatial distinctness and some lesser degree of self-containment.

Even before this proposal for London, the second Labour government had in 1931 set up a Ministry of Health Departmental Committee chaired by Lord Marley to investigate and make recommendations about garden cities and satellite towns.[90] Its report, long delayed by the political, economic and financial crisis of 1931 and its aftermath of financial austerity, appeared in 1935, endorsing Unwin's distinctions between the two types of settlement and making rather similar proposals. This was hardly surprising since Unwin and Sir Theodore Chambers, chairman of the Welwyn Garden City Company, were prominent Committee members.

The Committee's report had little impact. Within government its detailed proposals on ways to implement either satellite towns or garden cities were regarded as impractical,[91] and there were doubts about the whole policy of creating satellite towns and garden cities as a way to shape the growth of large urban areas rather than relying on peripheral suburban expansion. Ministry of Health officials felt that the views of Unwin and Chambers had been excessively indulged by the rest of the Committee. Yet political circumstances had changed radically since its inception and the report was received not by a (relatively sympathetic) Labour government but by a Conservative-dominated National government preoccupied by the economy. Nor did it help the Committee's credibility that Marley was seen as a man who was becoming excessively sympathetic to the Soviet Union following his two-month visit there in 1932.[92] Perhaps most important of all, the government still saw the rampant 1930s private suburban housing boom primarily as a solution and not yet as a problem.

Wythenshawe

Nevertheless, some local authorities during the 1930s did start to build actual satellite towns. Best known was Wythenshawe in Manchester, intended to house around 100,000 people (a figure reached in the mid-1960s, though which had fallen below 70,000 in the early twenty-first century) (Figure 4.12).[93] Even within the garden city movement it attracted divergent opinions. Its sympathisers labelled it the third garden city, while critics dismissed it as a mere suburb, another Becontree.[94] Shortly after the Great War ended, Manchester City Council recognised the scale of its housing needs and the limited space in and around the city for major schemes. It was advised by the already noted (and later renowned) planner Patrick Abercrombie that the largely unbuilt area south of the River

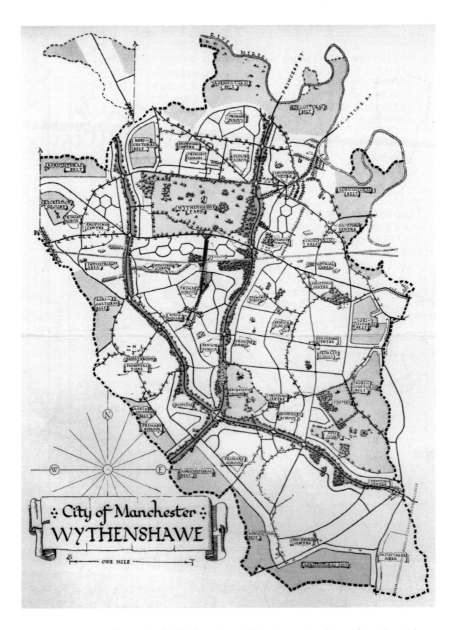

Figure 4.12 Barry Parker's plan for Wythenshawe, Manchester, developed from the mid-1930s. The innovative concept was for a socially mixed satellite town for up to 100,000 inhabitants, with a high degree of self-containment and autonomy. The reality fell well short of the more ambitious aims. (author's collection)

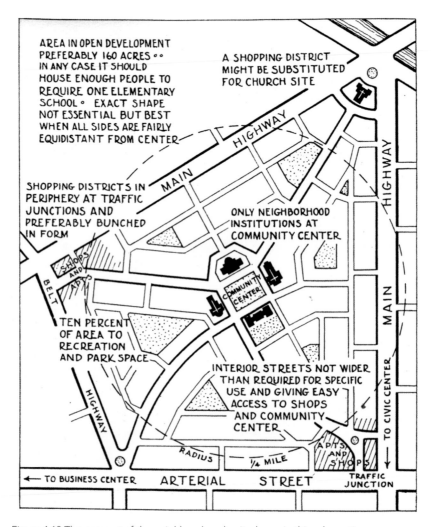

AREA IN OPEN DEVELOPMENT PREFERABLY 160 ACRES °° IN ANY CASE IT SHOULD HOUSE ENOUGH PEOPLE TO REQUIRE ONE ELEMENTARY SCHOOL ° EXACT SHAPE NOT ESSENTIAL BUT BEST WHEN ALL SIDES ARE FAIRLY EQUIDISTANT FROM CENTER

A SHOPPING DISTRICT MIGHT BE SUBSTITUTED FOR CHURCH SITE

SHOPPING DISTRICTS IN PERIPHERY AT TRAFFIC JUNCTIONS AND PREFERABLY BUNCHED IN FORM

ONLY NEIGHBORHOOD INSTITUTIONS AT COMMUNITY CENTER

TEN PERCENT OF AREA TO RECREATION AND PARK SPACE

INTERIOR STREETS NOT WIDER THAN REQUIRED FOR SPECIFIC USE AND GIVING EASY ACCESS TO SHOPS AND COMMUNITY CENTER

SHOPS AND APTS

BELT

HIGHWAY

HIGHWAY

MAIN

COMMUNITY CENTER

HIGHWAY

MAIN

TO CIVIC CENTER

RADIUS — ¼ MILE

APTS AND SHOPS

← TO BUSINESS CENTER   ARTERIAL   STREET   TRAFFIC JUNCTION

Figure 4.13 The concept of the neighbourhood unit, shown in this schematic representation in the Survey for the New York Regional Plan, was developed in New York during the 1920s. It entered British thinking during the 1930s and was central to planning the first post-war New Towns, albeit with variations. The original location of retailing on the edges of the neighbourhood differed sharply from British practice. (author's collection)

Mersey would be ideal for large-scale housing development. He warned them, however, of the problems of adequately controlling the development that might arise if the area remained outside the city. These would be more acute than most authorities experienced because the area was in another county, Cheshire, where the county council and that of the local Bucklow Rural District completely opposed any Mancunian incursion.

The political driving forces behind the scheme were two Manchester Aldermen, William Jackson and Ernest Simon (and later his wife, Shena). The Simons also played a key philanthropic role by purchasing Wythenshawe Hall and Park and then presenting them to the city at an early stage to encourage waverers on the council that the project was attainable. The critical acquisition came in 1926, when the 2,568 acres (1,040 hectares) of the Tatton estate finally came into the city's hands. Barry Parker, Unwin's former partner, was appointed to prepare a plan for a municipal satellite town covering an area of 5,567 acres (2,254 hectares), with municipally owned land forming the key part. In 1931, after much effort, the city boundary was extended to incorporate this whole area. The city gradually bought more land and by 1939 68 per cent of the site (3,787 acres or 1,533 hectares) was in its ownership.

The plan was an extensive updating of garden city planning based more consciously on the neighbourhood unit, an idea developed in the United States by sociologist Clarence Perry during the 1920s (Figure 4.13). Its essential feature was that housing was provided in clearly defined 'cells', each with its own local shopping and other social services and facilities. The individual neighbourhoods were physically defined by landscaped roads called 'parkways', another American idea of this period which set main motor routes (as distinct from local residential roads within the neighbourhoods) within wide landscaped belts. These would link the proposed satellite town centre with the outer agricultural belt that enclosed the town. There was provision for local employment on industrial estates, though this was never intended to be sufficient for all local workers.

Overall there would be up to 25,000 new dwellings, around four-fifths of which would be municipal, with the remainder privately developed. Where the land was municipally owned plots for private housing would be sold on a leasehold basis, as in the two garden cities. By the time war broke out some 8,000 municipal dwellings had been completed, with just over 800 dwellings built privately on municipal land. The population had reached around 35,000, already larger than the combined totals of Letchworth and Welwyn Garden City at that time. Additionally, 930 workers were employed in Wythenshawe, of whom around 500 actually lived there. The city's main airport also moved in 1938 to an adjoining site at Ringway and in the long term this was to have an important impact on employment and growth in the satellite town.

Speke

The other significant interwar attempt to create a satellite town was at Speke in Liverpool.[95] It was, however, much smaller than Wythenshawe, being originally intended for 25,000 inhabitants (soon scaled back to 22,000) and some 7,000 dwellings. As in the Manchester case, the area was originally outside the city, but there was less resistance either to the city buying the land or incorporating the area within its boundaries, which was mainly accomplished in 1932. Designed by the city architect, Lancelot Keay, and his department, the plan had a more formal layout than Wythenshawe, with fewer planning innovations. A full range of local shopping, social and cultural facilities were intended, as was a sports stadium (never built) to the south of the housing area near the riverside. Unlike Wythenshawe, there was no provision for private house construction, though there were significant numbers of unsubsidised council dwellings. These gave some social mix in an area otherwise rehousing former dwellers of slum and overcrowded districts. Residential construction and the development of social facilities occurred slowly, however. By 1939, only about 800 houses had been built.

Speke's most striking feature was, however, the growth of local employment, which ran far ahead of housing development, so that by 1939 there were around 7,000 local jobs. A major industrial estate was being developed by the city under special local legislation immediately north of the residential area. Liverpool's airport (which had opened in 1933) also adjoined the western side of the satellite town. In 1937 it attracted a large airframe factory as part of the government's shadow factory scheme, intended to shift strategically important production away from areas vulnerable to bombing. This was placed on the airport site, rather than the industrial estate, requiring the layout of the residential area to be adjusted to make space for it. (In the 1960s the airport also expanded south of the residential area, in the area where the stadium had been envisaged.)

Limitations of the municipal satellite-town model
Other municipal satellite towns were also being planned by the late 1930s, the most notable being at Seacroft in Leeds.[96] When this scheme originated in 1936 the intention was for 11,000 dwellings housing around 40,000 people. However, World War II delayed its development in earnest until the 1950s and 1960s. In the 1940s another even larger satellite for Liverpool (though outside its boundaries) was also envisaged at Kirkby the development of which began in 1950, adjoining a wartime Royal Ordnance Factory, which subsequently became part of Kirkby industrial estate, recently renamed as Knowsley Business Park.[97] By the early 1960s the satellite town housed over 50,000 people. Other large predominantly council-housing schemes of the early post-war years tried to adopt aspects of the satellite-town formula.

For a combination of reasons, none of the municipal satellite towns established themselves as really positive planning models. Even when they lay within their sponsoring city council's area they never entirely escaped the big-council-housing estate syndrome of being unable to provide shopping, community facilities and public transport links in step with housing provision. Although big local authorities were able to avoid the fundamental financial problems which dogged the two garden cities, housing was always the priority and the more ambitious social facilities were typically the most difficult to fund. This was especially so because of the threat and the reality of war, which delayed spending on any 'frills'. The satellites also often found it difficult to attract privately provided services and good-quality shopping because their populations overwhelmingly comprised lower-income groups. The readjustment problems of such families, often moving from former slum areas, could be severe, contributing to wider social problems and vulnerability to economic changes.

These factors and the sheer size of these satellites often produced a degree of stigmatisation in terms of the general perceptions of such areas. Kirkby, for example, became notorious as the crime-prone fictional 'Newtown' in the 1960s television series Z-Cars. There were also governance problems in that, despite their initial conception as 'townships' enjoying some partial autonomy, they usually ended up as subordinate entities of the whole city. Thus the special Wythenshawe Committee that existed before 1939 was soon abolished. However, Kirkby did become a local authority in its own right (albeit with another, much bigger authority, Liverpool, owning most of its housing). None of the municipal satellite towns gained the civic identity of the two garden cities (or, later, the New Towns).

The Barlow Commission

By 1937, as Wythenshawe and Speke were underway, the government began to accept that the various problems of growth and decline evident within British cities, between town and country and between different regions of Britain might be linked. In 1934 the Commission for the Special Areas had been established to channel extra assistance to the most depressed regions of the country. The Commissioners' powers were weak but the Commissioner for England and Wales, Sir Malcolm Stewart, a successful and respected businessman, became a powerful advocate for change. In his final 1936 report he argued that the excessive growth of Greater London should be curtailed in order to give other regions the opportunity to grow.[98]

There were doubts about the proposed policy, with its implication that there would have to be some kind of government direction of industrial location. Yet public opinion, including voices from the trades unions and industrialists, left no doubts that the thinking behind Stewart's argument had to be taken seriously. Various sections of government identified other factors that needed to be considered, not least the growing issue of the vulnerability of the most rapidly growing parts of Britain to aerial bombing. Since late 1934 the country had been classified for air defence purposes into danger, unsafe and safe zones based on distance from Germany – the presumed primary enemy – and the range of contemporary bomber aircraft.[99] At that time much of the active capacity for armament production was located in the dangerous south and east of the country or the unsafe midlands and south-west. Over the next few years new arms production was added in the safe zone (including Speke's airframe factory), benefiting some of the more depressed and less favoured areas of the country.

To identify all the various aspects of the problem and find a way of reconciling the different opinions within his government, the new prime minister, Neville Chamberlain, established a Royal Commission in 1937. Its brief was to investigate the geographical distribution of the industrial population and likely trends for change with particular reference to the social, economic and 'strategical' disadvantages of the urban and regional concentration of industries and people. Chaired by a former minister of labour, Sir Montague Barlow, it included representatives of business, trades unions, the civil service, the professions and academia. The planner Patrick Abercrombie was also a notable member.

The Commission received evidence from a wide range of interested parties (including the GCTPA and the companies developing the two garden cities) during 1938. It completed its report during 1939 but the outbreak of war delayed actual publication until early 1940. The Commission's report has assumed landmark proportions in the history of modern British planning, though it was notable mainly for acknowledging and analysing the spatial development of the national territory in a comprehensive and holistic manner.[100] There was a general presumption within the report that industrial activity and population were excessively concentrated in cities and particular regions, yet there were no decisive recommendations as to how the problems it presented should be addressed. About these the Commission was divided, so that a majority report, a note of reservation, a minority report and a dissentient memorandum were issued.

The main points of difference between these groups lay in how far the locational decisions of private industry should be controlled and actively shaped by the state and how strong central planning powers should be. Generally the majority opted for minimum constraints to stop industrial development in Greater London and generally preferred advisory rather than mandatory action. The minority view, supported by Patrick Abercrombie, wanted industrial location powers to go further, with restraint extending beyond Greater London and powers to give incentives to locate in less favoured areas. They also pushed for a much stronger central planning authority.

These minority recommendations were similar to those which had been urged by the GCTPA's evidence (written largely by Osborn)[101] and which finally ended the era of the Association's advocacy of 'town planning on garden city lines'. The Association's arguments also pressed for a comprehensive policy on the understanding that it would also be likely to include garden cities as a way of decongesting the big cities throughout the country, especially around London, or providing places in less favoured regions to which new industrial investment and employment could be attracted. The Commission, being largely concerned with bigger questions of policy, did not go as far as this, but garden cities and satellite towns were reported upon favourably with a definite sense that they might well form part of any policies to disperse excessive concentrations of industry and people, even those proposed by the most cautious members of the Commission.

War and a central planning authority

Though privately disappointed with the indecisive nature of the Barlow Report's recommendations, the GCTPA decided to be publicly positive in welcoming it.[102] This proved a sensible decision, because the Commission's hesitancy was soon decisively overtaken by the circumstances of war, which made the more radical minority report seem the best option.[103] The pre-war fear of bombing had brought some of the first governmental interventions in national industrial location. The reality of war triggered a decentralisation of both industrial production and people from big cities on a scale far beyond anything that the Barlow Commission had ever contemplated. Industrialists became accustomed to working closely with government over locational and other decisions. Meanwhile, bombing and the restraints on finance brought a fall in urban land values and, with it, a lowering of the confidence of the property sector. The result was that landowners and developers no longer saw planning as the irritating distraction of pre-war days. Now it began to look like something that could restore confidence and generally support their efforts. To the mass of the population, suffering the losses and deprivation of war, planning became a provider of hope for the post-war world, a pointer to the better life that would make all the sacrifice worthwhile.

During the worst of the bombing, in 1940–41, the wartime coalition government acted to commit itself to creating new central machinery for planning.[104] The immediate instrument of these changes was Lord Reith, the former head of the BBC, who was appointed minister of works and buildings. His ministry temporarily became the new central planning ministry (as the Ministry of Works and Planning), though in early 1943 a Ministry of Town and Country Planning was established (existing until 1950). Its first minister was a moderate and well-liked Conservative, William S. Morrison, who presided over a small and rather specialist agency rather different to the stronger body that Reith had sought. Morrison was therefore dependent on others to press his ministry's case in the cabinet and was weakened in dealing with larger ministries such as the Ministry of Health or the Board of Trade that directly affected his ministry's work. This problem was to dog the ministry's life, especially during Morrison's tenure before the 1945 election.

During his own brief and turbulent ministerial tenure, however, the autocratic Lord Reith, unco-operative and difficult though he was in his relations with other ministers, had already set in motion many important planning initiatives that were not easy to stop. They included two committees that were key to future planning policy, dealing with the critical question of compensation and betterment (on which the future effectiveness of the whole public planning system in relation to the rights of private land owners depended) and land utilisation in rural areas.[105] Neither committee was directly relevant to the new policies that would shortly emerge for planning decentralisation from the big cities to new planned settlements, but it seems unlikely that these last policies would have arisen independently of broader changes across the entire planning front.

Pressure and preparation

One of the reasons for drawing the conclusion above was that the garden city movement, by now led by Frederic Osborn (Figure 4.14), was actively positioning itself at the epicentre of this astonishing wartime fluidity of thinking about planning, within and outside government.[106] In 1941 the GCTPA renamed itself as the Town and Country Planning Association (TCPA). It retained its status as a pressure group, pressing its case on the public, government and private interest groups, but its original label was now seen as outmoded and too specific. The Association was eager to show that its concerns had moved on and, more than ever, spanned the entire planning field. But there was no relapse into the simple suburban revisionism of 'town planning on garden city lines'. What was now proposed was a truly comprehensive approach to all aspects of planning.

Yet, although planning was acknowledged as involving much more than Howard's ideas, this did not mean that the original desire to create new freestanding settlements was being forgotten. What was now being decisively

Figure 4.14 Frederic Osborn's leadership of the Garden City movement during the later 1930s and 1940s played a central role in ensuring its ideas were key in the formulation of thinking. This photograph dates from the 1950s. (author's collection)

changed was the preferred mode of their creation. It was a change that had first been heralded in 1918. Then, of course, Howard himself had still been around to press, against all the odds, his vision of a second garden city that would be privately, rather than state-developed. Now, however, well after his death, the ideas of the other New Townsmen of 1918 for a government-led new towns programme could be safely revisited.

So it was that *New Towns after the War* was republished in 1942 and its arguments soon gained a resonance far greater than in 1918.[107] Interwar experiences, the Barlow Report and the circumstances of war meant that the principle of planned decentralisation was becoming more widely accepted than ever before within professional, reformist and government circles. So too were the arguments that the state would have to be the main agency by which planned new settlements would be realised. Throughout the war, the TCPA and other planning bodies kept up the pressure, feeding the heightened interest in planning with publicity, conferences, exhibitions and other events to inform and shape opinion.

Yet it was not just the 'usual suspects' of the garden city movement who were forming part of this growing front in favour of planned new settlements. As noted earlier, the planner Thomas Sharp had in 1932 excoriated the garden city movement for its pernicious effects on interwar suburban development. By 1940, however, he had changed his message. His best-selling Pelican paperback, *Town Planning*, was enthusiastic about properly planned satellite towns as an alternative to metropolitan sprawl.[108] He felt the garden city movement was still muddling the satellite town ideal with 'another dream – perhaps not wild but certainly rather woolly – the dream of the romantic "garden city"'. He preferred the term 'sub-centralisation' to the garden city movement's 'decentralisation', but he also found things to admire in the garden cities, especially in the more formal neo-Georgian housing groups of Welwyn Garden City. By 1943 he was working with the Bournville Village Trust (which still followed a path close to the 'true' garden city line) in producing a widely admired plan for an imaginary satellite town that was featured in the Trust's wartime film *When We Build Again* (1943).[109] Despite arguments with his client about density, he designed it on much more urban principles than Letchworth or Welwyn Garden City, winning praise within the Ministry of Town and Country Planning.[110]

Some of the ministry's own professional planners were also working on similar approaches. In 1942, for example, Gordon Stephenson, head of the planning technique section of the ministry, produced a simplified plan of an imaginary new town for distribution as a wall chart to schools.[111] It had many features in common with Sharp's more elaborate proposals. In addition, many of the architects who were attracted to modernist principles, being suspicious, like Sharp, of the garden city's links with more romantic, traditional architecture, were also showing early signs of interest in the design of entirely new towns.[112] This trend should not, however, be exaggerated and its main impacts did not come until the 1960s. But the fact that the TCPA was from the 1940s consciously reaching out to a wider constituency perhaps helped in making this process possible.

The Greater London Plan 1944

Incontrovertibly, the most important wartime initiative that advanced government policies to achieve planned decentralisation and develop new settlements was the Greater London Plan. It was prepared for the Standing Conference on London Regional Planning (the successor body to the Greater London Regional Planning Committee, for which Unwin had worked). However, it would not have happened at all if Reith had not commissioned it and the

Ministry of Town and Country Planning had not then supported it and given a home to the planners who prepared it.[113] The plan was produced in 18 months by a small team led by Patrick Abercrombie (including Gordon Stephenson, Peter Shepheard and Tom Coote, who shortly afterwards planned the first actual New Town, as will be discussed in the next chapter).[114]

Apart from the scale and ambition of the work, the team had to face other challenges. Shortly before the plan was competed their offices within the ministry were bombed by German aircraft. Fortunately the plan itself was saved from the flames by a team member. A draft was delivered to the ministry in the spring of 1944 and the final version in December.[115] Appearing in print early the following year, it elegantly and forcefully articulated three of what were to become the four main strategic concepts of post-war planning orthodoxy: decentralisation, containment and redevelopment.[116] It also rested explicitly on the fourth – regional balance. Not all of this was entirely new, of course, and its planning ideas had been well rehearsed before 1939, not least by Unwin's proposals in his two reports of 1929 and 1933 for the Standing Conference's predecessor, described above. But the authoritative linking together of these proposals made it into one of the most significant plans ever produced anywhere.

In it, London was represented as four rings: the inner, tightly developed ring; the lower-density suburban ring; the green belt; and the outer country ring. Following Sir Malcolm Stewart's 1936 proposal, the plan now proposed that entirely new industrial development in the plan area should be prohibited (though extensive relocation of existing factories was envisaged). Planned redevelopment would occur within the inner ring, as already spelled out in the 1943 County of London Plan.[117] The green belt was to be greatly enlarged from pre-war efforts and it would be enforced by stronger planning controls, rather than simply public ownership and restrictive covenants, which the London County Council had begun to use in 1935.

Yet the most radical proposal, and the one most relevant to this story, was the planned decentralisation of over a million people from the inner ring mainly to the outer ring. In addition to the expansion of existing towns, there were to be eight completely new towns. (Although, further confusing the terminology, Abercrombie mainly referred to them as 'satellite towns'). In total, these new settlements were to house a population of just over 383,000, with full local employment and community facilities.[118] Ten possible sites were suggested, though only two of these (at Stevenage and Harlow) eventually became actual New Towns. A possible layout for one of the proposed sites at Ongar in Essex was prepared, Peter Shepheard's fine colour illustrations giving a vivid impression of

Figure 4.15 *The Greater London Plan 1944* was in several ways seminal to the subsequent New Towns programme. One of its suggested new satellite towns would have been at Ongar in Essex and some suggestive initial studies of how it might be planned were included. Its proposal for a pedestrianised central shopping centre was prophetic. (author's collection)

the kind of planned environments that, within a few years, would appear in the first New Towns (Figure 4.15).

Early preparations for a programme

Even as the plan was underway Ministry of Town and Country Planning officials were considering the legal, administrative and technical questions that planning and building new towns would involve.[119] The initial thinking was that local authorities, principally county councils, would be responsible for these with special central funding. In early 1944 an internal interdepartmental committee under George Pepler, the ministry's chief technical adviser, began to examine these questions in greater detail, broadly reinforcing the same line of thinking, although with several local-authority-based variants being proposed. There was, however, some scepticism from other officials as to whether local authorities, faced with so many other post-war tasks across the whole of their areas, would have the resources or the ability to concentrate on such a specific project as a satellite town. This resulted in a central-government-appointed development association being added as a further option.

By May 1945 a special Satellite and New Town Committee had been created within the ministry with Ministry of Health and Treasury representatives. There were, however, no specific plans for legislation to give force to these ideas by the time of the July 1945 general election. It was uncertain whether, should a Conservative government be elected, it would wish to proceed with a new satellite town policy. Already, however, specific questions were arising, notably at Stevenage (to be discussed in the next chapter). In February–April 1945 there had also been the intriguing proposal of the Co-operative Building Society to develop a private-enterprise new town at either Ongar or Brickendonbury, south of Hertford. It was indicated that the chairman of the company who intended to buy the land for this venture would be Lewis Silkin MP, the man who, after the change of government, would become the new minister of town and country planning. Nothing came of this, but it did serve to keep alive the idea of privately developed new towns for some time.

In the final days of Churchill's caretaker administration, after the 1945 election but before the results were announced, Morrison, the minister of town and country planning, defined his position regarding the satellite towns in readiness for the possibility of a new Conservative government. He made clear that he was thinking of only one or two satellite towns as demonstration projects and to show that an incoming Conservative government would mean business, if only on a modest scale. However, he finally rejected the idea that local authorities would directly act as the developing agencies, favouring either a development corporation formed by groups of local authorities or the government or a limited-profit private company.

The Reith Committee

Of course, neither he nor the Conservatives had any opportunity to act on this thinking. The results, when the ballot papers all finally came from those on active service across the world, produced a massive Labour victory. On the planning front the expectation was that much of the wartime planning agenda would now be acted upon. Even so, there were still worries about how far commitment to new satellite towns went. There was nothing in the Labour election manifesto[120] about new settlements and it was reasonable to wonder what, if any, priority they would have in a government assailed by many other pressing needs.

The new minister, Lewis Silkin, had been a local London politician who had shown a fondness for higher-density inner-city housing rather than dispersal.[121] This raised fears in Osborn and the TCPA that the new minister might reject arguments for planned dispersal, but he was not immune to the pressure being exerted by the TCPA and it soon became clear that, if there ever had been any real basis for Osborn's fears about Silkin, that was now past. And there was a real ally at the heart of the new government in the person of the new deputy prime minister, Herbert Morrison.[122] Herbert shared the same surname but was not related to the Conservative minister of town and country planning. This Morrison had been the Labour leader of the London County Council when it had introduced its green-belt policy in 1935 and (as noted in Chapter 2) was an old friend of the garden city movement and of Osborn in particular since Morrison's days as a World War I conscientious objector working in Letchworth.

Silkin pushed forward with Stevenage immediately (see Chapter 5) and within a few weeks set up a Departmental Committee to advise on the establishment, development, organisation and administration of New Towns as part of a government programme to achieve planned decentralisation from congested urban areas.[123] The Committee was also asked to suggest specific guiding principles that would ensure these towns grew to be 'self-contained and balanced communities for work and living'. The Committee was chaired by Lord Reith, and its members included Osborn and several others associated with the TCPA or the garden city movement. Other members included Sir Malcolm Stewart and a woman who was to play a brief but important role in the New Towns programme, the social scientist Monica Felton. Overall it was a group that could be expected to produce helpful and informed guidance with almost complete unanimity (and certainly not to question the programme in any significant way).

The Committee worked with extraordinary speed, producing three reports in January, April and July 1946.[124] While Reith took pride in his speed and decisiveness in going about any task, haste was essential in this one because the first stages in the creation of Stevenage had already begun in the autumn of 1945. Later, what was to have been the first of Labour's planning bills to be put before parliament (on development rights, provisions later incorporated in the 1947 Town and Country Planning Act) had to be postponed. This gave Silkin the unexpected opportunity in March 1946 to bring forward the New Towns Bill much earlier than anticipated, so that having all the Committee's findings immediately became paramount. Even so, the final report was submitted only a few days before the Bill received the Royal Assent.

Being able to work so quickly was facilitated by the extensive previous work on the subject that had already been carried out within the ministry. A draft Bill had been considered internally even before the Reith Committee was appointed, meaning that there was already a high level of prior agreement on many key aspects of New Towns policy. Reith was somewhat perturbed when Silkin told him what the form of the development body (a central government-sponsored corporation) was going to be.[125] In fact, however, the Committee also suggested the options of an 'authorised association' or a local-authority-sponsored corporation. But in general the Committee provided an independent legitimation for decisions already framed by the ministry as much as genuinely coming up with new thinking.

Their recommendations were very largely those that were followed in the New Towns programme. A New Town was to be fixed in size at the outset, the Committee suggesting that 30,000–50,000 would be an appropriate population target, or up to 80,000 where the New Town expanded a significant earlier town. All the land needed for the New Town should be acquired by the development body as soon as possible, by compulsory powers if necessary. Land being developed by others should be transferred only on a leasehold basis. There was advice about the phasing and pace of development, noting the prior need for building labour and for infrastructural development in advance of housing and other construction. The social basis of the plans should be carefully thought through and there would ideally be a mix of classes in all the districts of the New Town, avoiding the social polarisation of much interwar housing development (even of Welwyn Garden City). There were also recommendations about industrial development to ensure a range of local jobs, and about the creation of shopping, cultural and other services.

The New Towns Act 1946

There was much else in the detail of the Reith proposals that elaborated desirable practice in the planning, development and populating of the New Towns. Generally, there was much political and popular support for the measure.[126] Silkin's predecessor, W.S. Morrison, welcomed it. Despite the Bill's very radical features, not least the emphasis on a very statist form of planning, with an unelected state corporation creating a town entirely on its own land, it had unopposed second and third readings. The only parliamentary voice raised in protest was that of Viscount Hinchingbrooke, who argued that it was 'frankly totalitarian' and would produce 'havoc, bitterness and grave social damage'.[127]

The main concerns at Westminster came not from parliament but from Silkin's fellow ministers, who worried about the apparent focus of the policy on the London area and neglect of other, especially less prosperous, regions. This was to remain a major bone of contention within New Towns policy throughout its entire history, especially under Labour governments. Much of the Party's support came from the older industrial regions, which had been far more vulnerable to unemployment before the war. Regional policies intended to steer new industrial development from the London area to the development areas in the North, Wales and Scotland had just been introduced under the 1945 Distribution of Industry Act.[128] The fear was that these policies would be heavily compromised by the creation of New Towns with attractive facilities for new industrial development around the capital, which might well deter industries from moving to the development areas.

Meanwhile, events were also unfolding at Stevenage, where Silkin was already pressing forward under existing powers and meeting major local opposition. It was these events which prompted Hinchingbrooke's sour remarks during the Bill's passage and which will be examined in detail in the next chapter. Nevertheless, the Act was passed and it received the Royal Assent on 1 August 1946. For Silkin, this was undoubtedly a great early personal success, though he was soon to find himself mired in difficulties and delays. Never again did he enjoy the high political standing that he achieved at this time.

Conclusions

This chapter has stressed the essential mutability of Howard's visionary idea. Howard himself, although he reluctantly acquiesced in the pre-1914 revisionist shift towards 'town planning on garden city lines', always remained close to his original ideal of a strategy of creating freestanding garden cities through a combination of limited-profit private and voluntarist efforts. But many of those around him, including some of his closest supporters, soon began to find other paths. Howard's great holistic vision of an alternative way of living was disassembled and its constituent concepts recombined with others to produce new kinds of town-planning solutions to the questions of how and where people might live materially better and happier lives. These new possibilities were essentially ones that were deemed more attainable than the 'purer' expressions of Howard's peaceful path at Letchworth and Welwyn Garden City.

In the social and political context of Edwardian Britain, the garden suburb or garden village seemed a far more realisable goal than a 'true' garden city. Yet the huge changes produced by World War I and its aftermath completely changed the ways that housing was provided in Britain. The limited-profit co-partnership or quasi-philanthropic company as a means of delivering garden cities or garden suburbs now came to seem like a minor option, well-intentioned and with some advantages but wholly incapable of meeting the scale of housing needs. From 1919 housing provision was transformed with, henceforth, a large state-subsidised municipal sector and a recast private-housing sector geared towards building houses for owner-occupation. The interwar decades proved the most productive years up to the present day for house building and, to widely varying degrees, both sectors followed some of the principles of 'town planning on garden city lines'. Of the two, the municipal sector was closest, taking low-density garden-city-style housing and sometimes other aspects of Howard's thinking to very many working-class people. Although both municipal and privately developed environments had their weaknesses, they nonetheless represented a massive contribution to human welfare.

By the later 1930s these weaknesses and wider problems were beginning to outweigh the positive aspects of a broadly garden-suburb approach to urban and regional planning. New paths were sought, with the beginnings of green-belt policies and the emergence of the idea of the satellite town as a municipal garden city that came a little closer than ordinary suburban housing estates to being a self-contained and freestanding settlement. Ultimately, however, in the circumstances of war, there was return to the idea, first suggested in 1918, that the state should lead a comprehensive programme for planned metropolitan decentralisation to what soon became known as New Towns. The dominance of the state within this approach ran counter to Howard's belief in co-operative action but in 1946 it underpinned what became the largest New Towns programme undertaken by any Western country. It is to this that we now turn.

Notes

1   Ray Thomas, cited in M.R. Hughes (ed.), *The letters of Lewis Mumford and Frederic J. Osborn: A transatlantic dialogue* (Bath, 1971), Letter Osborn–Mumford 18.4.1969, p. 454.

2   The New Townsmen, *New towns after the war*.

3   Harrison, *Bournville*.

4   Hubbard and Shippobottom, *Port Sunlight*.

5   Waddilove, *One man's vision*.

6   Miller, *Raymond Unwin*, pp. 35–45.

7   Hardy, *Garden cities to new towns*, p. 73.

8   Stern et al., *Paradise planned*.

9   R. Unwin, *Nothing gained by overcrowding! How the garden city type of development may benefit both owner and occupier* (London, 1912).

10 J.N. Tarn, *Five per cent philanthropy: an account of housing in urban areas between 1840 and 1914* (Cambridge, 1973).

11 Hull City Council, *Garden Village Conservation Area character statement* (Hull, 1997).

12 M. Miller and A.S. Gray, *Hampstead Garden Suburb* (Chichester, 1992).

13 Miller and Gray, *Hampstead Garden Suburb*, p. 20.

14 E.G. Culpin, *The garden city movement up-to-date*, 2nd edn (London, 1914), p. 31.

15 Miller, *Raymond Unwin*, pp. 78–103.

16 Unwin, *Nothing gained by overcrowding!*

17 Skilleter, 'The role of public utility societies', pp. 125–65; Birchall, 'Co-partnership housing', pp. 329–58.

18 A. Reid, *Brentham: A history of the pioneer garden suburb 1901–2001* (Ealing, 2000).

19 Culpin, *Garden City movement*, 2nd edn, pp. 51–8.

20   Liberal Land Enquiry Committee, *The land, vol. 2: urban* (London, 1914), p. 104.

21   Miller and Gray, *Hampstead Garden Suburb, passim,* esp. pp. 51–2, 100–101.

22   Bournville Village Trust, *The Bournville Village Trust 1900–1955* (Birmingham, 1955), pp. 23–32.

23   Culpin, *Garden City movement,* 2nd edn, pp. 13–17.

24   H.R. Aldridge, *The case for town planning: a practical manual for the use of councillors, officers and others engaged in the preparation of town planning schemes* (London, 1915), pp. 157–60, 187–330.

25   M. Harrison, 'Thomas Coghlan Horsfall and "the example of Germany"', *Planning Perspectives,* 6/3 (1991), pp. 297–314.

26   A. Sutcliffe, 'Britain's first town planning act: a review of the 1909 achievement', *Town Planning Review,* 59/3 (1988), pp. 289–303.

27   J.S. Nettlefold, *Practical town planning* (London, 1914), pp. 426–35.

28   T. Adams, 'The origin of the term "town planning" in England', *Journal of the Town Planning Institute,* 15/11 (1929), pp. 310–11.

29   J.S. Nettlefold, *Practical housing,* 2nd edn (London, 1910).

30   Nettlefold, *Practical housing,* pp. 156–7; Cherry, *Birmingham,* p. 100.

31   Sutcliffe, 'Britain's first town planning act'.

32   Nettlefold, *Practical housing,* pp. 153–4; Nettlefold, *Practical town planning,* pp. 98–102.

33   Aldridge, *The case for town planning, passim,* esp. pp. 305, 613–42.

34   Culpin, *Garden City movement,* 2nd edn; see also Ward, 'Introduction'.

35   Culpin, *Garden City movement,* 2nd edn.

36   H.W. Richardson and D.H. Aldcroft, *Building in the British economy between the wars* (London, 1968), pp. 25–6.

37   Bournville Village Trust, *When we build again* (London, 1941), pp. 12–14.

38   M.J. Daunton, 'Introduction', in M.J. Daunton (ed.), *Councillors and tenants: local authority housing in English cities, 1919–1939* (Leicester, 1984), pp. 2–38.

39   A detailed summary of all important housing legislation is given in S. Merrett, *State housing in Britain* (London, 1979), pp. 307–19.

40   Skilleter, 'The role of public utility societies'; Birchall, 'Co-partnership housing'.

41   Royal Commission on the Distribution of the Industrial Population, *Report* (Cmd 6153) (London, 1940), p. 67.

42   London County Council, *London housing* (London, 1937), pp. 1–5, 130–32; Liverpool Housing Committee, *City of Liverpool housing* (Liverpool, 1937), pp. 6–7; Culpin, *Garden City movement,* 2nd edn, pp. 35–8.

43   Tudor Walters Committee, *Report of the committee to consider questions of building construction in connection with the provision of dwellings for the working classes in England and Wales, and Scotland* (Cd 9191) (London, 1918); Miller, *Raymond Unwin,* pp. 161–88.

44   R. Home, *'A township complete in itself': a planning history of the Becontree/Dagenham estate* (London, 1997).

45   London County Council, *London housing,* pp. 147–50, 166–71.

46   Liverpool Housing Committee, *City of Liverpool housing,* p. 16.

47   H.J. Manzoni, *The production of 50,000 municipal houses* (Birmingham, 1939), esp. p. 46; Cherry, *Birmingham,* pp. 113–16.

48   R. Jevons and J. Madge, *Housing estates: a study of Bristol Corporation policy and practice between the wars* (Bristol, 1946), esp. p. 17; R. Finnegan, 'Council housing in Leeds, 1919–39: social policy and urban change', in M.J. Daunton (ed.), *Councillors and tenants: local authority housing in English cities, 1919–1939* (Leicester, 1984), pp. 134–5.

49   E.g. University of Liverpool Social Science Department, *Population problems of the new estates with special reference to Norris Green* (Liverpool, 1939), especially pp. 25–38.

50   Miller and Gray, *Hampstead Garden Suburb*, p. 20.

51   T. Young, *Becontree and Dagenham: a report made for the Pilgrim Trust* (London, 1934), pp. 277–8.

52   Purdom, *Satellite towns*, 2nd edn, p. 84.

53   P. Willmott, *The evolution of a community: a study of Dagenham after forty years* (London, 1963), quotation from p. 109.

54   Home, 'A township complete in itself', p. 27.

55   P. Collison, *The Cutteslowe Walls: A study in social class* (London, 1963).

56   G. Weightman and S. Humphries, *The making of modern London 1914-1939* (London, 1984), pp. 109–10.

57   University of Liverpool Social Science Department, *Population problems*, pp. 8–9.

58   Bournville Village Trust, *When we build again*, pp. 95–6.

59   Bournville Village Trust, *When we build again*, pp. 95–8; Cherry, *Birmingham*, pp. 115–16.

60   University of Liverpool Social Science Department, *Population problems*, p. 9.

61   The Glasgow Story, 'Knightswood Housing' <http://www.theglasgowstory.com/image.php?inum=TGSA00787&t=1&urltp=story.php?id=TGSEA10>, accessed 20 October 2015.

62   A.A. Jackson, *Semi-detached London: suburban development, life and transport, 1900-1939* (London, 1973), pp. 297–8.

63   Bournville Village Trust, *When we build again*, pp. 62–77; University of Liverpool Social Science Department, *Population problems*, pp. 16–18; London County Council, *London housing*, pp. 243–50.

64   Home, 'A township complete in itself', p. 30.

65   Bournville Village Trust, *When we build again*, pp. 98–100.

66   J. Burnett, *A social history of housing 1815-1985* (London, 1986), p. 240.

67   G.C.M. M'Gonigle and J. Kirby, *Poverty and public health* (London, 1936), pp. 203–17.

68   Royal Commission on the Distribution of the Industrial Population, *Report*, p. 67.

69   Richardson and Aldcroft, *Building in the British Economy*, pp. 79–108, 300–321.

70   T. Sharp, *Town and countryside: some aspects of urban and rural development* (Oxford, 1932), p. 140.

71   A.T. Edwards, 'A further criticism of the garden city movement', *Town Planning Review*, 4 (1913), p. 318.

72   A.T. Edwards, *Good and bad manners in architecture: an essay on the social aspects of civic design* (London, 1945 [orig. 1924]).

73   Cited in Hardy, *Garden cities to new towns*, p. 177.

74   D. MacFadyen, *Sir Ebenezer Howard and the town planning movement* (Manchester, 1970 [(orig. 1933]), p. 97 (and pp. 92–8 more generally for his defence of Howard against Sharp's charges).

75   S.V. Ward, 'Thomas Sharp as a figure in the British planning movement', *Planning Perspectives*, 23/4 (2008), pp. 523–33; J.R. Pendlebury, 'The urbanism of Thomas Sharp', *Planning Perspectives*, 24/1 (2009), pp. 2–27.

76   Hughes, *Letters*, Letter F.J. Osborn–L. Mumford, 21.10.1945, p. 107.

77   Royal Commission on the Distribution of the Industrial Population, *Report*.

78   S.V. Ward, *The geography of interwar Britain: the state and uneven development* (London, 1988), pp. 207–31.

79   C. Williams-Ellis (ed.), *Britain and the beast* (London, 1937); J. Sheail, *Rural conservation in interwar Britain* (Oxford, 1981).

80   Unwin, *Nothing gained by overcrowding!* pp. 2, 19.

81   D. Schubert, 'Theodor Fritsch and the German (völkische) version of the garden city: the garden city invented two years before Ebenezer Howard', *Planning Perspectives*, 19/1 (2004), pp. 3–35.

82   Stern et al., *Paradise planned*, pp. 290–93, 749–53.

83   K.S. Domhardt, 'The garden city idea in the CIAM discourse on urbanism: a path to comprehensive planning', *Planning Perspectives*, 27/2 (2012), pp. 173–97.

84   B. Störtkuhl, 'Ernst May and the Schlesische Heimstätte', in C. Quiring, W. Voigt, P. Schmal and E. Herrel (eds), *Ernst May 1886–1970* (Munich, 2011), pp. 32–49.

85   C. Mohr, 'The new Frankfurt housing construction and the city 1925–1930', in C. Quiring, W. Voigt, P. Schmal and E. Herrel (eds), *Ernst May 1886–1970* (Munich, 2011), pp. 50–67.

86   Purdom, *Satellite towns*.

87   Purdom, *Satellite towns*, 2nd edn, pp. 41–2.

88   Greater London Regional Planning Committee, *First report* (London, 1929), pp. 44–9; S.V. Ward, 'What did the Germans ever do for us? A century of British learning about and imagining modern town planning', *Planning Perspectives*, 25/2 (2010), pp. 117–40, especially pp. 121–2.

89   Greater London Regional Planning Committee, *Second report* (London, 1933), pp. 93–109.

90   Marley Committee, *Garden cities and satellite towns: report of the departmental committee* (London, 1935).

91   NA HLG 52/741, *Consideration of report of Marley Committee 1935–37*, Memorandum on report of the committee on garden cities and satellite towns, 3/2/37.

92   N. Taylor, 'The mystery of Lord Marley: Nicole Taylor on the trail of an English peer in Stalin's Jewish Autonomous Region', *The Jewish Quarterly*, 198 (2005) <http://www.jewishquarterly. org/issuearchive/article8d4f.html?article id=113>, accessed 21 July 2011; S.V. Ward, 'Soviet Communism and the British planning movement: rational learning or utopian imagining?' *Planning Perspectives*, 27/4 (2012), pp. 499–524.

93   D. Deakin (ed.), *Wythenshawe: the story of a garden city* (Chichester, 1989) <http://www. wythenshawe.btck.co.uk>, accessed 15 October 2014.

94   Ibid. and Purdom, *Satellite towns*, 2nd edn, 46–7.

95   Liverpool Housing Committee, *City of Liverpool Housing*, pp. 54–7; Royal Commission on the Distribution of the Industrial Population, *Report*, [The Barlow Report] Cmd. 6153 (London, 1940), pp. 282–3; City of Liverpool Post-War Re-development Advisory (Special) Committee, *Town planning exhibition* (Liverpool, 1947), pp. 33–7.

96   Finnegan, 'Council housing in Leeds', p. 134.

97   City of Liverpool Post-War Re-development Advisory (Special) Committee, *Town Planning Exhibition*, pp. 30–31, 38–9.

98   Royal Commission on the Distribution of the Industrial Population, *Report*, pp. 3–5.

99   Ward, *The geography of interwar Britain*, pp. 74–99, especially p. 95.

100 Royal Commission on the Distribution of the Industrial Population, *Report*, pp. 185–243.

101 Garden Cities and Town Planning Association, *Royal Commission on the Geographical Distribution of the Industrial Population: Evidence of the Garden Cities and Town Planning Association* (London, 1938), pp. 282–3.

102 Hardy, *Garden cities to new towns*, p. 246.

103 S.V. Ward, *Planning and urban change* (London, 2004), pp. 74–9.

104 G.E. Cherry and P. Penny, *Holford: a study in architecture, planning and civic design* (London, 1986), pp. 101–34; S.V. Ward, 'Gordon Stephenson and the "galaxy of talent": Planning for post-war reconstruction in Britain 1942–1947', *Town Planning Review*, 83/2 (2012), pp. 279–96.

105 Uthwatt Committee, *Interim report of the Expert Committee on Compensation and Betterment* (Cmd 6291) (London, 1941); Uthwatt Committee, *Final report of the Expert Committee on Compensation and Betterment* (Cmd 6386) (London, 1942); Scott Committee, *Report of the committee on land utilisation in rural areas* (Cmd 6378) (London, 1942).

106 Hardy, *Garden cities to new towns*, pp. 240–93.

107 The New Townsmen, *New towns after the war*.

108 T. Sharp, *Town planning* (Harmondsworth, 1940), pp. 64–8. Quotation from p. 65.

109 Pendlebury, 'Thomas Sharp', especially pp. 14–16.

110 Ward, 'Gordon Stephenson', especially pp. 288–9.

111 G. Stephenson and C. DeMarco, *On a human scale: a life in city design* (Perth, 1992), pp. 86–7.

112 J.R. Gold, *The experience of modernism: modern architects and the future city 1928–1953* (London, 1997), pp. 194–200.

113 Cullingworth, *Environmental planning: vol. III*, pp. 4–5.

114 Stephenson and DeMarco, *On a human scale*, pp. 82–8.

115 Cullingworth, *Environmental planning: vol. III*, p. 5.

116 Abercrombie, *Greater London Plan 1944*.

117 J.H. Forshaw and P. Abercrombie, *County of London plan* (London, 1943).

118 Abercrombie, *Greater London Plan 1944*, pp. 33, 160–65.

119 This section is based on Cullingworth, *Environmental planning: vol. III*, pp. 3–13.

120 Socialist Unity, '1945 Labour Party Manifesto' <http://socialistunity.com/1945-labour-manifesto/>, accessed 11 November 2014.

121 R. Weight, 'Silkin, Lewis, first Baron Silkin (1889–1972)', *Oxford dictionary of national biography* (Oxford, 2004); online edn <http://www.oxforddnb.com/view/article/31684>, accessed 6 December 2010; Hughes, *Letters*, Letter Osborn–Mumford 14–17 August 1945, p. 91; Letter Osborn–Mumford 21 October 1945, p. 107.

122 Hebbert, 'Frederic Osborn', especially p. 179.

123 A. Homer, 'Administration and social change in the post-war British new towns: a case study of Stevenage and Hemel Hempstead 1946–70', PhD thesis (University of Luton, 1999), pp. 20–55.

124 Reith Committee, *Interim report of the new towns committee* (Cmd 6759) (London, 1946); Reith Committee, *Second interim report of the new towns committee* (Cmd 6794) (London, 1946); Reith Committee, *Final report of the new towns committee* (Cmd 6876) (London, 1946).

125 BBC Written Archives 560/5/8/2, Reith Diaries, 24 September 1945; see also Homer, 'Administration and social change', pp. 26–7.

126 Cullingworth, *Environmental planning: vol. III*, pp. 15–26.

127 Cited in Cullingworth, *Environmental planning: vol. III*, p. 25.

128 A. Booth, 'The Second World War and the origins of modern regional policy', *Economy and Society*, 11/1 (1982), pp. 1–21; D.W. Parsons, *The political economy of British regional policy* (Beckenham, 1986), pp. 1–95, especially pp. 77–86.

CHAPTER FIVE

Stevenage

Silkin's New Towns

Between 1946 and 1950 Lewis Silkin, the first Labour minister of town and country planning, had designated no fewer than 13 New Towns.[1] He had also secured the designation of the fourteenth, though the actual legal formalities did not occur until shortly after he left office at the 1950 general election. By any standards this was a remarkable achievement, quite unparalleled on the peaceful path or any variants of it before or since. This and the next chapter will focus on the Hertfordshire New Towns, which owe their existence to him, and Chapter 7 will give a briefer discussion of the other New Towns. However, we begin by outlining his complete programme in order to make fuller sense of what will shortly follow.

As shown in the last chapter, the Abercrombie Greater London Plan proposed eight new 'satellite towns' to serve Greater London. Eight New Towns were duly designated by Silkin during 1946–9, though only two were at the actual locations the Abercrombie team had selected. The programme began in one of the locations his planning team had selected at Stevenage in November 1946 and other New Towns followed in quick succession. Crawley, Hemel Hempstead and Harlow (the latter being the other 'Abercrombie location') were designated in January, February and March 1947. Hatfield and Welwyn Garden City then followed in March 1948, Basildon in January 1949 and Bracknell in June of the same year. A further six were designated in other parts of Britain. In Scotland East Kilbride and Glenrothes were designated in May 1947 and June 1948. In County Durham Newton Aycliffe was designated in April 1947 and Peterlee in March 1948. Cwmbran then followed in south Wales in November 1949 and Corby in Northamptonshire in April 1950.

These bald facts about how the programme unfolded inevitably give the story a sense of orderliness that was rarely apparent when viewed at closer quarters. In fact, the New Towns programme opened at Stevenage with a public relations disaster so serious that it could have destroyed the whole programme before it had even begun. This was despite over a year's work that ought, perhaps, to have better prepared the ground. Well before the 1945 election, the wartime coalition government's minister of town and country planning (W.S. Morrison) began actively examining the satellite-town locations recommended by Abercrombie in the 1944 Greater London Plan. From autumn 1944 Morrison's civil servants, chiefly Samuel Beaufoy, started consultations with local officials about the Plan's various proposals.[2]

Making Stevenage's master plan

Stevenage soon emerged during 1945 as the front-runner of Abercrombie's proposed satellite towns for early action. Seeking to advance the idea (even though the appropriate instrument for their development was as yet undecided), it was agreed within the ministry to prepare a master plan for such a town at Stevenage. It did not become the official master plan (in slightly modified form) until 1950 but was in nearly all essentials devised in 1945–6. Beaufoy originally wanted Thomas Sharp, pre-war scourge of the garden city movement but now a well-respected private planning consultant, to prepare the plan and had approached him informally in February 1945. Beaufoy's colleagues were, however, unhappy with making such decisions this way and the Treasury refused to sanction the funds to hire a consultant.[3] Instead an internal ministry team was set to work in July 1945. In the absence of New Town powers (not to be available for another year), legal authority for government to plan a New Town came from an obscure clause, never previously used, of the 1932 Town and Country Planning Act. Though regarded as legally rather dubious, the ministry considered it gave sufficient authority to allow the minister at least to initiate the development of a garden city.

The ministry planning team was led by the 37-year-old head of the ministry's planning technique section, Gordon Stephenson (Figure 5.1), mentioned in the last chapter in connection with his wartime work in progressing what became the New Towns programme.[4] He was a University of Liverpool-trained architect who, after graduation, had studied at the Institut d'Urbanisme in Paris in 1930–32, simultaneously becoming the first Briton to work in the atelier of the iconic modernist architect and planner Le Corbusier. Also one of the first British planners to visit the Soviet Union (for a two-month period in 1934), he studied city planning in 1936–8 at the Massachusetts Institute of Technology in the United States. No other British planner at that time, certainly of his age, had such widely based experience of his subject. His colleagues, including two other Liverpool architect-planners, Terry Kennedy and Peter Shepheard, were mainly

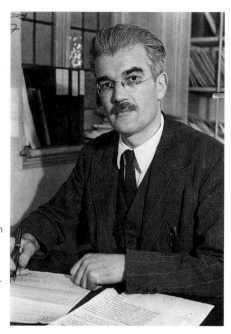

Figure 5.1 The leader of the team which in 1945–6 made the first plan for Stevenage, Gordon Stephenson, photographed in November 1947. He chose not to remain as Stevenage's chief architect and planner but had a significant later involvement as a private consultant. (Liverpool University Special Collections and Archives)

similar in age. The others were an older surveyor, Tom Coote, and an engineer, Eric Claxton, seconded from Surrey County Council, who, in the event, had a bigger impact than any of the others on the town that followed.[5]

As mentioned in Chapter 4, Stephenson, Shepheard and Coote had worked with Abercrombie on the Greater London Plan, experience which fed directly into their work at Stevenage. Stephenson and Coote had identified sites for Abercrombie's proposed satellite towns and it was they who had selected Stevenage. Stephenson and Shepheard worked on the principles of community planning which were adopted in the Stevenage Plan and Shepheard had also worked on the indicative plan for the proposed (but never built) Abercrombie satellite town of Ongar.[6] Stephenson had overseen the whole planning process at Stevenage, leading meetings with local and other interested parties (where necessary aided by other civil servants), supplying ideas and acting as critic. Coote prepared the site and ownership survey. Shepheard largely elaborated the detailed design, with Claxton providing the engineering input. Kennedy's great practical experience in designing and realising large building projects ensured that the team's bold ideas did not stray too far into fancy.

Stevenage in 1946 was a small country town of around 6,200 inhabitants straddling the Great North Road and with a small railway station on the London and North Eastern Railway mainline out of King's Cross station. The town was built mainly of local brick and had grown up gradually and organically, with an underlying unity of building materials, vernacular style and scale. There was also a pleasing informality (which is still visible) that came with varied building and roof lines set on each side of the wide main street, with many mature trees. Although there had been some more recent buildings, such as a local cinema, which seemed to jar with the historic character, this had not 'spoilt' the small town and it had not suffered any destruction during the war.

Functionally it provided shops and other services for the surrounding, predominantly agricultural area. There were also several comfortable historic inns, some of which had provided accommodation for visitors since its days as a coaching stop. Rather as the areas of Letchworth and Welwyn Garden City had been before their development had begun, it was surrounded largely by farms and some woodland. There were a few small clusters of houses and other buildings at several places, but, other than Shephall Green, these were not big enough to be described as villages. Two country houses – Aston House and Shephalbury – lay a little south of Stevenage town and its countryside also contained a few smaller gentry houses and rather more farmsteads. There were also nine factories in and around the town, mainly very recent arrivals.[7] The largest three of these manufactured gantries and conveyors, school furniture and similar products, and motorcycles. Together all the factories employed around 2,000 workers, around three-quarters of them living in Stevenage. The other main employers were in services (mainly retailing and professional services and transport) and agriculture. Though not a commuter town, some of its middle-class population travelled by train to London to work.

Overall, therefore, most of the Stevenage area before the New Town had changed only relatively slowly over time. While he was involved in making the plan, Stephenson recalled meeting a farm worker who lived where he worked and rarely travelled more than the two miles from his home to Stevenage High Street.[8] He had been to London only rarely, and not at all since 1939. On the other hand, against such seemingly unchanging ways of living were set the town's growing numbers of metropolitan commuters and the surge in wartime local industrial growth. These were signs of accelerating change, quite regardless of what was about to occur in the form of the New Town.

Like the Ongar example that Shepheard had worked up for the Greater London Plan, the 1946 Stephenson plan for Stevenage was based around six residential neighbourhood units, each planned for roughly 10,000 inhabitants (exactly so in Stevenage's case), with a single large industrial area (Figure 5.2).[9] The main railway line north from King's Cross station separated the industrial

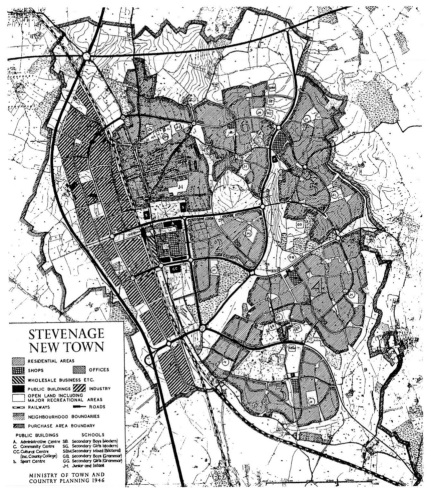

Figure 5.2 The Stephenson team's plan defined the key features of the New Town. It formed the basis of the 1949 official master plan and was significantly modified only in 1966. (author's collection)

(to the west) and the residential (to the east) areas. An entirely new town centre was planned, also to the east, lying between the residential areas and the industrial area. There was some criticism of this location, which was 'off-centre' as far as the residential areas were concerned, though the planners argued that its position between the employment and living areas would maximise use of central shopping and services. The old town of Stevenage was incorporated within neighbourhood 1, north of where Stevenage's new centre was to be. The planners thought (correctly) that this would allow the attractive historic qualities of the original town to be protected, since otherwise the old town would be the obvious location for major shops and other town centre activities. The Great North Road, which bisected the old town, was to be entirely bypassed on the western boundary of the new town, removing through traffic and giving easy access to the industrial area without vehicles needing to enter the rest of the town.

Good standard primary distributor roads without direct frontage development were also planned for vehicle circulation within the town. Despite this, it was not the truly car-orientated plan that it might now appear to have been. Very high cycle use was predicted (up to 50 per cent of all movements between inner residential areas and both the town centre and industrial area, based on estimates of contemporary patterns in Welwyn Garden City). It was suggested, largely at Claxton's prompting, that a proper cycleway system might be provided.[10] Significant numbers were also expected to walk from nearby residential areas to the new town centre. For the centre itself, the team very radically suggested that it might be pedestrianised (another idea rehearsed in the Ongar plan).

Completed in July 1946, the Stephenson plan thus presented a quite detailed vision of an actual New Town, one that, with a few changes, was to shape Stevenage's development for many years. All that was missing was the legal authority to put it into practice. The Attlee government and Lewis Silkin were, however, reasonably confident that this would be a straightforward process. How completely wrong they were.

'... a first class press story'

During the plan's preparation Stephenson and his team liaised with local council officials on technical matters relevant to the plan. Although those officials probably kept their council leaders informed, it was some time before direct meetings began between non-technical civil servants dealing with the bigger political questions and the elected representatives of the local authorities. Even then, however, Beaufoy and his colleagues preferred to deal with Hertfordshire County Council and the Executive Planning Committees for different sections of the county. Legally, county councils did not become the actual planning authorities until after the 1947 Town and Country Planning Act became operative. However, since the 1930s many county councils, including Hertfordshire, had begun to encourage the creation of executive committees, bringing together the district and municipal boroughs which were the actual planning authorities on a voluntary basis.

The aim was to pool their legal powers and share them with the county council to enable co-ordinated planning across the county. It was an interim measure that, by its nature, confused planning responsibilities, although it gave the ministry an apparently simpler means of consulting with local councils over post-war plans such as those for the New Towns. But, significantly, ministry officials did not usually consult directly with the district councils themselves until much later. This proved a serious mistake in the small country town of Stevenage and its surrounding area, which, by the spring of 1945, was set to be the government's first satellite town.[11] In Stevenage, as in most proposed future New Town areas, there would be at least some local resentment about actual or feared loss of property, especially from farmers, and about the more general inevitable dramatic changes to an established way of life.

Reluctance to address this at Stevenage may simply have been a product of inexperience at a time when government departments had got used, during wartime emergency conditions, to taking peremptory action without public consultation. But there may also have been other factors specific to Stevenage. In July 1945 two senior ministry officials met Walter Gaunt, former estates manager at Letchworth in its early days, future member of Lord Reith's New Towns Committee and, at the time, chairman of Hertfordshire County Council's planning committee. Privately Gaunt told them he thought Stevenage the best location for a satellite town but warned of local unrest, especially from farmers. He also showed that he had not lost the reputation for plain speaking which, as we saw in Chapter 2, had upset many during his days with the Letchworth Company. Thus he also advised the ministry to steer clear of the affected area's main local authority, Stevenage Urban District Council, which he thought 'a stupid body'.[12] He seems to have feared that the council would be deliberately obstructive. The officials were surprised at this directness, but it certainly appears to have put them on their guard.

It was not until the autumn of 1945 (by which time Silkin had become minister) that a ministry official, Beaufoy, first met Stevenage's local elected representatives. Although it was intended to be confidential, a garbled account of the meeting appeared in the local press, worsening mutual suspicions.[13] Yet, despite frequent consultations with Stevenage's officials, the ministry's small planning team prepared the outline plan for a satellite town (ultimately of 60,000 people) during late 1945 and early 1946 without further incident. The local council was not, in fact, averse to significant growth. In the late 1930s it had already planned for Stevenage to expand to a population of well over 30,000 (roughly five times the 1946 population).[14] Pressed by a Labour councillor, Philip Ireton, a railway clerk who was enthusiastic and well-informed about town planning (and certainly not 'stupid'), the council had established a special development committee in 1944. Again at his prompting, it gave guarded support the following year to the Abercrombie proposal that Stevenage should be a new satellite town.

Yet, for all his energy and vision, Ireton's was not the only voice on the council.[15] There were a few other white-collar railway workers, mainly Labour or sympathetic to the party, who broadly favoured the project. However, they were not a majority and the council also included a few neutrals and others who opposed it with varying degrees of vehemence. They included a stone-deaf farmer aged about 80 who said nothing in meetings, hated the idea of the New Town and could be relied upon to oppose the ministry. There were a few others who were also instinctive opponents. It might have been these councillors that Gaunt had in mind; at any rate, this new stage of the peaceful path was to be anything but.

Lack of real information greatly strengthened the hand of those who opposed the proposals, particularly as local planning applications began to be rejected from February 1946 because they might cut across future proposals for the satellite town. In early April the writer E.M. Forster, who knew the area well and had used it as the setting for his celebrated novel *Howard's End*, broadcast his own opposition to the satellite town, calling it instead a 'meteorite town'.[16] Already, a 'hands off our homes' poster campaign had begun.[17] On 25 April 179 home-owners received official letters telling them that the sites of their properties, mainly in the Fairview Road area, were going to be used for the satellite town. Though the letters offered to buy properties by agreement, it was also made clear that compulsion was ultimately an option. Although many affected homes lay in the proposed industrial zone west of the railway (subsequently reduced in size, so that the houses are still there), this element of the plan meant, bizarrely, that the New Town was instantly equated, during a grave housing shortage, with the proposed – though never implemented – demolition of perfectly habitable dwellings.

Astonishingly, it was only later that same day that the ministry planning team finally met the council face-to-face to explain their planning proposals.[18] Beaufoy was pleased with the meeting but sensed a dominant mood of 'polite antagonism'. Silkin himself had already agreed to visit the area, meet the council and address a local public meeting (Figure 5.3). Despite mounting opposition, he seemed confident of carrying the day and requested that a story be prepared for release to the world's press to announce the triumph he anticipated: '[t]here is a first class press story here on May 6th [the day of his visit]: "A new town is born"'.[19] His assessment was prescient, though not initially in anything like the way that he had hoped. Others more accurately foresaw immediate events. On

Figure 5.3 Minister of town and country planning, Lewis Silkin, speaking at a difficult public meeting in Stevenage on 6 May 1946. The wavy-haired man in the dark jacket seated beyond Silkin is Samuel Beaufoy, the ministry's planning official, who had been liaising with local councils in the area. (Stevenage Museum P2635)

30 April the London *Evening News* carried the grim headline 'DOOM TOWN PROTEST RISING'. As yet the protesters had no formal organisation that brought together their concerns, but the following day the Stevenage Residents' Protection Association was formed and quickly attracted members.

Throughout his visit Silkin heard many objections, especially from local people. There were two main sources of public opposition to the New Town. The first came from farmers who were to lose their livelihoods in the area and those residents who (it seemed at the time) would lose their homes. Yet many more general concerns were also voiced at the evening meeting. The essence of them was that Stevenage was bearing the costs of a national experiment, that its history was being uprooted and that it was all being done in a dictatorial fashion. Over 350 people were crammed into the Stevenage Town Hall with (possibly) as many as 3,000 people outside, listening avidly to the loudspeaker relay on the old High Street. Inside the hall, although there were some cheers, things did not go well for the minister, his own speech frequently being interrupted by jeering.[20] He tried to appeal to the audience's highest instincts:

During the war years we in this country stood together and suffered together, whilst
fighting for an ideal, for a democracy in which we all believed. I am sure that this
spirit is not dead in Stevenage, and if you are satisfied that this project is worth
while, and for the benefit of large numbers of your fellow human beings, you will be
prepared to play your part to make it a success.[21]

Yet such arguments did not assuage the protesters, who thought him
profoundly anti-democratic. Nor did Silkin's own attempts to deal with
interrupters always help: the riposte to one that 'it's no use jibbing, it's going to be
done' was countered with 'Hark, hark the dictator'.[22] At another point there was
a loud cry of 'Gestapo' from one protester. Towards the end of his speech Silkin
stated that 'The project will go forward, because it must go forward. It will do so
more surely and more smoothly, and more successfully with your help and co-
operation.' He also assured listeners that soon 'People from all over the world will
come to Stevenage to see how we here in this country are building for the new
way of life.'[23] He left the hall to find that a tyre of his official car had been deflated
and (it was suspected) sugar put in the petrol tank.

'Silkingrad'

For several years the deflated tyre and disabled engine were more apt as
metaphors for Stevenage's fortunes than were Silkin's expressed hopes at the
stormy meeting of 6 May. The New Towns Bill received its second reading only
two days after Silkin's visit to Stevenage and did not become law until August
1946.[24] The government publicity machine duly swung into action, but for
several years local reality scarcely matched the official narrative that was being
promoted. The early mishaps of the meeting and what had preceded it were not
easily overcome and new problems (several partly of the ministry's own creation)
were to arise, including a badly presented case for the New Town at the public
inquiry on the designation, staffing and leadership mistakes or misfortunes and
a serious financial crisis. Local opposition to the New Town was actually not as
numerically strong as might be supposed. A poll of local electors held by the
council (at which only 52 per cent actually voted) showed 1,316 entirely opposed,
913 in favour and 282 giving qualified support,[25] while the Residents' Protection
Association grew in strength to over 1,100 members by the summer. Yet it was
the vehemence rather than just the scale of opposition that was important. It did
not help that the advisory committee established in August 1946 to oversee early
progress on the New Town included only two councillors from Hertfordshire,
only one (Ireton) from Stevenage itself.

In October 1946 a local public inquiry in Stevenage considered objections to the proposed order to designate it formally as a New Town under the new Act. Unlike the May public meeting, at which the raw feelings of the original residents of Stevenage had been expressed, this related more to the planning arguments for and against the New Town and the actual boundaries of the designated area. It therefore involved discussion of specific matters such as the fear of the New Town coalescing with nearby towns, details of how and on what terms existing farmers would be displaced and implications for drainage and water supply. Silkin's peculiarly contradictory legal position as both promoter and judge of the scheme limited the rigour with which his ministry could simultaneously press his own arguments in favour. Even so, the ministry was poorly represented, with no positive advocacy of the New Town and no cross-examination of objectors. Some piquancy was given to the proceedings by the appearance of Ewart G. Culpin to articulate the local council's opposition.[26] As shown in the last chapter, he had been a leader of the Garden City Association's revisionist move towards garden suburbs before 1914, and had also been a Labour colleague of Silkin and Herbert Morrison on the London County Council between the wars. But for Culpin, just a few months before his death, this was personal in another way – Stevenage was his birthplace and he considered that approving the New Town would encourage a large urban agglomeration of Stevenage, Welwyn Garden City and Hatfield.

The inspector's confidential report to Silkin, though expressing surprise at the ministry's apparent complacency in failing to contest any objections, accepted that the counter-arguments held some validity.[27] Although he did not say that Stevenage should not be a New Town, he felt that Stevenage would *not* be a good setting in which to launch the whole programme. He recommended that this particular New Town should be delayed until the more serious objections (which had come from the water and river authorities and were about proposed arrangements for surface drainage) had been addressed. The ministry's chief inspector, reading the Stevenage inspector's report, added his own view that the size of the New Town should be reduced.

These misgivings (which were not, of course, made public) were certainly not what Silkin wanted to hear. With cabinet backing he decided to address the perceived (though not actually serious) drainage problems but otherwise press on regardless. Beaufoy wrote to the local authorities in the designated area explaining the minister's reasons and the designation order was confirmed in early November 1946, further hardening local opposition.[28] The Stevenage New Town Development Corporation was formally created a few weeks later.[29] Its composition reproduced the advisory committee set up in August 1946, with

Figure 5.4 Shortly after Stevenage New Town was formally designated in December 1946, local protesters replaced the station name-board with the name 'Silkingrad'. Donations to the Residents' Protection Association flowed in as the campaign was publicised nationally and internationally. (Stevenage Museum P9316)

Clough Williams-Ellis remaining as chairman. He was an architect and Welsh landowner who created the fanciful village of Portmeirion on his estate, a fact which frightened some who feared that Stevenage might suffer the same fate. He was also a charismatic advocate of the idea of planning and of rural protection. Yet he was not a natural chairman of any New Town, let alone one that would be able to do almost nothing for several months.

Shortly after the New Town was formally designated, two local residents who were set to lose their properties, with the help of some friends, surreptitiously put painted hardboard signs bearing the name 'Silkingrad' on the Stevenage railway station entrance and platform nameboards (Figure 5.4).[30] In the first snow of what would soon become the worst winter in living memory this new name, coined by one of the perpetrators, Clarence Elliott, consciously evoked Soviet totalitarianism. It seemed to the opposition movement to express perfectly how local interests were being disregarded in a dictatorial fashion. The action was quickly publicised and the story soon spread around the world, attracting support and funds for a legal challenge to Silkin's decision that, days later, was lodged in the High Court.

The Residents' Protection Association and the local branch of the National Farmers' Union wanted to quash the designation order.[31] They argued that Silkin's advocacy of the New Town at the public meeting in May had led him to treat objections in a biased way at the public inquiry. The High Court upheld this view in February 1947. Silkin and the government considered their options, but quickly decided they had to fight this decision in the Court of Appeal, otherwise not only would the entire Greater London New Towns programme very probably have been stopped in its tracks[32] but it would also have been far more difficult for Silkin personally to steer the major Town and Country Planning Bill then before parliament into law. Silkin triumphed in the Appeal Court in March 1947, whereupon the Protection Association raised more funds to carry the battle to the House of Lords. Eventually, in July, this supreme court decided in favour of the New Town and, at last, it seemed, the new Development Corporation could do its job of developing the new Stevenage.

'Sweet Stevenage! loveliest town they never built'
Or at least it could try to. The impact of the dollar crisis of 1947 put great pressure on public spending and work on all the New Towns was severely curtailed. Despite the early start at Stevenage, legal delays, during which the Development Corporation could do little more than mark time, had swallowed up that advantage. Now limitations on capital spending and staff appointments created another hiatus. Stevenage was in a worse position than any of the other three London New Towns which had by then been designated. In October 1947 an unknown poet published 'The Deserted Satellite' (mimicking Oliver Goldsmith's 'The Deserted Village') in the political journal *New Statesman and Nation*.[33] The verses satirised Stevenage as the 'loveliest town they never built', the 'Fairest of London's stillborn satellites'.

Stevenage was also to suffer other, more specific setbacks.[34] In November 1947 the first chairman of the Development Corporation, Clough Williams-Ellis, resigned in frustration at his own inability to achieve anything. His departure signalled the start of a phase of great discontinuity in the Development Corporation's leadership: his successor, the former civil servant Thomas Gardiner, took the post for only a year and *his* successor, the Reverend Charles Jenkinson, the well-known and widely respected socialist leader of Leeds City Council, died after a few months in August 1949. The most disastrous appointment of all then followed in the person of Monica Felton. There was nothing wrong with her record. She had been a member of the Reith Committee and the original deputy chairman to Williams-Ellis at Stevenage. Silkin then promoted her to chair the Development Corporation of the coal-mining New Town of Peterlee in County Durham before bringing her back to Stevenage in August 1949. She and Silkin had served together on the London County Council from 1937 and were very close personally (she was very probably his mistress during at least some of this time).[35] Not uncommonly for many of those associated with the early New Towns programme, she had strong left-wing (in her case Marxist) sympathies. She also possessed very great abilities: a strong intellect with clear views about planning and a strong character capable of dominating committees, badgering civil servants and getting things done. The real problem was that she also showed astonishingly poor judgement at times, most notably at Peterlee, where her style sharply divided local opinion between those who judged her strong and fearless and those who thought her a dictator. Despite working in the extremely male-dominated local society of the County Durham coalfield, she also allowed herself to become the subject of scurrilous rumours by being perceived as overfamiliar with some of her male staff. This might be viewed differently today, but she was judged by the standards of the time. However, the circumstances of her undoing were entirely unambiguous. She was absent without permission when she was supposed to be reporting Stevenage's progress to a parliamentary committee in June 1951. Her actual location at this time was also profoundly relevant: she was in North Korea on a Soviet-organised six-week trip at the height of the Korean War. This was a period of great paranoia about the Soviet Union (the defection of two senior British diplomats, Burgess and Maclean, about to be unmasked as Soviet spies, occurred at almost exactly the same time). It is doubtful whether even Silkin would have been able to have saved her career and political reputation. By this time, however, he had been replaced with the minister of local government and planning Hugh Dalton, who summarily dismissed her a few days later. She was the only New Town chairman ever to be sacked and there were later calls for her to be indicted for treason. Silkin might no longer be minister but, as far as Stevenage was concerned, Felton's real Soviet connections now seemed to be perpetuating the idea of 'Silkingrad'.

This poverty of leadership of the Stevenage Board in the early years might not have mattered as much if the general manager had been a stronger figure. Unfortunately, the legal challenges had made it difficult to attract an outstanding candidate.[36] Eventually, in 1947, the second chairman was able to appoint Major-General Alan Duff, who had had a distinguished military career, latterly as a senior administrative officer (several of the first generation of general managers were from senior military backgrounds). Yet, despite his high rank and unfailing courteousness and decency, Duff was not a natural leader in a civilian context. He found it difficult to respond sympathetically to the new residents' organisations, bolstering the idea that the New Town was a remote and unresponsive organisation. Neither could he counteract the severe discontinuities higher up or the lack of cohesion within the Corporation itself. Early uncertainties had also contributed to difficulties in the retention and effective team-working of other officials, not least in planning.

For a while it seemed that several of the Stephenson planning team might continue as officers of the new Development Corporation. Stephenson was tempted by the post of chief architect and planner but in July 1947 declined, disappointing both Williams-Ellis and the ministry.[37] Shortly afterwards he moved to a career that combined academia and consultancy, first in Liverpool and then in the Commonwealth, based first in Toronto and subsequently in Perth in Western Australia. (He did, though, play one significant further role in planning Stevenage, as we will see.) Shepheard was to have been his deputy and actually held this post for a short time. He was, however, unable to work with the chief architect appointed instead of Stephenson, Clifford Holliday, who at the outset appeared to want a different master plan.[38] The only member of Stephenson's original team who stayed in the long term was Claxton, who spent the remainder of his career at Stevenage. Despite his own periodic frustration with Holliday and others in the Development Corporation and beyond, he did much to uphold and deliver the promise of the 1946 plan.

Naturally, the publication of what would become the first official master plan in 1949 and the subsequent public inquiry provided some scope for a partial re-run of earlier battles with the Residents' Protection Association.[39] But the Association's impact was no longer as great as it had been in 1946–47, when its opposition had almost sunk the entire project. The Development Corporation now gave much more attention to public relations and a local information bureau was opened in October 1948. The main changes to the 1946 plan were to the primary distribution road system, including, eventually, the dropping of the proposed primary road along the Fairlands Valley.[40] The factory area was also slightly reduced in size and, although the industrial zoning for the houses in Fairview Road was not yet actually dropped, it was made clear that these dwellings would be removed only in the very long term (which never came).

However, Holliday's early interest in resiting the town centre more centrally within the town and the residential areas, on the Bedwell–Pin Green ridge, did not survive long. The then deputy architect Shepheard, who had played the key role in the 1946 design, intensely disliked this idea.[41] He recruited his former colleagues in the ministry to press Holliday to maintain the original vision. The plan was approved by the ministry in 1950. It was never seen as an absolute final blueprint for the New Town and underwent regular revisions, most fairly minor, every five or six years. The most important of the changes will be highlighted in later sections.

Gradually, then, with the establishment of an agency to develop the New Town and the acceptance of its plan, Stevenage had moved if not yet to reality then to being a more robust vision. The 1947 financial constraints were eased by the effects of the Marshall Plan and a massive American loan, but other problems of labour and material shortages remained. Moreover, some officials were also slow to respond to new opportunities as the 1940s ended. The result was that early housing output (only 28 permanent dwellings completed by 31 March 1951) was derisory, rather worse than in the other London New Towns, even though they had been designated after Stevenage.[42]

Building the New Town

Following its painfully protracted gestation, birth and early infancy, Stevenage experienced sturdy, at times prodigious, growth throughout the 1950s and, despite fluctuations, the 1960s. The Felton fiasco finally brought much better leadership to the Development Corporation.[43] Thomas Bennett was appointed as chairman and seemed a good candidate to be able to give the stability and direction that had been lacking. He was also chairman of Crawley New Town (which was performing much better than Stevenage) and a successful architect with expertise in managing large building projects. This led him to intrude more than necessary into professional and technical matters, often irritating officials; yet his proved a caretaker appointment and, on doctor's advice, he resigned after two years. It was only in 1953 that real continuity of leadership arrived in the form of Roydon Dash, a retired civil servant who was already deputy chairman at Bracknell New Town and remained chairman at Stevenage until 1962. Despite varying judgements about him, it seems that Dash was able to get the best out of the Development Corporation. This was especially so after Duff retired and was replaced as general manager by R.S. ('Sedge') MacDougall, previously county treasurer of Hertfordshire and better attuned to the sensitivities of local politics and society.

As this more effective organisation gradually evolved, so its operations moved into higher gear. First the process of buying the farmland needed for development began to accelerate. The Corporation had powers to acquire, by agreement or compulsion, all 6,156 acres of the designated area at its pre-New Town value,[44] but it still required central government approval and money on

Figure 5.5 Early houses built by the Development Corporation on the Stony Hall estate in Neighbourhood 1 (Old Town), completed in the early 1950s. (author photograph)

a year-by-year basis to do it. By 1952 about a third of the designated area had been bought by the Development Corporation and by 1960 roughly half. By 1980, when the Development Corporation was wound up, about four-fifths of the designated area had been purchased. It was estimated that about two-fifths of acquisitions had involved compulsory powers.

There was normally a further delay before ownership of acquired land could become full vacant possession, allowing construction to begin in earnest. Even so, housing completions rose significantly in the early 1950s and then soared. From the mid-1950s Stevenage was averaging around 1,000 house completions a year. By 31 March 1960 8,783 houses had been built by the Development Corporation.[45] A few others had been built by the local council (to meet pre-existing housing needs) and by private developers, but these together were rather less than a tenth of the total construction. The New Town proper was well underway and no longer a mere vision. Apart from further development in the Old Town (neighbourhood 1) (Figure 5.5), the first entirely new neighbourhood units began to take shape with developments in neighbourhood 2 (Bedwell), neighbourhood 3 (Broadwater) and neighbourhood 4 (Shephall). Neighbourhood 5 (Chells) was also started by the end of the 1950s.

Building was not, of course, just a governmental process undertaken solely by the Development Corporation. It also involved private building firms tendering for and undertaking the various construction contracts. A major problem in the early post-war years was the sourcing of sufficient building materials at a time when the big cities were tackling their own housing needs and other New Towns were being built. The initial desire was to build as much as possible in brick, but as housebuilding began to accelerate nationally from the end of the 1940s bricks proved to be in short supply. Practically every other material was also scarce at one time or another. Even the supply of hardcore for foundations ran short as the rubble from London's wartime bomb damage ran out.

Where possible, local builders were used, but they lacked the capacity to handle really big contracts. As a result national contractors soon dominated, especially Terson, Carlton, Wimpey and (later) Mowlem.[46] Between them these firms constructed about three-quarters of the more than 20,000 dwellings built for the Development Corporation between 1950 and 1980. In general, big contractors also tended to be the winners in the struggle to get hold of scarce building materials in the early 1950s.[47] As a consequence Stevenage actually did better in this respect than most other New Towns, particularly those which used more and smaller building firms. Even if material supply problems did arise, big contractors (especially Wimpey and Mowlem in Stevenage) were more able to handle the non-traditional construction methods that could offset both these and skill shortages. In early 1950s contracts Wimpey built terraces of housing in Stevenage using its 'no-fines' technique,[48] which involved concrete made without sand (that is, 'fines') being cast in situ between huge moulds to form the walls of terraces in just one pouring operation. No-fines concrete had wet-handling and insulation advantages over conventional concrete. Although the walls still needed a final render or other finish, the moulds could be used repeatedly and this method needed less skilled labour than did traditional all-brick construction.

Despite these expedients, labour supply was a continuing problem. It was very difficult in the New Towns because they were undertaking building programmes so far in excess of their existing populations, especially so in Stevenage. Many efforts were made to attract and keep construction workforces. Contractors' buses daily ferried building workers from London to Stevenage. The Development Corporation also provided hostel accommodation (initially in temporary prefabs). But the real incentive for many workers compared to working in London was the promise of getting, after just a few months of working in Stevenage, the tenancy of a good-quality new house, well equipped and with a garden. Many building workers (like thousands of others) were living in cramped, inadequate accommodation in London, with several families often sharing the most basic domestic amenities. So the prospect of decent housing secured far sooner than would be possible in London was a very real draw.

Not that this growing commitment to Stevenage meant that building workers simply complied with everything the building contractors demanded; working on large sites also facilitated large-scale labour organisation. Moreover, many London building workers already had a strong sense of the value of collective action, an attitude quickly strengthened by the very effective local leadership of the Amalgamated Union of Building Trade Workers. The most prominent single figure was a Communist bricklayer from London, Jim Collman, who came to Stevenage in 1951.[49] Though seen by some as divisive and abrasive, he was a natural leader and soon won the respect of workmates for his ability to get the better of contractors in disputes. It is clear that he encouraged other prominent union activists, such as Jim Cunningham, Bert Lowe and Pat Sullivan. Inevitably the early months of working in Stevenage had to be ones of acquiescence, but once the precious home was secured by a growing proportion of the workforce it was increasingly possible for the building unions to flex their muscles to seek improvements to what were often primitive working conditions, poor wages and the threat of arbitrary dismissal. They were particularly zealous in eliminating the so-called 'lump', whereby labour-only sub-contractors were used. This involved sub-contractors who supplied teams of nominally self-employed workers with fewer rights who accepted much poorer working conditions than those directly employed by the main contractors. While this practice did not disappear entirely, it soon became rarer in Stevenage than elsewhere.

Generally Stevenage became the most highly organised location for New Town building labour. Local union leaders estimated that around 90 per cent of Development Corporation housing was built on unionised sites,[50] and there were many short-term disputes. So, on top of its early problems, Stevenage also began to get a reputation for labour militancy. But this should not be seen simply in negative terms, as the fluctuations over time in dwelling completions were not the result of labour disruption. The reality was that the building workers brought a great deal that was positive to the emergent New Town. They and their families, many of them of Irish origin, dominated the first wave of New Towners.[51] In building the places that they, their workmates and their families would call home, they had a real stake in maintaining both housing output and quality. Increasingly, as discussed later, they also provided important social and political leadership within the wider New Town community.

Attracting jobs

Although building provided most of Stevenage's early employment growth, continued expansion depended on a major increase in manufacturing jobs. As for building workers, having a job in Stevenage was the key to being allocated a Development Corporation house. Only in this way could the central ideal of people living and working in the same town, inherited from the garden city movement and refined by Abercrombie and Reith, be fulfilled. Fortunately Stevenage was a place with clear potential for industrial growth. There were already several factories there in 1946, providing jobs for most of the existing working population.[52] Local industrialists, eager to expand, were important supporters of the New Town project.

As noted, the master plan made generous provision for new factory development in the future Gunnels Wood industrial estate west of the railway. Industrialists were initially reluctant to set up on what were, in 1950, still largely untouched fields. Combined with the slow start to house-building, this difficulty compounded the early hesitancy in Stevenage's growth: people would not move to Stevenage without having houses and jobs available. When he became chairman Bennett pressed the Development Corporation to build the first factories and roads on the industrial estate as a catalyst. Along with some astute negotiation with potential employers and central government, the effect was remarkable. The first new factories duly opened in 1953 and a spate of new employers followed within a few years.[53]

Almost from the outset military aerospace became the dominant manufacturing sector in Stevenage. De Havilland Propellers (later Hawker Siddeley Dynamics), already established in nearby Hatfield, opened in 1953. An even bigger prize, English Electric (later British Aircraft Corporation), arrived in 1955.[54] By 1961 they were already employing around 5,800 workers between them, representing 26 per cent of all Stevenage jobs and 37 per cent of those in manufacturing.[55] Two other important early employers that had preceded the New Town were King's (general engineering) and the Educational Supply Association. King's employed almost 1,800 workers in 1961. Another significant arrival was the photographic firm Kodak, which arrived in 1954 and employed 1,600 workers by 1961. Over the next few years further key employers moved in, including British Visqueen (later ICI Plastics), British Tabulators (later the computing conglomerate ICL), both in 1954, and Mentmore (pens and pencils) in 1956.[56] Although each of these three employed fewer than 1,000 in 1961, they subsequently exceeded that figure. In 1962 the last two of Stevenage's major employers during its New Town years arrived.[57] These were Taylor Instruments, which grew to around 1,100 employees by the early 1970s, and Bowater (packaging), which also peaked at the same time with around 600 workers.

Yet decision-making in industrial location at this time was not simply a function of Stevenage's natural and artificial advantages, the persuasiveness of the Development Corporation and industrialist preferences. Following the 1945 Distribution of Industry Act the location of factories during this period was heavily affected by central government policies.[58] From 1947 the key instrument of control was the industrial development certificate (IDC), which applied to any new factory development or extension of over 5,000 square feet. By issuing or withholding IDCs the Board of Trade could decide where new manufacturing could or could not take place. The broad policy was that the development areas (regions or parts of regions which suffered unemployment persistently higher than the national average, largely in the north, Wales and Scotland) would be most favoured. The Greater London New Towns became a secondary priority for IDCs, in instances, for example, where firms were moving out of Greater London or had other valid reasons to stay in the region. All other areas, especially the biggest cities in prosperous regions (and particularly Greater London) had lowest priority. However, IDC policy was applied with various degrees of zealousness. It depended very much on the prevailing national levels of unemployment and various political factors. On the whole (and a little oddly, given their general enthusiasm for New Towns) Labour governments were most reluctant to sanction big factory projects outside the development areas.

As Stevenage shows, however, the 1950s proved a boom period for factory development in the Greater London New Towns.[59] It helped in the granting of IDCs for factory developments in New Towns if other central ministries could be persuaded to support the cause, and in this it was useful to be able to argue that new industrial developments were of national strategic importance (which usually meant producing defence equipment and/or involved very advanced technology). Potential exports from new factories were another factor in gaining IDCs in the Greater London New Towns. These points are critical to understanding why military aerospace became so entrenched in Stevenage. English Electric had originally wanted to expand in Luton, but could not get enough skilled workers there. The Ministry of Defence suggested that they try Stevenage, also pressing the Board of Trade to grant the IDC. The firm seized on this, immediately buying the biggest site available, one of 70 acres (28 hectares). Once established, the export sales of the more successful products (often to rather repressive Middle Eastern regimes) were used to justify further expansions on the site. Although its work edged increasingly into space technology, similar considerations applied to De Havilland/Hawker-Siddeley.

What Howard might have thought about this or what former conscientious objector Osborn did think about this warlike path is not known. Yet there were local protests from trades unions and anti-nuclear organisations in Stevenage itself against its increasing dependence upon the global arms trade.[60] There was also a downside, in that changes in government thinking on product development (usually state-funded) could affect job numbers. Stevenage was adversely affected by the cancellation of both the Blue Streak battlefield missile project in 1960 and the Blue Water medium range ballistic missile in 1962.[61] In the longer term, most of the other manufacturing firms that had come to the New Town also proved to have their own particular vulnerabilities, partly because they were branch factories of larger undertakings.

As in most other London New Towns in the 1960s, Stevenage's working population mainly comprised male workers doing manual jobs, typically skilled or, to a lesser extent, semi-skilled.[62] Unskilled workers made up a smaller proportion than the national or regional average. Professional and semi-professional occupations were noticeably overrepresented, reflecting the higher expertise required in several industries (and in building and servicing the rapidly growing New Town). Employers, managers and the self-employed were a smaller proportion of working Stevenage than the national average. This reflected the dominance of a few large, mainly branch firms whose managers chose not to live in the town itself and the more general lack of a small-business 'culture'. As Stevenage started to mature as a fully fledged town during the 1960s there was also a steady rise in service employment, as retailing, public services of all kinds and a variety of office-based activities started to appear. These growing activities also began to diversify the employment base.

As this change occurred, so too did the range of labour that was needed, with more professional and other non-manual jobs and growing numbers of jobs for women and juveniles. Much of the growth in service employment mirrored the existing picture, with the non-manual equivalents of skilled and semi-skilled jobs predominating. This meant it was common for children to leave full-time education during secondary level, many before the age of 18, and enter employment in which they could then often build up their skills. In this, Stevenage was not so different from many other places and the recent industrial investment there made it more fortunate than most. Later, however, this lack of post-16 and even post-18 education would begin to matter for Stevenage's school leavers. In the heyday of the post-war boom, however, it was the plentiful nature of jobs and the absence of unemployment that were important. This was a young town of relatively affluent workers.

Figure 5.6 The first houses completed (in 1951) at Stevenage New Town at Broadview, off Sish Lane in the Old Town neighbourhood. Then, mothers had to push their children's prams and pushchairs through the mud of a construction site. This is now a much easier task and such family duties are more likely to be shared between mother and father. (author photograph)

The first neighbourhoods

But what did the New Town actually look like as its plan began to be realised, and what was it like as a place to live? Inevitably there was much uniformity, even monotony, in the face of the new Stevenage that emerged from the early 1950s (Figure 5.6). Given the short period over which the New Town appeared, it could hardly have been otherwise. The effect was compounded by the overwhelming dominance of one development agency working to a common, if evolving, set of master plan principles. Most of Stevenage consisted of large areas of low-rise public rental housing, often using fairly uniform housing designs and layouts, produced in large construction operations by a few national contractors. It was impossible under such circumstances to reproduce the varied and complex textures of the older, slower and more 'organic' process of growth more typical of Hertfordshire. The effect was also more striking than in the garden cities because they grew less quickly than did the New Towns. Even so, different parts of Stevenage New Town had noticeably different townscape 'textures'. A few examples will highlight this.

The face of the historic Old Town itself remained largely unaffected (though later road changes disrupted its visual integrity) (Figure 5.7).[63] Some peripheral demolitions also occurred to allow the first large area of New Town housing to be built in neighbourhood 1 (Old Town) at Stony Hall. Mainly of traditional brick construction, this area reflects the high social housing standards prevalent in the later 1940s when it was conceived and the first parts of it built. There is a greater sense of spaciousness than in later schemes, with more semi-detached houses, more short terraces, wider grass verges and trees on its roads. The six-storey Chauncy House, built in 1952, and nearby lower flat blocks were controversial exceptions that were intended for small middle-income households. (All the original flat blocks have now been redeveloped.)

From 1952 the first completely new neighbourhoods began to take shape, first at Bedwell and shortly afterwards at Broadwater and Shephall.[64] Unlike in the case of the first neighbourhood, focused on the Old Town, existing building development had very little impact on their layouts. At Shephall, the tiny existing village at Shephall Green remained around its church and small green as a striking contrast with the quite new residential pattern which was inserted around it. But this relic feature of a former rural landscape was exceptional: a protected historic enclave within the new neighbourhood that took shape around it.

Figure 5.7 The historic environment of the Old Town itself was largely unaffected by the New Town. There has been some limited redevelopment of individual buildings but the main changes have come from the longer-term growth of motor traffic. (author photograph)

Figure 5.8 The Broadwater neighbourhood began to be built from 1953. A common house type was the PP77 short terrace built by Wimpey using their no-fines concrete system. Another was the C23 flat-roofed house, shown beyond. Compared with the first housing, there are more signs of a search for economies, though the failure to provide for cars is common in all early schemes. (author photograph)

One of the first entirely new neighbourhoods, Broadwater, begun in 1953, typified these earlier residential areas in the boom years of housing output.[65] In line with the original 1949 master plan, it was planned at just over 12 dwellings per acre (30 per hectare). The first contract comprised 150 Wimpey no-fines three-bedroomed terraced houses of the Development Corporation's PP77 standard type (Figure 5.8).[66] This housing type was essentially a variation of a standard Wimpey design and similar in appearance to houses developed elsewhere at the same time. With a pebble dash cement surface finish, the houses are mainly arranged in straight rows of six or eight dwellings fronting the estate roads in a conventional manner. There were small open front gardens with a pavement and a very narrow grass verge with no street trees. Larger enclosed gardens were provided behind the houses. The area typifies the plainness of many neighbourhoods built in Stevenage and other New Towns when the pressure to produce more houses was growing.

There was little initial provision for cars, reflecting low car ownership at that time. Only 15 garages were originally provided, in a group behind these 150 houses, though the slightly more generous plan for the whole neighbourhood envisaged providing one garage per eight dwellings overall. The original development also included other dwelling types, such as the C23, a flat-roofed design, and the B9, a maisonette design with a stepped elevation that allowed a less conventional relationship to the road. These two housing designs were produced by the chief architect's department and were more distinctive in appearance than the PP77 type. Both involved more use of brick and were followed by later terraces and even semi-detached housing with entirely brick external walls as material shortages lessened.

As more housing appeared and families arrived, local primary schools were added on sites within housing areas. The shops came a little later and, after local complaints, six then unoccupied houses on Broadwater Crescent were opened as temporary shops with a small Co-op in a caravan parked across the road.[67] Broadwater's heart was a local three-storey shopping centre (mainly of brick) built in 1957, with small ground-floor shop units and flats above (Figure 5.9). It was arranged in two blocks, with a new neighbourhood church (built in 1955) forming the third side of an enclosure facing one of the main neighbourhood roads. The area between the buildings contained a small paved pedestrian precinct, a grassed area and some car parking spaces. Adjoining the shops was a public house (also built around 1957). In 1968 a six-storey brick-faced block of flats for elderly residents was added and in 1971 some single-storey housing for disabled residents in brick and timber. A local health centre was opened at about the same time.

Figure 5.9 Broadwater neighbourhood shops, built in 1957, with flats above. Nearby are a church, a pub, flats and old people's housing, providing a central point within a large neighbourhood. Over time, more parking provision has been needed and what were originally several small food shops have become one convenience supermarket. (author photograph)

What, then, was the experience of the early residents of these new areas? The reflective personal histories which are the richest source of information give the memories of those who remained in the town.[68] A minority, it is clear, had found too much to bear the wrench of leaving behind the lively and busy streets of inner London, where family and community ties were often strong. But the great majority of those who came stayed. Almost without exception they were very pleased to have their own new house, several bedrooms, a bathroom and an inside toilet (in the bigger houses sometimes two). As one who moved there at the end of the 1950s commented 'to get a house was lovely. We lived in rented rooms in London with two children …. We came to look at houses; the one in Penn Road [Bedwell] was really perfect.'[69]

Another mother with four children who came with her husband and family to Bedwell in 1957 from rented rooms in a house in Islington recalled:

> Never before had we had the luxury of a bath, hot water on tap and, best of all in our children's eyes, our own stairs. They ran up and down them on that first day calling out 'these are our stairs' and they all kept flushing the toilet. This was a great improvement on our former house, where the toilet was in the backyard.[70]

Also appreciated were the small touches of modern sophistication, such as 'an open porch that even had a light on it, so that when people came you could put this light on and welcome them into the house – we could not believe it …'.[71] Yet many families that had formerly lived in one or two rooms lacked sufficient furniture for the larger house into which they were now moving.[72] Moreover, while having a garden was a wonderful new experience for most residents, the debris of building had to be cleared before serious cultivation could begin. As one early resident said, '[t]he houses looked as they had been tipped out on to piles of rubble and mud'.[73] The closeness to the countryside at this early stage was generally pleasant, but cows straying up to as yet unfenced homes was unsettling and periodic plagues of earwigs a downright menace.[74]

Other problems reflected human emotions of separation.[75] Although they stuck it out, new residents, particularly housewives, often missed their wider families and the familiar faces and places they had known in their London lives. This was also, however, a spur to early socialisation among new residents. There were also many practical daily problems. Most pressing was the daily struggle to keep the family fed. It was not simply that rationing remained operative until 1954, as that affected the nation as a whole; more problematic was that, in the earliest years, the only shops and the market were in the Old Town. Even from the first estate at Stony Hall in the Old Town neighbourhood, this could be a daunting trek along unmade pavements beside roads traversed by builders' lorries. In wet weather the experience could be dreadful; in dry summer weather very dusty. The treks as Bedwell and Broadwater began to be developed grew even longer, but by then retail traders were responding with mobile shops and the Development Corporation, as we have seen, allowed temporary shops to be opened in advance of permanent arrangements. However, a range of local permanent shops was appreciated, and when they opened they typically included a grocer, baker, butcher, greengrocer, occasionally a fish shop and, a little later, a laundrette.

While the local shops, schools and other services helped to give clear definition to the neighbourhoods, their physical distinctiveness partly came from having clear edges derived from the landscaped road system. Between the neighbourhoods the primary road network was gradually constructed, with limited access into the residential areas via roundabouts.[76] In 1950 it was decided to adopt Eric Claxton's suggestions in the 1946 and 1949 master plans to create a fully segregated cycleway system. This was created alongside the new roads, paralleling the pedestrian routes.[77] Despite the expense, full segregation of road, cycle and pedestrian routes was maintained even at the greatest danger points, the roundabouts. Eventually Stevenage had 26 miles of cycleway forming the country's most comprehensive system. Despite this, however, actual cycle use quickly declined. From the projected 40 per cent of journeys to work, the actual figure was down to 13 per cent in 1964 and just over 7 per cent by 1972. (In 2011 it was just 1.7 per cent, marginally lower than the national average.) Alongside this, the car became the dominant mode of travelling to work.

The car also began to have many other effects on the New Townscape. As car ownership increased, more garage blocks had to be retrofitted into older residential layouts and more generously provided in new ones. The unbuilt, originally grassed, area at the Broadwater neighbourhood centre was also reapportioned to create more parking. These centres were also affected by larger changes in retailing patterns. Following the end of rationing (in 1954) and resale price maintenance (1963), smaller shops gradually became less viable, unable to compete with bigger retailing chains. Sooner or later the small food shops which originally characterised all the early neighbourhood centres were displaced in favour of a single larger retailer.

Changing the New Town

By 1961 Stevenage's population had grown to 43,600, over two-thirds of the original goal. Yet the 1960s saw a period in which the New Town's housing production fluctuated and was generally lower than in the later 1950s. This certainly did not reflect any decline in the national or regional needs for housing because the pressure was for more, not less, construction. The key reason for the drop in building in Stevenage was indecision within central government about how big the New Town should ultimately be.[78] This was a period when national (and global) population forecasts pointed to much higher increases than actually occurred. It was also expected with reasonable confidence that the economy would be able to grow alongside this population surge. In these circumstances, it was clear that the need for new housing would be very high. The problem was compounded by the aggressive programmes of slum clearance the older cities had embarked on from the later 1950s. Moreover, despite rebuilding at high densities, these cities were not able to rehouse all those displaced families within their own boundaries.

These factors again made governments turn to New Towns. As we will see in Chapter 7, there was a second phase of the New Towns programme in the 1960s in which further New Towns were designated with generally higher target populations than in the first phase. Alongside this there was also a push to increase the target populations of the existing New Towns. This was especially so in places such as Stevenage, which had now proved so successful in attracting people and jobs. It was also important that, unlike the other Hertfordshire New Towns, it seemed set to stay in the hands of its Development Corporation, which had (eventually) become an efficient development machine. It also seemed that the 'heavy lifting', politically speaking, regarding accommodating growth without serious delays had already been done. But just how much that extra population growth should be and therefore how many more houses would be required remained as questions that were never to be fully answered.

The first specific signs of change had come in 1958, when Henry Brooke, the Conservative minister of housing and local government, provisionally decided to increase Stevenage's target to 80,000.[79] His successor, Keith Joseph, doubtless alarmed by the advice he was then receiving about the expected scale of south-east population growth, moved the debate onto a quite different level.[80] In July 1964 he asked the Development Corporation whether (and how) Stevenage might be expanded to 150,000 inhabitants. In response, the Development Corporation (which was already considering growth options) counter-proposed an expansion to 130,000–140,000 – still more than twice the original target. Yet strong local opposition soon showed that much 'heavy lifting' remained to be done if this scale of expansion were to go ahead. In the event it did not. Joseph's Labour successor, Richard Crossman, rejected this proposal in 1965.

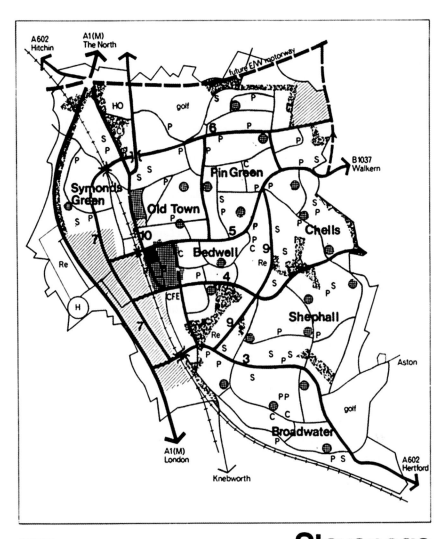

Figure 5.10 The 1966 master plan attempted to accommodate an increased target population. The most obvious changes from previous plans were the replacement of the industrial zone in the north-west with the new residential neighbourhood of Symonds Green. A small new industrial area was also zoned in the north-east. (author's collection)

Although the alarmist high national population growth forecasts were at this stage beginning to recede, reducing the pressure for extra housing, political factors undoubtedly played an important role in this decision. The first Wilson government of 1964–66 had only a tiny majority and the highly marginal Hitchin and Stevenage constituency had changed hands from Conservative to Labour in 1964. The very astute new MP, Shirley Williams, had objected to the proposals, doubtless influencing Crossman's thinking.

The approved 1966 master plan (Figure 5.10) finally settled on a target of 80,000 during the 'in-migration' phase with a broad (though never formalised) understanding that natural increase might then take this to 105,000. The man who had to give practical form to these various meanderings in policy thinking was the Development Corporation's chief architect and planner, Leonard Grange Vincent.[81] He joined the Corporation in 1949 and was head of his department from 1954 until 1962. He then formed a private consultancy with other members of his department which did most of the New Town's planning and much architectural work until the Development Corporation was dissolved in 1980. Along with Eric Claxton, he was the person who had the biggest impact on the face of Stevenage.

The policy challenges of the late 1950s and early 1960s that confronted Vincent were substantial planning problems. The most obvious way to increase population was to build housing at higher densities. However, the more development occurred on the originally planned fairly low-density basis, averaging about 12 dwellings per acre (30 per hectare), the less scope there was to follow this option without densities a great deal higher on remaining sites. Limited infill higher-density development was possible on unbuilt pockets of land within existing neighbourhood areas. Another option was to rezone land from non-residential uses to housing. This might involve actually increasing the proportion of the designated area of the New Town that was to be built on by reducing its green belt and other open spaces. Finally, the most radical option was to expand the boundaries of the New Town.

All these options were, in varying degrees, adopted. Vincent saw advantages in a major expansion west of the new route of the A1 Great North Road (which had only finally bypassed the New Town in 1962).[82] His view was that such an extension would correct the original plan's often criticised lopsidedness that had put all housing on its eastern side. Crossman's rejection of the most ambitious expansion proposal saw this off but he did approve a small 100-acre (40-hectare) extension in the north-east. This was to be a new employment area, compensating for the rezoning of the northern part of the original western industrial zone for a seventh residential neighbourhood (Symonds Green). In addition, the planned populations of neighbourhoods 5 (Chells) and especially 6 (Pin Green) were expanded and built at higher densities.[83] A large new high-density area (St Nicholas), equivalent to a new neighbourhood, was added north of Pin Green in the 1970s and 1980s. New residential land was also added at the edges of some of the older neighbourhoods, especially Broadwater (neighbourhood 3) on the southern boundary. Small infill sites were also found in several areas.

Later neighbourhoods of the 1960s and 1970s

These last were, however, simply adjustments to areas that were already completed or significantly developed. More profound were the differences in the urban design and physical character of the planned neighbourhoods, particularly Pin Green. This was primarily because of the adoption of 'Radburn' residential layouts. Radburn was a residential area in New Jersey developed in the later 1920s as the first part of what was to have been an American garden city designed for the motor age (aborted after the Wall Street Crash of 1929).[84] Planned by American architects Clarence Stein and Henry Wright, the one area that was completed had a lasting influence on housing layouts and other aspects of planning, not least in Stevenage. Its key feature was that it completely separated vehicle and pedestrian access. One side of the house gave on to a service road to be used by cars and service vehicles, while the other side opened onto a purely pedestrian pathway system that (in the original Radburn) led to a glorious 'inner park' system with amenity, recreational and cultural space and buildings and safe access to schools, health clinics and local shops. Where roads had to be crossed, pedestrian subways (the first ever in residential areas) were provided.

It was an idea that began to appear in Britain in the post-war years (the first example, incidentally, designed by Gordon Stephenson at Wrexham in 1949).[85] From the later 1950s it became common in all New Towns, urged at Stevenage by Vincent and Claxton, who both knew the original Radburn.[86] The first sizeable area developed in this way was Elm Green in Chells neighbourhood from 1959. Virtually all areas designed from the 1960s to the mid-1970s then followed this pattern. It was applied on a very large scale in Pin Green (Figure 5.11), especially at areas such as Sishes End, Trotts Hill and, in a less rigid way, at nearby St Nicholas.

A format originated for a predominantly middle-income housing area such as Radburn became diluted when applied to public rental lower-income housing in the UK. Although Stein had himself designed lower-cost housing in this format, he evidently did not particularly like the British interpretation.[87] In part this was because its widespread adoption coincided with growing central

Figure 5.11 Housing of the1960s built on the Mowlem system at Pin Green in Radburn layouts. This shows the front of the houses, with no motor vehicles, which are served by cul-de-sac garage courts at the rear. At its best the visual effect is attractive, but can also be very confusing. (author photograph)

government pressures to build more cheaply and adopt new construction methods. In Stevenage, large areas with Radburn layouts were built using non-traditional methods, overwhelmingly a variant of the Mowlem system.[88] This used lightweight concrete poured in situ, the external walls faced with brick, tile or weatherboarding, the internal walls so smooth as to need no plastering. Alongside this, densities were also being increased. St Nicholas, for example, had an average density of 16 dwellings per acre (40 per hectare), a third higher than in the earliest neighbourhoods. Pedestrian pathways were narrowed and the inner park's amenity green space and play areas were much less spacious than in the original Radburn.

Overall, the Radburn layout created a quite new townscape where the traditional idea of the residential street, present still in earlier neighbourhoods, was abolished (Figure 5.12). The idea that houses would be aligned parallel to the road, separated from it by a front garden and a public pedestrian path alongside the road, was gone. Similarly, the conventional idea of a more attractive front house façade being the public face and the back of a house being more functional was completely confused. In Stevenage's Radburn layouts, the vehicle side often presented an austere public face of garage walls and doors, with the private gardens entirely hidden behind adjoining high walls. The pedestrian side, with the benefit of landscaped corridors, was much the more attractive but became the functional side of the house, with kitchen, bathrooms and toilet(s). In part, such changes from the 'pure' Radburn formula reflected the responses of residents of early schemes.

For the visitor, these types of layout, particularly at the higher densities, can be unsettling and it is easy to get lost, even more so in Radburn layouts, where garages were not directly linked to the respective gardens.[89] This was a problem, for example, for delivery vehicles, and the long garage culs-de-sac are much disliked by refuse disposal drivers because of the need for constant reversing. Yet the layout offers some real compensations in the form of public amenity. Where the densities are a little lower and where the topography also helps create greater visual interest, as in parts of Pin Green, the pedestrian sides at least can be very pleasing, the individual house gardens fronting onto landscaped corridors with mature trees. At times residents have shown some unwillingness to conform to some Radburn layouts, imposing their own behaviour patterns on its more rigid applications (something also experienced to a lesser extent at the original Radburn itself). Paved pathways were ignored if other desire lines for movement existed; children often enjoyed playing in the garage areas. On balance, those who opted to live and stay in them seem to have come to terms with them,

Figure 5.12 In Radburn layouts pedestrian underpasses entirely avoid road crossings, as here in Pin Green. There is, however, a pedestrian sidewalk alongside the road as well, which was avoided in the full Radburn concept but reflected actual pedestrian behaviour. The road safety records of such layouts are very good. (author photograph)

and there is no evidence that they have been shunned as more formerly rental housing has been sold (and resold) in recent years.

Yet experience also changed other things, not least the concept of the neighbourhood itself. From the outset, many professional planners had pondered whether 10,000 people was too many, especially when combined with fairly low housing densities. A single neighbourhood shopping centre was likely to be too distant for the convenience needs of houses farthest from it. Accordingly, sub-centres had proved necessary even in the early neighbourhoods. Over time, other factors came into play. As a response to Stevenage's increased population target, Pin Green was planned (in 1962) as a massive neighbourhood for 20,000 residents. Early assumptions about shopping and other social provision in neighbourhoods also had to change. The early neighbourhoods showed shoppers increasingly relying more heavily on the main town centre, wanting fewer local shops.

Gradually a new pattern became apparent in later neighbourhoods and housing areas, with rather less of the rigidities of the original plan and its 1940s' assumptions. Thus, there were no exact equivalents of the main neighbourhood centres within the early neighbourhoods. Pin Green secured something similar in size to earlier examples at the Oval, opened in 1969.[90] Unlike the early examples, however, it was located at the edge of the neighbourhood most distant from the main town centre, giving it the maximum customer catchment area and also making it available to adjacent areas beyond Pin Green itself. Combined with higher housing densities and a larger population living nearby, it was thought this would prove more viable than the original concept. By the time the New Town Development Corporation was wound up, the neighbourhood unit concept had become so blurred as to be barely recognisable, much less referred to in policy documents. The Oval, for example, was labelled as a 'district' rather than a neighbourhood centre. Nevertheless, something of the idea of grouping shops and service provision at convenient points alongside housing persists even in very recent development.

The spaces between

The use of the green spaces between and within the neighbourhoods was something that evolved over time. The Stephenson plan was largely indicative in this respect, pointing out existing amenity areas and broad possibilities rather than earmarking any particular locations.[91] It suggested a major town park on the high ground at Pin Green and another smaller one that retained the private park at Shephalbury. A key idea, however, was that the primary road corridors would be wide landscaped parkways, a planning idea that had developed in the interwar period, especially in the United States. This made the roads visually very attractive to drive along, while the absence of building development immediately along the sides of the roads meant they were not used for very short journeys within neighbourhoods. Yet their usefulness as parks for people to walk in and quietly enjoy was limited as motor traffic increased. This was acceptable around most neighbourhoods, particularly as actual local parks began to be completed during the 1960s at Town Hall Gardens, Elm Green in Chells and Hampson Park at Pin Green, with other smaller areas around the town. Others followed in the new neighbourhoods of the 1970s.[92]

None were to be the main park of the New Town, however. This opened in summer 1972 in the Fairlands Valley between Bedwell, Shephall and Broadwater. The valley was an especially attractive area, recognised as such in the 1946 Stephenson plan. Yet the original primary road proposals for the area scarcely seemed consistent with protecting and enhancing those qualities. Proposed road nine along the valley was removed in the 1949 master plan with the new intention that the area would remain in agricultural use, though with improved public access for walkers and cyclists. Those who grew up in Stevenage at this time remember the freedom and pleasure of playing unsupervised all day long during summer holidays in the area as it was then.[93] The problem was that, allocated in this way, the valley remained vulnerable to future development, a fate that began to look likely as pressures to increase the ultimate size of the town grew in the early 1960s. The people of Stevenage were not having this, however, and mounted a strident and very effective local opposition in 1961, resulting in the idea being dropped.[94]

In retrospect, there seems a certain inevitability about how, over the following years, a firm proposal for the New Town's major park emerged. Even so, it took some time for the idea to take hold. This was then embedded in the 1966 revised master plan, though the effect was counteracted by the reappearance in the same plan of the proposed primary road nine along the valley, albeit along an improved eastern route.[95] Another fierce local campaign of opposition followed which persuaded the highways authority, namely the county council, to keep deferring the actual building of the road. For its part, Stevenage council certainly wanted to be rid of any threat of this road that would so compromise the beautiful public space that it began to lay out in earnest in the early 1970s. As created, Fairlands Valley Park covers 120 acres (just under 49 hectares) including 17 acres (just under 7 hectares) of water, mainly as a large boating and fishing lake.[96] From the very outset it has been a hugely popular amenity for the town and surrounding area, hosting many activities both organised and informal.

Figure 5.13 The central pedestrianised shopping area with its iconic clock tower has become a symbol of Stevenage and the New Town movement generally. Yet it came about only after a great struggle involving people, planners, politicians and retailers. (author photograph)

The road proposal was only finally dropped in 1978, at last guaranteeing the tranquillity of the expansive green space which had by then been open for several years. The price of this, as the Corporation's engineers and planning consultants had argued in the 1966 plan, was greater traffic on nearby and less suitable roads. Yet the Corporation was no longer minded to press the argument, leaving the matter entirely to local decision. Had the road ever been built it would undoubtedly have had a blighting effect on what has, in so many ways, been Stevenage's crowning glory as a New Town. In recent years the park has seen many detailed enhancements[97] and it is today a public amenity of which Howard would surely have been immensely proud.

The town centre

Another key part of Stevenage New Town that ought perhaps to have been more of a crowning glory was the New Town's centre (Figure 5.13). Its development, which forms an important facet of New Town history, embroiled the town in great controversy because of its innovative design as the first fully pedestrianised planned town centre in Britain and among the first in the world when its first shops opened in 1958. Several older cities had slightly earlier precincts, notably Coventry and Rotterdam, though these formed only part of their central areas.[98] A fully pedestrianised centre had already opened in the Stockholm satellite town of Vällingby (somewhat smaller than Stevenage) in 1954. Its planners did not, however, have to contend with anything like the amount and variety of opposition experienced in Stevenage.

At first, the idea of a pedestrianised centre seemed set for speedy acceptance. No one seriously questioned that a new centre was necessary. The historic Old Town would have been ruined by attempting to redevelop it as the shopping and administrative centre for the far bigger town that was emerging. The main question, so it seemed, was where the new centre should be. Holliday, the first chief architect and planner, had had his doubts about whether the 1946 plan location was best, given that its catchment area was skewed to the New Town's eastern side. This was also a major controversy in the inquiry over the approved 1949 master plan. Yet Holliday's endorsement and elaboration of the 1946 plan concept of a pedestrianised centre went unchallenged. The then chairman, Monica Felton, was also keen. The next step, in 1950, was to commission Gordon Stephenson, with Holliday, to prepare preliminary proposals for such a town centre in the originally proposed location. Stephenson also added Clarence Stein, a distinguished American architect–planner with unique experience of planning for the separation of motor traffic and pedestrians.[99]

Notable as co-designer of the original Radburn, Stein was already intending to come to Europe to visit Stockholm when Stephenson seized the opportunity to involve him.

The three planners produced an ambitious and generously proportioned pedestrianised precinct plan which was widely approved locally in Stevenage and even, despite misgivings in its estates section, by the ministry.[100] After detailed adjustments, a more worked-up plan based on their proposals was initiated and seemed set for acceptance. By this time, however, for their various reasons, Felton, Holliday, Stephenson and Stein had all left the scene. When Thomas Bennett arrived as chairman he soon decided that a pedestrianised scheme would be commercially unviable, reflecting the opinions of major retailers at the time. Although he carried enough of the Board with him, many Development Corporation officials and a minority of the Board were unhappy. In Claxton's words: 'Everybody seemed determined that the town centre shopping centre should be wholly pedestrian – except that is for one man … the Chairman …'.[101]

The next chairman, Royden Dash, though instinctively sympathetic to commercial considerations, was also sensitive to the strength of feeling in Stevenage – old and new. His concern, however, was whether the Development Corporation could go back to the ministry having changed its mind yet again without looking ridiculous. He rationalised (perhaps bowing to the inevitable) that letting the pro-pedestrian centre movement build up a head of steam and then having a public meeting so it could be let off was the best tactic. This could then be used to orchestrate the reversal of the earlier stance. The meeting duly occurred in January 1954 and showed that the people of Stevenage who expressed a preference, like the district council, were strongly in favour of a pedestrianised centre. However, ministry officials, not wanting to irritate the Treasury, were in a cautious frame of mind. The Board of the Development Corporation itself remained divided, with estates officials worried about the difficulties of securing major retailers to 'anchor' the centre. Yet they also recognised that lingering uncertainty about what kind of centre would be built was an even worse position from which to negotiate with retailers.

Despite the uncertainties, the Board requested that Vincent and Claxton prepare a revised plan that would be less frightening to retailers than the expansive Stephenson/Holliday/Stein layout. Visits by Board members and officials of the Development Corporation to the nearly completed Lijnbaan, the pedestrianised shopping area of Rotterdam, and Vällingby also helped calm nerves about the retailing viability of a pedestrianised scheme.[102] (The visit, interestingly, was at

Figure 5.14 Such was the recurrent pressure to allow motor vehicles into the centre that the more spacious earlier plans were abandoned in favour of a rather narrow mall that could never subsequently be converted into a motor street. The centre thus suffered for being an innovator. It never attracted a major department store, yet it remains a focal point for the town's people. (author photograph)

the suggestion of Terry Kennedy, one of original 1946 Stephenson Plan team, who, by 1954, was chief planner in the ministry.)[103] The scheme Vincent and his staff, mainly Ray Gorbing, and Claxton produced was altogether more compact than earlier proposals and had much closer integration with the bus station. The pedestrian routes were also narrower and public squares smaller. These features were to be a source of later criticism, because they gave a cramped feel to the shopping centre. Yet, at the time these features had the advantage of discouraging any future vacillation at Board level over whether to allow conventional traffic access by rendering it physically impossible (Figure 5.14).

The ministry continued for a few months to think that it could make a better job of it than Vincent, Claxton and their team members, with their combination of boldness and caution. Eventually, however the latter's proposals were approved at the end of 1954.[104] Following further refinement and sometimes tortuous discussions between letting agents and major retailers, construction began in mid-1956 and the first shops opened two years later.[105] By late 1959 more than 100 shops were established in the centre and were soon thriving. Vincent later recalled the continuing opposition of the retailers more generally, even as the centre was taking shape:

I remember addressing the Multiple Traders Association on our proposals for Stevenage and they just thought I was round the bend. They thought I was one of these ... long haired ideologists that hadn't really a clue what it was all about you see and had a bit of a rough time quite frankly but I was proved right. In fact so much so that one of the big advocates of non pedestrian centres, one of the Directors of the firm that advised many, many people said to me in a letter, which I thought was very nice, he said Mr Vincent you were right and I was wrong .... This was in 1970ish .... When of course all the town centres were being thought of being changed to pedestrian centres.[106]

In Stevenage itself further shops and other activities followed during the 1960s, although the uncertainties about whether and by how much Stevenage might expand also affected the scale of this. The cautious thinking which had constrained the original conception in the 1950s also began to cause other problems. Contrary to the original thinking, important offices and public buildings and even the town centre gardens are now separate from the pedestrianised retail core, east of a major 'barrier' road, St George's Way. During the 1960s the Development Corporation became eager for more office development in the town centre.[107] Initially the Corporation itself acted as developer, and the occupiers were often public sector agencies. Yet office growth proved increasingly difficult to attain when central government introduced national controls comparable to those for factory development in 1965. An office development permit (ODP), similar to the IDC, was henceforth needed and, once more, the Greater London New Towns were not seen as priorities.

This control could also damage the viability of other developments, particularly where commercial developers were involved (as was increasingly the case by the 1970s). The problem was that office rents were often the most reliably profitable ones and could hold the key to securing other, less profitable aspects of development (such as car parking and even more ambitious retailing projects). Unless the office development could go ahead, the other aspects would not. This thwarted a project for a major department store on a former car park in the early 1970s. However, more predictably profitable retailing developments could themselves be the key to securing other needed developments. In 1973, for example, a major store development by Tesco effectively facilitated the creation of a large cinema.

Also in the same year, Stevenage's new railway station was finally opened on the western edge of the new town centre, replacing the old station on the northern side of the old town. Immediately across Lytton Way from the station, at an important entry point into the centre, the Borough Council began to build a large arts and leisure centre.[108] This was funded on a then unconventional sale-and-leaseback deal with a merchant bank, which reduced the capital needed to fund such facilities, spreading the cost over a long period. (This kind of funding arrangement became more common in New Towns as public expenditure began to be squeezed during the 1970s.) The new centre filled what for at least ten years had been seen as two major gaps in the now much bigger Stevenage, limiting how far the New Town could really mature as a community. Although there was no enthusiasm on the part of their respective local organisations in favour of bringing arts and leisure together in one building, funding either of them separately proved impossible. Neither the Development Corporation nor the local Arts and Sports Trusts were able to do this until the council stepped in. The Arts and Leisure Centre, incorporating the Gordon Craig theatre, was opened in 1975 and remains a major resource for the town, albeit now without the much criticised bright orange plastic panelling so redolent of the period that originally adorned its exterior.

As these and other cultural and leisure facilities appeared, Stevenage's town centre began to come of age. In the longer term it has successfully served the town and, to some extent, the wider hinterland, even though the quality and mix of its shops have never given the town any real distinctiveness. It is as if retailers have never quite forgiven Stevenage for having the temerity in the 1950s to be a pioneer. Since the 1980s the architectural integrity and stylistic consistency of the shopping centre has also been compromised. The 1988 designation of the original core of the pedestrianised shopping precinct as a conservation area has helped protect this,[109] but more recent adjoining developments, such as the Forum and the Plaza, reflect strikingly different architectural and urban design thinking and use different materials. These later developments have also produced a northward shift of retailing within the town centre, triggering some deterioration of the southern parts of the original pedestrian area. Local planners have tried to limit off-centre car-based retailing development to stores that do not directly compete with those in the town centre, for example at the Roaring Meg Retail Park in Monkswood, opened from 1984, yet there have inevitably been some impacts on the town centre. Since then, there has also been even more off-centre growth, including a leisure park and occasional superstores elsewhere in the town (about which a little more in Chapter 8). Even so, the square and the northern part of what is now the 'historic' New Town centre still shows some vitality and is extensively used by the New Towners and the generations which have followed.

Who were the New Towners?

The coming of the new Stevenage centre was an important landmark in the creation of a largely self-contained New Town. Those who moved to the New Town and followed this important new branch of Howard's path could now live, work and find within it all the services and leisure enjoyments that they needed on a regular basis. It is clear that these goals were met relatively quickly, certainly compared with the two garden cities, although short-term delays (such as those for the town centre) meant that it did not always seem so at the time.

On the main indicator of self-containment, local employment, the achievement was very impressive. As the in-commuting building workers got their houses and the new factories came during the 1950s, the degree of employment self-containment rose.[110] By 1966 76 per cent of jobs in Stevenage were filled by its own resident workers. Most of the rest came from nearby districts, particularly the Hitchin area. Just 15 per cent of Stevenage resident workers commuted out, the lowest proportion of any of the Greater London New Towns, which all (except Hatfield, where the equivalent figures were very misleading, as will be shown) performed extremely well in this respect. Although growing car-based mobility and other factors soon began to affect this pattern, it has been a relative characteristic that has persisted.

One factor which produced this proximity of work to home was that, to get a Development Corporation house in Stevenage, it was almost imperative to have a job there or, at least, employment skills that were relevant to local labour market needs. By 1978 job-related categories had accounted for 74 per cent of all housing allocations, and in the earlier years that dominance had been near-total. Most new arrivals, preferably (though not invariably) those who had previously lived in London, were directly nominated for housing by an employer.[111] Central government also placed great faith in the Linkage Scheme (from 1949) and the Industrial Selection Scheme (from 1953), later known as the New and Expanded Towns Scheme (NETS).[112] These were intended to identify suitably skilled workers from London who could be matched through the labour exchange system with the New Town job markets. In practice, the schemes were always rather cumbersome and unpopular with employers, and the NETS was effectively abandoned by the late 1970s.

However, employer nomination and the various schemes described above had important exclusionary social consequences, especially during the 1950s and 1960s.[113] Thus the low proportion of unskilled workers in Stevenage (and its fellow New Towns) was striking. There were simply far fewer unskilled jobs being provided in the new industries than existed in the more congested parts of Greater London, whose multiple problems the New Towns were intended to ease. The overwhelming emphasis in housing allocation, especially in the early years, was also on male employment. The assumption was that men would be the breadwinners who would support their wives (and children).[114] The ability to get a house thus largely reflected the man's job; only slowly was the emerging reality of women working outside the home and being important contributors to household income recognised. The system also inherently discouraged retired or disabled migrants. However, this aspect was certainly eased to allow older or more dependent relatives to join their extended families, often at times when directly work-related housing demands were lower. By 1978 8 per cent of Stevenage Development Corporation's total housing allocations had been to parents of New Town residents, a proportion that had grown sharply during the 1970s.

Finally, the system was also racially exclusive, creating a persistent underrepresentation of non-white ethnic minorities in the New Towns. In part this reflected the reality that, especially in the 1950s and 1960s, many Commonwealth immigrants either did not have or were not recognised as having suitable skills for most New Town jobs. This contrasted with the Irish building workers, many unskilled, who moved to Stevenage to work and, for some, to settle.[115] As far as the more recent Commonwealth immigrants were concerned, they were also disadvantaged by local housing policies in the 'exporting' areas of London. These based housing entitlement partly on length of residence in that area, something which then reproduced itself in New Town housing allocations. Over time, however, this has changed, especially since the 1970s. Yet even in 1991 just 3.8 per cent of Stevenage's population was non-white.[116] Two decades later (on a broader definition of non-white, including mixed race) it was over 12.2 per cent.[117] Yet this remains around two percentage points below the national average, and the differential is much bigger compared with many 'normal' urban areas in prosperous regions. In nearby Watford, for example, 30.2 per cent of inhabitants are non-white.

It is, of course, arguable that all these social characteristics would have arisen anyway. Young upper-working-class families were likely to be more desirous to change and improve their lives than those with less to offer. Even as more women went out to work, men's income was typically higher, so individual family housing decisions would almost certainly have been based largely on that. Historically, the old and disabled have rarely (though not invariably) formed the vanguard of migration flows. And there were (for a variety of reasons) strong clustering tendencies apparent among recent Commonwealth migrants that affected their willingness to disperse. But the point here is that the way that

Stevenage and other New Towns were populated *reinforced* these factors. By the 1970s there were mounting criticisms that the New Towns had 'creamed off' the more able and ambitious working-class populations from the big cities, leaving a more dependent and problem-prone population behind.[118] The more extreme criticism was that the New Towns had created the newly recognised 'inner city problem'. Yet this was wildly exaggerated because most of the jobs that came to the New Towns were not the result of factory relocation from inner-city areas and most of the people who left inner-city areas did not end up in New Towns. But perhaps they had not ultimately been quite the solution to the (changing) problems of the big cities that Abercrombie, following Howard, had envisaged.

Much of the close relationship between employment and housing depended on housing being rented from the Development Corporation; the system could not have been so tightly controlled if housing had been rented from private landlords. Even the Stevenage local authority was obliged to give priority to its existing population (although over time the meaning of this changed, gradually coming to include children of New Towners). Still less was there a possibility of controlling the allocation of housing for owner occupation, which nationally was becoming an increasingly popular aspiration. By the later 1960s there was a growing recognition that the New Towns were anomalous in this respect. Early in Stevenage's development, the Development Corporation realised that many of the New Town's managers and professional workers were choosing *not* to live there, and increasingly it was feared that its better-off working class would follow suit if they could not buy housing in Stevenage. The same was true for most other New Towns.

In 1966 central government policy shifted decisively to favour a 50:50 housing tenure balance in all New Towns, similar to the national average at that time.[119] There were accordingly more moves to promote private housebuilding in New Towns, although major housing developers were not easily persuaded that building-for-sale markets in places such as Stevenage were going to be sufficiently strong to warrant really large-scale investments. The more obvious route was to allow sales of Development Corporation housing, something which was encouraged in the New Towns before the Thatcher government's 'right-to-buy' policy was introduced in 1980. After some initial hesitancy in both the application of national policy and local resident responses, the effect in Stevenage during the 1970s was nothing short of spectacular. In 1972 just 16.1 per cent of the town's households were owner-occupiers. By 1978 it was 37.8 per cent, the most dramatic rise in any New Town. Since then, sales of both former rented housing and new private building have grown. In 2011, 58.3 per cent of

Stevenage households were owner-occupiers, still below but much closer to the national average of 63.6 per cent (which itself is now shrinking).

How far did the newcomers shape Stevenage?

The appearance of a widening 'property-owning democracy' in Stevenage in the later twentieth century was certainly an important shift, with other changes allowing a greater flexibility in the way more of its people lived their lives. It is tempting but misleading to see New Town history simply in terms of, first, a planned, collectivist era in which the people of Stevenage were passive recipients of benevolent actions by planners and bureaucrats, followed by an individualist era in which its inhabitants were increasingly free to pursue their own dreams in their own ways. Rather, as this section will show, the people of the new Stevenage exerted a growing influence on the way their emerging hometown took shape from a very early stage in the New Town's history.

The first signs of this were evident in the way that the New Town community cohered. Those who planned and developed Stevenage and the other New Towns incorporated many planning concepts that were intended to promote social cohesion.[120] In particular, the neighbourhood unit was seen as a way of both organising the localised provision of public and private services and, in a looser sense, creating a quasi-village unit (rather a large village of 10,000 people in Stevenage's case) that gave a local social and physical identity to the area.[121] At a more detailed level the layout of housing areas was intended to reinforce that sense of local identity. In other ways, the Development Corporation's officers did much to encourage social interaction to breathe life into these physical arrangements. Thus they encouraged newcomers by, for example, organising early social events and ensuring that people did not feel isolated during the early weeks after their arrival in Stevenage.

In practice, the sense of community grew very rapidly, but most signs are that this was largely for unplanned reasons.[122] There were growing professional doubts about the all-embracing idea of the neighbourhood unit and, even for those who accepted it, there were doubts about its proper size. Whereas the 10,000 unit adopted by Stevenage's planners matched the population threshold needed for some local services, it did not fit others. The standards had been based on the advice given by other ministries concerned with education, health, transport and so on to the Ministry of Town and Country Planning, the Abercrombie Greater London planning team and the Reith Committee in the 1940s. Stephenson and his team had played a central role in collating and formulating these standards and reckoned that the pattern they proposed at Stevenage in 1946 constituted the 'best fit'. Yet some other 1940s New Towns deliberately used smaller neighbourhoods, reckoning that the local 'frame of reference' for local shops, primary schools and health care would be less than 10,000. The reality of some of this was also accepted in Stevenage. For example, in the Broadwater neighbourhood local shops were developed at Roebuck, Oaks Cross and Bragbury End as well as in the main neighbourhood centre at Marymead.

By the time the 1960s New Towns (or later local centres in Stevenage) were being planned it was realised that changes in retailing and mobility favoured larger units. Quite apart from this, it was also difficult in the early days to ensure that the neighbourhood units worked as intended because there were usually delays in finishing the non-housing elements of the areas, so that schools (the responsibility of the County Council), local shops and other facilities were not always provided to match growth. School catchment areas sometimes failed to match neighbourhood boundaries,[123] and children had to attend schools more distant from their homes than intended. The same applied to shops, medical facilities, churches, pubs and much else.

What actually created social cohesion were largely the common experiences of people who had chosen to seek a new life in a different setting.[124] Many, especially women with young children or expecting babies, missed the emotional and practical support networks of their families, which spurred the creation of various groups, ostensibly for other reasons but also providing ways for women to socialise and find babysitters.[125] New arrivals did not, on the whole, cringe shyly in their much appreciated but still strange new homes waiting for the Stevenage Social Development Officer to invite them to a welcoming event. Such activities played a part, but could not be said to be formative of social cohesion. Mother and baby care, sometimes at mobile health clinics in the neighbourhoods, provided another opportunity for meeting up.[126] But in the main newcomers embraced their new life eagerly and quickly began to interact with their neighbours. The neat fencing that began to be provided to clearly separate individual gardens created an individualised residential environment very different from what people had come from in London. Despite some rumours that it was deliberately intended to reduce gossiping, the fences were not a barrier preventing neighbours from talking to each other.[127]

Relations with the old Stevenage were not quite so fluid or positive. Many tradesmen welcomed the new business they brought, especially in the Old Town, which necessarily served as the main shopping centre in the early years. But, after the town's traumatic birth, some original inhabitants could not come to terms with the dramatic change that was underway.[128] Some looked askance at the Londoners who trekked from their new houses over still unmade roads and pavements to buy the necessaries of life on the Old Town High Street, which did not encourage the newcomers themselves to be particularly forthcoming. Yet the opposition gradually softened (probably more quickly than in Hemel Hempstead, as we will see in Chapter 6). As one newcomer later reflected:

> Other than using the shops I don't think we had a lot to do with the people in the Old Town. I think it was later I began to get to know people .... We didn't find any hostility towards us, it was more a gentle leg-pull than anything really serious. I think I always used to explain to the people in the Old Town just how grateful we were to move out of bomb-ravaged London into a new town with a new house. I realised what they had given up.[129]

Gradually the interests of new and old residents began to grow closer together, especially around broader concerns such as the nature of the new Stevenage town centre and the protection of the Fairlands Valley.

The lack of properly surfaced roads and pavements, accessible services, street lighting, post and telephone boxes, bus services and so on in the early days were themselves triggers for early community engagement and collective action.[130] In 'normal' towns the local council would have been the obvious target for such complaints, but in Stevenage there was a delay before electoral wards were formed for the new areas. Moreover, the unelected Development Corporation had usurped many of the roles normally overseen by local democracy. In these circumstances new 'grass-roots' organisations soon appeared to voice complaints about all aspects of New Town development.[131] From 1951 Residents' Associations appeared, serving local housing areas within the neighbourhoods. They were quickly followed by a New Town-wide Residents' Federation that was recognised as a negotiating body by the Development Corporation in 1954. Initially the Corporation leadership viewed the Federation as excessively politicised in its campaigns (though much of what it and the Associations were doing was holding the Corporation to its own master plan). The Federation's lively monthly tenants' organisation news-sheet, the *Stevenage Echo*, first appeared in 1952, initially as simple mimeographed sheets. It soon got under general manager Alan Duff's skin.

We have already noted how building workers, who dominated the earliest newcomers, quickly emerged as community leaders. They did so principally through the Associations and the Federation, which were soon being led by figures such as Alf Luhman (a carpenter), Mick Cotter and Fred Udell (bricklayers). Their workplace disputes were chiefly with contractors, but also to some extent with the Development Corporation. Because their offer of a house tenancy was conditional on working in Stevenage, the union leaders argued that the Corporation had a moral responsibility to ensure they were not exploited as a result. Such early skirmishes made the union activists into natural leaders for the new Associations and the Federation, which began to challenge the Corporation on many other matters.[132] However, other New Towners also played their part, including factory workers and housewives, who most directly faced the early daily challenges of living on the raw new estates. Some, most notably Hilda Lawrence, who edited the *Echo*, also became prominent figures in Stevenage's life.[133]

Other bodies also played important early roles in community formation, including the Community Centre Committees, which were established to run the new social centres that were appearing in the neighbourhoods from 1953, and the Town Forum, also formed in 1953. This was a body which grew from an initiative of the widely respected Development Corporation housing manager, Mary Tabor. It encouraged a more informed debate about Stevenage's development and organised lectures by Development Corporation officers and other professionals. Although there was overlapping of those involved in these various organisations, they differed in their social character. Generally the Development Corporation found the Federation and Residents' Associations more challenging than the other bodies, which it had helped nurture.

Towards the end of the 1950s, however, the original Tenants' Associations and the Federation began to fade as active agencies challenging the Development Corporation. In part this reflected an easing of the problems as the Corporation and building contractors responded to the complaints and learned how to avoid them arising. Material shortages eased during the 1950s, so that residents no longer had to wait quite so long for pavements or made-up roads. Social facilities also improved as local schools, community centres and pubs began to open. However, an important change in governance occurred from the later 1950s, as the New Towners turned Stevenage Urban District Council into a body that more effectively responded to and articulated their concerns.

Earlier in the decade building union activists had already drawn it into disputes with contractors, alerting the Council's building inspectors to the poor workmanship associated with skill dilution.[134] Now the new community leaders, with building workers in the vanguard, began themselves to become councillors. By the end of the 1950s, almost half the twelve-strong Urban District Council comprised building workers.[135] The first was Alf Luhman, but Fred Udell, Con Carey, Mick Cotter and others soon followed.[136] So too did other newcomers, such as Hilda Lawrence and her husband Bill, an engineer in an electronics factory who later worked for British Aerospace. Another important figure who came through the Residents' Associations to the council was Stan Munden, a worker at English Electric. Both Mick Cotter and Hilda Lawrence later served on the county council.[137] So significant were these two as local leaders that they were invited on to the Development Corporation Board in 1964 and 1965 respectively, serving until it was wound up in 1980.

Although some industrial workers and others played a part, no other group was as significant in Stevenage's new local leadership as the building workers. In part their early arrival and their direct role in shaping the New Town put them uniquely into this position, but this effect was clearly greater in Stevenage than in Hertfordshire's other New Towns. This was partly because it was more completely a New Town than were the others, where stronger existing identities persisted. Yet the collective strength of the building workers in Stevenage and the individual calibre of several of the local union leaders also gave this particular New Town a unique character that other New Towns did not have to such an extent. Politically speaking, their presence gave Stevenage Urban District and, after 1974, Borough Council an overwhelming Labour dominance. The builders especially brought a more radical variety of Labour, forged partly by working alongside influential Communists such as Jim Collman. This contrasted with the more traditional moderate brand of Labour represented by Philip Ireton (who left the party in 1981 to join the short-lived Social Democratic Party), with whom they had sometimes crossed swords in early disputes over schools and other matters.[138] It also espoused radical causes that did not always sit easily with the interests of other Stevenage workers. In 1959, for example, the Amalgamated Union of Building Trade Workers organised a strike to highlight the increasing nuclear militarisation of Stevenage's aerospace factories.[139]

Of course, community is not simply about the emergence of leaders. Stevenage's community life embraced many activities outside politics or trade unionism. Space does not permit any detailed treatment, but we can note the blossoming of cultural and sporting activities, which were to some extent fostered by the Development Corporation and later the Council as the formal institutions of the New Town. But they also rested on considerable voluntary efforts by arts and sports organisations that had emerged out of the New Town's people. And, as the children of Stevenage newcomers grew up with more disposable income than their parents had had, they embraced the burgeoning youth culture of the 1960s and 1970s. In 1968 the New Town was used as a setting for the feature film *Here We Go Round the Mulberry Bush*,[140] which portrayed a young population willing to embrace the latest, more revealing fashions, louder popular music and less inhibited dancing and, importantly, with the optimism and money to do so.

This was certainly no equivalent of the conscious attempts to find new ways to dress and live that occurred among the earnest early residents of Letchworth. Nor is there any reason to suppose that this loosening of morality or willingness to embrace social change was any more pronounced in Stevenage than many other places. But Stevenage New Town's very identity as an essentially young town, less obviously subject to the traditional order of things, made it an appropriate setting to portray these shifts. The film, it must be said, had no great artistic merit and was not even the best feature film set in a New Town.[141] Ultimately, though, its many scenes at readily identifiable locations around Stevenage give a unique and valuable picture of the New Town when it was, like the film's main characters, beginning to move towards adulthood.

Conclusion

Stevenage was the first New Town and most other first-generation New Towns, especially those built around Greater London, developed in a similar way. It had, of course, its own unique features and its early years were marked by a series of blunders, many reflecting its role as the prototype, and accidents that affected no other New Town to quite the same extent. It was also arguably more completely a New Town than almost any other Greater London New Town (except perhaps Harlow): that is, its previous identity, though fiercely defended, was ultimately more completely overwhelmed by the fact of its becoming a New Town. It is also a place that still proudly identifies itself as the first New Town. Unlike their equivalents in many of the others, its local historians have put the experience of being a New Town at the very heart of its story. Its council planners have, also to an unusual extent, seen the physical essence of the New Town as something that is worth conserving, evidenced by designated Conservation Areas for the town centre and in several neighbourhoods.

None of this is to claim that Stevenage, now a town of around 85,000 people, does not continue (or need to continue) to evolve and change (Figure 5.15). The last chapter will consider how successful the New Towns, especially Stevenage and the others to be examined in the next chapter, have been in the long term. Certainly, national economic fortunes, social aspirations and political fashions have changed since 1946 and even since 1980. In the early twenty-first century New Towns are primarily remembered, rightly or wrongly, as expensive and overly planned 'top-down' exercises in urban development. Scarcely anyone would now see them as exact models for future development. Yet, as the

Figure 5.15 Mural created to harness the youthful energy and creativity in St Nicholas, one of the last of the New Town neighbourhoods. It also reminds us that Stevenage, like any other town, is more than just the result of its planning and building; it continues each day to be reshaped by the lives and actions of its people. (author photograph)

experience of Stevenage amply shows, they were also testaments to a truly noble and, at the time, widely accepted early post-war belief: that it was possible and worthwhile to give ordinary working people a decent home and setting for their lives that did not simply depend on their individual abilities to compete in the market. In large numbers, they grasped that opportunity and made new lives for themselves and their families. They were part of a profound post-war social change that was occurring across Britain and whose full significance we have barely begun to grasp.[142]

The age was a different one to that of Ebenezer Howard, one that embraced the state as a benevolent agent of human welfare in a way that he never did. But the grandiosity of the vision behind Stevenage and those New Towns that came after was fully in the spirit of Howard, a worthy and bold step on what has become, to date, the most important variant of the peaceful path. It was, as we have seen, a project only partly realised, though more completely than was the original Garden City vision. Since 1980, when Stevenage Development Corporation was dissolved, opinions about the New Towns have shifted, until recently for the worse. Yet, unless we can equal or better them, the lessons of Stevenage remain ones that we should remember and from which we can certainly learn.

Notes

1   Cullingworth, *Environmental planning: vol. III*, p. 603.

2   NA HLG 91/74, S.L.G. Beaufoy Memo, 4.4.1946.

3   NA HLG 91/267, Memo S.L.G. Beaufoy–G.L. Pepler, 16.2.1945.

4   *Town Planning Review*, 83/3 (2012) (Special Issue on Gordon Stephenson), especially J. Gregory and D.L.A. Gordon, 'Introduction: Gordon Stephenson, planner and civic designer', pp. 269–78 and Ward, 'Gordon Stephenson'.

5   J. Balchin, *The first new town: an autobiography of the Stevenage Development Corporation 1946–1980* (Stevenage, 1980), pp. 65–6; M. Ashby and D. Hills, *Stevenage: a history from Roman times to the present day* (Lancaster, 2010), p. 138.

6   Stephenson and DeMarco, *On a Human Scale*, pp. 82–96; Interview with Sir P. Shepheard in Planning Exchange, *New Town Record*, DVD, (Glasgow, 1995). Now available from <http://www.idoxgroup.com/knowledge-services/idox-information-service/the-new-towns-record.html>; E. Claxton, *The hidden Stevenage: the creation of the substructure of Britain's first new town* (Lewes, 1992), passim.

7   NA HLG 91/80, Industrial Activity in Stevenage January 1945.

8   Stephenson and DeMarco, *On a Human Scale*, p. 94.

9   LUSCA, D307A/1/1/1/2, Ministry of Town and Country Planning, Stevenage – New Town Report on Planning and Development Proposals, 31 July 1946.

10 E. Claxton, 'The cycle and pedestrian ways of Stevenage', in H. Rees and C. Rees (eds), *The history makers: the story of the early days of Stevenage new town* (Stevenage, 1991), pp. 60–65.

11 H. Orlans, *Stevenage: a sociological study of a new town* (London, 1952), pp. 5–76

12 NA HLG 91/267, G.L. Pepler Memo, 24.7.1945.

13 NA HLG 91/74, S.L.G. Beaufoy Memo, 4.4.1946.

14 Ashby and Hills, *Stevenage*, pp. 40–46.

15 NA HLG 91/74, Stevenage UDC 1946–47 Council, 18.4.1946.

16 E.M. Forster, 'The challenge of our time', *The Listener*, 11 April 1946, as reproduced in E.M. Forster, *Two cheers for democracy* (Harmondsworth, 1965), p. 68.

17 NA HLG 91/74, S.L.G. Beaufoy Memo, 4.4.1946.

18 NA HLG 91/74, S.L.G. Beaufoy, Memo, 27.4.1946.

19 NA HLG 91/77, L. Silkin annotation of F. Hellings(?) Memo, 11.4.1946.

20 NA HLG 91/77, typescript newspaper story for *Manchester Guardian*, 7.5.1946.

21 NA HLG 91/77, Text of speech by minister at Stevenage 7.5.1946, 19.

22 NA HLG 91/77, typescript newspaper story for *Manchester Guardian*, 7.5.1946.

23 NA HLG 91/77, Text of speech by Minister at Stevenage 7.5.1946, 19–20.

24 Cullingworth, *Environmental planning: vol. III*, pp. 25–6.

25 NA HLG 91/74, Letter G.V. Berry, Clerk of Stevenage U.D.C.–Secretary Ministry of TandCP, 22.5.1946.

26 Ward, 'Introduction', p. xxiv.

27 NA HLG 91/74, Report of Public Inquiry…, 25.10.1946, 8–9.

28 NA CAB 124/870, Stevenage New Town (Designation) Order, 8.11.1946.

29 Cullingworth, *Environmental planning: vol. III*, p. 30.

30 Ashby and Hills, *Stevenage*, pp. 58–59.

31 Orlans, *Stevenage*, pp. 67–70.

32 NA HLG 91/542, especially L. Silkin, Memorandum on the Stevenage decision (undated).

33 Cited Orlans, *Stevenage*, p. 71.

34 Balchin, *The first new town*, pp. 15–29.

35 This has long been suspected. Yet neither of them ever openly admitted this or left any private papers to indicate the nature of their relationship. However, the erstwhile planner of Peterlee,

Berthold Lubetkin, was a soulmate of Felton's and a fellow Marxist. He kept a diary of his time at Peterlee which casts much light on the Silkin–Felton relationship, based substantially on his conversations with Felton and his presence at some of their private meetings. It indicates, for example, that Silkin suggested marriage to her in 1948 (his first wife having recently died). RIBA Archives, *Berthold Lubetkin Papers*, LUB 15/20/1, passim, especially 30.6.1948; 8.8. 1948. See also M. Clapson, 'The rise and fall of Monica Felton, British town planner and peace activist, 1930s to 1950s', *Planning Perspectives*, 30/2 (2015), pp. 211–29.

36   Balchin, *The first new town*, pp. 31–2.

37   Ward, 'Gordon Stephenson', pp. 279–96.

38   *New Town Record*, Sir P. Shepheard, interview.

39   NA 91/474, Report of Public Inquiry on Master Plan 18th and 19th October 1949.

40   Balchin, *The first new town*, pp. 134–5.

41   *New Town Record*, Sir P. Shepheard, interview.

42   Orlans, *Stevenage*, p. 225.

43   Balchin, *The first new town*, pp. 22–41.

44   Ibid., pp. 109–11.

45   Ibid., p. 153.

46   B. Mullan, *Stevenage Ltd: aspects of the planning and politics of Stevenage new town 1945–1978* (London, 1980), p. 332.

47   NA HLG 91/427. Memo G.R. Coles, 26.9.1952.

48   Geo Wimpey and Co, *No Fines Concrete* (London, c.1954), especially pp. 18–19.

49   C. Wall, L. Clarke, C. McGuire and M. Brockmann, *Building a community – construction workers in Stevenage 1950–1970* (London, 2011), especially pp. 21–3.

50   Wall et al., *Building a community*, p. 17.

51   The Irish Network Stevenage (edited by T. Barnes) *From the Emerald Isle to the green belt of Stevenage: an oral history of Irish settlers in Stevenage* (Stevenage, 2013).

52   LUSCA, D307A/1/1/1/2, Ministry of Town and Country Planning, Stevenage – New Town Report on Planning and Development Proposals, 31st July 1946 13–14; NA HLG 91/80, Industrial Activity in Stevenage, Note by Joan Campbell, 9.2.1945.

53   Balchin, *The first new town*, pp. 183–91.

54   A.R. Adams, *Good company* (Stevenage, 1976), p. 58.

55   Mullan, *Stevenage Ltd*, pp. 222–34.

56   Balchin, *The first new town*, p. 186.

57   Mullan, *Stevenage Ltd*, pp. 323–4.

58   Cullingworth, *Environmental planning: vol. III*, pp. 543–63.

59   Balchin, *The first new town*, pp. 188–90.

60   Ashby and Hills, *Stevenage*, pp. 153–4; 309.

61   Ibid., pp. 155–6; 311.

62   M. Aldridge, *The new towns: a policy without a programme* (London, 1978), pp. 117–24; Mullan, *Stevenage Ltd*, pp. 26–30.

63   Built Environment Advisory and Management Service, *A review of Stevenage Conservation Areas* (Stevenage, 2005), pp. 37–59.

64   Built Environment Advisory and Management Service, *Stevenage Conservation Areas*, pp. 59–69.

65   Built Environment Advisory and Management Service, *Broadwater (Marymead) conservation appraisal 2009* (Stevenage, 2009).

66   The designatory letters and numbers were simply a way to differentiate house designs, allowing them to be signified briefly on estate layout drawings with immediate cross-reference to drawings of the actual dwellings.

67   J. Campbell, 'Marymead Shopping Centre c1960' <http://www.ourstevenage.org.uk/page_id__99.aspx?path=0p164p61p>, accessed 17 August 2015.

68   H. Rees and C. Rees (eds), *The history makers: the story of the early days of Stevenage new town* (Stevenage, 1991), remains the best account of this phase. See also G. Clements, 'Matchstick trees and builders' rubble' <http://www.ourstevenage.org.uk/page_id__4.aspx?path=0p3p>, accessed 17 August 2015.

69   G. Clements, 'More great memories of Stevenage from the Good Friends Group' <http://www.ourstevenage.org.uk/page_id__342.aspx?path=0p3p>, accessed 17 August 2015.

70   M. Cousins, 'Early residents (viii)', in H. Rees and C. Rees (eds), *The history makers: the story of the early days of Stevenage new town* (Stevenage, 1991), pp. 112–14, quotation from p. 112.

71   K. Cope, 2013 [orig. 1999]: Wonderful, quoted in M. Ashby, *Voices of Stevenage* (Stroud, 2013), p. 103.

72   For example, M. Cotter, *Memories of Michael Cotter* (Stevenage, 1986).

73   M. MacLoed, 'Early residents (iii)', in H. Rees and C. Rees (eds), *The history makers: the story of the early days of Stevenage new town* (Stevenage, 1991), pp. 77–82, quotation from p. 78.

74   T. Sultzbach, 'Early residents (i)', in H. Rees and C. Rees (eds), *The history makers: the story of the early days of Stevenage new town* (Stevenage, 1991), pp. 69–74; C. Rees [unpaginated illustrative section between pp. 104–5] in H. Rees and C. Rees (eds), *The history makers: the story of the early days of Stevenage new town* (Stevenage, 1991), reproduces her exchange of correspondence on the earwig problem with R.S. MacDougall 14.8.1962 and 20.8.1962.

75   G. Drackford, 'Early residents (vi)', in H. Rees and C. Rees (eds), *The history makers: the story of the early days of Stevenage new town* (Stevenage, 1991), pp. 93–102.

76   Balchin, *The first new town*, pp. 125–49. Claxton, *The hidden Stevenage*, pp. 135–204.

77   HALS, CNT/ST/17/1/7 Stevenage Development Corporation, *Road System in the New Town*, 22.7.1949, 5–8; Balchin, *The first new town*, pp. 138–40.

78   F.J. Osborn and A. Whittick, *New towns: their origins, achievements and progress* (London, 1977), p. 122; Balchin, *The first new town*, pp. 72–86.

79   Ashby and Hills, *Stevenage*, pp. 159–68.

80   Ministry of Housing and Local Government, *The South East study 1961–1981* (London, 1964), especially p. 75.

81   Ashby and Hills, *Stevenage*, p. 137; Balchin, *The first new town*, pp. 70–72; Talking New Towns, 'Leonard Vincent' <http://www.talkingnewtowns.org.uk/content/category/towns/stevenage/leonard-vincent>, accessed 17 August 2015.

82   Balchin, *The first new town*, pp. 87–91, 127–9; Ashby and Hills, *Stevenage*, p. 152.

83   Stevenage Development Corporation, *Stevenage master plan 1966 summarised report* (Stevenage, c.1967).

84   C.S. Stein, *Toward new towns for America* (Liverpool, 1951), pp. 37–69.

85   Stephenson and DeMarco, *On a Human Scale*, pp. 121–6.

86   Balchin, *The first new town*, pp. 162–4.

87   L. Vincent, 'Leonard Vincent about traffic, residential areas and cycleways in Stevenage', <http://www.talkingnewtowns.org.uk/content/topics/developing-a-new-town/leonard-vincent-traffic-residential-areas>, accessed 18 August 2015.

88   L. Vincent, 'Leonard Vincent about building issues: which kind of buildings and which techniques?' <http://www.talkingnewtowns.org.uk/content/topics/developing-a-new-town/7075-leonard-vincent-about-building-issues-which-kind-of-buildings-and-which-techniques>, accessed 17 August 2015; Cresswell Film Unit/Stevenage Development Corporation, *Rationalised building – the Mowlem System* [Film] (Stevenage, 1964); Balchin, *The first new town*, p. 167.

89   Ibid., pp. 201–7.

90   S. Mortimer, 'The Oval Shops. 1969' <http://www.ourstevenage.org.uk/page_id__131. aspx?path=0p2p33p>, accessed 17 August 2015.

91   LUSCA, D307A/1/1/1/2.

92   Balchin, *The first new town*, pp. 162–4.

93   S. Taylor, 'Sharon Taylor about playing by Aston Brook' <http://www.talkingnewtowns.org. uk/content/towns/stevenage/sharon-taylor/sharon-taylor-playing-aston-brook>, accessed 19 August 2015.

94   H. Rees, 'The Valley 1961 and Road 9 1966', in H. Rees, and C. Rees (eds), *The history makers: the story of the early days of Stevenage new town* (Stevenage, 1991), pp. 126–9.

95   Balchin, *The first new town*, pp. 134–6.

96   Stevenage Borough Council, 'History of Fairlands Valley Park' <http://www.stevenage.gov.uk/ about-stevenage/fairlands-valley-park/28583/>, accessed 27 August 2015.

97   Recent improvements, <http://www.stevenage.gov.uk/about-stevenage/fairlands-valley-park/ 28585>, accessed 27 August 2015.

98   S.V. Ward, *Planning the twentieth-century city: the advanced capitalist world* (Chichester, 2002), especially pp. 168–9, 197–9, 203–5.

99   Stephenson and DeMarco, *On a human scale*, pp. 97–101; Stevenage Development Corporation, *Principles proposed for the planning and development of the town centre*, 8 September 1950.

100 Balchin, *The first new town*, pp. 267–81.

101 Claxton, *The hidden Stevenage*, p. 205.

102 Ashby and Hills, *Stevenage*, pp. 111–14

103 Stephenson and DeMarco, *On a human scale*, p. 104.

104 Built Environment Advisory and Management Service, *Stevenage Conservation Areas*, pp. 79–96.

105 Ashby and Hills, *Stevenage*, pp. 121–5.

106 L. Vincent, 'Leonard Vincent about Stevenage pedestrianised town centre' <http://www. talkingnewtowns.org.uk/content/topics/developing-a-new-town/leonard-vincent-about-stevenage-pedestrianised-town-centre>, accessed 19 August 2015.

107 Balchin, *The first new town*, pp. 284–5.

108 Ashby and Hills, *Stevenage*, pp. 196–9.

109 Stevenage Borough Council, *Town square conservation appraisal 2010* (Stevenage: 2010).

110 A.A. Ogilvy, 'The self-contained new town: employment and population', *Town Planning Review*, 39/1 (1968), pp. 38–54; A.A. Ogilvy, 'Employment expansion and the development of new town hinterlands 1961–66', *Town Planning Review*, 42/2 (1971), pp. 113–29.

111 Balchin, *The first new town*, pp. 174–5.

112 Aldridge, *The new towns*, pp. 108–13, 123–4; Cullingworth, *Environmental planning: vol. III*, pp. 399–415.

113 Aldridge, *The new towns*, pp. 122–3.

114 J.A. Moss, 'New and expanded towns: a survey of the demographic characteristics of newcomers', *Town Planning Review*, 39/2 (1968), pp. 117–39.

115 The Irish Network Stevenage, *From the Emerald Isle, passim*.

116 J. Wrench, H. Brar and P. Martin, *Invisible minorities: racism in new towns and new contexts* (Coventry, 1993), p. 146.

117 2011 Census Table KS201EW.

118 Aldridge, *The new towns*, pp. 146–56.

119 Ibid., pp. 92–102.

120 Department of Planning Oxford Brookes University, for Department for Communities and Local Government, *Transferable lessons from the new towns* (London, 2006) <http://www. futurecommunities.net/files/images/Transferable_lessons_from_new_towns_0.pdf>, accessed 19 March 2015, pp. 39–46.

121 LUSCA, D307A/1/1/1/1/2, Ministry of Town and Country Planning, Stevenage – New Town Report on Planning and Development Proposals, 31st July 1946, pp. 27–8; HALS, CNT/17/1/6, Stevenage Development Corporation, *The Neighbourhood structure of Stevenage New Town*, undated c.1948.

122 Homer, 'Administration and social change', especially pp. 265–7.

123 A. Luhman, 'The builders (ii)', in H. Rees and C. Rees (eds), *The history makers: the story of the early days of Stevenage new town* (Stevenage, 1991), pp. 27–8; C. Rees, 'The first neighbourhoods', in H. Rees and C. Rees (eds), *The history makers: the story of the early days of Stevenage new town* (Stevenage, 1991), p. 55.

124 Homer, 'Administration and social change', pp. 167–8.

125 Drackford, 'Early Residents', pp. 93–102.

126 Ashby and Hills, *Stevenage*, p. 115.

127 Talking New Towns, 'Mrs Galliers is frontline news' <http://www.talkingnewtowns.org.uk/content/topics/building-communities/mrs-galliers-frontline-news>, accessed 19 August 2015.

128 F. Udell, 'The builders (i)', in H. Rees and C. Rees (eds), *The history makers: the story of the early days of Stevenage new town* (Stevenage, 1991), pp. 19–20; M. McLeod, 'Early residents (iii)', in H. Rees and C. Rees (eds), *The history makers: the story of the early days of Stevenage new town* (Stevenage, 1991), p. 80.

129 J. Amess, 'How grateful we were', in Ashby, *Voices of Stevenage*, p. 105.

130 Rees and Rees, *The history makers*, passim.

131 Homer, 'Administration and social change', pp. 147–82; Balchin, *The first new town*, pp. 241–6.

132 M. Cotter, 'Stevenage Oral Interview Heritage Project, Tape No. A014/2', Interview by K. Cotter, 10 April 1986; The Irish Network Stevenage, *From the Emerald Isle*, passim.

133 Balchin, *The first new town*, p. 248; W. Fowler, 'Early residents (vii)', in H. Rees and C. Rees (eds), *The history makers: the story of the early days of Stevenage new town* (Stevenage, 1991), pp. 103–11.

134 Luhman, 'The builders', pp. 28–9.

135 Udell, 'The builders', p. 21.

136 Ashby and Hills, *Stevenage*, pp. 130–33.

137 Balchin, *The first new town*, pp. 27 and 247–8.

138 T. Collings (ed.), *Stevenage: images of the first new town 1946–1986* (Stevenage, 1987), pp. 41–5; Ashby and Hills, *Stevenage*, pp. 192–3; 217.

139 Collings, *Stevenage*, p. 60; Ashby and Hills, *Stevenage*, pp. 154–5; Wall et al., *Building a community*, p. 30.

140 C. Donner (dir.), *Here We Go Round the Mulberry Bush* (1968).

141 Which must surely be Bill Forsyth's charming 1981 film *Gregory's Girl*, set in Cumbernauld.

142 M. Clapson, *Invincible green suburbs; brave new towns: social change and urban dispersal in postwar Britain* (Manchester, 1998) is the most coherent articulation of this argument.

CHAPTER SIX

Hertfordshire's other New Towns

We saw in the last chapter how the New Town programme opened with Stevenage, making it the first milestone on this main post-Howard variant of the peaceful path. The mistakes, mishaps and triumphs that marked its experience in becoming a New Town certainly had some entirely unique aspects. Some arose from its role as as a pioneer and, in several respects, an innovator. But that experience also highlighted many features common to other New Towns designated in the years 1946–50 by the Labour government's minister of town and country planning, Lewis Silkin. As we noted briefly at the start of Chapter 5, Silkin's programme also created three other New Towns in Hertfordshire, which meant that it had more than any other county. Though their stories have always seemed a little 'quieter' than that of Stevenage, they too are a key part of the larger story, highlighting in different ways the themes and variations of wider New Town experience. This chapter therefore examines, albeit more briefly, these stories.

Hemel Hempstead
'One of those New Towns you keep hearing about'
In July 1951 a short black-and-white film about the New Town of Hemel Hempstead was premiered. Called *A home of your own* it was shown widely in London and suburban cinemas and elsewhere, especially during the Festival of Britain, which was in full swing during that same summer. It was well received and at least a million people had seen it by early 1952.[1] In style and construction *A home of your own* contrasted with most promotional films made over the years for New Town Development Corporations.[2] Typically, these were rather high-minded instructional presentations of the wonders of New Town planning. In making this one, however, the director Tony Thompson acknowledged a fundamental tenet of good film-making: that the best way to tell a big story is to find a compelling small one.

In this case the hope and promise of the New Town were encapsulated in the story of the Wilson family, George, Jenny and two daughters, who lived in two cramped rooms in an old shared house in Willesden in London. George goes off on a coach trip into the country with his mates and is struck by how beautiful the countryside is compared with where he lives. The coach stops in the old town of Hemel Hempstead, where a lively carnival (that of 1948) is in progress, largely to celebrate the town's history. He sees people showing real pride in the place where they live and he learns from some of them that this old town is to become 'one of those New Towns you keep hearing about'. He remembers that he has had a letter about this from Willesden council, inviting people on their housing waiting list with suitable work skills to apply to move there. George, a bricklayer, is taken with the idea that he and his family could be among those people, living in a real community that offers a better life for his family.

When he returns home, a weary and rather frazzled Jenny thinks he has had too much beer and fears his dreams will just bring more disappointment and hurt in their long search for a decent home. But he persists and applies to move there. A brief interlude then shows the early work of the Development Corporation, as plans for the new surface water drainage are finalised. But the filmmakers resist the temptation to give planning the central place in their story, as often occurred. The story soon returns to the Wilson family, as George is about to go to the local housing office about the application. Outwardly Jenny and he are both anxious and reluctant to express their real thoughts to each other but the film voices their inner hopes and fears. The film then cuts to show the local mayor speaking at the laying of the foundation stone on Hemel Hempstead's first housing estate in Adeyfield. George is shown nearby laying bricks on the estate, now at least working in what will become the New Town. He does the best work he can because he knows his only chance of getting one of the houses he is building depends on it.

And then, one day, the New Town housing officer comes along to the site and tells him that his dream has come true – he has a house. The mood of the film changes, and George and Jenny are shown planning how they will live in their new home. As they plan out the new space they will have and where the furniture will go, we hear Jenny's thoughts about their new life and the things that really matter in life. The scene fades into one of her waking up in their new home and undertaking housewifely tasks in a state of serene contentment. The dream has become reality. Soon they go out to a folk dancing welcome event organised by the Development Corporation and are drawn into the new society that is forming. Ultimately, though, the film emphasises the individual dimension as they return to their new house, somewhere they finally feel is a home of their own.

Even nearly 70 years later this technically quite simple film, seen now by generations for whom the concept of a home of your own means actual ownership rather than renting, retains a surprising capacity to move the viewer. It gives a real insight into the hopes of the people of early post-war Britain and the part that the New Towns played in addressing those. Actual recollections of the first Londoners to move to Hemel Hempstead in the period in which the film was released show how much that cinematic dramatisation really did speak to those hopes. One woman living with her husband and two children in accommodation shared with another couple in Wembley recalled just how difficult it was trying to get a council house around 1950:

> ... they told us we'd have to have another 60 points at least [in the numerical calculation of their housing need] before we stood a chance of having a place. And we'd always planned to have four children so I said to Ben 'let's have another baby, we'll get a house then'. So, after a lot of persuading, we decided and we had another baby. And we got down there then and they said, 'We're very sorry Mrs Adams but about 300 other couples did the same as you that night'. And we were back to square one, in a worse position really with another baby on the way and no place to put it.[3]

A complex reality

Meanwhile, the location of the New Town to which this growing family subsequently moved also presented its own challenges. As well as showing why the New Town was needed, the film was also a remarkably skilful representation of a local situation in Hemel Hempstead that, at the outset, was arguably even more difficult than that at Stevenage. Even before the New Town, 21,200 people lived in the area, largely in the existing small town of Hemel Hempstead and other separate areas of settlement at Boxmoor, Apsley and Leverstock Green (Figure 6.1). Apsley and neighbouring Frogmore End were well known for paper mills and stationery production, associated mainly with the long-established John Dickinson company, which had a strong brand reputation and employed around 5,000 workers. This and a few other industries, together with farming and the shops and services of Hemel Hempstead itself, had been the main sources of income in the area. The area's relatively good rail links also encouraged some commuting to work elsewhere.

As at Stevenage, there was strong opposition to the designation of a New Town. However, unlike Stevenage, Hemel Hempstead had not even been

Figure 6.1 The old town of Hemel Hempstead was the main settlement before the New Town. Its historic qualities have been conserved and commercial pressures shifted southward, to the new town centre. (Jane Housham)

identified as a suitable location for a satellite town in the Greater London Plan. Abercrombie and his team had instead favoured nearby Redbourn, but the ministry's planners thought a New Town there would be unviable. Around it were towns (St Albans, Harpenden and Hemel Hempstead) with greater potential for spontaneous growth, and the ministry planners considered that these would prevent Redbourn establishing itself. Trying to force the issue would merely produce a much larger and centreless urban coalescence. At Hemel, by contrast, better communication links facilitated a viable, freestanding and coherent town of about 60,000 inhabitants. In July 1946 Silkin received approval to proceed along these lines from his ministerial colleagues.[4]

These arguments by ministry planners cut little ice with existing inhabitants. Reflecting prevailing local opinion, Hemel Hempstead Borough Council often appeared even more against this New Town than had been the case at Stevenage. Gilbert Hitchcock, the only Labour councillor, was at the outset a lonely political voice in favour.[5] Although he was obliged to serve his council, the young town clerk, Charles Kirk, also quickly saw its potential benefits. Initially, however, it was the opposition which dominated. A Hemel Hempstead Protection Association soon appeared and the local newspaper, the *Hemel Hempstead Gazette*, gave much coverage to it and other opponents.[6] Yet the ministry had learnt from its earlier mistakes at Stevenage and was more careful with this, the third New Town (Crawley was second). Nor was the opposition as well organised as at Stevenage.

The public inquiry over the designation order, held over three days in early December 1946, saw a more effective presentation of the ministry's case (by Beaufoy) and the opposition unable to offer a coherent or credible set of objections. The council was 'peeved' (the inspector's word) at being supplanted by a Development Corporation and, though it was willing to see growth of a further 10,000, had done nothing previously to inspire confidence that even this modest growth would be coherently planned.[7] The inspector even felt sympathy for the borough council's advocate's having to present such fundamentally unconvincing arguments. Given the decisive way in which it rejected most opposition arguments, it was perhaps just as well that the inspector's report remained confidential. The Protection Association would clearly have been incensed if they had known that their case had been dismissed as 'inadequacy of compensation, loss of freehold, and a superiority complex. They feared the 40,000 persons to be brought to Hemel Hempstead might not be very nice to know.' Not surprisingly, the inspector upheld the designation order, though reduced the affected area, removing the originally intended area south of the main railway line (within which were the John Dickinson paper mills, the biggest existing manufacturer in the Borough) and avoiding the severing of various farms around other parts of the periphery.

Silkin and his staff acted on these recommendations, pleased to have such decisive support for the original intention while demonstrating that they were not unyielding where objections were judged soundly based. The New Town was formally designated in February 1947, although this did not quieten local opposition.[8] As one original resident later remembered:

> If I walked down Marlowes, I suppose, if I didn't know everybody, I recognised everybody and everybody knew everybody and so I suppose we didn't realise exactly what would happen but of course it's subsequently changed completely to what I would have preferred it to be. But then that's only because it was … [t]he town I was brought up in and was used to.[9]

As in Stevenage, the designation order was appealed but here the High Court dismissed the appeal (in July 1947), so the uncertainty was less prolonged.[10] Even so, local resentment rumbled on for several more years.

Another sign of this opposition came in the autumn of 1950, when the Development Corporation announced its proposed film.[11] The council, other local bodies and the local newspaper all feared a work of blatant propaganda and quickly distanced themselves or sounded objections. Strikingly, however, the mood had softened by the time they actually saw the film. In part, they had doubtless begun to bow to the inevitable. Yet some were clearly won over by the way the traditions of Hemel Hempstead were showcased in the film, with the newcomers taking their place within a town that already had deep roots. The *Gazette* considered that the film made an 'excellent impression'. It was also difficult to dismiss its very human portrayal of the real need for better housing that existed and the dire living conditions still prevalent in London.

The first actual newcomers had, of course, appeared by the time the film came out. Although this fictionalised account had made no reference to how existing residents reacted to the newcomers, there are many actual accounts of initial and, among some old towners, persistent frostiness.[12] It seems that this was probably more serious than in Stevenage, where the newcomers quite soon became the majority population. In later reflections more of the early New Towners in Hemel Hempstead mentioned the tensions with the original population. One, who arrived in 1951 and was hospitalised while having her baby, found the experience particularly upsetting. 'I had to go into St Paul's Hospital, which wasn't very good because we hadn't found the Hemel people very friendly and when I went in nobody spoke to me or anything, until one time the matron I think she was, she wasn't very nice, she upset me and I started to cry ....'[13] She also recalled a later incident while waiting to be served in a shop: '... the lady came and served me and suddenly someone said "that's right, serve the foreigners first"'.

Another new resident, arriving as late as 1954, commented that

> ... at first it was a bit hard, cos the people of Hertfordshire was a lot quieter than Londoners. Well there's a nice little village of their own and they didn't particularly want lots of houses, they liked it as it was, but they got used to us in the end. In Dickinson's, where I worked, no-one would talk to me. One day I said to them, 'Why is it you don't talk to me?' They said, 'Well you're a Londoner'. I said, 'Well does that make me have two heads or something?' and then we was friends again.[14]

These types of experiences created a not-always-justified expectation on both sides that there would be endemic hostility between the 'Londoners' and the 'Swede-bashers'. Despite the best efforts of the Development Corporation staff, the Hemel Hempstead Council of Social Service and generally sympathetic local leaders, such as clergymen, who urged mutual tolerance and understanding, these suspicions took time to diminish. One early source of resentment was the belief that Londoners were getting houses in their town (at what were incorrectly believed to be far cheaper rents than were actually charged) and the locals were not. Such was the extent of the hostility that when the local councillor (a rare supporter of the New Town) greeted one recent arrival, his genuine welcome was met with the rejoinder '...but what?'[15] He was evidently the first person she had met who had been able to do this without also carping in some way.

Planning a 'dream city in the valley of the Gade'

As at Stevenage, some local resentment showed itself in the process of planning, which gave further rich opportunities to criticise the fact, scale and nature of the New Town. The ministry commissioned a consultant planner, Geoffrey Jellicoe, to produce tentative proposals for Hemel Hempstead's development in November 1946. Jellicoe, aged 46, was an architect, a planner and a founding figure in the nascent profession of landscape architecture. During the following year he produced more elaborated proposals for the new Development Corporation.

Despite all the local political difficulties, Silkin had noted that, from the physical point of view, Hemel's site was the most promising of all of the first New Towns.[16] Its terrain comprised lightly timbered hills and valleys bisected by the river Gade, which also, with the river Bulbourne, formed its southern periphery. This presented Jellicoe with a fine opportunity to create a wonderfully attractive place. Unfortunately for him, however, he proved more eager to exploit the dramatic landscape possibilities of the site than were those whose approval was needed before his plan could proceed.

During 1947 Jellicoe and his team elaborated the master plan, despite some confusion as to what timescale it was supposed to cover. Jellicoe's direct role ended before the process was complete, but many of his most idealistic ideas survived. The Corporation submitted what was essentially a toned-down Jellicoe plan for approval to Silkin in August 1949 and a public inquiry followed in November. In his subsequent report the inspector, K.S. Dodd (who had almost immediately judged it a 'bad plan'[17]), listed several very serious defects, many resulting 'from Jellicoe's delightful but impractical dream-city in the valley of the Gade'.[18] The major objections he reported had already been voiced locally, broadly reflecting the profound difficulties of creating a New Town in the same location as a smaller old town. There were many and continuing local fears about the proposed number of demolitions, high costs[19] and many other detailed aspects.[20] Dodd particularly criticised the excessively low densities, the over-provision of roads, the expensive road alignments and the overly monumental approach to

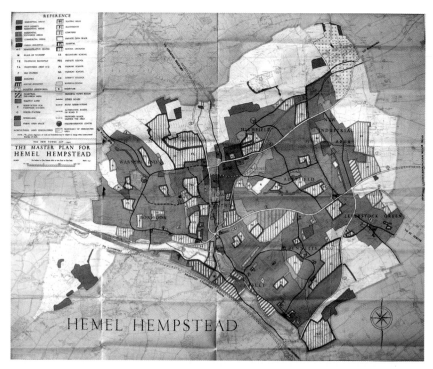

Figure 6.2 After much dispute, this was the finally approved master plan, showing the clear emphasis on neighbourhood units (though of varying size), the central position of the town centre and the large new industrial area at Maylands on the eastern side. (author's collection)

planning the town centre. In June 1950 the plan was returned for modifications. Published in a further version in September 1951, it was only finally approved in June 1952 (Figure 6.2).

While many New Towns experienced difficulties finalising their master plans, nowhere was the process as fraught as at Hemel Hempstead. With hindsight, it is clear that Jellicoe's conception, born of the very early post-war mood of idealism, had fallen prey to increasing fears about costs and delays within government programmes that took hold within a few years. Yet the main thinking behind this first attempt at the Hemel Hempstead master plan was hardly challenging. At the conceptual level, many proposals simply reflected the emergent orthodoxy of contemporary New Town planning, particularly the neighbourhood unit concept. Yet, because there was so much existing development within the designated area, it was not possible to start with the relatively 'clean sheet' of Stevenage. The initial proposal in 1947 was for seven neighbourhoods (subsequently reduced to six) varying from over 11,500 to just 3,500 people.[21]

Even as late as January 1952, the borough council had still not accepted that the New Town itself was a legitimate venture.[22] Sensing a fresh opportunity to procure its abortion, councillors lobbied the new Conservative housing minister, Harold Macmillan, arguing that the whole area was topographically unsuited for development on the scale intended. Instead, the Council proposed that the Development Corporation should be recast as a body composed solely of the borough and county councils, undertaking expansion to only half the extent intended. Within government Macmillan was repeatedly being pressed during these years to consider scrapping or scaling back the whole New Towns programme. He successfully argued against these proposals, recognising that the pressures for housing and metropolitan decentralisation would not simply disappear and that the alternative would just be a 'nasty mess'.[23] Equally, he parried Hemel Hempstead Borough Council's attempt on the life of this particular New Town.[24]

Despite this outward support from their minister, however, many ministry officials, feeling obligated to try and find economies in the New Town programme, were clearly exasperated with the Development Corporation. Beaufoy and his colleagues considered that many of the plan's proposals would be too costly. In their view, Jellicoe's originally proposed densities were simply too low, and with too much green space. The outcome was that densities were increased further after the referral of the 1949 plan. The number of neighbourhoods was also reduced to six (the one dropped, Grove Hill, was eventually developed to provide for natural increase in the 1960s). Many other detailed aspects were criticised, particularly Jellicoe's aesthetically pleasing but costly preference for putting housing on sloping sites instead of maximising the use of such level sites as there were.

The most serious concerns were about how the New Town's centre should develop.[25] There was general agreement on the proposed site, south of the existing Hemel Hempstead High Street, along the Marlowes. Centrally located in the New Town area, this was already a minor shopping street that ran north–south parallel to the river Gade slightly above the valley floor. There was a large though little-used railway viaduct (later removed) over its southern end. Over time, alternative plans emerged. In 1947 Jellicoe proposed a hillside retail and commercial development rising from the Marlowes on the eastern side.[26] The western side along the valley bottom would remain largely open, with seven linked water gardens alongside the Gade. Taking inspiration from Princes Street in Edinburgh and The Promenade in Cheltenham, it was this which most prompted the 'dream city' jibe.

Figure 6.3 A 2013 view of the southern part of Marlowes. Originally a normal traffic street, this section was pedestrianised from 1992. The town has become a major shopping centre and expansion continues. (author photograph)

A second option favoured within the Development Corporation was a more compact shopping development on the valley floor on the western side of Marlowes with offices to the east. Jellicoe added a further variant in April 1949 that combined some elements of his original with development on the west side of Marlowes. The ministry's planners, meanwhile, were pressing for a two-sided high street with less development on the slopes and a northward shift to link up with the old town. The outcome was essentially a compromise between these last three options, though it has changed greatly since it first appeared. From 1992, shortly after new shopping development had been completed, the main shopping core along the southern part of Marlowes began to be pedestrianised (Figure 6.3). More recently, the Riverside development has taken the pedestrianised retail core even further south.

Back in 1950, however, Jellicoe had been left feeling very bruised by the way his original bold plans, conceived amid early post-war hopes, were treated as these were overtaken by desires for economy.[27] He vowed to have nothing more to do with planning Hemel Hempstead. His practice did, however, undertake some architectural commissions designing housing. And, as a landscape and garden architect, Jellicoe was tempted back to design a more modest version of the Water Gardens. It took all the charm and tact of the then chairman, Henry

Figure 6.4 The Water Gardens were a fine embellishment to the New Town and remain a restful oasis despite their alarming deterioration in recent years. A major restoration is currently underway. (author photograph)

Wells (about whom more below), over a couple of drinks at a London hotel, to persuade Jellicoe to undertake this project. In doing it, Jellicoe surprised many by damming the Gade to create a lake with a fountain. What resulted, created between 1957 and 1962, was among the UK's finest post-war urban landscape designs (Figure 6.4).[28] Though sadly deteriorated in recent years, the heritage importance of the Gardens is now widely acknowledged. They also remain as the most tangible expression of Jellicoe's frustrated aspiration to create what in 1949 he had referred to as 'a classical composition in what might be described as the grand manner of landscape'.[29]

Developing the New Town

The long delays in finalising plans did not, however, prevent construction starting. Once the legality of Hemel Hempstead New Town was confirmed development was pushed forward far more effectively than at Stevenage. By 1953 housing completions exceeded those of any other contemporary New Town and continued at around 1,000 each year for the rest of the decade. Its population reached 54,000 in 1960 and two years later the Corporation was judged to have completed its work. Charge of the town's remaining development, largely to cater for its natural increase, passed to the national Commission for the New Towns.

It was thus one of the first two New Towns (the other was Crawley) to reach the end of its 'active' (planned migrational) growth phase.[30]

There were several reasons why, comparatively speaking, Hemel Hempstead did so well. It helped, of course, that the scale of growth, from 21,200 to 60,000, was more modest than that of Stevenage or many other New Towns. In 1957 Henry Brooke, the housing minister, responded to the nationally high birth rate by increasing Hemel Hempstead's ultimate target to 80,000,[31] but it was, eventually, spared further rises or growth uncertainties. More important, however, was the ease with which new employers could be attracted.[32] This amply demonstrated Hemel's economic growth potential to governments, virtually ensuring their approval for a very active housing programme to keep pace. As at Stevenage, a few building firms played important roles. By 1960 Wimpey alone had built around a third of the total new homes, using both traditional and 'no-fines' construction methods, with other contractors such as Leslie and the St Albans firm Miskin also very significant house-builders.[33]

From 1950 new manufacturing employers began to appear, many moving directly from London to expand. Notable new firms which had a big impact in consolidating Hemel's position were Rotax (later Lucas Aerospace), which arrived in 1952 and Kodak, in 1957, but there were many others. Overall the 6,200 local jobs in 1947 had risen to 28,500 by mid-1966.[34] Over 80 per cent of the resident workforce by then worked in the New Town and many others worked in the borough but outside the New Town (mainly at Dickinsons).[35] As well as the basic employer attractions that any New Town could offer – well-planned sites and a good living environment for workers – many firms were attracted by Hemel's especially good (and improving) communications. In 1959 the long-awaited new 'London–Birmingham Motor Road' – the M1 motorway – opened, skirting the New Town's eastern boundary. This was very close to the large new industrial estate at Maylands, where almost all new factory development from 1953 occurred.

Many employers had undoubtedly anticipated the motorway's arrival and expanded further over succeeding years, while Hemel Hempstead's potential as a distribution centre and location for office growth was boosted by the new road. During the later 1960s and 1970s these sectors became major sources of employment growth, both in the centre and in the Maylands area. The latter benefited because of its immediate links to the M1 and status as an entry point into the town. This is a trend which continues today and the area, now rebadged as the 'Maylands Gateway', continues to be one of major significance for economic development in both town and county, underlining the wisdom of decision-making by a small number of people very early in the New Town era.

Organisational and personal factors also contributed in other specific ways to Hemel Hempstead's rapid growth, especially at the very beginning. Its Development Corporation avoided the problems that Stevenage suffered in terms of attracting and retaining leadership and professional expertise. Despite his difficult reputation, the first chairman, Lord Reith, was already a towering figure (in all senses) in public sector management, capable of outstanding achievements when insulated from the day-to-day machinations of elective local or national politics. He came to Hemel Hempstead determined that it would be the first New Town to be finished and firmly implanted this ambition in the Development Corporation.

In November 1950, however, Reith left for the more demanding chairmanship of the Colonial Development Committee. He was replaced by Henry Wells, an urbane and exceptionally able surveyor who, during the 1940s, had distinguished himself in the Ministry of Town and Country Planning. Wells was already a Board member (and from 1949 to 1950 also deputy chairman of Bracknell New Town), and remained chairman at Hemel Hempstead until the Development Corporation was wound up in 1962.[36] It was a mark of his success that he subsequently became chairman of the Commission for the New Towns, the national body which replaced all New Town Development Corporations as they finished their work.

Reith and Wells presided over a very able professional staff that quickly coalesced to form an effective team. At the helm was an outstanding general manager, William O. Hart. Although his usual deftness of touch curiously failed him in finding a swift compromise to the master planning problems already described, this was exceptional. Hart's stature was such that when he left in 1956 it was to become clerk (i.e. chief executive) of the UK's largest local authority, the London County Council. The corporate vision of Reith, Wells and their officials affected all aspects of making the New Town during the 1950s. Years later, Philip Bee, one of the Corporation's architects, recalled how he and his colleagues toured the building sites with large cartons of cigarettes.[37] Packets of twenty were given to plasterers and bricklayers as an added incentive if they worked through weekends to finish jobs early. This is not to say that site tensions of the kind identified at Stevenage were unknown but, as this anecdote suggests, the general tone of labour relations was altogether less challenging.

The new Hemel Hempstead

These more moderate workplace relations also appear to have softened the tenor of community politics, which, as in Stevenage, soon appeared in the new neighbourhoods. In part this may, despite the early tensions between existing residents and newcomers, have reflected the more established nature of Hemel Hempstead as a place with the traditional, conservative values of a country town. On the other hand, these factors were mirrored by a Development Corporation not unduly worried by the demands arising from new local associations formed by the newcomers. These concerns emerged at the same stage and for reasons similar to those at Stevenage. Here, however, they were more encouraged by the Development Corporation. There was less confrontation and fewer worries of excessive politicisation of the kind that had troubled the general manager at Stevenage.

An important intermediary who helped to cultivate these links was the Hemel Hempstead public relations officer, Gerald Brooke-Taylor. He also worked hard to build better links with the old towners and the borough council. As at Stevenage, the New Town certainly brought social and other changes, so that Hemel Hempstead's politics shifted leftward within a few years. The original anti-New Town lobby also faded within a short period. By 1956 Labour was in a strong position on the borough council and Gilbert Hitchcock became that party's first mayor. In the longer term, Hitchcock played a role similar in some respects to that of Philip Ireton at Stevenage, another local man and white-collar trade unionist who from the first had championed the New Town. His membership of the borough and county councils and involvement in other local institutions made him an excellent interface between the locality and the

Figure 6.5 Some of the first New Town housing in the Adeyfield neighbourhood. The familiar 1950s problems of failing to anticipate the rise of motor car use are especially apparent but the houses themselves, of traditional construction, remain attractive and popular. (author photograph)

Development Corporation (and the local office of the Commission after 1962). Working closely with Brooke-Taylor, Charles Kirk and the county council, he helped Hemel Hempstead to become a New Town pioneer in the joint provision of community facilities.

Hitchcock's ward as borough councillor included the Adeyfield area, the first and largest of the New Town neighbourhood units (Figure 6.5).[38] Construction began here in 1949 and the first houses were occupied the following year. As the first residents remembered, '[a]ll we saw were open fields, four, five houses, some being completed, tons and tons of cement, ballast and bricks. Pouring wet, pouring with rain. It wasn't a very good impression really, the first impression we had. But we liked the house very much.'[39] Other early New Town residents recall an altogether more emotional experience on first seeing the house they had been allocated:

> Well, we came in and we had a look at the house and … got all excited because it was the kind of house we'd always said we wanted. And when I went upstairs to explore there was one bedroom, and another bedroom, and a bathroom, and an airing cupboard, and another door down the end – wonder what that it is. So I went and had a look and I had three bedrooms which made me come downstairs, sit on the bottom step and howl. I wept simply because I was so happy. We had a garden for the child to run it – well, a garden of sorts because by then it was only rubble. They'd taken off the top soil and left a beautiful layer of yellow clay which walked into the house *everywhere*. But nevertheless we had a house, a home of our own where we could shut the front door and didn't have to worry about anybody.[40]

The first neighbourhood at Adeyfield was largely complete by 1953. It mainly comprises short terraces of brick-built, pitched-roof houses with front gardens, and a few low-rise flats.[41] The housing is arranged fairly conventionally alongside streets or set back around small greens. Even from the beginning, established trees helped soften the inevitable rawness of a new building estate and many new ones were planted. More than six decades later, the landscape has matured and it is clear that the buildings have lasted very well and remain popular and well-kept. Adeyfield Secondary School is centrally located in the neighbourhood and there are two primary schools. The neighbourhood centre at The Queen's Square (commemorating its official opening by the new queen in July 1952) fully exemplifies the contemporary thinking about neighbourhood planning (Figure 6.6). Parades of shops, church, public house, community centre and library, and the neighbourhood's largest block of flats form the square, with a local road passing diagonally through, on each side of which are parking and public space.

Figure 6.6 The shopping parade at the Adeyfield neighbourhood centre at Queen's Square. Opened by the Queen in 1952, it has been refurbished and remodelled in recent years with a changed roof design and new brick pillars to create a more robust colonnade than in the original. Yet the initial conception remains and the centre is well used. (author photograph)

Figure 6.7 Designed by Geoffrey Jellicoe and Partners, Long John in Bennetts End neighbourhood (1953) ingeniously combines groups of standard Wimpey row housing punctuated with flats one storey higher to create a unique terrace rising up the slope. A separate crescent at the top completes the visual effect. (author photograph)

Adeyfield showed the usual late 1940s/1950s underestimation of the level of car use, although because of a generally spacious layout the impacts of on-street parking are less obvious than in areas developed even a few years later. Development at Bennetts End began in late 1951, at Chaulden and Warners End in 1953 and at Gadebridge in 1955.[42] The more hilly terrain of these areas gave greater possibilities for more interesting designs and layouts, the most striking example of which was Jellicoe's notable composition at Long John in Bennetts End, built in 1953. Here was created an extremely long continuous rising frontage of two-storey Wimpey-built terrace houses with changes of ground level in the façade marked by several intervening three-storey dwellings ('poppers-up', as Jellicoe termed them).[43] The vista up the hill was then closed by a separate short three-storey curving terrace (Figure 6.7).

Over time there was the same increase in building densities as at Stevenage, which was especially noticeable by the time that Highfield was begun in 1959.[44] Yet, compared with Stevenage and other New Towns, where more housing development occurred later in the 1960s and 1970s, there was little use of Radburn layouts, designed more explicitly to cater for the car. There are some examples in later neighbourhoods at Highfield and especially so in the last, Grove Hill, where development began in 1967.[45] In the following decade, as sales of rental housing saw 40 per cent of households owning their homes by 1978, more completely private sector residential development began to occur, notably at Woodhall Farm.[46]

Final thoughts

The New Town area of Hemel Hempstead had close to 86,000 inhabitants in 2011. This exceeded its final New Town population target and made it the biggest of the Hertfordshire examples. Its economy was (and remains) prosperous, even though it had undergone a great deal of change. While much of the physical legacy of its New Town era remains, it is also a place which has moved on more completely than Stevenage. Fewer people today have much awareness of Hemel Hempstead as even a 'former New Town'. Echoing a theme of the 1951 film, the New Town experience itself has now become just one episode in a longer process of urban evolution and change.

Hemel's pre-New Town size perhaps meant that the impact of its New Town 'period' was less profound than for its sister on the other side of the county. This was especially so since Reith's ambition to finish it before any of the other New Towns was fulfilled, its Development Corporation being wound up eighteen years before Stevenage's. The Commission for the New Towns which followed it operated on a much smaller scale and with a lighter touch that was less self-consciously 'new' and allowed a stronger local input. Apart from the Water Gardens, which are nationally registered as gardens of historic interest and currently (in 2015–16) undergoing major restoration, no other measures recognise or protect the New Town's built or landscape legacy. Unlike in Stevenage, there are no New Town conservation areas. With the one exception of Scott Hastie's commissioned history, local historians have previously given the New Town surprisingly little attention, though recent work by oral historians is changing this.[47] Yet it remains a key formative period in the town's history, one that established a momentum for change which continues indirectly to shape the town in the twenty-first century.

Welwyn Garden City New Town
'... the narrowest ideological grounds ...'

The anger at Silkin's decision during 1947–8 to designate Welwyn Garden City as a New Town with a Development Corporation came from quite a different quarter and was expressed in quite different terms to that unleashed at Stevenage and Hemel Hempstead. There the objections were from disgruntled local residents objecting to impending changes in their locality, property appropriation and demolition, from farmers defending the integrity of their holdings and from local councillors resenting the loss of their powers. Here the objections came overwhelmingly from Welwyn Garden City Ltd, the company which had developed the garden city since its inception. The chairman, Sir Theodore Chambers, complained bitterly about a decision to replace the company with a public development corporation. It was a decision which, he said 'ignores its history and achievements and is difficult to understand except on the narrowest ideological grounds'.[48]

The point of dissent was not, therefore, whether a substantial new settlement should be built – that was already a partially accomplished fact. And what had resulted was a widely admired model of the advantages of planning and building afresh, away from the congested cities. Rather, it was a question of the proper instrument for achieving this. Should it be an established privately owned company that had been building a garden city for nearly two decades, or a newly established and untried government corporation? Welwyn Garden City Ltd had, of course, a strong public interest tradition but, since the 1934 reorganisation, there was no longer any restraint on the size of dividend that it could pay to shareholders. In this respect, whatever its traditions and track record, it had diverged from a central principle of Howard's 'peaceful path'.

Even so, it is not clear exactly why Silkin wanted to nationalise the company. Abercrombie and his team had not contemplated making Welwyn Garden City into one of the new satellite towns. When Silkin first presented his proposals for planning the London region to a key ministerial policy committee in spring 1946 he also followed this line, bracketing Welwyn Garden City with Letchworth as places that 'could and would prefer to look after themselves'.[49]

Figure 6.8 Welwyn Garden City and Hatfield were designated as twin New Towns, neighbours but firmly separated by intervening green space. (author's collection)

Then, in September, the Labour-controlled Welwyn Garden City Urban District Council met secretly with him, asking that he take future development out of the Company's hands.[50] They objected strongly to the Company's promotion of residential social segregation and its restrictive policies towards cinemas, public houses and shopping.[51]

Whether or not the local council's intervention had anything to do with it, Silkin had by November changed his mind. There is certainly no evidence that pressure came from fellow ministers to do this. Actually the reverse was the case, with the Treasury questioning all new major financial commitments.[52] The minister now argued that Welwyn Garden City and neighbouring Hatfield should be New Towns, sharing a single development corporation. The case at Hatfield was, as we will see, very strong. Even the Company was prepared to accept a 'shadowy suzerainty' over it (in the deputy secretary of the ministry's words) by a new Hatfield-focused Corporation.[53] The problem was that the intended scale of Hatfield's expansion on its own was insufficient to justify a fully-fledged development corporation. Actually taking over nearby Welwyn Garden City, rather than just supervising the Company, made such a corporation viable by increasing the scale of the operation. And, from the planning point of view, though there was no intention to merge the two, Hatfield was so close to Welwyn Garden City that it made sense to manage their expansions in tandem (Figure 6.8).

More fundamentally, Silkin had become convinced that it was unwise to allow a private company to implement key public policies. These were not simply about growing a New Town but also ensuring that it grew in as self-contained a way as possible and was directly integrated with the outward movement of population and employment from Greater London. He did not explicitly say that a private, profit-seeking company (that had promoted Welwyn Garden City partly as a middle-class commuter town before 1939) could not be trusted to respect the new policy priorities. Yet those fears were there, albeit shared by few others at the time. Among the many doubters was his own inspector at the designation inquiry, who recommended that the Company's record as a model of town planning and enlightened estate development was such that it should be allowed to continue.[54] The leader of the garden city movement and a champion of the New Towns programme, Frederic Osborn (a Labour Party member), also thought that Silkin's decision was unnecessary and doctrinally motivated. So too did the *Times*, the *Economist*, the *Architect's Journal* and many others.[55] Tellingly, however, Osborn later acknowledged that Silkin's fears may have been soundly based.[56] And, as we saw in Chapter 2, in Letchworth (where the First Garden

City was not nationalised) the abandonment of the limited dividend principle triggered a retreat from Howard's public spirited principles by the late 1950s.

'...a NEW TOWN NOT a GARDEN CITY'

Despite contemporary objections Silkin did not give way, but he was thwarted over a related issue: what the New Town would actually be called.[57] The draft designation order referred to 'Welwyn New Town'. Silkin and his officials wanted to avoid 'Welwyn Garden City New Town', and not just because it was a cumbersome name. They did not want New Towns to be viewed simply as rebadged garden cities, which they saw as an outmoded concept. Instead, they wanted places where a modern post-war society, less class-bound and with more social mixing, would develop. The clear east–west residential segregation of classes evident in Welwyn Garden City in 1948 certainly did not fit the new model. Yet the same obstacles that had faced the Company over the name question remained: there was already a settlement called 'Welwyn' whose inhabitants had steadfastly ensured that it remained quite distinct from 'Welwyn Garden City'. The idea of an entirely new name was considered briefly but soon rejected as impractical. Local opinion in both the 'Welwyns' and more widely in the county was that the names and the differentiation between them were now permanent and could not be undone. Silkin and his officials were very unhappy about all this. One exasperated civil servant commented, 'what is going to be constructed is a NEW TOWN NOT a GARDEN CITY. This is 1948 A.D.'[58]

But they were obliged to concede. The new 'Welwyn Garden City New Town Development Corporation' was constituted in May 1948.[59] (Hatfield Development Corporation, legally a separate body, was identically constituted.) Its/their Board(s) differed significantly from the others discussed in that there was stronger representation of local council interests,[60] reflecting the high degree of local government support for both New Towns. The chairman was Reg Gosling, a Board member of the Co-operative Wholesale Society, former president of the London Co-operative Society and much involved in the political wing and other facets of the co-operative movement. There was an irony in this because the expiring Welwyn Garden City Company had for some years not permitted a Co-op store in what, until 1936, was their own retail subsidiary's monopoly territory. This had annoyed the local Labour movement and Silkin may possibly have appointed a Co-op man as chairman with this in mind. (Not that either of them ever brought up this old resentment.) With public speaking skills first acquired on East End street corners, Gosling was an effective chairman who enjoyed and responded well to counter-argument at both Board and public meetings.

The only Board-level continuity with Welwyn Garden City Ltd was the new Board's vice-chairman, Dick Reiss, who had previously held the same role with the Company.[61] Silkin knew him from their work together on the London County Council Housing Committee in the 1930s. The minister wanted the new Board to be able to draw on his long experience, though Reiss was shunned by some former associates for agreeing to serve the new body.[62] There was other continuity in several aspects of the Company's administrative and technical expertise,[63] the most notable of which were the retention of Louis de Soissons as town planning consultant and Malcolm Sefton as landscape architect. The new Corporation's comptroller and chief engineer had also filled equivalent roles in the Company and there were several others in more minor posts. The general manager was, though, a new appointment – James McComb, a Stowe-educated former Spitfire pilot decorated for his distinguished service leading 611 Squadron during the Battle of Britain. During his long tenure (until 1962) he proved an extremely able manager of the twin Corporations, working especially well with Gosling (despite their very different backgrounds) until the latter's death in 1958.[64]

The Corporation's first significant action came during 1949, when it acquired most of the property of the Company it was superseding and two of its subsidiaries.[65] Because the Company had acquired its site from previous owners and kept the freehold intact as a unified estate, site acquisition at Welwyn Garden City was more straightforward than in any other New Town. A valuation of £2.8 million was agreed for the assets needed to develop the New Town (a price the ministry later thought overgenerous). The assets were, however, substantial, comprising a mansion (Digswell House), six large houses and over 1,600 houses, flats and cottages, 1,979 acres of undeveloped land and freehold ground rents on residential, industrial and commercial properties. A few subsidiaries of Welwyn Garden City Ltd were left untouched, including Welwyn Stores Ltd and Welwyn Builders, which came under the control of a new private body, the Howardsgate Trust.[66] The Company's land outside the designated area also remained, controlled by a new company, Danesbury Properties. Digswell Nurseries briefly remained independent, but soon this too became part of the Development Corporation.

Another very early action was to prepare and approve a new plan. De Soissons produced a new plan that was exhibited and discussed locally in May 1949 and submitted for central approval in October.[67] The basic aim was to plan for an increase from 18,500 to 36,500 inhabitants. This was less than the 50,000 target proposed by the Company in its 1947 plan, which was controversially to be achieved by a major extension north of the Mimram valley (entirely avoided in the 1949 plan). Instead, growth was to be achieved by major housing extensions to the north-western and south-eastern areas, by rounding off existing development in the south-west and by adding a major new 'residential unit' in the north-east. In line with earlier plans, the term 'neighbourhood unit' was pointedly not used. Certainly, the 'residential units' lacked the clear physical distinctiveness associated with fully articulated planned neighbourhoods at that time. But, in truth, their planned distribution and the clustering of community facilities did not differ hugely from that now favoured model. The industrial area was to be extended to the north-east and south-east, the town centre completed and a large area of playing fields provided to the east. A large part of the north-east was reserved for gravel extraction (though never used). The dropping of this reservation in 1954 allowed the target population to be increased to 50,000 without any incursion north of the Mimram. This change was ratified in the 1957 revised master plan.[68] (In 2011 the former New Town area's population, approximately 46,600, was approaching this final target.)[69]

Compared with Stevenage and, especially, Hemel Hempstead, the plans for Welwyn Garden City New Town caused little controversy and were readily accepted by the ministry. In essence, this was because both plans were essentially sensible elaborations of de Soissons's pre-war conception of the planned town of Welwyn Garden City. This is ironic, given Silkin's hope that the 'Welwyn New Town' he had wanted would mark a clear break from the old garden city era. However, one of his concerns was acknowledged in the explicit desire in the 1949 plan (and reiterated in the 1957 revision) to rebalance Welwyn Garden City's social geography. The overwhelming pre-1948 dominance of private home ownership on the western side, especially in the north-west, was to be countered by many more weekly rental, lower-cost dwellings in that area. Similarly, the eastern side was to include more homes for sale and more expensive monthly rental housing.

Making the garden city into a New Town

These concerns were immediately apparent in the construction efforts of the Corporation. Its early reports specifically highlighted new housing schemes intended to reduce the impact of this residential 'Iron Curtain'.[70] The opinions of those who lived there about how serious this divide actually was after 1945 clearly varied. One woman who moved from Barnet with her husband (who also happened to be Ebenezer Howard's grandson) and children in 1952 to a new Development Corporation house on the east side remembered enjoying the sense of real community there.[71] She never herself felt any strong sense of an unequal divide. Difficulties in getting to the better shops in the town centre on the western side were clearly apparent, but better bus services had improved matters compared with the pre-war days. Her husband, however, had quite a different perception and felt the social divide was still quite strong even then.

But there were also more immediately pressing problems for the Development Corporation. It was, of course, subject to the same national financial constraints and materials shortages that affected other New Towns, but it and its Hatfield twin faced unique local problems as they tried to accelerate housing construction from the late 1940s. The main one stemmed from another peculiarity: existing local employers within the town boundaries or nearby were already generating a high and expanding demand for male workers that met both New Towns' foreseeable needs in this respect. It was a position similar to that in the provincial New Towns of Aycliffe and Corby, but unique among those around Greater London.

In most respects this was an enviable position, but one with several downsides (more so in Hatfield, as will be shown). Obviously it intensified the pressing need for housing, not just to relieve London's housing pressures (the main purpose of the New Towns programme) but also to service needs arising from expanding local employment. The local economy had grown markedly since the late 1930s, but without properly accommodating either the firms or their new workers. Especially pressing for both New Towns were housing needs associated with the fast-growing de Havilland aircraft works. These adjoined Hatfield, although they had many workers living (or hoping to live) in Welwyn Garden City. As will be shown in the discussion of Hatfield, de Havilland's activities were a very high national priority, critical to Britain's early post-war defence and export earnings.

The most immediate consequence was that the twin Development Corporations were short of building workers.[72] As in other towns with boom industries paying high wages, workers were reluctant to do less lucrative jobs. Yet, whereas Stevenage and Hemel readily attracted building labour with the early promise of a house, this was less easily achieved when existing and incoming factory workers were also claiming priority.[73] Welwyn Garden City was not quite so badly off in that the former Company's building activities had fostered the growth of a local workforce, but the shortage was still serious and, in an effort to attract new workers, the Corporations opened a building workers' hostel in an old RAF camp between the two New Towns.[74] Gradually, however, the problems were overcome and the hostel was closed in 1954 without prejudicing the by now growing housing output.

The twin Development Corporations, especially the one at Welwyn Garden City, initially favoured smaller construction contracts and smaller, fairly local firms.[75] The latter included Welwyn Builders Ltd, the former subsidiary of

Figure 6.9 Housing in Knightsfield dating from around 1960. Although there is some modernisation compared with pre-war designs, the continuing impact of the de Soissons approach is evident in the design and grouping of the buildings. (author photograph)

Figure 6.10 A local shopping centre, also of around 1960, in the Haldens area in the north-east of the town. Again the emphasis is on simple, classically inspired elegance. (author photograph)

Welwyn Garden City Ltd. In part this approach arose because the Corporation, mindful of the general shortage of building labour in the area, wanted to maintain a local building capacity to allow longer-term maintenance and repair work. Yet, although smaller local builders usually produced to a high quality, they were slower than bigger firms when working on larger contracts. This was partly because they struggled much more than bigger firms to secure scarce building materials. Perhaps for this reason, it soon became difficult to fill the smaller and medium-sized construction contracts. Inevitably, therefore, bigger firms came to play a bigger role, though less than in Stevenage or Hemel Hempstead.

There was also less use of non-traditional construction methods than in other New Towns. The structural and other problems that had become apparent at the Company's 1920s concrete housing estate at Peartree (eventually completely demolished in the early 1980s) may also have discouraged further constructional experimentation.[76] De Soissons had generally endowed Welwyn Garden City with a well-mannered, neo-Georgian aesthetic that reflected local traditions and materials. The same aesthetic continued to dominate construction in the New Town era, especially when de Soissons himself was in charge (to 1955) (Figures 6.9 and 6.10). For similar reasons, combined with the earlier completion of Welwyn Garden City's active New Town phase, there was little interest in the Radburn housing layouts that became common in Stevenage and many other New Towns. Instead, more conventionally arranged layouts continued to be preferred, with houses parallel to tree-lined roads (in some cases with open fronts), along with some culs-de-sac with small greens.

After a very hesitant start because of the problems mentioned earlier and delays in main sewer construction in the Mimram valley, rates of house-building began to improve. By March 1955 just over 2,300 dwellings had been built by the Development Corporation in Welwyn Garden City, around 40 per cent for factory workers, mainly incomers working for pre-existing firms.[77] The 'Londoners first' approach to housing allocation followed in the New Towns left pre-existing housing needs mainly to the local council. Here, however, the former Welwyn Garden City Company rental housing now in Corporation ownership gave greater flexibility because it was not subject to the normal strictures about who could become tenants, in contrast to housing built in the New Town era. In any case, the more acute housing shortages eased over time. By December 1961 the Corporation's own dwelling completions had grown to over 4,700, and they exceeded 6,000 when the Commission for the New Towns took over from the Corporation in 1966.[78] The Commission itself added further housing, though at a slower pace.

Meanwhile, the already well-developed local economy grew further during the 1950s and 1960s, albeit now more closely matched by the housing programme. There were fears in the early 1950s that housing might actually overtake local job availability, largely because the Ministry of Supply kept postponing approval of a building licence for a large new factory for one of the big existing local employers, Murphy Radio.[79] However, the feared problem (not one that many other New Towns had the luxury of worrying about) never materialised. Comparatively speaking, Welwyn Garden City was always more quantitatively significant as a centre of employment than as a residential town.[80] In 1966, for example, available jobs outnumbered resident local workers by some 4,000.[81] The net result was that there was a little over 17 per cent more jobs than workers in Welwyn Garden City.

Yet this net figure concealed a complex pattern of in-commuting (of, as one civil servant earlier put it, 'cloth-caps'), mainly to local factories, and out-commuting ('bowler hats'), mainly to better-paid office jobs in London and nearby towns.[82] The sum of both groups of commuting workers in 1966 was equivalent to over two-thirds of all workers actually living in Welwyn Garden City New Town. This pattern was, of course, markedly at odds with employment self-containment, a core aspirational target of New Towns policy, yet other New Towns had also begun to experience these same trends. In the increasingly mobile society of the 1960s more workers were able to live further from where they worked. In this, as in other ways, the New Town model of the 1940s reflected less and less the emergent way of life of the 1970s and beyond.

The enduring garden city

As its experience of being a New Town passed, it was clear that Welwyn Garden City's character had been less profoundly changed than had Stevenage's or even Hemel Hempstead's. Silkin's original ambition had been to overlay the garden city with a more modern and socially mixed New Town appropriate to the post-war era. In many ways, though, the place's identity as a garden city has proved resilient. In a purely physical and aesthetic sense, much of this reflects the uniquely enduring hand of de Soissons. Although his garden city planned vision was less apparent in the outer and later estates, it still dominates the place as a whole. But other factors are also involved. There is still recognisably a larger section of the local population that is more affluent than in other New Towns, deriving originally from the promotion of the garden city by the Company before 1939 to middle-class rail commuters. And although a Welwyn Garden Residents Association that appeared in 1956 reflected more the concerns of the less affluent new (and old) Welwyn Garden citizens,[83] many local social and cultural institutions continue to be shaped more by the most affluent section of the population. And, despite the efforts of New Town planners, the old east–west social distinctions can still be seen: muted, perhaps, but unmistakable.

The garden city era also dominates the heritage and collective memories of the town, especially in the very large conservation area covering the town centre and western residential districts.[84] Although the New Town period is represented by the Beehives conservation area in the south-east, which protects an area built in the 1950s for relatively affluent residents in an attempt to shift the social geography. Despite its date, however, it recalls the classic neo-Georgian garden city image in its design and building materials. Aspects of the New Town era are also remembered in present-day Welwyn Garden City most notably in the naming of the Gosling Sports Park after the first chairman of the Development Corporation. Yet the most prominent public monuments in the town centre honour the heroes of the original garden city in three separate pieces of commemoration along the Parkway–Campus axis to Howard, de Soissons and Chambers. There is no record of what Chambers, so bitterly opposed to New Town designation, thought of what became of the garden city after it left his charge. Writing in July 1948, he expected what followed to be 'lifeless, extravagant and ineffective'.[85] He died in 1957 but it is fair to suggest that he would be surprised at how far the legacy of the Company he led has persisted and the degree to which it is cherished in current planning policies.

Hatfield
'[A] confused medley of housing'
Hatfield was that extremely rare thing: the New Town that everyone wanted. Well, almost everyone: there were a few minor objections from local farmers. Yet the National Farmers Union, which generally handled cases where agricultural objections were more widely based, was not even involved in the Hatfield designation inquiry. This outbreak of near unity reflected the unfortunate state of Hatfield's development at that time. There was a small, beautiful and historic old town east of the mainline from King's Cross, nestling beneath the gates of the large Hatfield Park estate, for centuries home to successive Marquesses of Salisbury (Figure 6.11). Wisely, Silkin made no attempt in the New Town proposal to test the Salisbury dynasty's general sympathy for Howard's principles by routing this latest stage of the peaceful path onto their home ground. In any case, the opening of the park to Hatfield residents for much of the year provided a major amenity for the town.

Figure 6.11 Old Hatfield, looking towards the Gatehouse into Hatfield House and Park. New Town policies ensured that this was protected, with most new development occurring west of the railway. (author photograph)

The main arguments for a New Town at Hatfield lay on the other side of the main London and North Eastern Railway tracks, following the opening of the de Havilland aircraft factory in 1934. In 1920 the original factory had been sited at Edgware, in what was then open country. Quickly, however, it had become hemmed in by suburban housing following the 1926 surface extension of the London Underground. At Hatfield, alongside the new Barnet bypass (the present Comet Way, opened in 1926 to bypass the old Great North Road through old Hatfield), de Havilland acquired a very large open site. This quickly became its new manufacturing base, growing from 900 employees in 1934 to 4,280 in 1939 and 7,000 in 1949. And it was still growing, with many workers commuting from London and elsewhere. In 1939 another new factory was built nearby on a prominent site adjoining the new road at the northern end of the future New Town. This was Jack Olding's, the British importer of American Caterpillar tracked vehicles; on this site they were assembled, prepared, adapted and maintained. During the war the factory, popularly known as 'Caterpillar Island', was used extensively for all kinds of tracked vehicles, including tanks. By 1949 it had 1,000 employees. A few smaller factories had also arrived by 1939.

Although some de Havilland and Olding workers lived relatively locally in Welwyn Garden City, St Albans and elsewhere, this sudden economic growth also created local pressures to expand the hitherto small commuter residential

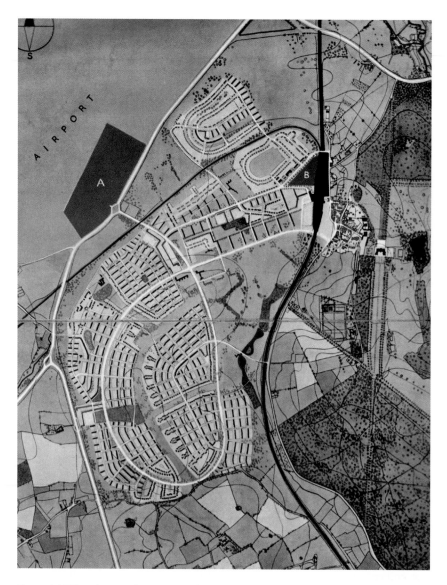

Figure 6.12 The Abercrombie proposal for the expansion and formalising of Hatfield's development (though he did not actually propose it as a satellite town). The position of the aircraft works and airfield which shaped the New Town's economic destiny is shown at 'A'. (author's collection)

area west of the railway. By 1948 Hatfield's population had grown to 8,500. During the later 1930s private developers began building what the Abercrombie plan described as 'a confused medley of housing'.[86] Some was ribbon development along the new bypass facing de Havilland, the rest disconnected estates and accretions to existing villages and hamlets. Although it developed a council estate at Birchwood from the late 1930s, the local authority, Hatfield Rural District, found it otherwise very difficult to insert any order into the inchoate pattern that was emerging. Like other small district councils, it lacked the financial, political and technical resources to contemplate the larger scale and expensive 'front-end' planning that was necessary to develop a satellite town.

The 1944 Abercrombie plan – some parts of which later appeared in the New Town plan – proposed Hatfield as a planned expanded town to allow more of its workers to live there and give it greater physical and social coherence (Figure 6.12). Yet no recommendations were made about the institutional mechanism by which the planned expansion was to be achieved, and it was not until 1952 that the Town Development Act finally created a legal mechanism for small local authorities in Hatfield's position to receive financial and other assistance from congested metropolitan areas seeking to export population and central government. Yet, with de Havilland set to grow even more and a major drug company actively considering moving there (though never actually doing so), this issue could not wait.

In November 1946 Silkin proposed to a cabinet policy committee that Hatfield become a New Town in conjunction with Welwyn Garden City.[87] The Treasury resisted for a while, one official arguing that Hatfield Council could soldier on, guided by ministry planners, and that 'on sunny afternoons they can cross the fields to Stevenage and pick up hints'.[88] Such arguments were not taken seriously, but the viability of the small development corporation needed for Hatfield alone was certainly questionable. As noted earlier, the real dispute was about how the future growth of Welwyn Garden City was to be managed. Once that was decided in favour of a New Town, however, the idea of a New Town at Hatfield was never in doubt, although its originally intended size of 30,000 was reduced to 25,000.

The proposed designation sailed through the March 1948 inquiry and was confirmed in May.[89] The designated area, comprising some 2,340 acres (947 hectares), was the second smallest of the London New Towns (only Bracknell was smaller). It was an elongated, curving site between Hatfield Park and the Barnet bypass, though excluding the town's main workplace, the de Havilland works, which was on the road's western side. The Lea valley formed its northern boundary and the village of Welham Green marked its southern limit. The largely undeveloped southern part of the site rose gently to an elongated chalky ridge, its slopes well-endowed with many attractive mature trees. Compared to the northern part, which was flatter and heavily compromised by existing building, the south offered many possibilities to create a town that might be something special.

Planning a New Town on a 'traffic island'

This, at least, was the hope with which Hatfield's planning consultant, Lionel Brett, embarked on his task. In all but this respect, Hatfield Development Corporation was composed identically to the Welwyn Garden City Corporation. But, whereas de Soissons continued as planning consultant to that Corporation, the 36-year-old Brett became at Hatfield the youngest of the New Town planners.[90] Educated at Eton and Oxford (where he read history), he had qualified as an architect only in 1939 and designed his own home and a house extension for an aunt. After war service in the Royal Artillery he stood unsuccessfully as a Liberal parliamentary candidate in 1945. Having become interested in planning during the war he set up as a consultant, working with Clough Williams-Ellis and Abercrombie on abortive plans for three small towns. Despite this very limited professional experience he obviously impressed these two luminaries with his design ability and intellectual qualities. And, one presumes, his self-belief. As he later wrote, 'what had been drummed into me by 23 years of elitist education, was solid idealism plus the use of words. With these, I thought, one could set about the rebuilding of England.'[91]

Brett's plan for Hatfield (Figure 6.13) aimed for a more compact pattern of residential development than in most other New Towns.[92] One reason for this was the way in which existing and proposed roads, particularly the North Orbital Road (the present A414) along the southern edge of the Lea valley, made the core of the designated area into a 'traffic island', edged by important flows of longer-distance traffic which Brett wanted to discourage from unnecessary entry into the town. He endorsed proposals for a southern perimeter road (South Way) to link the old Great North Road to the Barnet bypass, which had the effect of dramatically reducing traffic on the old Great North Road through Old Hatfield that otherwise would sever it and the biggest publicly accessible open space at Hatfield Park from most of the New Town. South Way and the North Orbital at the other end of the town effectively gave new 'hard edges' to the town, marking the boundary of the built-up area. Beyond both roads the designated New Town area was open land which Brett retained, reserving for agriculture or predominantly unbuilt land uses. Although these green areas gave

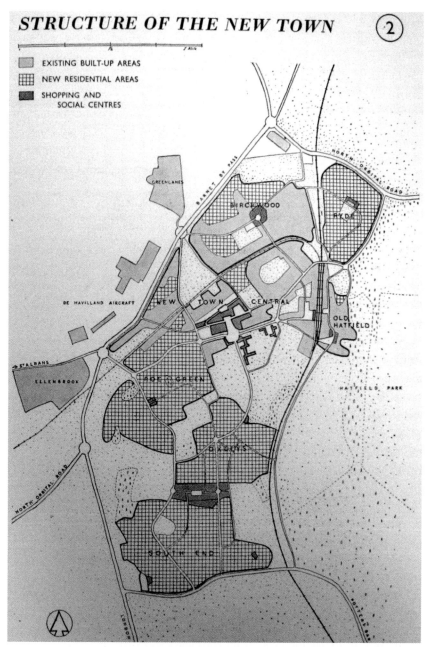

Figure 6.13 The master plan for the New Town. Compared with other New Town plans of the period, it was much more compact, with little open space within the designated area, and the main industry beyond. (author's collection)

'soft edges' to the north and south of the town, they actually reduced the amount of the designated area that was available for building, intensifying the need for a relatively dense urban layout within the 'traffic island'.

Other factors also encouraged the notion of a more tightly developed urban pattern. The unfortunate nature of the existing piecemeal development pattern itself strengthened the appeal of a plan that drew the town more tightly together. Moreover, Brett himself was sensitive to the latest currents in architectural and planning thinking and wanted to avoid any repetition of what was then increasingly regarded as the excessive spaciousness of Welwyn Garden City.[93]

Having thus created a basic physical framework for the New Town, the 1949 plan defined seven basic residential units within it.[94] In the case of old Hatfield, which became (at 1,000 inhabitants) the smallest of these, it was merely a case of protecting and enhancing its character by removing through traffic and making some minor changes. More recent existing development would see more infill building to form two residential units and related social facilities and services at Birchwood (3,000) and New Town Central (5,500). Apart from Ryde (2,500), which was east of the railway and north of old Hatfield, the entirely new residential units and local service provision would be in the southern half of the town at Roe Green (5,000), Oxlease (3,000) and South Hatfield (5,000).

Like de Soissons, Brett preferred to conceptualise and label these as residential units rather than as full-blown neighbourhood units. In Hatfield's case, however, there were much stronger differences from the neighbourhood unit model.[95] Certainly its local areas were not clearly differentiated physically from each other as occurred in Stevenage or, to a lesser extent, Hemel Hempstead (but especially at Harlow). Hatfield had almost no space within it to provide the areas of parkland, playing fields or road landscaping that elsewhere gave this physical separation. Local retailing, school and other social provision were also organised on a less formulaic basis, with more expectation that these facilities would be shared with adjoining areas.

Even more so than in the case of its twin neighbour, there was no quantitative need at Hatfield to attract new employers. Its major industries were already present (albeit the main ones just beyond the designated area). Nor, especially in the case of by far the biggest, de Havilland, was there any need to worry about whether there was enough room for industrial expansion. Yet this did not mean that the Development Corporation could simply ignore industry and employment, which had provoked the single objection to the plan at the January 1950 inquiry. The problem was rather a lack of balance, with little employment available for women or to offset an excessive dependence on the aircraft industry. And, while de Havilland at Hatfield had both military and civil sides to its operations, both were subject, especially in the early post-war years, to the vagaries of government policy. Although neighbouring Welwyn Garden City had a much more diverse manufacturing employment base, it was anticipated that, apart from a little manufacturing, most new non-de Havilland employment in Hatfield would be service-related. The plan used the town and local centres as the spaces where this additional employment would be located.

De Havilland had another, quite different impact on the thinking of Brett and the Development Corporation, which arose because of the noise impact on the New Town of jet aircraft testing sheds and flight paths from the aircraft works.[96] As the plan was being formulated, de Havilland was making two runways.[97] The principal one was broadly parallel to the Barnet bypass, but a secondary grass runway was created at right angles to the main one, to be used when the wind direction and speed made the main runway difficult to use. It was this which created the problem, because on the relatively few days of the year when it would be used aircraft would take off directly across Hatfield. They would then pass, at low altitude, over the slopes of Roe Green, precisely where much of the New Town's first areas of new housing were to be built.

The Corporation, which wanted the right to build up to three storeys if necessary up to the brow of the ridge, were adamant that they could not sterilise a swathe of land in an already tight site and Brett suggested that tree belts could mitigate the impact a little. James McComb (no stranger to early jet aircraft) also contended that noise over the whole New Town area and beyond whenever jet engines were being run (on the ground or in the air) was already intolerable and it would not be significantly worse directly under the flight path. In the event a compromise was reached and the particular Roe Green problem rarely arose. In practice, the secondary runway was little used by de Havilland not so much because of noise considerations as for operational reasons: pilots and the company considered that the point where the grass runway crossed the main concrete runway created an avoidable risk. Although this specific problem did not materialise to the expected extent, therefore, the general problem of aircraft noise remained. One Roe Green resident recalled that when 'the Comet was running its engine … we couldn't have any windows open if we wanted to talk'.[98] So, in a way that seems surprising today, Hatfield's people simply adapted to living with a tremendous and potentially damaging nuisance associated with the place where most of the New Town's workers directly or indirectly earned their living.

'Am I building a New Town or am I earning dollars'?

Approval for the plan came in August 1950, but it was not to be the only shaper of the town's destiny. The plane that produced most of Hatfield's noise during its early years as a New Town, the Comet, made its first test flight in 1949 and entered commercial service in May 1952. It was the world's first jet airliner and promised to be a world beater. Governments of the time gave it the highest priority, hoping its potential for export sales would make a major contribution to Britain's economy and renew its international prestige. Yet by September 1952 production remained very slow, with only one plane completed each month. Meanwhile, the cabinet ruled that the housing of workers needed to fulfil the armaments programme should be given the highest priority,[99] while it was also hoped that military jet planes would be another major source of foreign currency earnings. These 'top-level' concerns directly affected Hatfield because de Havilland was a key hub of the aircraft industry at a national level. The main problem was getting enough skilled workers, to which the lack of housing in the Hatfield area was a major obstacle. Although some de Havilland workers were already living in the town or nearby, many still lived in London. They either faced gruelling journeys to work or had to live much of the time away from their families in local lodgings.

Wherever they lived, few were satisfactorily housed. To remedy this, Hatfield Development Corporation had to overcome the same early problems as did its twin in Welwyn Garden City. Building labour and especially material shortages appear to have been more acute than in Stevenage or Hemel Hempstead, and there were also specific local delays in completing the Colne valley sewer. The Corporation was very much aware of the additional national pressures upon it. As McComb admitted asking himself in September 1952, 'am I building a New Town or am I earning dollars – and I answer it by saying that unless we earn dollars or other foreign currency there won't be a New Town'.[100] In one sense it was useful to have these additional pressures on the ministry to expedite materials supply. But McComb still insisted that building and other essential workers also needed housing. They also had to be given priority because otherwise more houses could not be built and schools, health care or other services would not be provided.

All of this also sat very uneasily with the principal objective of the Greater London New Town programme, which was not to cater directly for the growth of industries that were already present but to achieve the decentralisation of population and industry from London. Housing de Havilland's workers from London was approved of, but those who had already moved to Hatfield or the surrounding area could not now in theory be housed by the Development

Corporation. They would have to look to the local council, which, for its part, saw the New Town as a way of minimising its own housing responsibilities for de Havilland. This 'Londoners first' policy was especially irritating to McComb and Gosling, who felt a strong sense of obligation to those who had already moved (they also wanted more flexibility to attract and retain good building workers, whether or not they were Londoners).[101] The situation also created tensions among de Havilland's workforce. As one said, '[t]here was an awful lot of fiddling going on with people claiming that they lived in London, claiming they were married and all kinds of things...'.[102] He referred to someone who used a post restante address in Barnet while in fact living in Hatfield in order to get a Development Corporation house. Eventually Corporation officers suspected this was happening on a sufficient scale to warrant inspecting where applicants claimed they lived in London, including where they slept.

Yet, if there were these kinds of strains, the wider tensions between newcomers and existing inhabitants were really rather muted compared with those in Stevenage and especially Hemel Hempstead. As one newcomer, who came to set up a chiropody business, observed:

> people who had been much more established in the town were certainly slightly separate at times from some of the others, but that's natural it is purely a question of having known people for so long. I can't say I noticed a reaction to newcomers in Hatfield as might have happened in some places. I don't really think that there was any animosity to newcomers.[103]

This is borne out by a noticeable silence in subsequent oral history reflections. In other respects, however, early experiences of arrival and of settling in and socialising appear to have much in common with those in other New Towns.

Over time, the 'Londoners first' mantra was less strictly enforced, which all Development Corporations, especially Hatfield, welcomed. By 1953 the shortage of building labour had also eased, so Hatfield could increasingly concentrate on de Havilland workers. The Development Corporation's housing completions increased markedly in the mid-1950s before dwindling at the end of the decade and then undergoing some fluctuation during the 1960s. By 1967, when the Corporation had been disbanded, it had built just over 4,100 dwellings. Roughly half were allocated to the growing number of de Havilland workers, but many continued to live elsewhere. A further 1,200 dwellings had been built by the local council and 280 by private builders. The first area to be developed was at Roe Green (in 1950), followed by South Hatfield (from 1954) and Oxlease

Figure 6.14 Hatfield's housing was widely praised, notably this group designed in 1954 at Roe Green, combining attractive design with economies in materials and space. (author photograph)

(from 1957).[104] Contrary to original intentions, the Corporation decided in 1957 that Ryde neighbourhood should be entirely privately developed housing; construction began there in 1959.[105]

The designs and detailed layouts of the Corporation's housing, which made good use of the partially wooded slopes, attracted praise (Figure 6.14). There were usually small individual front gardens, often combined with more public green areas or verges and larger individual back gardens. As in other New Towns, provision for cars was very limited. The houses themselves were simple and unpretentious, brick-built so far as materials shortages permitted but with other walling materials, such as weather boarding and asbestos panelling (now replaced), often used. In 1954 housing in Roe Green designed by Lionel Brett with his partner Kenneth Boyd (who ran the architectural side of the business) received the regional housing medal. The partnership secured many detailed housing commissions in Hatfield during the 1950s. As early as 1949, Brett became interested in reducing housing costs, experimenting with more economical designs that saved money by reducing hallways and landings within houses. Many Roe Green houses, for example, used open-plan living/dining areas with stairs leading directly to the upper floor. These features, together with the greater exposure in upper parts of the town, may account for more early residents

Figure 6.15 This strikingly designed scheme in the most elevated southern part of the New Town was a modernist echo of Georgian terraces. Unfortunately the flat roofs did not prove to have been well attached during a 1957 gale shortly after completion. (Jane Housham)

mentioning in oral history accounts the difficulty of heating houses than was the case in the other New Towns (though, as was usual, no rented New Town houses had central heating until rather later).[106] Regardless of this, however, some of the design ideas for greater economy in space and building costs were taken up by the ministry when the Conservative government launched the 'People's House' nationally in 1952.

Hatfield Corporation also began to use more packaged forms of non-traditional housing. The Hazel Grove area of South Hatfield, developed from the mid-1950s, included over 380 dwellings built on the Wimpey 'no-fines' system. They were highly unusual in design (again by Brett and Boyd): flat-roofed and formed in long terraces which curved sinuously, following the contours up to the brow of the ridge. The effect was highly contemporary while echoing aspects of Georgian design and was much admired by contemporary architectural opinion (Figure 6.15). However, things went seriously wrong during a gale in November 1957 when the long flat roofs of several terraces took on the aerodynamic properties of aircraft wings. Being rather inadequately secured to the walls, they were wrenched free and thrown distances up to 70 feet.[107] The physical damage was repaired, with the contractor and the architects sharing the liability, but the reputational damage to Brett was serious. His partnership broke up and he did no further architectural work in Hatfield.

Economic worries

The incident echoed in certain respects the earlier catastrophic fate of Hatfield's great hope, the Comet. Rushed into service with inadequate understanding of the performance under stress of the many innovations it contained, it suffered a series of major fatal accidents during 1953 and 1954. Eventually, after extensive inquiries and investigations, it was recognised that the special alloys used in the original design were prone to metal fatigue and mid-air disintegration. Only in September 1958 did the improved Comet regain its certificate of airworthiness. By then, however, its advantage had been lost and the larger and more cost-effective Boeing 707 and Douglas DC-8 took what had been hoped would be its prime markets in transatlantic air travel.

For Hatfield the long-voiced fears about unbalanced employment now began to be realised, as redundancies reduced de Havilland from its peak of approaching 12,000 workers to around 10,000.[108] Government, meanwhile, was withdrawing its financial support for the civil aircraft industry. Cushioning guarantees for Comet orders from countries with weaker currencies or sympathetically timed orders from the RAF could no longer be so confidently expected.[109] Hatfield was also affected by the same cutbacks on the military side that hurt Stevenage. Overall, however, because of its central role in de Havilland's research and development work, Hatfield fared much better than the firm's other sites. Some work was relocated from elsewhere to Hatfield and redundancies were more limited than had originally been feared, while displaced workers were quickly absorbed into industries in surrounding areas.

Pursuing greater balance in Hatfield, the Development Corporation attracted a few small new industries, but these were to boost female employment – of which there was little at the aircraft works – rather than to genuinely diversify the local economy.[110] This still did not need seriously to be addressed. Yet, for de Havilland, things were never quite the same again and the fragmented structure of the British aircraft industry began to be consolidated. In 1960 de Havilland became part of Hawker-Siddeley and the marque itself was superseded in 1963. Eventually, in 1977, British Aerospace was formed. Hatfield had been the very centre of de Havilland's operations, but increasingly it was one production centre among several in Britain (and, later, Europe). The full playing out of the consequences of these changes occurred only in the 1980s and 1990s, culminating in the ending of production and the closure of the airfield in 1994.

For many New Towns, the growth of retailing and other services for the growing population began to diversify employment soon after the initial

Figure 6.16 The small New Town centre at Hatfield attempted to give some coherence to rather piecemeal pre-war shopping developments, with some limited success. There have been subsequent additions with a major supermarket and, more recently, regeneration. (Jane Housham)

growth phase had occurred. Partly because it was smaller than most other New Towns and so close to the by then more established centre of Welwyn Garden City (which from 1939 had its own department store), this proved less so for Hatfield. An existing shopping area had begun to grow incrementally before the New Town and Brett proposed that this could be incorporated into the New Town's main centre (Figure 6.16). Eventually this is what happened, though not before much argument about whether the plan and the centre's actual location should be changed. The centre that finally resulted added two new squares: one a market place lined on two sides by two levels of shops, one above the other; the other, White Lion Square, larger and lined by shops on three sides. Various new public buildings were also incorporated. The overall result pleased few and was still incomplete when the Development Corporation was wound up in 1966. In the absence of serious competition it served local needs adequately for several decades, though more recently has suffered real decline. Delayed by the financial downturn and continuing problems in the intended development partnership, a somewhat hesitant process of regeneration is now underway.

After de Havilland

In the longer term, however, the basis was laid, even before the New Town was designated, for an economic and social diversification that made Hatfield unique among the first generation of New Towns and unusual even when later ones were included. This is the University of Hertfordshire, the growth of which owed very little to the New Town but which, like much else in the town, stemmed from de Havilland.[111] In 1941 the company made an apprentice training agreement with Hertfordshire County Council and, three years later, the chairman of de Havilland presented a 90-acre (36-hectare) site in Roe Green to the county, stipulating its use for educational purposes. In 1952 Hatfield Technical College was established, becoming the Hatfield College of Technology in 1958, Hatfield Polytechnic in 1969 and the University of Hertfordshire in 1992. Today the university has about 27,000 full- and part-time students, over 90 per cent of them based in Hatfield, mainly on the original campus and most of the remainder on part of the former de Havilland site.[112]

Its impacts on Hatfield and the wider county are substantial, including direct provision of jobs, a large demand for local goods and services, a source of graduate workers for nearby employers and some important links with business innovation. The economic development officers of many former New Towns of the same era would doubtless have loved to have such a growing future asset. Resident students also have a noticeable impact on Hatfield. Although there is a sizeable amount of specialist student accommodation, there are now significant numbers of student households living in multi-occupied houses, many in former New Town estates in Roe Green and South Hatfield.[113]

The students add a different kind of 'social balance' to that envisaged by the Reith Committee, one about which local opinions are certainly mixed. Yet there is also much daily travel from the surrounding area to Hatfield to study (not just on the part of part-time students), while students resident in Hatfield reportedly often weekend elsewhere. Nor – although they may remain in the county – does Hatfield itself retain many of its graduates who were not already resident there. In this respect, Hatfield, a rather small university town with a character still largely shaped by the twin legacies of a particular twentieth-century manufacturing industry and its New Town experience, does less well than bigger metropolitan or medium-sized historic cities. Changing these perceptions will be very important to Hatfield's future and its potential to recapture, in a new era, an economic importance equivalent to that which it held in the mid-twentieth century.

The 800-acre (323-hectare) area formerly occupied by the de Havilland factory and airfield became another major potential asset in regaining that importance.[114] Although over half of the land was excluded from development because of its planning status as green belt, a new district of Hatfield has grown on the northern part of the area. Even before the demise of factory and airfield, the creation of the A1(M) motorway and the opening of the Hatfield Tunnel in 1986 began to change the area, with the former A1 becoming Comet Way. An early development immediately above the tunnel, bordering the de Havilland site, was the Galleria shopping development, originally opened in 1991 (and about which a little more in Chapter 8).

Conclusions

These vignettes on the three other Hertfordshire New Towns reveal many things in common with Stevenage but also some differences. These are not so much in their experiences as New Towns, for there were many important 'family resemblances' during their time as New Towns (to which we will return). However, there were some contrasts in the character of the bodies which oversaw development in each New Town and in the skills and personalities of the people who ran these bodies. There were also differences in how detailed planning was conducted – their town centres, the approach to framing the neighbourhoods/residential units and detailed aspects of housing design, for example. There were also important differences in their social histories. The enduring characters of Hemel Hempstead, Welwyn Garden City and Hatfield as towns have certainly been less determined than that of Stevenage by the fact of them having been New Towns. For them, the New Town experience did not last as long and other important facets of their identities that preceded their designations were either reinforced or at least not overlain by becoming New Towns. Thus the size of Hemel Hempstead as an established town, the strong continuities with previous planning and development at Welwyn Garden City and the many impacts of de Havilland in Hatfield all remained defining features.

Yet the main points to make remain the generic ones about New Towns and their many enduring qualities. For all the economic changes that have subsequently occurred, all the Hertfordshire New Towns remain places attractive to new employers with relatively high potential for innovation. This partly reflects their locations in London's outer metropolitan area and the way that subsequent investments in the road and rail infrastructure have strengthened their advantages. The economic frame of reference is now much more regional, in contrast to the great emphasis on self-containment in the early post-war decades. But, in other respects the persistence – now expressed in a new terminology of 'sustainable communities' – of relatively high percentages of workers still living and working in their own former New Towns remains impressive in the face of vastly increased car-based personal mobility.

And, to go back to the ideals expressed in the film with which this chapter began, all these New Towns remain decent places for most of their populations to live. That decency may seem a little limiting for their young people compared with the imagined excitements of the bright lights of the big city, but this is hardly peculiar to the former New Towns. Some of their shops and other services in the local centres might be undergoing or have undergone facelifts and occasional areas of housing more radical renewal. In the main, though, their once raw housing estates survive largely intact. They have been updated in some respects and many, through sales, are now part of the housing market, with all that that entails for good or ill. But they remain settings for the great majority of their inhabitants to live in pleasant and convenient places which present few obvious obstacles to happiness. They too represent important milestones on the peaceful path. Perfection in all these things still beckons, of course (a theme to which we will return in the last chapter), but these New Towns, like Stevenage, achieved much that has not subsequently been equalled.

Notes

1   NA HLG 91/61, Hemel Hempstead Development Corporation, 29th Report to Minister of Housing and Local Government, 24.1.1952, 5.
2   Anthony Thompson (dir.), *A home of your own* (Data Films for HHDC, 1951).
3   N. Adams, interviewed in BBC2 TV programme, *Now the war is over: a home of your own* (BBC, 1985); P. Addison, *Now the war is over: a social history of Britain 1945–51* (London, 1985), pp. 81–2.
4   Cullingworth, *Environmental planning: vol. III*, p. 52.
5   G. Hitchcock, 1995: interview by Joyce Hartley, in *New Town Record*, DVD (Glasgow, 1995). Now available from <http://www.idoxgroup.com/knowledge-services/idox-information-service/the-new-towns-record.html>; S. Hastie, *Hemel Hempstead: the story of new town development 1947–1997* (Hemel Hempstead, 1997), p. 25.
6   Hastie, *Hemel Hempstead*, pp. 20–22.
7   NA HLG 91/536, *Report of Inquiry*, 1946.
8   NA HLG 90/223, *Hemel Hempstead New Town (Designation) Order*, 31.1.1947.
9   T. and S. Waterson, 'Thoughts on the new arrivals' <http://www.talkingnewtowns.org.uk/content/topics/attitudes/like-idea-others-moving-hemel-hempstead>, accessed 19 August 2015.
10   Hastie, *Hemel Hempstead*, p. 22.
11   T. Price, '"Southern Victory" to hit Old Town', *Hemel Hempstead: the new town years 1947–1997* [special series], *The Gazette*, 13 (1997).
12   Hastie, *Hemel Hempstead*, pp. 22, 58–64; G. Hitchcock, interview in *New Town Record*.
13   U. Taber, 'What the people of Hemel Hempstead thought of the new arrivals' <http://www.talkingnewtowns.org.uk/content/towns/hemel-hempstead/una-taber/people-hemel-thought-new-town>, accessed 19 August 2015.

14   E. Bull, 'Fitting in with the locals' <http://www.talkingnewtowns.org.uk/content/towns/hemel-hempstead/eileen-bull/fitting-locals>, accessed 19 August 2015.

15   G. Hitchcock, interview in *New Town Record*.

16   NA HLG 91/60, Notes of an address by the Rt Hon Lewis Silkin MP during the 2nd meeting of the HHDC …, 26.3.1947.

17   NA HLG 91/66, K.S. Dodd, Memo: Hemel Hempstead Master Plan Inquiry, 6.12.1949.

18   NA HLG 91/234, Report of a Public Inquiry held in Hemel Hempstead on 15th, 16th, 17th, 18th and 22nd November 1949 into Representations with regard to the Master Plan.

19   NA HLG 91/234, Hemel Hempstead Protection Association, Report of the Executive Committee upon the Development Corporation's Third Plan for the Development of Hemel Hempstead into a New Town, October 1949.

20   NA HLG 91/63, W.O. Hart, Summary of Proposals and Criticisms received as a result of the Exhibition of the Outline Plan, 27.11.1947.

21   NA HLG 91/63, G.A. Jellicoe, *The Report accompanying a plan for Hemel Hempstead New Town*, 3rd June 1947.

22   NA HLG 91/438, especially Borough of Hemel Hempstead, Representations about the Hemel Hempstead New Town, 5th December 1951.

23   Cullingworth, *Environmental planning: vol. III*, 118.

24   NA HLG 91/438, Letter H. Macmillan–Mayor of Hemel Hempstead, 21.1.1952.

25   NA HLG 91/62, passim.

26   NA HLG 91/63, Jellicoe, *Report*, pp. 15–16.

27   Sir Geoffrey Jellicoe, 1995: interview by Tony Burton, in The Planning Exchange, *New Town Record*, DVD (Glasgow, 1995). Now available from <http://www.idoxgroup.com/knowledge-services/idox-information-service/the-new-towns-record.html>.

28   Allies and Morrison/The Landscape Partnership, *Water Gardens study: Hemel Hempstead*, (2011), especially pp. 1–23.

29   Quoted by K.S. Dodd in NA HLG 91/234, Report of a Public Inquiry…, p. 11.

30   Cullingworth, *Environmental planning: vol. III*, pp. 343–4.

31   HALS, CNT/HH/6/1/4, Hemel Hempstead Development Corporation, *Report on the New Master Plan for Hemel Hempstead* (HHDC, 1960).

32   Hastie, *Hemel Hempstead*, pp. 144–65.

33   Hemel Hempstead Development Corporation, *Hemel Hempstead – new town from old* (Hemel Hempstead, 1957); Hemel Hempstead Development Corporation, *Hemel Hempstead – new town from old* (Hemel Hempstead, 1960).

34   F.J. Osborn and A. Whittick, *The new towns: the answer to megalopolis* (London, 1969), p. 412.

35   Ogilvy, 'Employment expansion'.

36   HALS, CNT/HH/6/2/3, Commission for the New Towns, *Hemel Hempstead*, Commission for the New Towns, 1969.

37   Quoted in *Now the war is over: a home of your own*; Addison, *Now the war is over*, p. 81.

38   Hastie, *Hemel Hempstead*, pp. 74–85.

39   B. Adams, interviewed in *Now the war is over: a home of your own*.

40   B. Ford, interviewed in *Now the war is over: a home of your own*; Addison, *Now the war is over*, pp. 82–3.

41   HALS, CNT/HH/6/3/1, Hemel Hempstead Development Corporation, *Your house in Hemel Hempstead* (c.1955) shows all the dwelling types constructed during the early years, many in Adeyfield.

42   Hastie, *Hemel Hempstead*, pp. 86–121.

43   Jellicoe, interview in *New Town Record*.

44   Hastie, *Hemel Hempstead*, pp. 122–37.

45   HALS, CNT/HH/6/3/2, Y.J. Lovell, Hemel Hempstead Neighbourhood Development: Grove Hill Precinct 'A', Lovell, 1966.

46   Hastie, *Hemel Hempstead*, pp. 138–43.

47   See the relevant section of the recently created website http://www.talkingnewtowns.org.uk/content/category/towns/hemel-hempstead.

48   Chambers, in Purdom, *Satellite towns*, 2nd edn, p. xi.

49   Cullingworth, *Environmental planning: vol. III*, pp. 33–4. The paper was presented to a sub-committee of the Lord President's Committee which formulated new policies.

50   De Soissons, *Welwyn Garden City*, p. 119.

51   Cullingworth, *Environmental planning: vol. III*, p. 84.

52   Ibid., pp. 62–6.

53   NA HLG 91/286, memo, E.A. Sharp, 13.3.1947.

54   NA HLG 91/298, Report of Inquiry proposed designation order. 1948, p. 18.

55   De Soissons, *Welwyn Garden City*, pp. 115–19.

56   Osborn and Whittick, *The new towns*, p. 226

57   NA HLG 91/96, passim.

58   NA HLG 91/96, Memo L.F. Boden-M.M. Dobbie, comment by Dobbie, 11.2.1948.

59   NA HLG 91/297, passim.

60   NA HLG 91/210, passim.

61   NA HLG 91/210, Letter L. Silkin–R.L. Reiss, 11.5.1948.

62   NA HLG 91/210, T.H. Sheepshanks, Note to Parliamentary Secretary and Minister, 10.5.1950.

63   De Soissons, *Welwyn Garden City*, pp. 122–3.

64   F. Clayton, 1995: interview in The Planning Exchange, *New Town Record*, DVD (Glasgow, 1995). Now available from <http://www.idoxgroup.com/knowledge-services/idox-information-service/the-new-towns-record.html>.

65   NA HLG 91/494; De Soissons, *Welwyn Garden City*, pp. 125–7.

66   Rook, *Welwyn Garden City Past*, pp. 114–17.

67   HALS, CNT/WH/13/1/2/1, L. de Soissons, *Report of the Welwyn Garden City Development Corporation upon the outline plan* (Welwyn Garden City, 1949).

68   HALS, CNT/WH/13/1/2/2, Welwyn Garden City Development Corporation, *Report of the Welwyn Garden City Development Corporation on the progress and present development of the plan prepared in 1949 by Louis de Soissons* (Welwyn Garden City Development Corporation, 1957) especially pp. 19–20.

69   Town and Country Planning Association, *New towns and garden cities – lessons for tomorrow. Stage 1: an introduction to the UK's new towns and garden cities, appendix the new towns: five minute fact sheets* (London, 2014).

70   HALS, CNT/WH/13/3/2/9, Welwyn Garden City and Hatfield Development Corporations, *In Step … with Housing* (Welwyn Garden City and Hatfield Development Corporations, 1955), p. 15.

71   V. Godfrey, 'An east side home' <http://www.ourwelwyngardencity.org.uk/page_id__444.aspx?path=0p2p57p60p>, accessed 20 August 2015.

72   For example, HALS, CNT/WH/13/3/2/4, Welwyn Garden City and Hatfield Development Corporations, *The progress of Hatfield and Welwyn Garden City New Towns* (1952), pp. 5–6.

73   NA HLG 91/486 highlights many of these housing allocation issues, especially Letters McComb–Heady, 15.4.1952 and Heady–McComb, 21.4.1952.

74   HALS, CNT/WH/13/3/2/7, Hatfield and Welwyn Garden City Development Corporations, *In Step …with building labour* (Hatfield and Welwyn Garden City Development Corporations, 1954).

75   NA HLG 91/427, Memo by G.R. Coles, 26.9.1952.

76   S. Hall, '20 million plan to rebuild homes' <http://www.ourwelwyngardencity.org.uk/page_id__538_path__0p162p.aspx>, accessed 28 April 2015.

77   HALS, CNT/WH/13/3/2/9, *op.cit.*, 10 and 21. Though precise figures are given, the two sets are not strictly comparable, hence the approximation of the proportion. The dwelling completions figures include private dwellings on sites leased from the development corporation but not local authority housing.

78   Welwyn Garden City Development Corporation, *Welwyn Garden City new town* (Welwyn Garden City, 1961); de Soissons, *Welwyn Garden City*, pp. 240–41.

79   NA HLG 91/489, especially letter J.E. McComb–G.L. Barber, 14.3.1951. The building licence was a national control over whether building projects should be allowed to go ahead. It was introduced in wartime to ensure scarce building resources were effectively used in the national interest. The building licence system remained in operation until 1954 when all rationing was abolished.

80   Ogilvy, 'The self-contained New Town'.

81   Ogilvy, 'Employment expansion'.

82   NA HLG 91/489, Memo, R. Metcalfe–F. Schaffer, 6.11.1958.

83   De Soissons, *Welwyn Garden City*, p. 151.

84   Welwyn Hatfield Borough Council, *Welwyn Garden City Conservation Area appraisal* (Welwyn Garden City, 2007).

85   Chambers in Purdom, *Satellite towns*, 2nd edn, p. xi

86   *Greater London Plan 1944*, 1945, 172

87   Cullingworth, *Environmental planning: vol. III*, pp. 62–4.

88   Ibid., p. 64. Perhaps the official meant Welwyn Garden City.

89   NA HLG 91/298, Report of Inquiry proposed designation order. 1948, p. 18.

90   M. Spens, 'Obituary: Lionel Brett (4th Viscount Esher)', *The Studio*, 28 August 2004; A. Powers, 'Obituary: Viscount Esher', *The Independent*, 13 July 2004; Viscount Esher, 1995: in The Planning Exchange, *New Town Record*, DVD (Glasgow, 1995). Now available from <http://www.idoxgroup.com/knowledge-services/idox-information-service/the-new-towns-record.html>.

91   Cited in Powers, 'Obituary'.

92   HALS, CNT/WH/13/2/1/1, L. Hatfield Development Corporation, *Report upon the outline plan prepared by Lionel Brett* (Hatfield Development Corporation, 1949).

93   Esher, 1995.

94   HALS, CNT/WH/13/2/1/1, L. Hatfield Development Corporation, *Report*, pp. 18–19.

95   Esher, 1995.

96   HALS, CNT/WH/13/2/1/1, L. Hatfield Development Corporation, *Report*, p. 19; NA HLG 91/211, *passim* but especially memoranda P. Tennant. 15.9.1949, 26.9.1949.

97   The de Havilland Aeronautical Technical School Association (De Mercado, R.), *Hatfield aerodrome from the air* (Stockport, *c.*2010).

98   E.g. J. Smith, 'Days Mead to Bishops Rise', in A. Burke and M. Corbett with the Boomtime Group, *Voices of Hatfield from the '50s and '60s* (Stroud, 2011), p. 23.

99   NA HLG 91/427, Memorandum C.J. Southgate, 18.6.1952.

100 NA HLG 91/427, Letter J.E. McComb–T.D. Wickenden, 2.9.1952.

101 NA HLG 91/427, Letter J.E. McComb–T.D. Wickenden, 2.9.1952.

102 J. Parker, 'How to get a house', in A. Burke and M. Corbett with the Boomtime Group, *Voices of Hatfield from the '50s and '60s* (Stroud, 2011), p. 17.

103 G. Model, 'Setting up a new business in Hatfield' <http://www.talkingnewtowns.org.uk/content/category/towns/hatfield/mr-g-e-model>, accessed 19 August 2015.

104 Osborn and Whittick, *The new towns*, p. 141.

105 J. Cobern, D. Irving and C. Martindale, 'Part 4. New Town housing 1948–2008: the Development Corporation 1955–1966', in *Hatfield and its people: New Town housing, 1948–2008*, part 10 <http://www.ourhatfield.org.uk/page_id__222.aspx?path=0p106p114p>, [accessed 30.4.2013].

106   E.g. J. Vann, 'Cooler up the hill', in A. Burke and M. Corbett with the Boomtime Group, *Voices of Hatfield from the '50s and '60s* (Stroud, 2011), p. 21.

107   J. Axford, 'When the roofs blew off!' <http://www.talkingnewtowns.org.uk/content/topics/moving-in/jessie-axford-roofs-blew>, accessed 19 August 2015; K. Wright, 'The day I may have met Barbara Cartland!' <http://www.talkingnewtowns.org.uk/content/topics/work/ken-wright-day-may-met-barbara-cartland>, accessed 19 September 2015.

108   NA HLG 91/741, especially letter J.E. McComb–J.H. Waddell, 28.7.1959.

109   NA HLG 91/741, Memo R. Metcalfe, 15.9.1959; New Town needs peep into the future – Gloom at Comet redundancies, *Manchester Guardian*, 20 August 1959.

110   HALS, CNT/WH/13/2/1/2, Hatfield Development Corporation, *Hatfield New Town: Progress and present position of the plan* (Hatfield, 1957), pp. 10–11.

111   University of Hertfordshire, *The University of Hertfordshire: sixty years of innovation* (Hatfield, 2012); University of Hertfordshire, 'History of the University of Hertfordshire' <http://www.herts.ac.uk/about-us/history>, accessed 2 May 2014.

112   University of Hertfordshire, *Travel plan update* (Hatfield, 2010).

113   C. Lennon, 'Tighter planning rules for student homes in Hatfield', *Welwyn Hatfield Times 24*, 10 January 2012 <http://www.whtimes.co.uk/news/tighter_planning_rules_for_student_homes_in_hatfield_1_1172812,> accessed 2 May 2014.

114   Welwyn Hatfield District Council and St Albans City and District Council, *Hatfield Aerodrome: Supplementary Planning Guidance* (Welwyn Garden City, 1999).

CHAPTER SEVEN

Wider perspectives

Beyond Hertfordshire

In no other part of the United Kingdom (or indeed the world) was Howard's peaceful path, or close variants of it, as enthusiastically followed as it was in Hertfordshire. The county's five garden cities and New Towns were part of that twentieth-century search for a better way of living in an urban, industrial society, one that avoided many problems of the big, concentrated city. Hertfordshire might even be seen as the nearest existing equivalent to a 'Social City', Howard's polycentric cluster of small and medium-sized towns, all interconnected but each one also separate and distinct in its own identity and functions.

Yet Hertfordshire's unique experience, full though it was, is far from being the whole story. The garden suburbs and satellite towns of the interwar and early post-war years, examined in Chapter 4, were earlier variants of the peaceful path. Outside Hertfordshire, there were also significant variations from its experience among the other New Towns that were created after 1946. It is these, together with a briefer review of some of the wider international dimensions of new town planning – some quite different – which are addressed in this chapter. In turn, these wider perspectives give a better appreciation of the distinctive features of the Howardian approach to creating new settlements and the specific manifestations of it that are located in Hertfordshire.

The programme that began in Stevenage in 1946 led eventually to the creation of 32 New Towns (Figure 7.1). As noted at the beginning of Chapter 5, a total of 14 New Towns was designated between 1946 and 1950 under the two Attlee Labour administrations. All but one were designated by the town and country planning minister, Lewis Silkin, and he had secured cabinet approval for the last when he left office in February 1950, shortly before designation was completed. The Conservative governments that followed from 1951 to 1964 were initially less enthusiastic and designated only one further New Town in the ten years from 1951. During the last years of this period of Conservative rule, between 1961 and 1964, however, a further six were designated. The subsequent

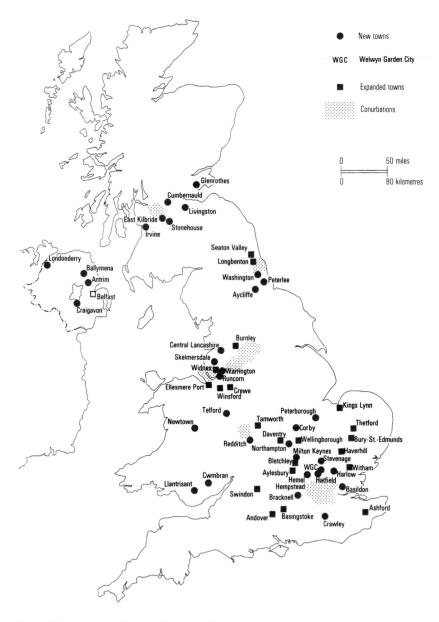

Figure 7.1 Map of the New and Expanded Town programmes at their greatest extent c.1973. It includes the very short-lived Stonehouse New Town in Scotland and Llantrisant in south Wales, which was never actually designated. Only the larger Expanded Towns are shown here. (author's collection)

Wilson Labour administrations designated ten more between 1965 and 1970. One further New Town was designated in 1973, but was soon terminated before any significant development had occurred.

The first New Towns

The initial emphasis was very much on addressing the problems of London by fulfilling the proposals of Abercrombie's Greater London Plan for new settlements to achieve planned decentralisation of people and jobs from the capital (Figure 7.2). Along with the four Hertfordshire New Towns, a further four were designated at Crawley in Sussex, Harlow in Essex (both 1947), Basildon in Essex and Bracknell in Berkshire (both 1949).[1] Patrick Abercrombie, this time with Robert Matthew, had proposed a similar strategy of planned decentralisation for Glasgow in the Clyde Valley Plan of 1946, specifically suggesting the site of East Kilbride in Lanarkshire, which became the first Scottish New Town in 1947. The original target populations of these other metropolitan 'overspill' designations were broadly in the same range as the main Hertfordshire examples.[2] Thus Harlow was to be for 60,000, Crawley and Basildon for 50,000 and East Kilbride for 45,000. The main exception was Bracknell, where strong local opposition led to a designation for only 25,000 – the same size as Hatfield – in the first instance. As with Stevenage and Hemel Hempstead, many targets were subsequently increased, ultimately to 80,000 at Crawley, 90,000 at Harlow, 140,000 at Basildon, 60,000 at Bracknell and 82,500 at East Kilbride.

A secondary function of the last named had been to attract new industry to the west of Scotland. Economic development was, however, to be the primary aim of Scotland's second New Town as it was designated in 1948. This was at Glenrothes in Fife, where projected new colliery development was expected to create many new jobs. Its original target was 32,000 inhabitants, but this was later increased to 55,000, mainly because, from 1959, it also became something of an overspill New Town, receiving population from Glasgow, especially so after what was to have been a major pillar of its local economy, the Rothes Colliery, was closed in 1961.

Various regional development needs were also important objectives in Silkin's other New Towns, such as Newton Aycliffe and Peterlee in County Durham, designated in 1947 and 1948.[3] The former was to provide housing for workers at a large industrial estate created during the war as a Royal Ordnance Factory in a relatively remote area and now being given over to civilian industry. It was originally planned for only 10,000, a figure later doubled and then, over-optimistically, raised to 45,000. Like Glenrothes, Peterlee was to be primarily a

"It's not fair. I want to throw for some sites for Satellite Towns in 1949. You picked them all last year."

Figure 7.2 The New Towns programme was initially focused on the needs of Greater London, although the process of choosing their locations was not as arbitrary as this cartoon suggests. It does, however, suggest something of how criticisms of the programme were building up as new sites were designated but with little immediate impact on housing needs. (author's collection)

coal-mining New Town; it was planned for 30,000 inhabitants and intended as an alternative to the pithead villages that were typical of the county (its history will be considered in a little more detail below).

The Welsh New Town of Cwmbran in eastern Monmouthshire was designated in 1949 in an area where there was already significant employment, but to which many workers had to travel long distances from their homes.[4] The intention was to create a town (originally for some 35,000 people, later raised to 55,000) which could house many workers and their families much closer to these factories. Finally, in 1950, Corby in Northamptonshire was designated (initially for 40,000, later raised to 55,000) to provide a more coherent pattern for development associated with the expansion of the Stewarts and Lloyds steelworks. This Scottish company had originally opened there in 1934 and, with major expansion occurring, it attracted yet more workers from central Scotland to this east midland New Town.

A latter day Edward I?

Overall, Silkin set a remarkable record, and was seen by some as a latter day Edward I.[5] It was the number of New Towns he founded that prompted the comparison, rather than the reasons. Motivated by a combination of military subjugation, administrative stabilisation and trade development, Edward had founded many new towns (rather more than Silkin, though over a longer period) in Gascony, Wales and England.[6] Yet Silkin had begun with grander hopes of founding 25 New Towns; however, his plans for overspill New Towns for provincial English cities, particularly Manchester, where several sites were considered, came to nothing. Neither did his interest in creating a New Town resort (he favoured Littlehampton), intended to help expand tourist capacity as the Holidays with Pay legislation started to have the major impact that war had delayed.[7] More generally, his ambitions were subverted by the legal challenges and wider economic problems that had such a big impact on Stevenage's early development but also affected the whole programme.

The enthusiasm of his ministerial colleagues also waned as they witnessed the controversies of the first months. Offsetting the 'London-centredness' of the programme by designations in Scotland, Wales and the regions allayed some concerns, but ministers also began to grasp how prolonged the development process would be, so that New Towns would make only a small contribution to meeting national housing needs in their early years. Silkin had originally hoped that it might take ten years to complete a New Town, an estimate very wide of the mark. Even those such as Hemel Hempstead and Welwyn Garden City that already had substantial existing populations took longer than this. The more completely 'new' New Towns took much longer.

A few glances at other 'first-generation' New Towns show that many of those around London, despite a few variations in their planning and local economies, had histories broadly similar to the Hertfordshire examples. Basildon, however, showed some important differences in that it was partly intended to replace an earlier phase of 'plotland' development.[8] Here small parcels of former arable land had been sold off with little or no infrastructure or services and developed piecemeal, mainly with chalet and shack developments of very light construction. There were around 6,000 such dwellings, which were condemned by officialdom as rural slums. The local councils had pressed for a New Town to be designated to allow these areas to be comprehensively redeveloped. In the event, clearing these areas proved very controversial, as plotland residents showed themselves much fonder of their homes than those wedded to the ideals of post-war planning had anticipated.

Farewell Squalor

Yet it was among the provincial New Towns of this period, especially those intended to boost regional development, that the main contrasts with Hertfordshire's experience were apparent. Peterlee is a case in point and several other factors in its development add to its interest. It needs to be seen in the context of a decline of coal mining in the west of County Durham and the recognition that the long-term reserves lay in the east, towards the coast.[9] As a result the 1951 County Durham Development Plan adopted the notorious 'D' village policy, under which old pithead villages so categorised would gradually be abandoned by being denied any future public or private development.[10] The proposed scale of long-term abandonment was nothing short of staggering. Almost a third of all the settlements in the whole county were originally judged to be in Category 'D', rising to around half in the county's western planning districts.

No abandonments were proposed in the Easington Rural District (the location of Peterlee), but pithead villages, even where collieries were still thriving, were seen as blots on the landscape: untidy, unlovely and insanitary. Peterlee would entirely supersede this ugliness, would be a place where miners and their families could live a better life; a place, too, that would attract new industries, allowing some longer-term economic diversification and occupational balance. There was much enthusiasm for the New Town in the local area, especially within the Easington Rural District Council and the county council, both solid Labour strongholds.[11] It was they and the Durham Miners Union who pressed for a New

Town to be designated. The New Town's very name honoured Peter Lee, a widely and warmly remembered leader of the Durham miners and of local government. Local professional expertise also played a part in the person of C.W. Clarke, the RDC's engineer and surveyor, who orchestrated this local commitment and helped frame many aspects of the project. He authored an important outline survey in 1946 that made the case for a New Town, subsequently extended and reissued the following year under the evocative title *Farewell Squalor*.

Responding to this local pressure, in March 1948 Silkin appointed his close associate Monica Felton, a former member of the Reith Committee and already deputy chairman at Stevenage, as first chairman of the Peterlee Development Corporation. The well-known modernist architect–planner Berthold Lubetkin, a Soviet emigré who had come to Britain in the 1930s, was commissioned to prepare the plan.[12] Both he and Felton had strong Marxist sympathies and wished to create a New Town quite different from all the others. It was to be one that, rather than being a garden-city-inspired collection of neighbourhood units dominated by individual garden housing, would embody and reproduce the strong social cohesion and class consciousness of the miners themselves. Lubetkin favoured a very compact and concentrated plan, fitting as he saw it for a cohesive mining community. He proposed high-density housing groups and a town centre which would give the town a strong identity as a 'miners' capital'.

Farewell Lubetkin

In any circumstances, it would probably have been very difficult to realise all Lubetkin's proposals. His rather singular desire to reroute the main A19 road to run through the town centre in order to intensify the sense of its regional centrality as a 'miners' capital', for example, would have required costly bridging work. However, Lubetkin was derailed primarily by the National Coal Board's insistence that as much as possible of the coal beneath the town should remain capable of easy exploitation. Since there were serious fuel shortages in the early post-war period, the Coal Board, predictably, won this argument. Lubetkin's radical plan was rejected, denying subsequent generations the chance to judge whether his bold vision would have made a better place to live than what was becoming the standard planning conception of the standard early New Town based on low-density neighbourhood units. Many architects would now argue that it would have been, but the actual record of the higher-density New Towns has been mixed, albeit for a variety of reasons. What is clear is that the defeat of Lubetkin's plan was facilitated by the departure of Felton to take up the chairmanship at Stevenage in 1949 and the replacement of Silkin himself early the following year (although he was already weakening in his support). Lubetkin's contract expired shortly afterwards and, unwilling to abandon his vision, he too departed.

Peterlee's planning was then taken over by Grenfell Baines and Hargreaves, who were also fulfilling the same role at Newton Aycliffe.[13] They prepared a much more conventional New Town plan, based on neighbourhoods of 5,000–7,500 inhabitants, each further subdivided into approximately three local units. Housing was mainly developed on fairly conventional lines, in small, low-density groups aligned to minimise the risks of damage through mining subsidence. Even so, this did not overcome the extreme difficulties of co-ordinating development with mining activities, and development was rather delayed. Large parts of the designated area could not be used because of subsidence risks. New industries were also slow to appear, which, combined with the weakening position of coal by the end of the 1950s, meant that the New Town grew much more slowly than originally anticipated. There was never any temptation to increase its original target population – as happened elsewhere – which in any case it never managed to reach.

The defeat of Lubetkin's plan also gave Peterlee a particular place in architectural history as the most acute symptom of a general timidity of approach to the planning and design of the early New Towns. There were, however, much deeper social and political concerns that transcended even this architectural disappointment. Local and national politicians and the Development Corporation signally failed to recognise the great loyalty which inhabitants of the existing mining villages felt to the places they already inhabited. Their long plain terraces, limited services and primitive sanitation might be very far from the romantic English village ideal, but people's attachment to these places ran very deep.[14] No existing villages in or around Peterlee were actually selected to die under the 'D' Village policy, but they were to be categorised 'C' (minimal investment), meaning that the New Town would be favoured over them, something that prompted real resentment.

A sense of a brave design ideal having been defeated did, however, persist in the Development Corporation's conscience, and as the south-west residential areas began to be developed it was decided to seek a boldness of design which had not previously been visible. The general manager of the Development Corporation wished to make better, more organic use of public space. The modern artist Victor Pasmore was hired in 1955 to collaborate with the Corporation's architects[15] and the results attracted much architectural interest, although some residents criticised the reduction or elimination of private garden space in favour of public space.

Even more controversial was Pasmore's 1969 Apollo Pavilion, a concrete sculpture which also functioned as a pedestrian bridge between two south-western housing groups. Although its artistic significance was judged considerable, the Pavilion also prompted local puzzlement. After the Development Corporation handed its care over to the local council in 1978 maintenance deteriorated and it became a venue for anti-social behaviour, bringing calls for its demolition. Eventually, however, it was restored in 2008–9 and in 2011 was given well-deserved protected status as being of historic and architectural interest. This extra care has signalled the undoubted artistic importance of the Pavilion and helped to reduce some, though certainly not all, of the local puzzlement.

The Town Development Act 1952

The new Conservative government which came to power in October 1951 almost immediately began to question the New Towns programme.[16] By the end of the year only 3,126 dwellings had been completed in all 12 New Towns in England and Wales combined; however, the new minister, Harold Macmillan, successfully defended the programme from Treasury suggestions that it should be abandoned. But a possible New Town for Manchester under discussion before the election, at Congleton in Cheshire, was completely dropped. More generally there was a shift to a more economical approach to developing the existing New Towns, which we have seen reflected in the four Hertfordshire examples.

The Conservatives' alternative approach to new planned decentralisation, at least in England and Wales, involved using the Town Development Act 1952.[17] This became yet another, though much less significant, variant of the 'peaceful path'. In the Greater London Plan Abercrombie had recognised that some planned decentralisation from the capital could be accomplished by the planned expansion of suitable smaller towns, a process that would be led not by purpose-made development corporations but by local authorities. Silkin considered this, but did not rush to legislation because he recognised that in the immediate post-war years urban local authorities, facing immediate housing and reconstruction needs in their own areas, would not want to start by building houses well beyond their boundaries. His successor, Hugh Dalton, began to work on it during the very short-lived Attlee government of 1950–51. By the time of the 1951 election a measure was set to come to parliament that was then taken over by the incoming Conservative government, which enacted it the following year. The measure applied only to England and Wales, however, and Scotland did not receive the same powers until 1957. As a result, there was no way until then of responding to the growing pressures in Scotland for planned decentralisation from the big cities other than by extending the New Towns programme. This factor contributed to the designation of Cumbernauld New Town (to be considered below) in 1955.

The 1952 Act (and that of 1957) essentially offered several ways for the local authorities involved to reach agreement about how an outward movement of population and employment from congested cities could be facilitated. Compared with the New Towns, much of the initiative rested at local level and was thus less likely to create the kinds of resentment of externally imposed decisions that were evident at Stevenage and Hemel Hempstead. Once agreement was reached on the principle to move population to a new location and the scale on which this was needed, some means of realising this was required. Essentially, a large city local authority wishing to move many people to a very small rural town would probably shoulder more of the responsibilities and costs, sometimes with the county council in the receiving area also being active. On the other hand, the district or borough council of an already sizeable rural town ambitious for some further growth would probably take more control itself. According to the nature of the agreement reached, there would be a transfer of housing subsidies and a contribution to sewerage and water supply costs from the exporting to the importing areas. Central government also provided extra funds to authorities involved in such schemes, especially if there was to be new or relocated employment in the receiving location.

Although the Expanded Towns (as town developments were collectively termed) programme avoided both governmental heavy-handedness and the expense of creating a development corporation, it was never as important as the New Towns programme. The inhabitants of potential reception areas were often just as suspicious of incomers from the big cities as were their equivalents in the New Town areas, but, in contrast, they could exert direct influence on their local councillors to prevent expansion happening or to limit its extent. The arrangements which worked best were where the receiving areas were 'growth-minded'. This would often arise because of an existential threat to the local economy, something worse than locally orchestrated expansion being threatened, and/or because local leaders were ambitious and able to transcend opposition. Over time, the London County Council and its post-1965 successor, the Greater London Council, also learnt how to overcome the fears of smaller local authorities in reception areas. They were increasingly able to do this by citing examples of earlier expansions that had gone smoothly and where the wider benefits of growth and better local services could be demonstrated.

The Expanded Towns

Despite all this, however, only two expansion schemes ever approached the size of a New Town. One was at Swindon, where exceptional local leadership combined with local fears for the future of the former Great Western Railway works following railway nationalisation to see the town's council use the 1952 Act from an early stage as a springboard for future growth and diversification.[18] The other came at Basingstoke from 1960 onwards,[19] where expansion arose because there was major opposition across the county to the London County Council's efforts in the late 1950s to promote its own New Town at nearby Hook.[20] This led to a period of negotiation, with Hampshire and the district councils instead agreeing a major town expansion at Basingstoke and a smaller one at Andover.

In total, 60 town expansion agreements were eventually negotiated in England and a similar number in Scotland (where the 1957 Act gave more incentives and direction to the programme). Around 89,000 dwellings were provided in England and Wales, well over half for London.[21] The average size of Scottish schemes was smaller and they were overwhelmingly devoted to Glasgow, with a national total of 11,000 dwellings built by 1974. Apart from the two large English expansions mentioned, almost all these schemes throughout Britain were rather small, typically adding one relatively large housing estate to small towns. As noted in Chapter 2, one such example was in Letchworth, where the 1,500-dwelling Jackmans Estate stemmed from a 1955 expansion agreement with the London County Council.

Even though the individual expansion schemes were modest compared with national or metropolitan housing needs, their physical, social and economic impacts on individual small towns could be dramatic. As at Swindon, though on a smaller scale, the agreements were often used to bring new industries to sleepy country towns, such as Haverhill in Suffolk, Thetford in Norfolk and Banbury in Oxfordshire.[22] The last of these was also unique in having expansion agreements with both London and Birmingham, introducing an unusual diversity within its population of newcomers. Haverhill, fictionalised as Angleton, was the setting of a 1965–69 BBC television soap opera, *The Newcomers*,[23] that dealt with human stories surrounding the move of a factory and its workforce from London to an expanding town, showing the problems of settling in including sometimes strained relations with existing inhabitants and between workers and managers in this new location. The treatment was rather caricatured, largely reflecting the perspective of incoming managers at the expense of rather narrow-minded workers and existing residents.

The long-term reality is that these expansions gradually brought the benefits of growth, eventually including better shopping, public service, leisure and cultural facilities and more employment opportunities. As was often the case with major new developments, however, housing growth often ran ahead of these other needs. Inevitably places were changed and some traditional aspects submerged, but the effect was less dramatic than in most New Towns. Under its town expansion scheme, for example, Thetford grew fourfold from 1958 to 1980 to reach about 20,000 when the 1952 Act expansion scheme was complete. Over a comparable period from 1946 to 1968 Stevenage had grown around tenfold to about 60,000 (and many more newcomers were still to follow).[24]

Cumbernauld breaks the mould

The only New Town designation of the 1950s after Corby came in December 1955 at Cumbernauld in central Scotland, which had originally been proposed in the 1946 Clyde Valley Plan.[25] Its intention was to provide for population decentralisation from Glasgow, much the most densely populated city in the United Kingdom. In the case of East Kilbride, the city council had been resistant to losing population. Now, however, the acute difficulties of meeting its housing needs within its own boundaries were undeniable.[26] (Moreover, as noted, it was not until a few years later that town expansion schemes became possible in Scotland.) Cumbernauld's initial target population, 50,000 inhabitants, was increased to 70,000 in 1960, 80 per cent of whom would come from Glasgow.

Preliminary proposals that formed the basis of the approved plan appeared in the spring of 1958. The vision was radically different to that found in any of the plans for the first-generation New Towns,[27] partly reflecting the severe physical constraints of the site. It was hemmed in to the south-west and eastern sides by coal and other mineral reserves, while other physical features such as peat bog and sharp slopes added further constraints. It had originally been intended that the designation would include an adjoining and more appealing tract of land within Lanarkshire, but this was opposed by the county council. The upshot was that the designated site was the most inhospitable of any New Town. It centred on an elevated ridge in the middle of the Forth/Clyde valley and was far more exposed to wind and driving rain than were surrounding areas.

Faced with this difficult site, the chief architect and planner, Hugh Wilson, seized the opportunity to make a radical break from the rather formulaic pattern of planning seen in the first-generation New Towns. He opted for much higher building and population densities than had previously been usual. Except in the case of two of the peripheral villages, the neighbourhood unit principle, the

Figure 7.3 Cumbernauld was radically different from the first New Towns. This photograph c.1968 shows the first phase of the elevated 'megastructure' that formed the central area. Notice the extensive open concrete walkways, the line of penthouse flats above the shopping level and the hotel (on the left). Following negative reactions, later central development has been much more conventional. (Architectural Press Archive / RIBA Library Photographs Collection).

cornerstone of early New Town plans, was rejected. Instead, most residential areas were closely adjacent to the town centre, which sat centrally on the top of the ridge. The intention was that this would be a compact settlement, inspired by Italian hilltop towns, where most residents would look primarily to the centre rather than to local neighbourhoods.

The key to realising this vision was the wholesale adoption in the New Town plan of the Radburn principle of separating vehicle and pedestrian circulation systems. We have seen how planners in Stevenage (and other early New Towns) began to adopt this principle in the later neighbourhoods. Cumbernauld was, however, the first sizeable town anywhere to be planned entirely around Radburn principles, so that fully segregated pedestrian routes connected the residential areas to the town centre, linking also with schools and other social facilities. However, despite some partial attempts to mitigate the effects of exposure to wind and rain by the design and grouping of buildings, the pedestrian journey to the town centre could be a daunting business. One commentator wrote about the 'Cumbernauld lean', a characteristic way of walking around the town to compensate for wind buffeting. There was also much sarcasm about the Italian design inspiration in such an inhospitable setting.

The first phase of the new central area took shape between 1963 and 1967, soon bringing further criticism (Figure 7.3).[28] It comprised an elevated 'megastructure', uncompromisingly modernist in design, with shopping, housing, hotel and other central activities. Despite winning much praise from many architects, it was the few initial notes of criticism – that it was coarse, 'verging on the megalomaniac' and blind to simple needs – which proved more prescient.[29] Criticisms grew when the second phase was completed in 1972. Further phases have largely abandoned the original concept in favour of large ground-level retail units, and the early stages soon experienced high vacancy rates. Eventually, in 2002–3, a large section of the first phase was demolished. Since then, however, the reputation of the town centre has substantially improved, especially since the opening of the new Antonine shopping mall alongside what remains of the original central megastructure in 2007. In a less dramatic sense, the wider town, now with a 2011 census population of around 52,000 people, has also changed, becoming rather more car-orientated than originally intended. Like most other Scottish New Towns, it also has rates of owner-occupation that are higher than the UK average (and markedly higher than those in any of the Hertfordshire New Towns, the long-term performance of which will be considered in the next chapter).[30]

A return to New Towns 1961–4

By the later 1950s the Conservative government was reluctantly moving back to the designation of further New Towns,[31] forced by a combination of circumstances.[32] After 1955 all the big cities embarked on major slum clearance programmes. It soon became clear that, even when multi-storey flats replaced old terraces and tenements (as they increasingly did), it was still impossible to rehouse the same number of people on the same area. This was something frequently misunderstood by politicians and public alike. It was not just slum housing which was being replaced by more roomy dwellings; there was also a need for new schools with proper playing fields, for modern roads and car parking, which all made new demands for space. The high-rise blocks also needed to be widely spaced to reduce overshadowing.

Meanwhile, green belt policies were increasingly preventing growth around most provincial conurbations, much as on the fringes of London and Glasgow since the 1940s. Expectations of slowing national population growth that had conditioned 1950s planning thinking were also being radically revised, so that in 1965 forecasters were predicting a UK population of around 72.5m by 2000.[33] In the event, the 2001 Census recorded just 58.8 million; however, the likelihood of a significant overestimate was not even realised until the late 1960s and the likely full extent of that overestimate not until the 1970s. Faced with early 1960s projections of population growth, therefore, the existing New Towns programme and rather puny Expanded Towns programme looked very inadequate.

So it was that Skelmersdale and Runcorn were designated as New Towns for Merseyside in 1961 and 1964, Dawley[34] and Redditch[35] for the West Midlands in 1963 and 1964, Livingston as a further Scottish New Town in 1962[36] and Washington for Tyneside in 1964.[37] In all cases the primary purpose was metropolitan overspill, though the last two were also intended to foster regional economic growth. The initial population targets of all of these new settlements were significantly higher than early New Town initial targets (although many of these were also being increased at around this time),[38] although most of these early 1960s designations tended to have more existing inhabitants than the first-generation New Towns.[39] Thus Skelmersdale, with 10,000 inhabitants at designation, was intended to grow to 80,000, and Runcorn from 28,500 to 100,000. Dawley with 21,000 would grow to 90,000, Redditch with 32,000 also to 90,000 and Washington from 20,000 to 80,000. The most optimistic of all was Livingston, set what turned out to be the hopelessly ambitious target of growing from 2,000 to 100,000.

The generally muted or positive reactions of the mainly sizeable existing populations to New Town designations in these areas contrast with the serious opposition in Stevenage, Hemel Hempstead and some other early Greater London New Towns. Over time, of course, there was more experience in smoothing the path to designation and allaying local fears. Politicians, civil servants and development corporation staff now better understood local needs for accurate early information. It was also important that the case for these New Towns had been argued through within a government that was naturally sceptical about New Towns. More widely, local or regional studies had usually already done much to make the case for each of them.

Most importantly, all these second-generation New Towns were designated in regions less prosperous than the Home Counties, more at risk of real decline (Figure 7.4). Earlier New Towns established in the less favoured regions had mainly proved themselves in attracting new manufacturing and other employment. In other words, existing local populations and politicians could see real advantages, economic and otherwise. This was especially so in areas such as central Scotland, County Durham and Merseyside. But, even in the generally

A town that has everything and is surrounded by countryside. It's a great place

TO LIVE

Living conditions are pleasant in Skelmersdale. There is plenty of modern housing in a wide variety of sizes and styles to rent or to buy. Pedestrian ways for safe walking and green open spaces, planned with nearly 2 million trees and shrubs to line the access to open country. The town's climate-controlled Concourse is one of Europe's most modern shopping centres. For their leisure, residents can use the superb hobby facilities in the local schools, if the more athletic pursuits of the indoor sports centre or the many splendid sports fields do not attract them.

Figure 7.4 The second-generation New Towns were located away from London and played important roles within their regions, offering modern settings for new industrial development. This promotional material (c.1977) for Skelmersdale was intended to appeal to businessmen, showing how the New Town could provide attractive surroundings for managers to live. (author's collection)

prosperous West Midlands, the existing small town of Dawley lay in a declining older industrial area of Shropshire, blighted by abandoned coal-mining and iron workings. The New Town embraced the existing town and its surroundings, offering modernisation, new jobs and environmental improvements. The economic hopes which were embodied in these second-generation New Towns did not mean that all local opposition melted away, however; the process of buying farmland, for instance, was rarely entirely painless. And where New Town centres were created in new locations potentially eclipsing the established centres, there were challenges: in Runcorn, for example, the existing town centre was threatened.

Examples of second-generation New Towns

Like Cumbernauld, all these New Towns were generally envisaged as being built at higher densities than the first generation.[40] There were, however, many variations in their plans compared with the rather formulaic patterns of the 1946–50 designations. In general, though, their housing was developed in more compact groups, with less emphasis on private gardens, at least in Development

Corporation rental housing. Again, as at Cumbernauld, urban design and architecture were, from the beginning, rather more strikingly modernist than in their early post-war predecessors. This was further emphasised by the growing use of industrialised building methods, important from the very outset in these New Towns.

Skelmersdale, for example, was planned by Hugh Wilson, the planner of Cumbernauld, though now working on a less challenging site.[41] Even so, his plan again rejected the neighbourhood unit, favouring the close grouping of most of the population within a short distance of the town centre at densities of around 18–20 dwellings per acre. Residential areas in Livingston were at an even higher density, making particularly heavy use of prefabricated and non-traditional construction in its early phases.[42] Yet certain 'traditional' aspects also persisted. Thus Peter Daniel, the Development Corporation's chief architect and planner, directing the master plan, favoured a modified version of the neighbourhood unit concept to group residential areas within the town.

Other New Towns of these years showed similar eclecticism. Washington, master planned by the consultants Llewelyn-Davies, Weeks and Partners, was framed around a strong road grid system, an idea that the same consultants later elaborated much further at Milton Keynes (Figure 7.5).[43] Within the square mile

Figure 7.5 Washington was a particularly successful second-generation New Town, a growth point in north-eastern England. Unlike those of some others of this period, its planners gave much emphasis to the motor car. From the outset residential development was geared to creating traffic-free living areas, as here at Donwell, photographed in 1972. (author's collection)

grid squares the living areas were typically grouped into three distinct 'villages', each averaging about 4,500 inhabitants. Housing densities were noticeably lower than others of the second generation, if still a little higher than those in the first-generation towns (and with less emphasis on private gardens).

Of these New Towns designated in the early 1960s, perhaps the most interesting from the planning point of view was Runcorn.[44] Its master plan was prepared by Arthur Ling, who framed the New Town around the unique structuring device of a basic figure-of-eight public transport route (with two additional loops). Together they linked residential areas, the new New Town centre at the crossover of the figure eight, the existing town and industrial areas. The initial hope was that a rail-based rapid transit or guided bus system would have provided the transport, but a simple dedicated busway using ordinary buses proved less costly. The corollary of this high reliance on public transport was that the New Town had to be compact, with most people living relatively close to the busway in quite high-density housing but with extensive public open space and other amenities.

How successful were the second-generation New Towns?[45]

In the long term, these second-generation New Towns have experienced more obvious problems than those earlier examples around Greater London. There were, of course, many variations between the different New Towns in the first and second generations. Yet the fact that, as a group, the 1961–4 examples were built in areas with less strong regional economies and therefore were often accommodating generally poorer populations than had moved to New Towns in earlier years obviously made it more difficult for them to appear as 'successful' in the long term as the first-generation towns which, again as a whole, were weighted towards the most affluent part of the UK.

It is also fair to say that the performance of many of the more innovative aspects of the planning and designs of the second-generation New Towns has been mixed.[46] To take just one example, the greater reliance from the outset of the second-generation New Towns on ambitious methods of housing design and construction also produced more failures than in first-generation New Towns, which tended to be more conventional in their design and construction. For instance, the Castlefields and Southgate housing estates at Runcorn were both innovative in design and construction but both soon failed structurally and socially. They have been completely demolished, the Southgate estate less than 15 years after it was built, and their sites have been redeveloped. However, earlier generation New Towns have experienced similar problems where they adopted comparable design and construction innovations in later phases of housing (in

Harlow, for example). The Hertfordshire New Towns have generally escaped this, as we will see in Chapter 8. Yet all this is far from being the whole story. Some of the second-generation New Towns, and especially Washington, have proved to be extremely successful growth points within their less affluent regions. Most (except Skelmersdale and Runcorn) also showed higher rates of owner-occupation in 2011 than the UK New Towns average. This put them above all the Greater London New Towns designated by Silkin (except Bracknell), including those in Hertfordshire. In part this was because most of the pre-existing New Town areas had bigger populations than the first-generation towns had had, with existing housing that, over time, has proved attractive for owner-occupation. It also reflected sales of newer housing formerly rented from the Development Corporation and the encouragement of new building for sale in the later phases of these New Towns. Overall, though, it reinforces the point made about Cumbernauld that most provincial English and the Scottish New Towns have over time proved attractive for would-be owner-occupiers. If they have failed in some respects, they have succeeded in others.

Regional concerns and third-generation New Towns

The regional consequences of the prevailing expectations about national population growth also formed an increasingly important part of the arguments for New Towns during the 1960s.[47] Two questions pervaded all official thinking at this time: how might space be found for the anticipated large population increases of the later twentieth century? And, relatedly, how might sufficient new employment growth be ensured for this new population without exacerbating the already marked drift to the South East and (to a lesser extent) the Midlands?

The new Labour government which took office in October 1964 inherited various recommendations from earlier regional reports.[48] A major White Paper on central Scotland in 1963 had suggested a further New Town at Irvine, on the north Ayrshire coast.[49] The Treasury, however, was not keen on the proposal because all the existing Scottish New Towns were costing much more than their equivalents elsewhere. This extra cost reflected the prevailing low levels of public sector housing rents in Scotland, meaning that greater subsidy was needed. It was difficult for the New Town Development Corporations to break out of this low-rent cycle because otherwise potential migrants would have been unwilling to move there. The result was that the designation of Irvine, another New Town that would face this problem, was delayed until 1966.

Still more protracted were the considerations of *The South East study 1961–1981*, published in March 1964.[50] Faced with the prospect of more rapid growth than in any other British region, the study's authors had proposed a mix of substantially new urban centres and major expansions of existing ones, notable because the proposed new settlements and major expansions would be far bigger than the first generation of New and Expanded Towns. The geography of these proposed growth areas also differed in that they were now being sited much further from Greater London and in several cases beyond the boundaries of the South East region. In essence, the 1944 Greater London Plan that had been the source of Hertfordshire New Towns was now being drawn onto a much larger canvas.

In the event, declining growth expectations meant that most of the study's suggestions were not pursued. Three large New Towns were designated at Milton Keynes[51] and Peterborough[52] (both 1967) and Northampton (1968).[53] The first was originally projected to grow from an existing population of 40,000 to 250,000. The other two towns, already large, were intended to grow from 81,000 to 180,000 and from 133,000 to 230,000 respectively. These projected increases were all on a larger scale than anticipated in the 1964 study. However, several other proposals for massive planned expansion in the Southampton–Portsmouth area and major growth at Newbury, Stansted, Ashford and Swindon were dropped or radically scaled back. A proposal for a similar scale of expansion at Ipswich got as far as the designation inquiry, at which much, largely agricultural, opposition was voiced.[54] Accordingly, the inspector recommended a smaller expansion, but the project was then completely dropped on cost grounds in 1969.

Third-generation New Towns in other regions

Manchester had long been considered as a major city with housing needs that could be alleviated by New Town development. Even under the Attlee governments, possible sites were seriously considered at Mobberley (rejected because of mining subsidence) and Congleton (which was not popular in Manchester and was rejected because of the high quality of the agricultural land which would have been taken).[55] Manchester City Council itself was still completing Wythenshawe in the first post-war years and also continued to seek sites in Cheshire for planned overspill under the 1952 Act, especially at Lymm.[56] Manchester's rather poisonous relations with the county council and local opposition prevented this location from being accepted, though it briefly resurfaced as a possible New Town site in the early 1960s. A major objection, however, was that it would have been essentially a commuter town, well-connected to Manchester and without significant local employment.

Risley, near Warrington, was identified as a possible New Town site in 1964, before the change of government.[57] Yet much of the site was unsuitable because the extensive presence of peat and projected coal mining under the area made it impractical for building. Eventually, in April 1968, a New Town was designated which incorporated the buildable parts of Risley within a wider area, including the already large town of Warrington. It thus became the New Town of Warrington and was developed on a similar pattern to Peterborough and Northampton, in this case originally being intended to grow from 124,000 to 205,000.

Alongside this, a much bigger project of the same type was under consideration in the Preston–Chorley area. Most government ministries were in favour because it would be a strong growth point and had an already robust industrial base. There was no loss of high-quality farming areas and no need to negotiate the minefield of relations with Cheshire. Yet Manchester's leaders were less than keen because of the distance from the city. There were also serious misgivings from the towns of north-east Lancashire because of fears that a New Town would damage their already uncertain economic prospects. Eventually, in March 1970, the Central Lancashire New Town, intended to grow from an existing 235,000 inhabitants to 321,000 (and eventually by natural increase much larger), was designated. It was much the largest existing and projected population ever to be included under the New Towns Act.

This trend towards using the New Towns Act within areas that already had sizeable populations was already very marked. It was evident, for example, in the West Midlands, where Dawley New Town area was greatly extended in December 1968 to include the neighbouring areas of Wellington and Oakengates.[58] The new enlarged New Town, soon renamed as Telford, was planned to grow from 70,000 to 220,000. The reason for this enlargement was that Dawley, by then almost six years beyond its original designation, comprised the most rundown part of Shropshire. Without any regional assistance to offer it was struggling to attract industry, in turn making potential residents unable or unwilling to move there. The adjoining areas were, however, altogether more promising because they already had significant employment and were much more attractive for private house-building. This enlargement generally had the desired effect and Telford began to grow more confidently than its predecessor.

The same broad trend was also apparent in Northern Ireland, which, until 1965, did not have any legislation to create New Towns. This was changed by the growing confidence in New Towns as powerful instruments of regional growth. Four New Towns were designated at Craigavon (1965), Antrim (1966), Ballymena (1967 – these two sharing a Development Commission, as they were called in Northern Ireland) and Londonderry (Derry, 1969).[59] The first was the most ambitious, with projected growth from 61,700 to 180,000. It was also the only one to propose a substantial new urban identity, uniting the Lurgan–Portadown area. Unfortunately that new identity was instantly labelled as sectarian by its very name, which honoured the first post-partition prime minister of the Province of Northern Ireland, who was, of course, a Unionist and Protestant. Antrim and Ballymena were substantial expansions around existing centres, set to grow from 32,500 between them to 100,000. Londonderry's growth was to be much more modest, from 82,000 to 94,500, but was notable for being essentially a piece of planned urban renewal, the first such example. In this respect it was a forerunner of the Urban Development Corporations that began to be created throughout the UK in the 1980s.[60]

Finally, against the general trend to ever larger New Towns, we should note the most unusual of all the designations of this period, Newtown, in rural mid-Wales (in December 1967). With a target population of just 11,000, it was intended to double the size of the historic Montgomeryshire market town (originally created as a new town in the thirteenth century by Edward I). Its purpose was essentially related to rural economic development and it grew from a proposal for a much

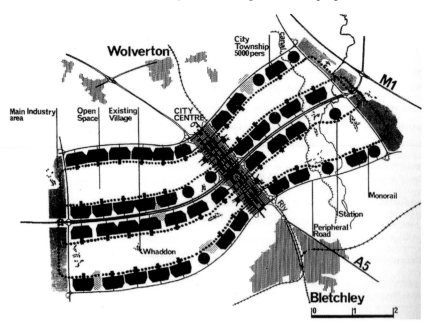

Figure 7.6 The original idea for a new city in north Buckinghamshire was promoted by the County Council as a radical monorail-based plan ('Pooleyville') to be developed by a public–private partnership. Both the partnership and the radical plan were rejected in favour of creating a normal New Town Development Corporation for what became Milton Keynes. (author's collection)

larger New Town based on Caersws. This would have been for 70,000 people, a figure that could have been reached only through what, for some Welsh opinion, was the very unwelcome prospect of taking overspill population from the West Midlands. Newtown was launched partly with a sense that its success might lead to the bigger project being revived (it never was). As the smallest ever New Town, it did not justify a full development corporation. Instead, that role was fulfilled by a more generalised Mid-Wales Development Corporation that used some professional staff from Cwmbran Development Corporation.

Milton Keynes

The most celebrated New Town of the third wave, and often seen as the most successful of the whole programme, was Milton Keynes (Figure 7.6).[61] Nearby Verney in Buckinghamshire (south-west of the present New Town) had been briefly considered as a possible New Town site in the later 1940s, but no action was ever taken.[62] From the mid-1950s a London County Council Expanded Town scheme had also been agreed for the existing town of Bletchley. Recognising the growth potential of this area (endorsed in the 1964 *South East study*), in the early 1960s Buckinghamshire County Council proposed to develop a large New Town of up to 250,000 inhabitants through a partnership involving itself, private developers and central government. In late 1964 the county architect, Fred Pooley, produced a futuristic figure-of-eight plan for what was called North Buckinghamshire New City, based around a monorail system with high-density clusters of residential development interspersed with employment areas.[63] It attracted great interest, but the ministry did not believe that the partnership was sufficiently robust to implement the scheme. In January 1967, therefore, it took direct control of the project and designated the site as a large New Town.

The adopted plan (Figure 7.7) also completely rejected the 'Pooleyville' concept,[64] vetoing a public transport plan with high-density development clusters in favour of a much lower-density car-based plan based around a kilometre road grid. Bletchley, the small towns of Stony Stratford and Wolverton, and 14 villages were encompassed within this grid. The basic approach was one which its planners, Llewelyn-Davies, Weeks, Forestier-Walker and Bor, had been moving towards in their plan (made under the name Llewelyn-Davies, Weeks and Partners) for Washington New Town, a few years earlier.[65] This latest plan was especially notable for the 'Americanist' thinking that underpinned it, personified by the involvement of the American Melvin Webber, who introduced the concept of a 'non-space urban realm'.[66] This asserted that modern communications such as the car and the telephone would encourage a growth of community

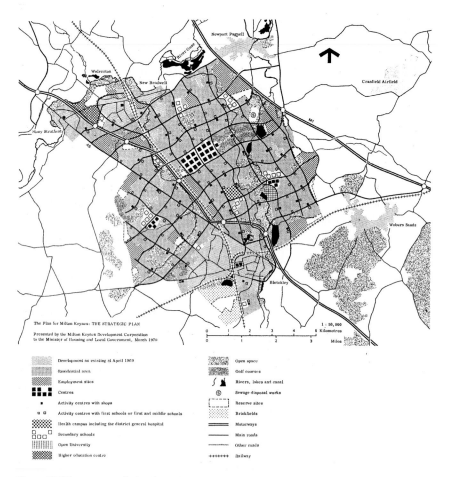

The Plan for Milton Keynes: THE STRATEGIC PLAN

Presented by the Milton Keynes Development Corporation
to the Minister of Housing and Local Government, March 1970

1 : 50,000

Development as existing at April 1969		Open space
Residential area		Golf courses
Employment sites		Rivers, lakes and canal
Centres	⑤	Sewage disposal works
Activity centres with shops		Reserve sites
Activity centres with first schools or first and middle schools		Brickfields
Health campus including the district general hospital		Motorways
Secondary schools		Main roads
Open University		Other roads
Higher education centre	+++++++	Railway

Figure 7.7 The approved plan for Milton Keynes, 1970. This was a car-based plan, framed around a grid road system which allowed high-speed car travel around the city. It was heavily influenced by American ideas and has proved very popular with most residents. However, it has not been conducive to good public transport provision. (author's collection)

that was progressively less related to spatial proximity. The patterns of people's lives would no longer be related to their immediate neighbours or a reliance on local employment or services. Instead of a city built around neighbourhood (or other locality-based clusters), a much more mobile population would develop social networks and use public and private services across the city as a whole, not necessarily in their neighbourhoods or a town centre. The master plan thus differed from earlier New Town plans. Local service centres were conceived of as being more outward-looking, serving the city as a whole rather than just an immediate locality. There was also less emphasis on the traditional notion of

Figure 7.8 Netherfield, an early rental housing development in Milton Keynes. Its radical design and metallic finish were not popular and there have been several attempts at 'makeovers'. Despite these, it remains one of the most deprived parts of what has generally been an economically successful and popular New Town. (Jane Housham)

centrality in the city. The city centre, such as it was, should have a rather different role, less dominant in terms of providing all the city's higher level functions.

In practice, that concept as approved was altered in some key respects.[67] Instead of a Los Angeles-style many-centred city, the main downtown centre was much more important than its master planners had imagined. (Yet, rather paradoxically, the centre's retailing came in the form of something along the lines of a rather stylish out-of-town car-based regional shopping mall.) The road grid was set in generously landscaped corridors, so much so that it was possible to drive at high speed along them without even being aware that a city surrounded them. Instead of American-style traffic lights at intersections, roundabouts were used, intensifying this sense. The grid squares also became inward-looking living areas, rather conflicting with the original planning intentions.

Overall, it soon became, for Britain, a unique and distinctive environment. After a somewhat shaky start, with several rather poor-quality Development Corporation rental housing schemes, notably those at Netherfield (Figure 7.8) and Bean Hill, Milton Keynes gained a reputation for good modern design and soon had an enviable record for employment growth. The diversity within the existing areas also meant that, unlike earlier New Towns, it was soon attracting a bigger proportion of professional and managerial groups as residents. This was further strengthened as more private housing construction occurred from the later 1970s. Its Development Corporation helped set a pattern for other New Towns by attracting the volume private house-builders to provide a growing

Figure 7.9 Early twenty-first-century private housing development in Milton Keynes, as seen from one of the grid roads. The town was one of the first to attract private housing developers on a large scale from the later 1970s and it has been an extremely attractive location for house purchasers. (author photograph)

proportion of housing (Figure 7.9). All these factors put it among Britain's fastest growing areas, encouraging more investment and better leisure and cultural facilities. The founding of the Open University in 1969 added a further distinctive element. However, its conception as a distance-learning institution did not foster a significant local student population, a gap which is still felt. Overall, although it still has its deriders, Milton Keynes generally justifies the label that has been attached to it: 'successful'.

The partnership New Towns

There had been an increasing tendency for the New Towns of the 1960s to include areas with larger existing populations than previously. In part this was because there were now few relatively empty areas to which employers and residents would wish to move that were not subject to green belt or other planning restrictions. Moreover, apart from the large expansions of Swindon and Basingstoke, the Town Development Act procedure of local-authority-orchestrated planned overspill was used cautiously by local councils, fearful of too much change in their areas. Increasingly, therefore, even Conservative governments were returning to the view that the much stronger resolve and powers of a New Town Development Corporation offered the surest way of ensuring that larger expansions would happen.

The first Hertfordshire New Towns had shown how tense relations could easily arise between Development Corporations and even quite small local councils. But use of this approach in already large towns, as implied by the *South East study* and other regional studies of the 1960s, created an even more intractable problem because much larger and stronger local authorities were involved. When they were designated as New Towns, Warrington and Northampton (and Ipswich, had it been designated) were county boroughs (i.e. unitary authorities), responsible for all local services at a time when local government was more powerful than it is today, and had extensive financial and technical capacity, important land holdings and other assets. Their status changed in 1974, however, when they were replaced by district and county councils. From the outset the existing settlement of Peterborough, despite having city status, had the more limited powers of a municipal borough. But it was a large one, much the most dominant centre in the small and short-lived county of Huntingdon and Peterborough, newly created in 1965 only to be superseded by an enlarged Cambridgeshire in 1974.[68]

By 1964, central government had accepted that the planned growth of such places could occur only as a partnership between development corporation and local authority.[69] In practice, the partnership in each New Town varied to suit local circumstances but was based on some general principles. As of right, the local authorities would be more substantially represented on the boards of the development corporations than under previous arrangements (though these never became elective posts). There would also be some sharing of technical staff. The local planning authority would not be supplanted by the development corporation as had previously been the case, though it was expected that the two would work closely together.

There was also a division of development roles. In Northampton, for example, the development corporation was responsible for infrastructure, housing, local shopping and employment development in the expansion areas.[70] The local authority would deal with the previously urbanised area and local housing and other needs arising from it, and would then deliver normal local services in the new areas as they were built. However, new major facilities, such as shopping, leisure and cultural buildings, were needed in the 'old' urban area to serve the enlarged population. In time, these would pay for themselves or be covered by local tax increases. But, as always with New Towns, there were heavy 'front-end' costs to be borne before matching financial returns appeared. This issue was a major stumbling block, especially so in the designation of the first partnership New Towns at Peterborough and Northampton, and remained a continuing source of dispute in the latter. To offset this, development corporations would transfer funds to cover any shortfall, though rarely satisfying the local authorities.

The path blocked

The decision not to go ahead with Ipswich in 1969 was the first sign that the New Towns programme might be becoming less relevant. As population projections fell, the growth pressures which had driven 1960s thinking began to ease. There was also growing public opinion by the late 1960s that policy needed to change within the big cities. Criticisms of 'clean-sweep' slum clearance and redevelopment policies were increasing,[71] local communities began to contest clearance proposals and the weaknesses of some replacement housing (particularly system-built and high-rise blocks) became ever more apparent. By 1969 there was a definite shift towards improving rather than demolishing existing older housing, implying less need to find additional space for displaced populations outside the cities.

During the 1970s this change was reinforced by a mounting awareness of a much wider inner-city problem – not just an issue of housing but one with much wider social and economic dimensions.[72] On most indicators of social disadvantage inner-city areas were at the most vulnerable end of the range, with more of their population dependent on social welfare benefits than in most other types of area. Some inner-city areas had large Afro-Caribbean or Asian populations which experienced substantial discrimination. Inner-city inhabitants in general were far more likely than those in other areas to lack work skills, be too old or young to be able to work, have lower educational attainment, worse English language skills or poorer health, or be living in fractured families. Crime and antisocial behaviour were also rising alarmingly.

Alongside this catalogue of social problems and an important causal factor in many of them was another series of economic problems. As the national economy weakened, the brunt was being borne in inner cities, as older factories in such areas suffered more acutely and historic dock areas were closed. The need for labour fell accordingly and, with this, went population decline. In the inner parts of the six main metropolitan areas (London, greater Manchester, the West Midlands, Merseyside, Tyneside and Clydeside) population fell by 8 per cent between 1951 and 1961, 26 per cent between 1961 and 1971 and 37 per cent between 1971 and 1981.[73] Not so long ago such decongestion of the inner cities had been consciously sought by public policies. Yet, as planned decline became unplanned freefall during the 1970s, especially in less economically favoured metropolitan areas such as Clydeside, Merseyside and Tyneside, the solution became a problem.

The New Towns programme had certainly not caused inner-city decline (though the view was commonly expressed). Even at the peak of the programme in 1974, the London New Towns had over the whole post-war period accounted only for around an eighth of the roughly 2 million people who had left the capital.[74] Yet, if New Towns were not the cause of the problem, they no longer seemed a relevant part of any solution. Despite Howard's original intention, restated by Abercrombie, that garden cities and New Towns should relieve the worst problems of the big cities, this had not been realised in practice. Admittedly only a small minority (again around an eighth) of jobs lost from inner-city areas had actually moved to the New Towns. More typically, New Town industries comprised new or much enlarged plants for growing industries or, increasingly, inward investments by foreign firms. Douglas Jay, president of the Board of Trade in the first Wilson government, had frequently worried that the New Towns, especially those for London, would deflect new industrial investment from the lagging regions, but he had not at that time been concerned about the impacts on jobs in inner-city areas.

He well understood that the main impact of New Towns on the inner cities was then primarily housing-related. Based on his experience as an MP for an inner-London constituency, he reported in August 1965 that it was 'virtually impossible ... for the worst housed families in central London to get a house in a New Town'.[75] By placing so much emphasis on having a local job before being entitled to a house, New Town policy, especially for the first generation of developments such as those in Hertfordshire, for at least two decades 'creamed off' the most able and ambitious working-class populations from the cities they supposedly served. As we noted for Stevenage, it was the unskilled, the unemployed, those who were not 'economically active', the old, the ill and disabled who tended to be left behind. Improved access to New Town housing for such groups began from around that time, especially in the third-generation New Towns, and was pursued more strongly in the 1970s, partly in response to the inexorable shift of strategic policies towards alleviating inner-city problems.

Decline and fall

Even so, additional New Town projects were still being actively considered. Following an earlier study, in 1972 Edward Heath's Conservative government laid a draft designation order for a New Town at Llantrisant on the edge of the south Wales valleys.[76] After a public inquiry at which there was strong local opposition, the proposal was dropped in 1974. Meanwhile, in 1973 the final New Town, Stonehouse, in west central Scotland, had been started as yet another overspill site for Glasgow's housing needs. In 1976, after 96 houses had been built, it was abandoned.[77] Over the water, all the Northern Irish New Town Commissions had been wound up in 1973, after existing for between just four and eight years.[78] In none of these cases can it really be claimed that it was the New Towns or would-be New Towns themselves that had in some way 'failed'. The reasons were altogether wider. For Llantrisant and Stonehouse, these reasons were largely economic. The leaders of towns in the south Wales valleys feared that a New Town at Llantrisant would fatally undermine their faltering economies, still based largely on coal mining. Despite their distinctive physical character, the valleys were places with many similar problems to those of the inner cities, though with mountains between their main streets. Stonehouse's fate was sealed by a realisation that, because the precipitate fall in population numbers in inner Clydeside was the worst of any inner-city area, planned decentralisation had simply become the wrong answer. The disbandment of Northern Ireland's New Towns in particular had more complex roots, reflecting the province's peculiar political problems, wildly inaccurate population forecasting and specific economic weaknesses following the onset of the 'Troubles'.

In April 1977 the environment secretary in the Wilson Labour government, Peter Shore, having already unveiled his policy for the inner cities, reported his department's review of the New Towns.[79] All pending proposed enlargements of designated areas were dropped and population targets for all 'active' New Towns were reduced. The Expanded Town programme was also brought to an end. The overall target for all the UK New Towns now became 1,993,000, which can be compared with the all-time high-point target for the same New Towns of 2,237,030 in 1970 (this figure including growth that had already occurred).[80] The London New Towns, especially Milton Keynes, Peterborough and Northampton, between them lost 148,000. Central Lancashire was also drastically trimmed. The Mid-Wales Development Corporation, responsible for the tiny Welsh New Town of Newtown, had been wound up just days earlier. Now the winding-up of eight development corporations in England was also promised. These comprised the first-generation New Towns not already handed over to the Commission for the New Towns (Stevenage, Harlow, Bracknell, Basildon and Corby), together with Runcorn, Redditch and Washington.

These disbandments (notably those of Stevenage, Harlow, Bracknell and Corby) were already well in train when Margaret Thatcher became prime minister in 1979. As was expected, the entire process was not easy to accomplish overnight, as the Commission for the New Towns did not want to take over departing Development Corporations that were still heavily in deficit or with major development work still underway. The life of Washington Development Corporation, for example, was extended to 1988, allowing it to play a key role in bringing the hugely successful Nissan car plant to the area during the mid-1980s.[81] In fact, these handovers were completed between 1980 and 1989 (though the last, Runcorn, was first merged with Warrington Development Corporation in 1981).

Along with the growing concern for inner cities, Margaret Thatcher's radical Conservative government added its own ideological objections to the New Towns programme as an exercise in 'big government'. In fact, the most active New Towns, especially Milton Keynes, Peterborough, Northampton and Warrington, were already favouring private housing development before 1979.[82] There had also been a significant increase in owner-occupation in many New Towns as former development corporation rental housing had begun to be sold to sitting tenants. Nevertheless, the new administration was eager to accelerate this process. Its strategists felt that the upper-working-class groups who had moved to the New Towns in the post-war boom years, personified as 'Basildon Man', might permanently switch their traditional political allegiance from Labour to Thatcherite Conservatism if they could be eased into home ownership.[83] Alongside this, they also wanted an accelerated winding-up of the whole programme and disposal of the assets held by individual New Towns and the Commission for the New Towns.

Several other Development Corporations were wound up during the 1980s, with just Telford, Milton Keynes and the Scottish New Towns remaining into the following decade. The first two were disbanded in 1991 and 1992 respectively and the Scottish New Towns in 1995–96. The latter's peculiar longevity (especially so East Kilbride and Glenrothes) partly reflected greater Scottish resistance to the harsh wind of Thatcherite change, but, more specifically, there was no Commission for the New Towns north of the border to complete a New Town's development and manage its assets. This meant that, compared with England and Wales, a larger proportion of a Scottish New Town's development had to be finished before its development corporation could be wound up. Half a century after the first New Town Development Corporation was set up, the last two (for Livingston and Irvine) were dissolved. It marked the end of a remarkable programme that had been one of the key stories of post-war Britain. Throughout (and even beyond) its life, the UK's New Town programme was widely studied and admired by policy makers, planners and relevant professionals from other countries. New Towns were also popular venues for official visits by dignitaries. Their success in attracting inward investment, increasingly from overseas, also meant that many companies eagerly examined what they had to offer. The overall numbers of these various visitors could be substantial; during the 1970s, for example, Stevenage Development Corporation annually received around 6,000–8,000 visitors of various kinds wishing to inspect the New Town, around half of whom were from outside Britain.[84] The pattern for other New Towns was similar. Aspects of the programme's overall conception and organisation, and some design aspects of New Towns, were also emulated elsewhere. Yet, for all the admiration of the British model, it would be quite wrong to imply that any of this represented a simple process of copying. Conscious decisions and underlying differences of context and circumstance meant that foreign equivalents of the New Towns developed in their own way. At their best, they became every bit as celebrated and influential as those in the UK.

Stockholm's satellite new towns

A much admired early post-war case that was often considered alongside the British examples was the Stockholm new town programme. Its conception drew on longstanding Swedish interest in the garden city tradition since the early years of the twentieth century.[85] Initially Swedish architects and planners drew on German learning about and interpretations of the work of the British movement. However, during the 1940s a keen Swedish interest grew in contemporary Anglo-American planning thinking and practice, especially in relation to community planning. The writings of the American theorist and author Lewis Mumford, particularly his book *The culture of cities*, which was published in Swedish in 1942, and the 1943 and 1944 plans for the County of London and Greater London, were soon shaping thinking about Swedish practice. Their importance was essentially in showing how urban areas could be planned to foster a sense of linked local communities with a strong sense of neighbourliness and a convenient relationship to places of employment, social facilities such as schools and health care, and shopping and cultural facilities. The neighbourhood unit that was so important to the first British New Towns was not slavishly copied, but rather the principles on which it had been based were absorbed into Swedish practice. This link was particularly evident in the first of Stockholm's new settlements at Vällingby (Figure 7.10).[86]

This was planned from 1946 and its first neighbourhood, Blackeberg, was finished in 1951. The main centre at Vällingby itself opened in 1954. The second new town was at Farsta (where actual building began in 1958). By 1966 Vällingby had reached a population of 55,000, with Farsta slightly larger, so that these were directly comparable to British first-generation examples. There was much mutual learning between the British New Towns and Stockholm: thus in developing their own plans Stockholm's planners had drawn directly on British 1940s thinking about neighbourhood planning, while Stevenage Board members and officials studied Vällingby's pedestrianised shopping centre while considering their own.

Despite these various interactions, however, Stockholm's new towns were differently conceived from those of Britain. Central to the idea was the so-called ABC typology, standing for *arbete* (work), *böstader* (housing) and *centrum* (centre). Vällingby itself was planned as a full ABC settlement that was the

Figure 7.10 Vällingby (here photographed c.1963) has been the most renowned of Stockholm's satellite towns. Developed by the city in conjunction with its metro system, the town never achieved the degree of employment self-containment achieved in British New Towns. Yet it proved an attractive and popular location for a socially mixed population and was widely admired internationally. (author's collection)

main focus of a cluster of adjoining neighbourhoods that were more completely 'B' settlements (i.e. residential communities). There was also to be significant development of the 'A' employment function across the whole cluster. Vällingby was planned on the assumption that half its resident workers would be employed there. Stockholm's new towns were never to be the entirely freestanding, self-contained towns favoured in Britain, where a numerical balance of local jobs and local workforce was normally sought and often came close to being achieved. In the Stockholm examples, however, even the lower level of employment self-containment that was sought still could not be achieved. In 1965 76 per cent of Vällingby's resident workers and 85 per cent of Farsta's commuted out to their place of work.

This was scarcely surprising because both settlements lay much closer than their British counterparts to the existing urban core, being built on land long owned by the city, and they immediately became part of the Swedish capital's travel-to-work area. Virtually from the first, these new communities were connected, like beads on a string, to the wider metropolitan area by the Tunnelbana, a brand new efficient and high-capacity metropolitan rail system that ran underground in the urban core. Public transport use was consequently extremely high (and has remained so, despite increasing motorisation). This also reflected the way the towns were planned. To function efficiently the Tunnelbana needed large populations in the immediate catchment areas close to stations, with the result that overall housing densities were higher than in British New Towns.[87] In both Vällingby and Farsta around three-quarters of dwellings were provided as apartments, the remainder as single family dwellings. Walking from Tunnelbana stations, it is striking how tall blocks of flats give way to medium and to then low-rise flat blocks, before terraced housing and finally detached houses with gardens dominate.

Planners in many other countries were attracted to the Stockholm new town model, which at its best was accompanied by attractive modern design of buildings and spaces with a softness and humanity that seemed to be lacking in other varieties of modern architecture. Features such as the design of pedestrian areas and the street furniture were often completed to an exemplary standard rarely matched in Britain. However, the Swedish social democratic utopia did not last for ever. The same pressures to build more housing that affected many comparable countries also touched Sweden. Quality suffered and the later Stockholm satellite communities developed on the post-war principles did not generally match the first ones. Thus Skärholmen, where the *Centrum* comprising the town centre and related housing was opened in 1968, soon became the subject of public criticism.[88] Yet its conception and form had actually owed more to the powerful interest groups representing the building industry, retailing and motoring than to genuinely community-focused planning and architecture.

By 1970 construction had been more completely industrialised, with extensive use of low- and high-rise apartment blocks built using prefabrication and many residential layouts conditioned by the operational requirements of the construction cranes.[89] The way the built environment was placed in earlier schemes within the often undulating, rocky topography of Stockholm and its surroundings gave way to sites levelled before construction so that tracks could be laid for the cranes. (This was rather less in evidence in Britain although largely, one suspects, because the terrain was less challenging and industrialised apartment construction less extensive than in Sweden.) The new areas, particularly at Tensta but also in other places such as Alby, soon proved less popular than the earlier ones and were increasingly occupied by groups experiencing various kinds of social problems, people with fewer choices about where they lived.

Other Nordic and Dutch examples

The developments seen in Sweden's neighbours shared some similarities with Stockholm's new town programme. Copenhagen's famous 'finger plan' of 1947 was an even clearer articulation of the notion of linear planned decentralisation from a major city along rail transportation routes,[90] in the form of 'fingers' of nodal urban development around the rail stations, with intervening green wedges (Figure 7.11). This concept was in sharp contrast to the Abercrombie Greater London Plan model of a surrounding green belt beyond which were freestanding New Towns. However, in the Danish case, the settlements along the fingers were less remarkable than those of Stockholm. There was also the crucial difference that there was less control by the City of Copenhagen over where development occurred than in Stockholm, where the city limits and city land holdings initially gave tight control. The result was that Copenhagen's intended green wedges between the fingers were soon compromised by infilling with development, especially to the north.

Helsinki was notable in having a small garden city (unusually, this term was still preferred over the more fashionable 'new town' or 'satellite town' labels) at Tapiola.[91] It was planned from 1946 on a forested site west of the capital city, with development beginning in 1952. Intended for up to 15,000 inhabitants, it was conceived as a socially mixed settlement developed as

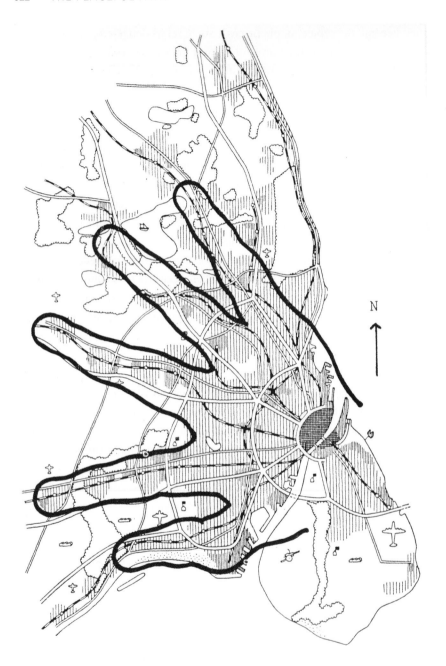

Figure 7.11 The Copenhagen 'finger plan', 1947, was based on a very different conception of managing urban growth from that in the 1944 Greater London plan. Linear development along rail lines was to be interspersed with green wedges, a contrast with the Abercrombie concept of a containing green belt with overspill developments beyond. (author's collection)

several neighbourhood units. It was also planned with (and has) extensive local services and employment. Developed by a non-profit housing association, about two-thirds of its dwellings were low-rise apartments (three to four storeys), with around 15 per cent terraced or detached houses and some higher-rise blocks. Overall densities were low, although the 'garden' aspect was mainly forest land and other public spaces, rather than the private gardens familiar from British examples. On paper, the numerical balance of local jobs to workers appears close, but because Tapiola closely adjoins Helsinki there is much in- and out-commuting, so that actual local employment of locally resident workers is very low. Like the Stockholm examples, however, it was soon winning plaudits around the world, especially from American architects and planners.

Although Dutch planners had long been aware of Howard and the garden city, their engagement with planning entirely new towns came mainly during the post-war years. The Netherlands experienced particularly high post-war population growth, and by the later 1950s a consensus was forming, similar in intention to the British 'Abercrombie model', that a policy of planned deconcentration of the biggest urban areas was needed.[92] As well as smaller locations for expanding existing small towns, three significant new town sites were identified: one at Zoetermeer near the Hague and two on the ongoing Flevoland polder reclamation in the Ijsselmeer.[93] These last two new towns became Lelystad (where the first buildings were finished in 1967) and Almere (first housing completions in 1976), and have been the focus of most international interest. Unusually in Europe, these two were truly 'new' new towns, built on land which a few years earlier had not even existed. Nevertheless, they soon became the main urban centres of the new province of Flevoland and helped relieve growth pressures in Amsterdam.

Almere (now with around 200,000 residents) has attracted the most international interest and has often been compared with Milton Keynes, which was studied closely by Almere's planners. They also drew on the experiences of other British New Towns, such as Runcorn, which provided some of the inspiration for Almere's somewhat larger busway system. Increasingly, however, British planners have been referring to Almere, not least its relatively low reliance on the car (in stark contrast to Milton Keynes) and, most recently, the strong encouragement its planners have given to people building their own homes. Although some have criticised the towns for their excessively suburban qualities, they have proved attractive places to live for those seeking these qualities and deserve much of the international attention they receive.

French *villes nouvelles*

French planners also came later to their new town strategy. Howard's thinking had helped shape French housing reform ideas about suburban expansion since earlier in the century, and attractive relatively low-density *cités-jardins* were developed in the fringes of many of the northern industrial towns, especially after 1919.[94] They were also built around Paris, although many of these were at somewhat higher densities and, by the 1930s, housing design more generally was shifting to favour more modernist, high-density approaches. Throughout the post-1945 period, however, there was French interest in community planning concepts associated with the garden city tradition, especially the neighbourhood unit. In 1949, for example, the first post-war master plan for Lyon included three distinct neighbourhood units at Bron-Parilly, Duchère and Montessuy.[95] Architecturally they look strikingly different from low-density, low-rise British expressions of neighbourhoods, but embody similar social planning principles. Increasingly, however, French sociologists became more involved in developing such principles, so that the direct connection became less obvious over later years.[96]

But the most significant change as regards substantial new planned towns in France came only with the 1965 *Schéma Directeur d'Aménagement et d'Urbanisme de la Région de Paris* (SDAURP, or, in English, the scheme of direction of land use planning and urban design for the Paris region) (Figure 7.12).[97] This plan, equivalent in significance to the 1944 Greater London Plan but far more growth-orientated and quite different in some key features, proposed major expansion of the Paris metropolitan region. Its earliest drafts envisaged that the Paris region would grow to 14 million inhabitants, though this number was subsequently scaled back. The intention was to improve on what had degenerated into a rather incremental and ill-considered process of peripheral expansion in the suburbs. During the 1950s and early 1960s many suburban areas of big cities had seen the growth of very large public sector housing projects (the *grands ensembles*), such as Sarcelles or Massy-Antony in the Paris region. Invariably such places were dominated by large blocks of apartments built with industrialised methods and for many years had very poor provision of community facilities and poor transport links. As a contrast to these, the 1965 SDAURP provided a clearer strategy with two great parallel axes of growth north and south of the historic centre.

Conceptually, the basic strategy was in some key respects a scaled-up version of the early post-war plans for Stockholm and Copenhagen, which the French planners had studied closely. As in Stockholm, there would be massive investment in a new metropolitan rail system, the RER (regional express network), which, with new roads, would provide the transport framework. To

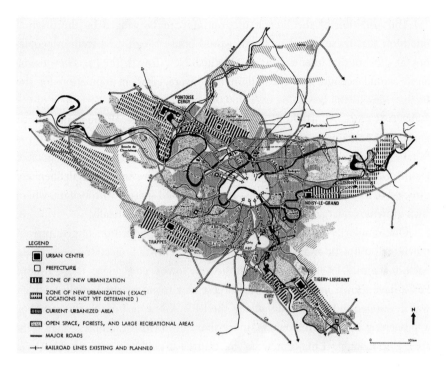

LEGEND

- ■ URBAN CENTER
- □ PREFECTURE
- ▥ ZONE OF NEW URBANIZATION
- ▦ ZONE OF NEW URBANIZATION (EXACT LOCATIONS NOT YET DETERMINED)
- ▨ CURRENT URBANIZED AREA
- ▦ OPEN SPACE, FORESTS, AND LARGE RECREATIONAL AREAS
- ━━ MAJOR ROADS
- ─┼─ RAILROAD LINES EXISTING AND PLANNED

Figure 7.12 The 1965 *Schéma Directeur* for the Paris region was an expansive plan, with satellite towns along major rail axes, effectively scaling up the Scandinavian approach for a much larger metropolitan city. The eight new towns originally proposed were scaled back to five very large settlements. (author's collection)

develop these axes, eight new towns had initially been proposed, soon reduced to five, at locations identified by the SDAURP at Marne-la-Vallée, Melun-Sénart, Cergy-Pontoise, Évry and Saint-Quentin-en-Yvelines.[98] Their development began in earnest in the late 1960s, though all incorporated existing urbanisation.

Each had the very fragmented pattern of small local governments (*communes*) typical of France. The largest Parisian new town, Marne-la-Vallée, has no less than 26 local *communes*, a situation quite inconceivable in Britain. To give the necessary decisive leadership to the development process, French officials wanted something akin to the centrally appointed British New Town Development Corporation and created their own version, the Établissement *Public d'Aménagement*. In common with Britain, there was also a political need to offset arguments that, in contrast to the previous post-war regional policies to redress the balance towards provincial France, new town policies favoured the Paris region. Accordingly, four provincial new towns were established near Marseille, Lyon, Lille and Rouen.

The ambition of the French programme can be gauged by the original intention that these nine new towns would house roughly 2.4 million people, not far short of that intended for all 32 British New Towns. The Paris new towns alone would account for 1.4 million. The average target population for the French new towns was to be over 260,000, with most of the Paris new towns 300,000 or more. All would be major employment centres, although the British goal of self-contained new towns was not pursued and all the Parisian new towns functioned as integral parts of the metropolitan labour market area. A notable feature was that major university and state research investment was deliberately directed to many French new towns. This contrasted sharply with Britain, where such growth was largely absent or occurred only opportunistically.

One similarity was, however, that the original population targets proved much too optimistic and were reduced sharply as growth projections were reined back in the mid-1970s. Nevertheless, the new towns, particularly those around Paris, have grown impressively. The largest new town, Marne-la-Vallée, which was developed in linear fashion along the RER 'A' line east of the city, now has approaching 300,000 inhabitants, more than any British examples. They were soon able to support major new service centres at public transport hubs. These had extensive shopping and office-based development and, close by, high-density apartment developments. Industrial areas and, increasingly, lower-density housing were developed at greater distance from these centres. It was the same basic pattern of activity and density zoning that had been evolved at Vällingby.

Like their British equivalents, the *villes nouvelles* around Paris have evolved since their inception. Certain aspects of the original conception have worked well. The RER-based public transport framework, which was taking shape as the new towns started to be built, has served them very well. It allows residents much easier access to a far greater labour market area of metropolitan Paris (and its many other amenities and attractions) than is as readily available to residents of the British New Towns close to London. The *villes nouvelles* have also effectively created real shopping and administrative centres in the outer parts of the metropolitan area of what was still, in the 1960s, an exceptionally centralised city. Regarding housing provision, the increasing role of private residential developers since a policy change in 1977 has heralded a bigger proportion of low-rise buildings and more individual houses and gardens than in the first areas of building, where public sector apartment blocks predominated. The shift to a form of development closer to the Anglo-American idea of the suburb has proved attractive to a widening section of French society, and was seen as a significant improvement on the usual French idea of the suburbs (the *banlieues,* most typically dominated by the *grands ensembles*) which presented much the same mix of social problems as had appeared in Britain's and the USA's inner cities by the 1970s.

New towns for America

The garden city idea had prompted much interest in the United States from the 1920s to the 1940s. As mentioned in earlier chapters, some American professionals and reformers had contributed new ideas, especially the neighbourhood unit and the Radburn layout. Yet not until the 1960s were entire new towns being developed with any of that sense of social purpose that animated the post-war British programme.[99] Two widely admired private sector new towns were developed close to Washington at Reston, Virginia (begun in 1962, for an original target population of 72,000) and Columbia, Maryland (1963, for 110,000).[100] Both had charismatic and visionary developers, Robert E. Simon at Reston (his initials are incorporated in the name) and James Rouse at Columbia. Both had the outlook and, with some difficulties, the funding to take a long view of the ventures. They studied the best British and European examples and had a genuine desire to promote socially mixed and cohesive communities with good design and local service provision.[101]

Columbia has usually been seen as the more innovative, with a hierarchy of shopping and other service provision comparable to that evident in British New Towns and Stockholm's satellite towns. The smallest community unit was the residential cluster, with four or five clusters making a village (of which nine were planned) and a town centre serving all the villages. Both, especially so Columbia, were successful in achieving racial mix, partly because they enthusiastically used federal subsidies, when these were available, for racially mixed developments. Rouse was immensely proud that the first child born in Columbia, in 1967, was to a black man and his white wife – this in a state that had actually legalised interacial marriages only in that year.[102] Social class mix proved more elusive, and it was difficult to attract the most affluent white residents, partly because of the greater presence of black people than in most suburbs of the Baltimore and Washington region, where it was located. The least well-off were also few in number, reflecting a shortage of really low-cost housing.

Both new towns were widely admired by garden city enthusiasts in the United States, Britain, Australia and elsewhere. Following land acquisition tactics that were similar to what had occurred at Letchworth and Welwyn Garden City, Simon and Rouse had achieved the land value capture and unified ownership that were the key preconditions of following the peaceful path. They appeared to have combined a privately orchestrated profit-seeking development process with many of the planning aspirations of publicly initiated new towns. At Reston, however, some of the original vision was lost as funding became pressured during the 1970s. The resources of the Rouse Corporation and the exceptionally deep pockets of the large insurance company that was his principal backer made Columbia more able to weather the storm. Yet it was another private new town of this period, Irvine, near Los Angeles, which proved the most commercially successful in that respect.[103] Also begun during the 1960s, it had fewer pretensions to the design, social and community ethos of the garden city legacy. Today it has about 240,000 inhabitants and hosts many major businesses which provide jobs for many more than just local workers.

These three examples suggested that new towns could be built without European-style direct government involvement. The federal new communities programme of the late 1960s and early 1970s appeared to mark a new boldness in relation to new towns for America.[104] It adopted the indirect mechanism of relying mainly on federal loan guarantees for private capital to build substantial and racially mixed new settlements. There was also some grant aid available through other federal programmes. Fifteen new communities were started under this programme. Two were 'in-town', at Cedar-Riverside in Minneapolis and Roosevelt Island in New York City, with the rest in urban–rural fringe locations, more directly comparable to British New Towns. Within a few years, however, severe financial problems saw the programme completely axed under President Nixon. The in-town examples subsequently prospered, but only two of the rest proceeded. The most impressive is The Woodlands, developed on a very large site near Houston. Now with just over 100,000 inhabitants, its planning, design and landscaping is of high quality, though, like Irvine, the town's developers have not seriously engaged with the social aspirations of the garden city/new town tradition.

Japanese and Australian new towns

Outside Western Europe and the United States there have been many other interesting examples of planned new towns showing varying degrees of connection to the Howardian tradition. Some were developed in circumstances quite different to those found in Britain. These included late colonial or early post-independence efforts to boost national economic development, to meet new governance needs or to accommodate new populations. The efforts of countries as diverse as India and Israel (and many others) contain examples of all these types. Many were planned with some nods, at least, in the direction of the British garden cities and New Towns. Yet there have been few attempts to emulate the economically diverse, self-contained and freestanding settlement planned with a strong social and community agenda that became the British New Town ideal. Many, such as those in Hong Kong and Singapore, were essentially large, high-density social housing schemes, without significant local employment, though in some cases with associated shopping and service centre development.[105] At their best they have been served by excellent metropolitan rail networks.

A similar pattern was also evident in Japan where, despite longstanding interest in the garden city tradition, its garden cities (*den-en-toshi*) and new towns have largely been suburban commuter developments.[106] A major commuter rail line in Tokyo is actually called the Den-en-toshi Line. Among other places, it serves a large *den-en-toshi* housing development promoted by the Tokyu Railway Company during the 1950s. The basic pattern, albeit at higher densities, has been similar for many public sector schemes, such as the huge Tama New Town in suburban Tokyo.[107] It was developed from 1964 by three metropolitan and national government agencies, predominantly as apartment housing. Originally planned for a projected 342,000 inhabitants, this figure proved wildly optimistic and Tama currently houses around 200,000, a reflection of Japan's stagnating population and economic growth. The pattern has been similar in similar new towns serving other cities, such as Kozoji New Town (in suburban Nagoya) and Senri (Osaka).

Ostensibly Australia began the post-war period relying very much on the British model of metropolitan planning. Yet, even here, there was much scepticism about reinforcing it with planned Abercrombie-style new towns. The main exception was Elizabeth, developed in the suburbs of Adelaide in South Australia (Figure 7.13).[108] Begun in 1950, with the first houses completed in 1955, it was created by the South Australia Housing Trust, the state's public housing agency. Planning closely followed the British first-generation New Town model. By the mid-1950s the British New Town 'tour' to Harlow, Crawley, Stevenage, Hemel Hempstead, Welwyn Garden City, Letchworth and Cwmbran was well-established for Trust officials. Yet development occurred without British-style legal and organisational frameworks or funding, which weakened implementation.

The main intention was to boost South Australia's growth and Elizabeth became a major reception point for recently arrived migrants from Britain's industrial towns seeking a new life in Australia. There was also major factory development, with a General Motors (Holden) car plant the main local employer for many years. Elizabeth's population peaked in the mid-1970s at about 34,000 inhabitants, since when it has declined. More acutely than British New Towns,

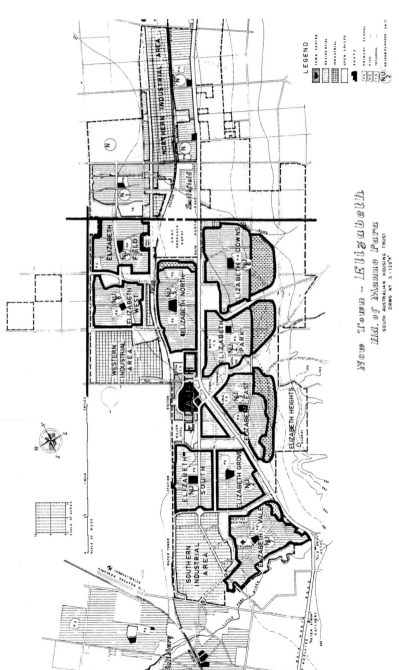

New Town – Elizabeth
Hd. of Munno Para
SOUTH AUSTRALIAN HOUSING TRUST
DRWG Nº S-120ᴹ

Figure 7.13 Elizabeth in South Australia was a New Town close to Adelaide developed very much on the British model, with particularly close links with Hemel Hempstead. In the 1950s and 1960s it housed many recent migrants from the 'old country', but its economy suffered when employment in the car industry declined in the later twentieth century. (author's collection)

however, it has suffered in recent decades from deindustrialisation and a continuing poor reputation as a public sector housing ghetto.

There were several later proposals for growth-related new towns, most of which were dropped or significantly diluted. Most interesting from the perspective of this book is one that proceeded more or less as planned: Joondalup, north-west of Perth.[109] It was developed, British-fashion, by a state development corporation from 1977. Like several proposals of the time, it reflected a marked interest in Scandinavian planning ideas within Australian metropolitan planning in the late 1960s and early 1970s.[110] This new approach favoured the creation of growth corridors, with Joondalup identified as a then undeveloped point for growth on Perth's north-west corridor. It was served, like Stockholm and Copenhagen, by the metropolitan rail system.The detailed planning was notable because Gordon Stephenson, responsible for the first plan for Stevenage, played an important formative role. British and American new town examples were studied closely. The former seemed more relevant from a broader planning point of view and the latter (Reston, Columbia and Irvine) more interesting for their detailed design and better business and private finance orientation. From this synthesis of thinking has grown a thriving new town. What was originally a very sparsely populated area currently has about 55,000 inhabitants.

Soviet new towns

The final example is chosen because it has intrinsic importance and also highlights a surprising interaction. A 1980 estimate suggested that around 800 new towns had been created in the Soviet Union since the 1917 Bolshevik Revolution.[111] Typically these were in association with new industrial complexes, though many were effectively new industrial suburbs of old established cities, sometimes renamed. The most celebrated, however, was Magnitogorsk, heralded as a showpiece of Soviet planning and development in the 1930s. It was established from 1929 in a completely new location, east of the Urals, under Stalin's first Five Year Plan. The area had vast iron deposits and the new city was intended to exploit these with a vast new iron and steel complex.[112] Although no others achieved Magnitogorsk's iconic status, these industry-related settlements continued to be the usual kind of Soviet new towns in the post-war years. Similar ones were also created in the wider Communist bloc. Particularly notable were the steelworks-based new towns of Nowa Huta in Poland, Stalinstadt (now Eisenhüttenstadt) in the German Democratic Republic and Sztalinvaros (now Dunaujvaros) in Hungary.[113]

Although there had been some early Russian interest in Howard's ideas, these post-1917 new towns showed little sign of this. However, the Soviet connection with British experiences became much closer under Nikita Khrushchev's leadership from 1953. There was much Soviet admiration of Western housing and planning achievements, and Soviet visits to Western Europe to learn about housing, planning and construction became common. Particularly admired were French prefabricated housing systems, the Swedish satellite towns and British New Towns.[114] In 1954, 1955 and 1957 Soviet officials and architects made important trips to examine British planning practice as part of exchanges with British delegations. Over the years following many Soviet groups visited British New Towns. Although exact itineraries varied, Hertfordshire's role in pioneering garden cities and New Towns was usually acknowledged.

This interest derived from Khrushchev's desire to ease relations with the West after the onset of the Cold War in the late 1940s. Soviet spending priorities might then shift away from armament spending, allowing real improvements in Soviet living standards. Housing and planning were an important part of this and it became fruitful to learn from Western post-war efforts. The housing and land availability pressures in the biggest Soviet cities were acute and, in this context, British and Nordic attempts to relieve these pressures held great interest. These connections also reduced international tension, creating a new 'cultural diplomacy' that also involved mutual exchange in artistic, scientific, technical, educational and related fields. They were a striking contrast to even just a few years earlier, before Stalin died, when all Soviet links were viewed with great suspicion, not least the ill-advised Moscow-organised North Korean trip by Monica Felton in 1951, described in Chapter 5. It is intriguing to speculate about how, had she been more careful and remained in office as chair of Stevenage, she might have used the much better Anglo-Soviet links of the Khrushchev era.

Actually the impacts of these planning-related links in the two countries were not obvious. Although many Westerners had been impressed with Soviet planning before 1939 and in the 1940s, the mood had shifted by the 1950s. By then Britain was moving away from favouring an increasingly state-led economy and policies, as had been the case in the 1940s. Instead the dominant thinking was to create a 'mixed economy' that gave a bigger place to the private sector and allowed the growth of a mass consumer society. In these circumstances, it was the American, rather than the Soviet, dream which began to seem the more relevant. When Henry Wells, chairman of Hemel Hempstead Development Corporation, returned from a Soviet visit in 1958 he was quite blunt in stating that 'the Russians have nothing to teach us on principles of town planning'.[115] Nevertheless, he and other British New Town planners and advocates were always flattered by Soviet interest in their work.

For their part, Soviet planners launched some *sputnik* (satellite) town projects around Moscow and Leningrad in the early 1960s with the intention that they would directly adopt some of the physical characteristics of British New Towns. There is little evidence that these hopes as to the built form were realised, however. As built, these areas are dominated by large apartment blocks; some sections are of lower-rise construction than typical Soviet schemes, but there is little sign of the row housing that appeared in the original drawings. The real impacts of Western contact were rather more subtle, helping shape Soviet planning methodologies in relation to, for example, the planning of hierarchies of community facilities. Soviet planners thus used British New Towns to help determine what population threshold was needed for a community to support facilities such as local shops, nursery, primary or secondary schools, health clinics and so on, all the way up to major shopping areas, universities or main hospitals. Soviet new towns, meanwhile, remained predominantly of the usual industry-related 'company town' type. One example, often shown to later Western visitors, was the new town of Tolyatti, built from the 1950s to replace the existing city of Stavropol, its site flooded under the Volga river project (Figure 7.14).

Figure 7.14 Tolyatti was a Soviet new town originally developed under the Volga River project. In the 1960s it became a major car manufacturing centre and was substantially expanded by adding the Avtozavodsky district, shown in this rare 1970s photograph. The contrasts with British New Towns are striking. (Town Planning Review)

The first new town sections were for hydro-electric workers, but a new motor manufacturing district, Avtozavodsky, was added from 1966. Its residential areas comprised huge apartment blocks mainly of nine storeys. Again, the smaller dwellings more typical of British New Towns were lacking.

Conclusions

We have seen how increasingly varied Howard's original path became, with parallel routes alongside it. Contrary to what he had wanted, it was the fundamental transformation to embrace the state as the principal development agency that became the real 'master key' that unlocked the large-scale development of new towns in Britain. Many British New Towns did eventually become profitable, although, since their funding came from national government, it was logically back to that source that surpluses flowed (though the position became more diverse over time, as we will show in the next chapter).

Other important changes to the Howardian formula were also evident in the British New Town programme as it grew. It became not just, as Howard had originally envisaged, a way of addressing the social ills of the giant congested city and the depressed countryside. The New Town programme unfolded as the countryside was becoming a much less vulnerable territory. Its agriculture was supported by governmental intervention, its natural beauty subject to effective planning protection, its lifestyle becoming ever more 'urban', though in a different way to how Howard had imagined it.[116] Instead of relying on the close proximity of country and town, rural electrification, the telephone, television and, latterly, the internet have allowed most benefits of urban living to penetrate even quite remote rural areas. Car-based mobility has also allowed easier rural access from the deeper countryside to urban services, employment and other opportunities. The 'traditional' rural way of life has certainly been strongly defended in recent years and rural areas have shown larger percentage population increases than have urban or mixed urban/rural areas. Yet those who directly earn their living from agriculture now comprise less than 1 per cent of the working population. The perpetuation of the rural way of life now relies on the likes of systems analysts, accountants and personnel managers living in the countryside, rather more than those actually earning their living from the land.

Meanwhile, however, the big city continued to be a site of social problems for many people and the New Town programme became a significant means of alleviating those concerns for some of those people. Most New Towns, like those in Hertfordshire, primarily served as a means of planned decentralisation from the biggest cities. Yet there was no desire to drive this to Howard's logical conclusion – the withering away of the big city. When that began to look like a possibility in the 1970s it was the New Towns programme that was made to wither away and the restoration of growth in the big cities became the new priority. Moreover, a significant minority of New Towns were designated to promote economic development rather than metropolitan overspill, primarily to offset regional (rather than rural) economic decline. A few were created primarily with the intention (which then changed over time) that they would service the growth of a single dominant industry.

The scale of New Towns also increased. Even the first-generation New Towns were a step up from Howard's original ideal, going further in the second generation. But the giant New Towns of the third generation, projected for over 200,000 inhabitants, were quite different propositions. Milton Keynes was intended for a population equivalent to an entire Social City. These changes reflected a shifting sense of what scale was necessary to make a fairly self-contained town in a far more mobile society. In several cases, these larger population targets arose because the New Town was already to a considerable extent also an old town, with a much larger existing population than in previous garden cities and New Towns. By the 1960s, the limitations of the 1952 Town Development Act were clear to all. These partnership developments marked a recognition that the powerful development instruments created to build New Towns would be more effective to manage the large-scale expansions of already large towns. This was stretching the notion of a New Town into the idea of a 'new-town-in-town', a precursor of the urban development corporations in the 1980s and 1990s.

If this variety was visible over time in the UK, how much greater was that apparent in other countries, though there were still some common features. With the main exception of the USA, some kind of governmental or quasi-government body was the usual way to develop new towns. A few American developers attempted, for profit, to build new towns that followed several aspects of the peaceful path formula. In practice, however, despite their good intentions, they were focused on more affluent populations than were the government-led new town projects of most other countries. Yet what was most striking about new town development elsewhere was how rare was the British ideal of self-contained, freestanding new settlements. Close integration of home and workplace was certainly attained in Soviet new towns, which were mainly Communist 'company towns', without the diversity of employers that was usual in most British New Towns. Soviet permits authorising a place of residence, so that permission had to be granted for permanent internal migration from one area to another, also fostered the close proximity of home and work.

Far more common in the advanced capitalist world was the less completely self-contained satellite town. It was more fully integrated, especially for employment, within larger metropolitan areas. At their best such places combined good local services and some employment opportunities with easy access to everything the big city had to offer, including greater choice of employment, services and cultural life. By comparison, British New Towns, following Howard, seemed to promise a life that turned away more completely from the metropolis. As car-based mobility improved and more New Town households began to buy their homes, however, a looser pattern began to evolve. Later New Towns, especially Milton Keynes, were planned partly with this loosening relationship in mind, though the virtues of as much self-containment as possible were still being championed. And, arguably, as we have embraced the ideals of sustainable development, they still are – a thought which takes us into the final chapter.

Notes

1   Cullingworth, *Environmental planning: vol. III*, pp. 32–115, uses original documents to give the central government perspective on the designation of all the first-generation New Towns. Apart from the other references cited, it is the key source for the origins and designations of all the New Towns.

2   U. Wannop, 'New towns', in B. Cullingworth (ed.), *British planning: 50 years of urban and regional policy* (London, 1999), p. 216.

3   G. Philipson, *Aycliffe and Peterlee new towns 1946–1988: swords into ploughshares and farewell squalor* (Cambridge, 1988).

4   P. Riden, *Rebuilding a valley: a history of Cwmbran Development Corporation* (Cwmbran, 1988).

5   Hughes, *Letters*, Letter F.J. Osborn–L. Mumford, 11.9.1951, pp. 197–8.

6   M.W. Beresford, *New towns of the Middle Ages: town plantation in England, Wales and Gascony* (Stroud, 1988).

7   Cullingworth, *Environmental planning: vol. III*, pp. 113–14.

8   D. Hardy and C. Ward, *Arcadia for all: the legacy of a makeshift landscape* (London, 1984), pp. 202–9; Cullingworth, *Environmental planning: vol. III*, pp. 82–6.

9   K. Patton, 'The foundations of Peterlee new town', in M. Bulmer (ed.), *Mining and social change: Durham county in the twentieth century* (Beckenham, 1978), pp. 218–33.

10   G. Pattison, 'Planning for decline: the "D" village policy of county Durham', *Planning Perspectives*, 19/3 (2004), pp. 311–32.

11   Philipson, *Aycliffe and Peterlee*, pp. 27–35.

12   J. Allan, *Berthold Lubetkin: architecture and the tradition of progress* (London, 1992), pp. 119–26; 463–518; J. Allan, 'Lubetkin and Peterlee', in T. Dekker (ed.), *The modern city revisited* (London, 2000), pp. 103–24.

13   Philipson, *Aycliffe and Peterlee*, pp. 49–75.

14   Ibid., pp. 88–91.

15   Ibid., pp. 97–119.

16   Cullingworth, *Environmental planning: vol. III*: 116–51.

17 Ibid., pp. 486–524; I.H. Seeley, *Planned expansion of country towns* (London, 1974).

18 M. Harloe, *Swindon: a town in transition* (London, 1975).

19 J.H. Dunning, *Economic planning and town expansion: a case study of Basingstoke* (Southampton, 1963). E.G. Stokes, *Basingstoke – expanding town* (Southampton, 1980).

20 Cullingworth, *Environmental planning: vol. III*, pp. 155–62; J.R. Gold, 'Revisiting the new town that might have been', in London County Council, *The Planning of a new town: design based on a study for a new town of 100,000 at Hook, Hampshire* (London, 2015 reprint of original 1961), pp. vii–xxviii.

21 P. Hall and M. Tewdwr-Jones, *Urban and regional planning*, 5th edn (London, 2011), pp. 70–71.

22 A. Alexander, *Britain's new towns: garden cities to sustainable communities* (London, 2009), p. 20. For an insight into the local impacts, see Thetford's Great Heritage, 'Town expansion and migration' <http://www.thetfordsgreat.org/eras.aspx?age-of--empire>, accessed 20 March 2015.

23 British Film Institute, 'The Newcomers' <http://www.screenonline.org.uk/tv/id/1401049/>, accessed 12 August 2015.

24 Figures from C. Carney, 'A Profile of Thetford' <http://www.keystonetrust.org.uk/wp-content/uploads/2015/05/thetfordprofile.pdf>, accessed 12 August 2015 and Balchin, *The first New Town*, pp. 81.

25 Cullingworth, *Environmental planning: vol. III*, pp. 38–41, 149–51; J. Taylor, 'Cumbernauld: the conception, development, and realisation of a post-war British new town', PhD thesis (University of Edinburgh, 2010).

26 Cullingworth, *Environmental planning: vol. III*, pp. 149–51.

27 J.R. Gold, *The practice of modernism: modern architects and the urban transformation, 1954–1972* (London, 2007), pp. 148–51, 155–64.

28 J.R. Gold, 'The making of a megastructure: architectural modernism, town planning and Cumbernauld's central area, 1955–75', *Planning Perspectives*, 21/2 (2006), pp. 109–31.

29 P. Nuttgens, 'Criticism: Cumbernauld town centre', *Architectural Review*, 141/850 (1967), p. 444, quoted in Gold, 'The making of a megastructure', p. 122.

30 Derived from figures in Town and Country Planning Association, *New Towns and Garden Cities*.

31 Cullingworth, *Environmental planning: vol. III*, pp. 164–206.

32 J.B. Cullingworth, *Housing needs and planning policy* (London, 1960).

33 Cullingworth, *Environmental planning: vol. III*, pp. 531.

34 M. de Soissons, *Telford: the making of Shropshire's new town* (Totnes, 1995).

35 G. Anstis, *Redditch: success in the heart of England – the history of Redditch new town 1964–1985* (Stevenage, 1985).

36 E. Wills, *Livingston: the making of a Scottish new town* (Maidenhead, 1996).

37 S. Holley, *Washington: quicker by quango – the history of Washington new town* (Stevenage, 1983).

38 D. Field, 'New town and town expansion schemes: part III: five new towns planned for populations of 80,000 to 100,000', *Town Planning Review*, 39/3 (1968), pp. 196–216.

39 Wannop, 'New towns', p. 216.

40 M. Willis, 'Sociological aspects of urban structure: comparison of residential groupings proposed in planning new towns', *Town Planning Review*, 39/4 (1969), pp. 296–306.

41 H. Wilson and L. Womersley, *Skelmersdale new town planning proposals. Report on basic plan* (Skelmersdale, 1964); Osborn and Whittick, *New Towns*, pp. 294–303.

42 Osborn and Whittick, *New Towns*, pp. 427–37.

43 Llewellyn-Davies, Weeks and Partners, *Washington new town master plan and report* (Washington, 1966); Holley, *Washington*, pp. 7–24.

44 A. Ling and Associates, *Runcorn new town. Master plan* (Runcorn, 1966); Osborn, and Whittick, *New Towns*, pp. 304–13.

45 Except where indicated, interpretations in this section draw on Town and Country Planning Association, *New towns and garden cities*.

46   Alexander, *Britain's new towns*, pp. 150–56, gives many examples of how housing schemes failed in New Towns, not just those in second-generation New Towns.

47   Cullingworth, *Environmental planning: vol. III*, pp. 207–88.

48   D.A. Bull, 'New town and town expansion schemes: part I: an assessment of recent government planning reports', *Town Planning Review*, 38/2 (1967), pp. 103–14; D.A. Bull, 'New town and town expansion schemes: part II: urban form and structure', *Town Planning Review*, 38/3 (1967), pp. 165–86.

49   White Paper, *Central Scotland: a programme for development and growth* (Cmnd 2288) (London, 1963); Irvine Development Corporation, *Irvine new town 1966–1996* (Irvine, 1995).

50   Ministry of Housing and Local Government, *The South East study*.

51   T. Bendixson and J. Platt, *Milton Keynes: image and reality* (Cambridge, 1992).

52   T. Bendixson, *The Peterborough effect: reshaping a city* (Peterborough, 1988).

53   H. Barty-King, *Expanding Northampton* (London, 1985).

54   Cullingworth, *Environmental planning: vol. III*, pp. 269–79.

55   Ibid., pp. 95–102.

56   Ibid., pp. 151–5, 220–22.

57   Osborn and Whittick, *New Towns*, pp. 314–23; Cullingworth, *Environmental planning: vol. III*, pp. 196, 219–23.

58   M. de Soissons, *Telford: the making of Shropshire's new town* (Shrewsbury, 1991), pp. 61–78; Department of Economic Affairs, *The West Midlands: a regional study* (London, 1965), pp. 62–74.

59   F. Schaffer, *The new town story* (London, 1970), pp. 296–300.

60   G. McSheffrey, *Planning Derry: planning and politics in Northern Ireland* (Liverpool, 2000), pp. 98–108.

61   M. Clapson, *A social history of Milton Keynes: middle England/Edge City* (London, 2004).

62   Cullingworth, *Environmental planning: vol. III*, pp. 113, 228–9, 500.

63   G. Ortolano, 'Planning the urban future in 1960s Britain', *The Historical Journal*, 54/2 (2011), pp. 477–507.

64   M. Clapson, M. Dobbin and P. Waterman, *The best laid plans: Milton Keynes since 1967* (Luton, 1998), pp. 3–58.

65   Bull, 'New town and town expansion schemes: part II'.

66   M.A. Webber, 'Planning in an environment of change: part I: beyond the Industrial Age', *Town Planning Review*, 39/3 (1968), pp. 179–95.

67   D. Walker, *The architecture and planning of Milton Keynes* (London, 1982).

68   Bendixson, *The Peterborough effect*, pp. 29–47.

69   Cullingworth, *Environmental planning: vol. III*, pp. 377–80, 513–20.

70   Aldridge, *The New Towns*, pp. 71–4; Barty-King, *Expanding Northampton*, pp. 21–44.

71   M.S. Gibson and M. Langstaff, *An introduction to urban renewal* (London, 1982).

72   P. Harrison, *Inside the inner city* (Harmondsworth, 1983).

73   I. Begg, B. Moore and J. Rhodes, 'Economic and social change in urban Britain and the inner cities', in V. Hausner (ed.), *Critical issues in urban economic development*, 2 vols (Oxford, 1986), Vol. I, pp. 10–49.

74   Aldridge, *The New Towns*, p. 147.

75   Cullingworth, *Environmental planning: vol. III*, p. 216.

76   Colin Buchanan and Partners, *Llantrisant – prospects for urban growth* (London, 1969); Cullingworth, *Environmental planning: vol. III*, pp. 283–6.

77   Aldridge, *The New Towns*, pp. 56, 150. Wannop, 'New towns', p. 218.

78   See, for example, BBC News, 'Craigavon town planning: British modernism 50 years on', 25 October 2014 <http://www.bbc.co.uk/news/uk-northern-ireland-29728971>, accessed 25 March 2015.

79   Aldridge, *The New Towns*, pp. 150–56.

80   Wannop, 'New towns', p. 220.

81   W.G. McClelland, *Washington, over and out: the story of Washington new town, 1983–1988* (Stevenage, 1988).

82   S.V. Ward, 'Consortium Developments Ltd and the failure of new country towns in Mrs Thatcher's Britain', *Planning Perspectives*, 20/3 (2005), pp. 329–59.

83   How justified this characterisation actually was is discussed in D. Hayes and A. Hudson, *Basildon: the mood of the nation* (London, 2001).

84   Balchin, *The first New Town*, p. 345.

85   T. Hall, 'Urban planning in Sweden', in T. Hall (ed.), *Planning and urban growth in the Nordic countries* (London, 1991), pp. 167–246.

86   P. Hall, *Cities in civilization: culture, technology and urban order* (London, 1998), pp. 858–85.

87   M. Andersson, *Stockholm's annual rings: a glimpse into the development of the city* (Stockholm, 1998), pp. 168–95.

88   H. Mattson, 'Where motorways meet: architecture and corporatism in Sweden 1968', in Swenarton, M., Avermaete, T. and Van Den Heuvel, D. (eds), *Architecture and the Welfare States* (London, 2015), pp. 154–75.

89   Andersson, *Stockholm's annual rings*, pp. 191–5.

90   T. Knudsen, 'International influences and professional rivalry in early Danish planning', *Planning Perspectives*, 3/3 (1988), pp. 297–310; B. Larsson and T. Thomassen, 'Urban planning in Denmark', in T. Hall (ed.), *Planning and urban growth in the Nordic countries* (London, 1991), pp. 6–59.

91   H. Von Hertzen and P.D. Speiregen, *Building a new town: Finland's new garden city – Tapiola*, revised edn (Cambridge, MA, 1973); L. Aario, 'The original garden cities in England and the garden city ideal in Finland', *Fennia*, 164/2 (1986), pp. 157–209.

92   K. Bosma and H. Hellinga, 'Dutch urban planning: between centralization and decentralization', in K. Bosma and H. Hellinga (eds), *Mastering the city: north-European city planning 1900–2000*, vol. II (Rotterdam, 1997), pp. 80–87.

93   C. Van der Wal, *In praise of common sense: planning the ordinary. A physical planning history of the new towns in the Ijsselmeerpolders* (Rotterdam, 1997).

94   J.P. Gaudin, 'The French garden city', in Ward, S.V. (ed.). *The garden city: past, present and future* (London, 1992), pp. 52–68.

95   A. Vollerin, *Histoire de l'Architecture et de l'Urbanisme à Lyon au XXe Siècle* (Lyon, 1999), pp. 73–6.

96   On the French approach to the post-war planning of social housing and new communities, see K. Cupers, *The social project: housing in postwar France* (Minneapolis, MN, 2014) and W.B. Newsome, *French urban planning 1940–1968: the construction and deconstruction of an authoritarian system* (New York, 2009).

97   In addition to the above references, see D. Van Hoogstraten, 'Paris 1965 Schéma Directeur d'Aménagement et d'Urbanisme de la Région de Paris', in K. Bosma and H. Hellinga (eds), *Mastering the city: north-European city planning 1900–2000*, vol. II (Rotterdam, 1997), pp. 324–9; L. Vadelorge, *Retour sur les villes nouvelles: Une histoire urbaine du XXe siècle* (Paris, 2014).

98   J.M. Rubenstein, *The French new towns* (Baltimore, 1978).

99   Garvin, *The American city*, pp. 313–54.

100   Tennenbaum, R. (ed.), *Creating a new city: Columbia, Maryland* (Columbia, MD, 1996); J.R Mitchell and D. Stebenne, *New city upon a hill: a history of Columbia, Maryland* (Charleston, SC, 2007); N.D. Bloom, *Suburban alchemy: 1960s new towns and the transformation of the American dream* (Columbus, OH, 2001).

101   M. Clapson, *Anglo-American crossroads: urban planning and research in Britain, 1940–2010* (London, 2013), pp. 99–122.

102 J. Olsen, *Better lives, better places: a biography of James Rouse* (Washington DC, 2003), pp. 196–8.

103 A. Forsyth, *Reforming suburbia: the planned communities of Irvine, Columbia and the Woodlands* (Berkeley, CA, 2002). Despite having the same name as the Scottish New Town, the pronunciation of their names differs. Irvine, California has a long last syllable; Irvine, Scotland could be spelled without the final 'e'.

104 W. Nicoson, 'The United States: the battle for title VII', in M. Apgar (ed.), *New perspectives on community development* (London, 1976), pp. 38–58.

105 M.R. Bristow, *Hong Kong's new towns: a selective review* (Hong Kong, 1989); O.J. Dale, *Urban planning in Singapore: the transformation of a city* (Oxford, 1999).

106 S.J. Watanabe, 'The Japanese garden city', in S.V. Ward (ed.), *The garden city: past, present and future* (London, 1992), pp. 69–87; K. Sakamoto, 'The theory of the Japanese garden city: its acceptance and development 1906–1942', in T. Saiki, R. Freestone and M. van Rooijen (eds), *New garden city in the 21st century?* (Kobe, 2002), pp. 75–97.

107 Tokyo Metropolitan Government, *A hundred years of Tokyo city planning* (Tokyo, 1994), pp. 66–7; A. Sorensen, *The making of urban Japan: cities and planning from Edo to the twenty-first century* (London, 2002), pp. 185–8.

108 M. Peel, *Good times, hard times: the past and the future in Elizabeth* (Melbourne, 1995).

109 T. Stannage, *Lakeside city: the dreaming of Joondalup* (Nedlands, 1996).

110 I. Morison, 'The corridor city: planning for growth in the 1960s', in S. Hamnett and R. Freestone (eds), *The Australian metropolis: a planning history* (London, 2000), pp. 113–30.

111 V.K. Stepanov, 'Union of Soviet Socialist Republics', in A. Whittick (ed.), *Encyclopaedia of urban planning* (Huntingdon, NY, 1980), p. 1146.

112 S. Kotkin, *Magnetic mountain: Stalinism as a civilization* (Berkeley, CA, 1997).

113 A. Åman, *Architecture and ideology in eastern Europe during the Stalin era: an aspect of Cold War history* (New York/Cambridge, MA, 1992); K. Lebow, *Unfinished Utopia: Nowa Huta, Stalinism and Polish society 1949–56* (Ithaca, NY, 2013); R. May, 'Planned city Stalinstadt: a manifesto of the early German Democratic Republic', *Planning Perspectives*, 18/1 (2003), pp. 47–78.

114 Ward, 'Soviet communism and the British planning movement'; I.R. Cook, S.V. Ward and K. Ward, 'A springtime journey to the Soviet Union: postwar planning and policy mobilities through the Iron Curtain', *International Journal of Urban and Regional Research*, 38/3 (2014), pp. 805–22.

115 H.W. Wells, 'A chartered surveyor looks at Soviet Russia', *The Chartered Surveyor*, 91/7 (1959), pp. 374–81.

116 DEFRA (Department for Environment, Food and Rural Affairs), *Statistical digest of rural England 2012* (London, 2012).

CHAPTER EIGHT

Where the path led

Population growth in garden cities and New Towns

The 2011 census showed that the 32 former New Towns in the United Kingdom (including Welwyn Garden City) and Letchworth Garden City together had a little over 2,794,500 inhabitants, about 4.4 per cent of the total UK population.[1] Directly or indirectly, the lives of all these people have been affected, to some extent, by the principal branches of the peaceful path. Obviously the growth that was directly attributable to New Town or garden city development was rather less. A simple measure of this is possible, in that the pre-existing populations of the areas of all New Towns and garden cities when they were initiated had been 1,108,300.[2] At a very crude level, therefore, we can point to an extra population of just over 1,686,200 people. This was a net addition close to, indeed slightly more than, the growth anticipated in the total of the population targets adopted when all those garden cities and New Towns were initiated, which was 2,791,000. (It was, however, rather less than the 3,123,000 total which represented the all-time maximum revisions of those targets, though this dated from a time when national expectations about overall population growth were extremely inflated.)

Of course, these are rather crude figures. On the one hand, it can be argued that many of the New Towns have moved on from that era, some (for example, most of those in Northern Ireland) quite soon after they were designated. Perhaps, therefore, not all the growth that occurred can be claimed as resulting from the New Town programme. Yet, against this, it can be very plausibly argued that the experience of being a New Town did not end when the Development Corporation was dissolved. Rather, the New Town experience set in train a process of growth that created an infrastructural capacity for further development and, among local populations and business interests, a 'growth-minded' mentality. It is, for example, inconceivable that Milton Keynes would have subsequently been groomed for such twenty-first-century expansion as is now contemplated had it not already proved its capacity for real growth as a New Town.

Population growth in Hertfordshire's garden cities and New Towns

As this begins to imply, the overall picture conceals a great deal of local variation, part of which we glimpsed in the previous chapter. Some New Towns were certainly built on wildly overambitious hopes resulting in a big shortfall of actual growth compared with targets, especially those set in the 1960s. This was especially so with several of the New Towns in Scotland and Northern Ireland. Here, however, we will concentrate on the Hertfordshire garden cities and New Towns which have been the particular focus of this book, making broader comparisons where appropriate. Their total 2011 population was 288,700 (almost 26 per cent of the Hertfordshire total), a net increase of 251,200 on the original population.[3] The 2011 garden cities and New Towns' total was significantly more than their original target population total of 213,500 and rather close to the most ambitious target of 292,000.[4]

As can be seen, this simple measure of growth shows the Hertfordshire garden cities and New Towns together performed better than the UK New Town average. Thus Letchworth Garden City, with approximately 33,200, had crept a little over Howard's notional 32,000 target. Stevenage, at just below 84,000, and Hemel Hempstead, at approximately 85,700, had more than met their revised targets of 80,000. At a time of excessive optimism among population forecasters, however, it had been informally expected that the former might grow to 105,000, which it did not.

Interestingly, there remains a strong local appetite for further growth in Stevenage, although the view is that this cannot be achieved without expanding over the town's tightly drawn boundaries, something now resolutely opposed by the adjoining authority, North Hertfordshire District (Figure 8.1). Since 1999, what is effectively a new small neighbourhood has been built by three private housing developers at Great Ashby, immediately north-east of the Stevenage boundary. But in recent years opposition to Stevenage extensions has grown, with a proposed large extension west of Stevenage, involving a substantial incursion into North Hertfordshire, seen as particularly unwelcome.[5] Changes to government policy in 2010 effectively strengthened the hand of North Hertfordshire to resist such expansion and the scheme has now been withdrawn.

Hatfield, already part of a larger local authority, Welwyn and Hatfield District, avoided these kinds of problems. It had apparently done particularly well in growing to a 2011 population of just over 39,000, which was well above the original 25,000 target; yet the 2011 figure should be treated with some caution, as it is based on present ward boundaries now including some existing villages and privately developed housing recently built on the old de Havilland

Figure 8.1 Stevenage's tightly drawn boundaries combined with local pressures for further expansion on the western side have created conflict with the neighbouring local authority of North Hertfordshire, despite a supposed legal 'duty to co-operate'. (© Robert Thompson)

site, both of which lay outside the very tight limits of the former New Town. Its neighbour, Welwyn Garden City, with approximately 46,600 in 2011, was the only Hertfordshire example not to reach its revised New Town projected target of 50,000 (though it comfortably exceeded its garden city target of 40,000).

Attracting employers

Generally speaking, these trends were typical of all the first-generation Greater London New Towns, where the wider regional economy has been sufficiently strong to create jobs and thus attract migrants from the capital or elsewhere. As noted, all the Hertfordshire New Towns experienced their greatest growth when the link between having a job and getting a house was most strongly enforced. Looking more widely, it is clear that New Towns with particularly disappointing growth were mainly those established in later policy phases, when population growth forecasts were excessively high and/or in parts of the country with weaker regional economies. None of these ever really applied to Hertfordshire's New Towns, though Stevenage was touched by the tendency for exaggerated forecasts in the early to mid-1960s.

Figure 8.2 Hemel Hempstead has become a major shopping centre, more so since the new Riverside development opened in 2005. Although its pedestrian area appears to be normal public space, it is actually private, subject to its own management and security. This differs sharply from the original conception of public space in the New Towns. (author photograph)

Economically, however, all these towns were very successful in attracting employers from quite an early stage. From the beginnings at Letchworth through to the present, Hertfordshire has benefited by its proximity to London and excellent communications, factors which encouraged industrial development. As the county's manufacturing base began to be established, various 'clustering' effects also became apparent. Thus information technology manufacturing in Stevenage from the 1950s grew very much from the initial British Tabulating Machine Ltd (later International Computers Ltd) base in Letchworth from 1920 and continued to expand after 1945. Another example was the pre-war move of de Havilland to Hatfield; its subsequent growth affected not just that New Town but also encouraged aerospace industrial development nearby, most obviously at Stevenage.

Recent economic resilience

Yet the real resilience of the economies of all the Hertfordshire garden cities and New Towns was tested by the dramatic national contraction of manufacturing from the 1980s. Formerly dominant industrial firms in all of them dramatically reduced employment and in many cases closed completely during the 1980s and 1990s. Kodak, for example, was once synonymous (in the UK) with Hemel Hempstead, but the firm's presence in the town is now the palest shadow of its former self. De Havilland, latterly British Aerospace, has completely gone from Hatfield. Although aerospace survives in Stevenage, it is focused on research and development and no longer provides mass factory employment. Virtually all Letchworth's original main manufacturers, such as Spirella, ICL, Shelvoke and Drewry, and Kryn and Lahy, no longer exist. The iconic Shredded Wheat factory in Welwyn Garden City is now completely closed, the company relocated.

Most New Towns (like the older industrial towns and cities) elsewhere suffered equivalent or worse economic body blows during the same years. Comparatively, however, Hertfordshire's garden cities and New Towns recovered remarkably well. The former de Havilland site in Hatfield, for example, now contains a business park and a second campus of the University of Hertfordshire, both intended to boost the town's and county's future economic development.[6] (Unfortunately, however, the Hatfield Tunnel prevents the park from being seen from the A1(M) motorway, limiting its prestige value and possibly its attractiveness to 'blue riband' companies.) In the other New Towns there has been more continuity in how former staple industries still provide a real basis, not just a site, for present and future business development. Thus some long-established firms (or successor companies which took over or grew from the ashes of former firms) have continued as important elements of their town's economies. We have already mentioned Stevenage's continued 'high-end' presence in aerospace, represented by the firms Astrium and MBDA, while Fujitsu's presence in computing is a reminder of ICL's former manufacturing significance. Long-established pharmaceuticals firm Roche similarly remains a key employer in Welwyn Garden City. However, there are also newer names. The most prominent is the pharmaceutical giant GlaxoSmithKline, which built its prestigious UK research centre in Stevenage in 1995. There have also been many rather smaller newcomers to all of these towns.

Many of the main employers in these towns are now predominantly service rather than manufacturing operations. They embrace a wide variety of activities. The larger former New Towns of Hemel Hempstead and Stevenage are most dominant in consumer services such as retailing (Figure 8.2). Distribution and administration related to retailing are also important in Hemel Hempstead – the headquarters of DSG (Dixons) consumer electronics retailing – and Welwyn Garden City – the headquarters of Tesco supermarkets. Business services and 'knowledge industries' of various kinds are also now found more commonly than actual manufacturing. Letchworth, for example, attracted many smaller firms of this type, especially to the former Spirella factory and ICL offices (the Nexus building). Public services, particularly local government, are major employers in several towns, notably Hemel Hempstead and Stevenage. Hatfield enjoys the unique presence of the University of Hertfordshire, still mainly located on its original site.

Social indicators

Overall, therefore, all these towns have proved relatively resilient in regenerating their economies, generally more so than New Towns in more peripheral regions. This does not mean that everyone in these towns has been fully sharing in this prosperity, however. In Stevenage, for example, many very good jobs requiring high expertise have been created in recent years, especially in pharmaceuticals and aerospace, yet relatively few of these are held by Stevenage residents.[7] Many are being taken by in-commuters living in nearby areas such as Hitchin or Letchworth, rather than those who wish to live in the town. The people of the town itself show a slightly higher level of deprivation than English (though not UK) New Towns as a whole.

This problem is less marked in most of the other towns, especially so the garden cities, which have largely remained attractive residential towns. But there are also disparities within the New Towns, where residents of some wards lack the skills to gain better-paid jobs. Thus, although Hemel Hempstead as a whole has lower deprivation than the English New Town and national average, a ward such as Highfield does noticeably less well.[8] There are also pockets of particular deprivation in central Stevenage and Hatfield. But these should not be exaggerated and Hertfordshire's New Towns, in comparison with all New Towns and especially older cities in less prosperous regions, have generally avoided or overcome the worst signs of deprivation.[9] This is generally borne out in the general health of their populations, with equal or higher proportions of their populations than the UK average in 2011 reporting themselves in good or very good health. However, other indicators suggest a more mixed emerging picture, with, for example, higher than national average obesity levels in Hemel Hempstead and especially Stevenage.[10] These characteristics, unless checked, are likely to damage the longer-term health prospects of those concerned.

Housing conditions

All the Hertfordshire garden cities and New Towns provide good housing conditions. Although some of their housing stock is aging, especially in Letchworth, standards have been maintained or improved in the main. A few instances of wholesale clearance and redevelopment have occurred, as in the cases of an estate of 1920s concrete housing at Peartree in Welwyn Garden City and part of the Stony Hall estate in Stevenage (Figure 8.3). But, compared with

Figure 8.3 Much of the original 1920s concrete housing development at Peartree in Welwyn Garden City was redeveloped in the 1980s. It was a relatively rare example of housing failure in the Hertfordshire garden cities and New Towns. (author photograph)

later New Towns or even some first-generation New Towns, such as nearby Harlow, all those in Hertfordshire were built mainly using fairly traditional methods and materials. Like much housing of the early post-war decades, some upgrading has been necessary, especially to improve heating and insulation. Yet the novel construction systems that were used (mainly Wimpey No-Fines and Mowlem in Stevenage, Hemel Hempstead and Hatfield) have not generally presented intractable structural problems to date.

All these planned Hertfordshire towns show what became a very characteristic New Town housing tenure mix, especially so in the earlier New Towns.[11] Despite the effects of right-to-buy since the 1970s and especially the 1980s, the proportion of households in owner-occupation in most of these planned towns still remains a few percentage points lower than the national average (much lower in Hatfield's case). It does not help that, in common with other areas in London and the South East, local house prices have risen dramatically in recent years. Generally they are highest in areas closer and with the most convenient links to London. However, the 'affordability gap' between average earnings and the cost of housing is less severe than in some older towns in the Home Counties and London itself.

In all Hertfordshire's planned towns social renting, largely of the inherited housing stock of development corporations, has remained higher than the UK average and in many cases the New Towns average. Stevenage and Hemel Hempstead each had around 28 per cent social renting in 2011, compared to 18.5 per cent nationally. Perhaps surprisingly, this difference is largest in Letchworth (32 per cent social renting), where housing association provision (21.5 per cent) is unusually important.[12] As elsewhere, however, social housing provision has in recent decades failed to keep pace with local housing needs. Renting from private landlords is lower than the UK average and especially that of the big cities, except in Hatfield, where, at 23 per cent in 2011, it is very much higher, reflecting the impact of the town's student population.

Broader planning considerations

All towns developed on a planned basis, especially over a relatively short period, are prone to certain long-term problems. The assumptions on which they were planned may well change, partly reflecting changes in the way people live their lives. In some cases the original planning or design concepts adopted were in some way flawed. Of course, these things will affect all places, but the fact that new settlements were typically developed in large sections means that the effect is magnified. For example, patterns of local retail and other social provision

Figure 8.4 Jarman Park in Hemel Hempstead is a leisure-park development with associated fast-food outlets and superstore, opened in 1994–5. It illustrates how new, more car-based, consumption-related development formats began to overlay the original planning conceptions during the late twentieth century. Subsequently, however, the main leisure operator closed, and major refurbishment has occurred, shown here. (Jane Housham)

adopted in the first generation of New Towns reflected an era before the major supermarket chains appeared, when car-based mobility was much lower and when much shopping and other service provision was far more locally based. This has created a need for the adaptation and regeneration of the original neighbourhood centres in all the New Towns. Stevenage, Hemel Hempstead and Hatfield have also seen a rather pragmatic later twentieth-/early twenty-first-century development of large-scale car-based retailing, leisure and related formats. These include superstores, retail warehouse parks, multi-screen cinemas and fast-food outlets built in off-centre locations not previously used for such purposes. The product of private developer rather than planner initiative, not all of these have been entirely successful and have experienced varying fates.

Thus Jarman Park in Hemel Hempstead, for example, was a former refuse tip and sewage-treatment site that in 1994–5 became a leisure park with a retail superstore (Figure 8.4).[13] After some early success the main leisure provider closed, leaving it in need of significant refurbishment (underway at the time of writing). However, a recent move to extend it with major retail development was rejected by the local authority, largely because it would have undermined the main town centre. The Hatfield Galleria shopping centre on part of the former de Havilland site had also initially faltered after opening in 1991, but then was

Figure 8.5 Tesco superstore at Broadwater, Stevenage is typical of early twenty-first-century retailing. Compared with the nearby Broadwater local neighbourhood unit centre (Figure 5.9) this more contemporary pattern offers a wider choice for car-based shoppers from a much wider catchment area. (author photograph)

relaunched more successfully as a designer outlet and leisure park in 1996.[14] That same year also saw the opening of the Stevenage Leisure Park on the former site of one of the few factories (originally King's) that had preceded the New Town designation.[15] Its proximity to the town centre and the railway station have helped its success and it was subsequently extended. Retail superstores built in the former New Towns away from the originally planned shopping centres in the 1990s and 2000s, such as the example at Broadwater in Stevenage shown in Figure 8.5, have generally proved successful.

There have also been important retailing and other changes in the central areas. The Hertfordshire garden cities and New Towns between them show the evolution of thinking on this matter, from conventional frontage development on traffic streets to purpose-built open precinct pedestrianisation to enclosed shopping malls, pedestrianisation of existing conventional streets and various combinations of all of these. The shift from access based on public transport, cycling and walking to increased car use has also placed a strain on these areas. Hemel Hempstead's town centre, commercially the strongest of Hertfordshire's planned towns, has gone through and shows the signs of all these phases. Stevenage, which began as the boldest, with its open pedestrian precinct, shows some of the problems of being an innovator. Welwyn Garden City, despite having a rather bland enclosed shopping mall built in the late 1980s, retains much of the original concept. Hatfield's town centre is the least satisfactory and is undergoing a rather hesitant regeneration at the time of writing.

Changing transport modes have also left their mark on other planning aspects. For example, the narrowness of the early residential streets of all the Hertfordshire planned towns and associated limited car parking arrangements leave continuing problems. The Stevenage cycleway system was a fine achievement but is very underused at present, which may compromise its chances of survival. In later neighbourhoods, especially in Stevenage, planned with Radburn or modified Radburn layouts, the idiosyncrasies of complete pedestrian/vehicle segregation have had mixed effects. Behind the attractively landscaped and pedestrianised house 'fronts' were austere and much less salubrious 'backs'. Yet the effects have been curious rather than truly failing. Hertfordshire's garden cities and New Towns have been spared the planned social housing environments, such as 'streets in the sky', that proved so calamitous in some inner-city locations.

How successful were the garden cities and New Towns?
On balance, although the picture is nuanced rather than clear-cut, Hertfordshire's planned settlements can be judged as successful towns. Everything depends, of course, on how 'success' is defined. Their economies and societies have, as shown, proved robust and enduring. At their best, in parts of the garden cities, they have created genuinely attractive built environments. The worst that might be said about the rest is that they are a little dull, though this partly reflects current tastes, which regard the architecture of the early post-war welfare state with a certain ennui. In this connection, however, it is worth recalling that Georgian and Victorian built environments were once also treated with some disdain. A future change of popular taste may also in time affect the plain simplicity of the early New Town neighbourhoods.

The truth was that, at the time, such places housed many people in far better conditions, at generally modest cost and sooner than would have been possible elsewhere, especially in London. In a larger sense, too, the alternative to them would almost certainly have been much less orderly development around existing towns throughout Hertfordshire and a more generalised sprawl out from London in the south of the county. There would have been more developments similar to that which occurred to some extent at Elstree and Borehamwood. By 1939 the scene had already been set for a major growth of Greater London suburbia into this area. Although this did not materialise as intended because of the war, the London County Council did build a sizeable 'out-county' estate there in the early post-war years.

Where Hertfordshire's planned towns were rather less successful was in addressing society's wider problems, in terms of who they benefited and who they excluded. Howard, it should be remembered, also wished to address the needs of outcast London, not just those a little higher up the social scale. Yet the very poorest and worst-housed of the capital, the unskilled, those with the misfortune to grow up in broken homes, single parents, the disabled, the old, the ill and overseas immigrants had far fewer opportunities to avail themselves of the better life chances that garden city and New Town living brought.[16] Not until much later, as the main growth phase of Hertfordshire's planned towns was coming to an end, did this begin to change. For the first 20–25 years after 1946 the path such people had to traverse remained a far more challenging one. Sadly, however, their under-representation in the earlier New Towns probably helped to ensure, by excluding the 'difficult' cases who were suffering multiple disadvantages, that the success of the programme could be demonstrated.

What happened to the Howard legacy?

There was another failure, one that lay even closer to the very centre of Howard's dream of the peaceful path. Apart from at Letchworth, and even there only partially, no way was ever found to realise his proposals to capture for the benefit of the local community the whole of the uplift in land value associated with the development of the original rural estate as a town. Who, then, did benefit from this uplift? The Treasury, having been the source of funding for the New Towns, received a great deal back as individual towns moved into profit, which generally they began to do as they were transferred to the Commission for the New Towns.

The Commission initially kept the commercial assets and undeveloped land. For housing and associated community assets, however, the pattern changed after 1976, as these were increasingly transferred from the Commission to local authorities. While this offered some potential for real local benefit, the extent to which this actually happened is debatable. At best, the benefit was extracted as funds to manage, maintain and, as necessary, improve or even replace the housing stock itself. Moreover, the community assets themselves, though they included neighbourhood shopping centres with some capacity for commercial rent generation, often needed some renewal to maintain their capacity to generate rents. Even if this was successful, the financial 'clawback' arrangements prevailing during the 1980s and 1990s reduced the possibility of retaining property income gains for wider benefit (although these rules were subsequently eased).

Increasingly from the 1970s and especially the 1980s property assets were sold outright. Much public sector rental housing was sold to occupiers, often at a discount, so that individual owners rather than the wider community benefited. Commercial assets and development land were also sold by the Commission for the New Towns and successor bodies, generating one-off income but removing the possibility of future public benefit from land value uplift by transferring it to new owners.

Have we come to the end of the path?

In his famous 'Three Magnets' diagram Howard posed the question: 'The people – where will they go?' His answer in 1898 was that they would want to find a balance between town and country living in the garden city. By the last quarter of the twentieth century, however, inner-city decline led policy makers (though not yet particularly the people themselves) to the thought that many people needed to be attracted back. The goal became to repopulate the cities, to prevent them from entirely emptying out and leaving great tracts of derelict land, abandoned factories and housing estates.

So it was that planned decentralisation and the New Towns programme were pensioned off as active policies. In the years that followed a great deal of effort was devoted to regenerating inner-city areas. Dereliction was recycled into heritage as former factories and warehouses became apartment complexes and hotels. Conference centres, cultural buildings such as art galleries and museums appeared. The volume private house-builders (who for many years had not dreamt of building in such locations) were tempted back and discovered that a market existed for such adaptive reuse and for new-build housing. In some locations major new commercial developments occurred, creating new employment hubs. The effects, especially in London, were striking, as population began to rise for the first time in many decades. This positive impact came more slowly in cities that did not have the capital's international status and economic dynamism, but few older cities and towns remained untouched by reurbanisation.

There is no doubt that big city living appeals to many, especially the young. All the features that Howard identified as forming the positive pole of his Town Magnet are still there, while many of those which constituted its negative pole have diminished. Cities are nothing like as unpleasant and unhealthy as they were when Howard wrote. Manufacturing industry, with all the noise and pollution that it brought to Victorian cities, has largely gone. Today's motor traffic certainly creates air pollution and has implications for health, but its effects are far more limited than the omnipresent coal smoke from industry and domestic fires that blighted older cities until the 1950s. Today, living in a city in the UK is rather less important as an intrinsic source of disadvantage than it was in the 1890s. The source of disadvantage is not so much now the city itself but rather wealth and income, regardless of the place in which one is rich or poor.

The continuing appeal of 'town–country'

Yet it is easy to exaggerate the appetite for reurbanisation. Even as the inner metropolitan populations of London and other big cities stabilised and then began to rise, there was an enduring strong demand for the town–country qualities that Howard articulated. Much reputable research in the early twenty-first century, before the economic crash of 2008, indicated strong preferences in England for essentially suburban forms of housing – detached and semi-detached houses and bungalows.[17] Some willingness to compromise was reported, especially among those setting out in the housing market. Yet in 2004 research suggested that around 70 per cent of first-time buyers would not consider a flat. Gardens remained extremely popular. We might assume that the subsequent travails of the housing market may well have increased the willingness to compromise, but even so it seems unlikely that underlying preferences have drastically changed.

Certainly in the aftermath of the New Towns programme there were important initiatives aimed at finding ways to offer something of Howard's vision of 'town–country'. In the face of local planning policies strongly favouring restraint outside the big cities, especially so in areas covered by green belt policies, this has not been easy. In 1983 Consortium Developments Ltd, a coalition of the ten biggest house-builders, tried to launch a programme for around 15 'new country towns' each of around 9,000–18,000 inhabitants (Figure 8.6).[18] Despite the encouraging ideological signals of Thatcherism, seeking to free the market and reduce state restrictions, it came almost immediately into conflict with implacable (largely Conservative-voting) local opposition. After bringing forward four detailed proposals, all refused, the Company was dissolved in 1991.

In Cambridgeshire there was local support for new settlements of this kind and a privately developed new village of 5,000 dwellings was begun at Cambourne in 1993 and has developed, albeit quite slowly, since then. And the first phase of another, larger 'mini-new town scheme', Northstowe, eventually of to 10,000 dwellings with a final population of perhaps 25,000, is now being developed, with state involvement recently helping the partnership of the private developer and local authorities overcome some of the final funding problems.[19] Already there were a few other small examples of new settlements developed by various combinations of private and local authority initiative,[20] and signs of real encouragement from central

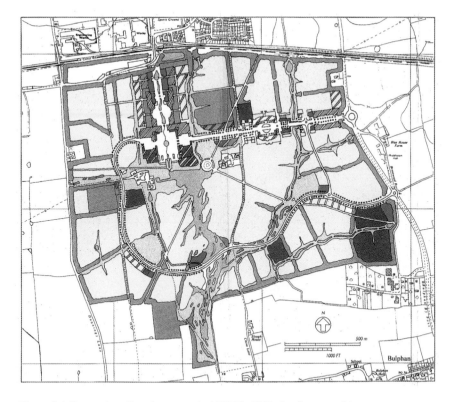

Figure 8.6 Consortium Developments Ltd (CDL)'s 1986 plan for a small 'new country town' at 'Tillingham Hall', Essex. None of their projects were realised, but CDL elaborated the idea of private sector new settlements with physical and social infrastructure funded from the development uplift in land values – the 'peaceful path' meets Thatcherism. (author's collection)

government since the early part of this century have also gradually been growing. The 2003 Sustainable Communities Plan identified several growth areas, including indicative proposals for small new communities, most notably at Ebbsfleet in Kent, at the Thames Gateway. There were also proposals to expand some of the by then ex-New Towns, such as Milton Keynes, Northampton and Harlow.

Eco-towns and new garden cities
In 2007 the Brown Labour government launched the Eco-towns initiative, essentially to encourage and support a few small new settlements or, in practice, town extensions with many advanced environmental features.[21] Four sites were approved in 2009 at Whitehill-Bordon in Hampshire (initially for 5,000 but later 4,000 dwellings), St Austell and Clay Country in Cornwall (initially 5,000 dwellings, though now the projected size is uncertain), Rackheath,

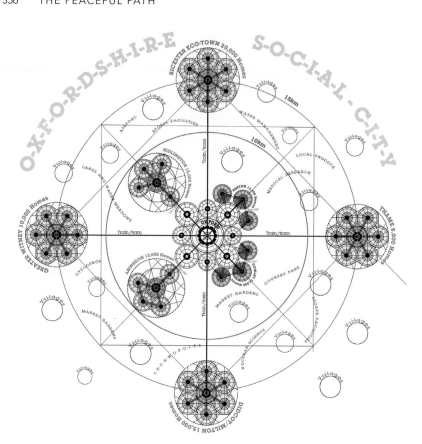

Figure 8.7 URBED's 2014 elaboration of a project to build a new garden city for Oxfordshire. The echoes of Howard's Social City are obvious, though with more town extensions rather than freestanding garden cities. Social concerns are less in evidence than they were in the original diagram. (Courtesy of URBED)

Norfolk (perhaps 5,100 dwellings) and North West Bicester, Oxfordshire (6,000 dwellings). The Cameron coalition government cut back on the Eco-towns initiative, which had generated much local opposition in several locations, contributing to the continuing uncertainty noted here.

However, the Cameron government also moved further in this general direction by reintroducing the term 'garden cities' into planning policy discourse in the new National Planning Policy Framework of 2012.[22] Both coalition partners, Conservatives and Liberal Democrats, have been to different degrees enthusiastic about the idea. A Conservative peer, Lord Wolfson, launched a major competition to demonstrate how a new garden city might be realised. The winner, announced in 2014, was the planning consultancy URBED, which proposed a series of discrete town extensions for the fictionalised historic city of Uxcester, doubling its size to

400,000.[23] The idea was then elaborated (while remaining still an intellectual exercise) for a real location as a neo-Social City proposal for Oxfordshire (Figure 8.7).

Also in 2014 a government policy document on locally led garden cities was issued, essentially encouraging local authorities to consider such ventures as a way of meeting local housing requirements.[24] During that year the government went even further by announcing where the first new garden cities would be.[25] In the spring it committed itself to providing financial assistance for a 15,000-dwelling project at Ebbsfleet in Kent in former chalk pits between Bluewater Shopping Centre and the new station on HS1 (the Channel Tunnel Rail Link).[26] This idea, far from being new, had been rumbling around for a decade with little progress because of the high costs of developing the site. A development corporation is being created with the intention of breaking the logjam. Towards the end of 2014 it was announced that the second new garden city would be Bicester, where the approved Eco-town project in the north-west of the town was wrapped up in a wider scheme to add a total of 13,000 dwellings to the whole town.[27] More new garden cities are promised, while Labour has been talking more ambitiously about reviving the New Towns programme. Since the 2015 election, the Conservative government has announced (very limited) support for two local 'garden towns' at Didcot in Oxfordshire and in north Essex.

A real need for housing

It is easy to be rather cynical about the new initiatives so far announced. Although we can be reasonably sure they will be interesting exercises in making new places, they are insignificant in relation to the huge scale of national housing requirements. Unless their numbers and/or the size of each one increases greatly, they will not achieve anything approaching the impact of the New Towns programme and its progenitors.

Yet there can be no doubt that a real need for homes exists.[28] A generation is being held back by the difficulties of finding a secure base on which to build their adult lives. For some years, but particularly since the housing crash of 2008, housing supply has fallen well short of demand, with the consequence that prices have risen very sharply. This is especially so in London, where house prices and rents have been rising even faster than in the rest of the country. With the average house price in London reported in September 2014 as £514,000, and rent levels to match, the cost to buy or rent even the tiniest flat in the least fashionable part of London is, for large sections of the population, quite prohibitive.[29] This is driving many people employed in London but unable to afford its house prices to look further afield. The same is happening to a lesser degree in other housing price 'hotspots', particularly where planning constraints such as green belts limit the possibilities for peripheral expansion in the 'hotspot' itself. (The Cambridgeshire new settlements programme was partly a product of this, responding to the problems of one such local 'hotspot', which is also significantly affected by the additional impact of London itself.)

All this shows that there is scope for a much bigger programme of new garden cities or New Towns, especially in places well connected to the capital or these local 'hotspots'.[30] The scale of the unfulfilled housing requirement is so great that new settlements could never, even on a much larger scale, be the only solution. Yet they could be an important contributor in the medium to longer term, especially if the new garden cities or New Towns were attractively designed and became congenial places in which to live. There are several key considerations which form preconditions to achieving this. It would be desirable if the need for long journeys to and from work could be reduced by having more local jobs, and the larger the new settlements that are envisaged, the more feasible this becomes. Ideally, too, such settlements, of whatever size, should be largely self-sufficient in their local service provision, especially in terms of shops, schools and local health care. Again, however, this becomes easier to achieve as settlement size increases.

Yet Howard's peaceful path was not simply about good planning. It involved a key principle of political economy, one hugely important in nineteenth-century reformism: how the rising land values that follow development might be harnessed for real and lasting community benefit. This was central to the original conception of the garden city. The scope for this appears much more limited in the new garden cities because they will be developed much more on market principles. Private profit-seeking landowners and developers are in position in all the new garden cities and similar places mentioned, though this could change. At present, however, there is no public sector development agency or limited dividend company which buys all the land needed for development, as was the case for the original garden cities and New Towns. At Ebbsfleet, for example, the site is entirely in the hands of the Land Securities property company, while the Gallagher property company is in a similar position at Northstowe.

As good as it gets?
The development mechanism being adopted is not so different from that proposed by Consortium Developments Ltd in the 1980s. In theory, if market conditions are right (which, in the aftermath of the property crash, they were not), part of the uplift in land value associated with development is surrendered by developers to fund some of the physical and social infrastructure and amenities integral to making the new garden city. In particularly favourable market conditions it can also be used to subsidise affordable and social housing

Figure 8.8 Ebenezer Howard as an old man. Do we have the courage today to return to the reformist path he imagined in the 1890s? (Town and Country Planning Association)

alongside ordinary market house-building. In theory, this involvement of profit-seeking developers avoids the chronic undercapitalisation that plagued both of the 'real' garden cities, causing their slow development. Whether this new mechanism will ever entirely avoid this problem is doubtful, however, because it is extremely sensitive to market conditions, even for 'patient' developers with reasonably deep pockets (which some of them certainly have). The prolonged negotiations of planning agreements with local authorities seeking social or environmental benefits have sometimes also slowed actual development.

But in strong market conditions the approach may prove a serviceable development mechanism, especially if central government becomes more willing to provide the funding, organisational framework and leadership that will offset developer uncertainties. This seems now as if it may be on the brink of happening, at least on a small scale. We may be sure, however, that the approach will never give significant long-term community benefits of the kind (as mentioned in Chapter 2) that are now disbursed annually in Letchworth. Expressed in the metaphorical terms of the Howard legacy, it is as if part of an inheritance is taken early to fund current needs, foregoing a larger inheritance in the long term. That long-term gain effectively disappears into developer and landowner profits and the wealth represented in future house value rises for house purchasers. This highlights an even more profound contradiction in this mechanism because it depends on a strong housing market, effectively one where prices are rising sufficiently to encourage private developers to build. Yet this is doing the exact opposite of fostering the creation of more affordable and social housing. It means, absurdly, that the general level of house prices has to rise in order that, for some, prices can become relatively cheaper.

Perhaps, in our neo-liberal age, this really is as good as things are going to get. Yet Ebenezer Howard imagined something better than this – and in an age when the free market was even more exalted than it is now. He saw that if development land could be entirely removed from the free market by some form of continuing collective ownership then it should be possible to provide the long-term security of decent living standards, perhaps not quite for all but for at least a wide cross section of society. The relevance of this idea is far greater today, when land is a much bigger proportion of housing costs than it was in Howard's day. Of course, neither he nor those who followed him ever worked out a fully satisfactory way of delivering on the possibilities which followed from this key principle. Yet, whatever their faults in this or other respects, in the post-war New Towns they came a good deal nearer to achieving this goal than we seem capable of doing today. The peaceful path is still there – if only we can again find the courage and the commitment to follow it.

Notes

1   Reproduced from Town and Country Planning Association, *New Towns and Garden Cities*, p. 25. This figure excludes the short-lived thirty-third New Town, Stonehouse. The population figure for Letchworth Garden City has been added to the TCPA figures by the present author.

2   Wannop, 'New Towns', p. 216. The figures are corrected to include the original population and target of Welwyn Garden City, not simply its population at the time the New Town was designated. The figure for Letchworth is also added and that for Stonehouse excluded.

3   Derived from figures in Town and Country Planning Association, *New Towns and Garden Cities*.

4   This figure includes the informal expectation (noted later in the main text) that Stevenage would eventually grow to 105,000, although this was never adopted as a formal target, which remained 80,000. If this lower target had been used instead, then the county's New Towns would have comfortably exceeded their highest targets.

5   M. Donnelly, 'Plans for 3,600 Stevenage homes withdrawn after 12-year wrangle', *Planning Resource*, 15 August 2013 <http://www.planningresource.co.uk/article/1207535/plans-3600-stevenage-homes-withdrawn-12-year-wrangle>, accessed 14 August 2015.

6   Regeneris Consulting, *Hertfordshire strategic employment sites study* (London/Hertford, 2011).

7   Town and Country Planning Association, *New Towns and Garden Cities*.

8   House of Commons, *Transport, local government and the regions committee publications – memoranda*, Session 2001–02, 'Memorandum by Dacorum Borough Council (NT 27)' <http://www.publications.parliament.uk/pa/cm200102/cmselect/cmtlgr/603/603m01.htm>, accessed 9 March 2015.

9   Derived from figures in Town and Country Planning Association, *New Towns and Garden Cities*.

10   Association of Public Health Observatories, *Health profile Stevenage* (London, 2009); L. Burge, 'Stevenage obesity levels are on the rise', *The Comet*, 19 January 2011.

11   Derived from figures in Town and Country Planning Association, *New Towns and Garden Cities* (except where other sources indicated).

12   Nathaniel Lichfield and Partners for Letchworth Garden City Heritage Foundation, *Economic assessment of growth options final report* (London, 2013), p. 18.

13   Hastie, *Hemel Hempstead*, pp. 214–17.

14   The Galleria, Hatfield <http://www.landsecurities.com/retail-portfolio/retail-property-portfolio/the-galleria>, accessed 19 August 2015.

15   Ashby and Hills, *Stevenage*, pp. 235, 353.

16   As well as the evidence of this discussed in Chapters 5 and 7, see also the moving personal story told in A. Johnson, *This Boy* (London, 2014), especially p. 235. After many years of poverty and deteriorating health in appalling housing conditions in London, Johnson's mother, with her two children, was finally offered a house in Welwyn Garden City in 1964. Unfortunately she had died a few days earlier. The offer was immediately withdrawn.

17   CABE (Council for Architecture and the Built Environment), *What home buyers want: attitudes and decision making among consumers* (London, 2005) <http://webarchive.nationalarchives.gov.uk/20110118095356/http://www.cabe.org.uk/files/what-home-buyers-want.pdf>, accessed 11 March 2015, examines the findings of these various surveys.

18   Ward, 'Consortium Developments Ltd'.

19   S. Bell, 'Treasury to trial "new housing delivery model" at Northstowe eco town site', *Planning Resource*, 2 December 2014 <http://www.planningresource.co.uk/article/1324694/treasury-trial-new-housing-delivery-model-northstowe-eco-town-site>, accessed 13 March 2015.

20   S.V. Ward, 'Public–private partnerships', in J.B. Cullingworth (ed.), *British planning: 50 years of urban and regional policy* (London, 1999), pp. 232–49; S.V. Ward, 'New garden cities and the lessons of the past', *Town and Country Planning*, 81/9 (2012), pp. 381–4.

21   DCLG (Department for Communities and Local Government), *Eco-towns prospectus* (London, 2007).

22   Ward, 'New garden cities'.

23   URBED, *Uxcester garden city: submission for the 2014 Wolfson Economics Prize* (London, 2014).

24   DCLG (Department for Communities and Local Government), *Locally-led garden cities* (London, 2014).

25   An excellent summary of recent policy developments can be found in L. Smith, *Garden cities, standard note: SN/SC/6867*. Last updated 31 December 2014 <http://www.google.co.uk/url?sa=t andrct=jandq=andesrc=sandsource=webandcd=5andved=0CDkQFjAEandurl=http%3A%2F% 2Fwww.parliament.uk%2Fbriefing-papers%2Fsn06867.pdfandei=hdMCVfryIfC07Qayk4H4C wandusg=AFQjCNESGeKdh38JINUSR5V8cLosn8rYmAandsig2=anP8rs79TJJiDrGpcGGWSg andbvm=bv.88198703,d.ZGU>, accessed 13 March 2015.

26   DCLG (Department for Communities and Local Government), *Ebbsfleet Development Corporation: analysis of consultation responses and next steps* (London, 2014).

27   P. Dominiczak, 'Bicester announced as new garden city', *The Telegraph*, 1 December 2014.

28   DCLG (Department for Communities and Local Government), *Household projections, 2008 to 2033, England*, Housing Statistical Release (London, 2010). This puts average annual housing needs for England at an additional 232,000 units, roughly twice the number currently being completed each year.

29   P. Inman, 'UK house prices hit new record as London average breaks £500,000', *The Guardian*, 16 September 2014 <http://www.theguardian.com/business/2014/sep/16/house-prices-record-bubble-interest-rates-uk>, accessed 11 March 2015.

30   This argument is essentially that elaborated in P. Hall and C. Ward, *Sociable cities: the 21st-century reinvention of the garden city* (London, 2014).

Aalen, F.H.A., 'English origins', in S.V. Ward (ed.), *The garden city: past, present, future* (London, 1992), pp. 28–51.

Aario, L., 'The original garden cities in England and the garden city ideal in Finland', *Fennia*, 164/2 (1986), pp. 157–209.

Abercrombie, P., *Greater London Plan 1944* (London, 1945).

Adams, A.R., *Good company* (Stevenage, 1976).

Adams, T., 'The origin of the term "town planning" in England', *Journal of the Town Planning Institute*, 15/11 (1929), pp. 310–11.

Addison, P., *Now the war is over: a social history of Britain 1945–51* (London, 1985).

Aldridge, H.R., *The case for town planning: a practical manual for the use of councillors, officers and others engaged in the preparation of town planning schemes* (London, 1915).

Aldridge, M., 'Only demi-paradise? Women in garden cities and new towns', *Planning Perspectives*, 11/1 (1996), pp. 23–39.

Aldridge, M., *The New Towns: a policy without a programme* (London, 1978).

Alexander, A., *Britain's new towns: garden cities to sustainable communities* (London, 2009).

Allan, J., 'Lubetkin and Peterlee', in T. Dekker (ed.), *The modern city revisited* (London, 2000), pp. 103–24.

Allan, J., *Berthold Lubetkin: architecture and the tradition of progress* (London, 1992).

Allen, W.A., 'Soissons, Louis Emmanuel Jean Guy de (1890–1962)', rev. Andrew Saint, *Oxford dictionary of national biography* (Oxford, 2004) <http://www.oxforddnb.com.oxfordbrookes.idm.oclc.org/view/article/32792>, accessed 14 August 2014.

Allies and Morrison/The Landscape Partnership for Dacorum Borough Council, *Water Gardens study: Hemel Hempstead* (Hemel Hempstead, 2011).

Åman, A., *Architecture and ideology in eastern Europe during the Stalin era: an aspect of Cold War history* (New York/Cambridge, MA, 1992).

Amess, J., 'How grateful we were', in M. Ashby (ed.),*Voices of Stevenage* (Stroud, 2013), p. 105.

Andersson, M., *Stockholm's annual rings: a glimpse into the development of the city* (Stockholm, 1998).

Angwin, M., 'Memories of Welwyn Garden City 1930s and 1940s' <http://www.ourwelwyngardencity.org.uk/page_id__515.aspx?path=0p3p>, accessed 20 August 2015.

Anstis, G., *Redditch: success in the heart of England – the history of Redditch new town 1964–1985* (Stevenage, 1985).

Ashby, M., *Voices of Stevenage* (Stroud, 2013).

Ashby, M. and Hills, D., *Stevenage: a history from Roman times to the present day* (Lancaster, 2010).

Association of Public Health Observatories, *Health profile Stevenage* (London, 2009).

Axford, J., 'When the roofs blew off!' <http://www.talkingnewtowns.org.uk/content/topics/moving-in/jessie-axford-roofs-blew>, accessed 19 August 2015.

Balchin, J., *The first New Town: an autobiography of the Stevenage Development Corporation 1946–1980* (Stevenage, 1980).

Royal Commission on the Distribution of the Industrial Population, *Report* [The Barlow Report], Cmd. 6153 (London, 1940).

Barty-King, H., *Expanding Northampton* (London, 1985).

BBC News, 'Craigavon town planning: British modernism 50 years on', 25 October 2014 <http://www.bbc.co.uk/news/uk-northern-ireland-29728971>, accessed 25 March 2015.

Beevers, R., *The garden city utopia: a critical biography of Ebenezer Howard* (Basingstoke, 1988).

Begg, I., Moore, B. and Rhodes, J., 'Economic and social change in urban Britain and the inner cities', in V. Hausner (ed.), *Critical issues in urban economic development*, 2 vols (Oxford, 1986), vol. I, pp. 10–49.

Bell, S., 'Treasury to trial "new housing delivery model" at Northstowe eco town site', *Planning Resource*, 2 December 2014 <http://www.planningresource.co.uk/article/1324694/treasury-trial-new-housing-delivery-model-northstowe-eco-town-site>, accessed 13 March 2015.

Bellamy, E., *Looking backward, 2000–1887* (London, 1888).

Bendixson, T., *The Peterborough effect: reshaping a city* (Peterborough, 1988).

Bendixson, T. and Platt, J., *Milton Keynes: image and reality* (Cambridge, 1992).

Beresford, M.W., *New towns of the Middle Ages: town plantation in England, Wales and Gascony* (Stroud, 1988).

Bevir, M., *The making of British socialism* (Princeton, 2011).

Birchall, J., 'Co-partnership housing and the garden city movement', *Planning Perspectives*, 10/4 (1995), pp. 329–58.

Bloom, N.D., *Suburban alchemy: 1960s new towns and the transformation of the American dream* (Columbus, OH, 2001).

Bonham-Carter, E., 'Planning and development of Letchworth Garden City', *Town Planning Review*, 21/4 (1951), pp. 362–76.

Booth, A., 'The Second World War and the origins of modern regional policy', *Economy and Society*, 11/1 (1982), pp. 1–21.

Bosma, K. and Hellinga, H., 'Dutch urban planning: between centralization and decentralization', in K. Bosma and H. Hellinga (eds), *Mastering the city: north-European city planning 1900–2000*, vol. II (Rotterdam, 1997), pp. 80–87.

Bournville Village Trust, *The Bournville Village Trust 1900–1955* (Birmingham, 1955).

Bournville Village Trust, *When we build again* (London, 1941).

Bradshaw, J., 'Newspaper tycoon', *Journal of the Northumberland and Durham Family History Society*, 15/3 (1990), pp. 72–3.

Briggs, A. (ed.), *William Morris: selected writings and designs* (Harmondsworth, 1962).

Bristow, M.R., *Hong Kong's new towns: a selective review* (Hong Kong, 1989).

British Film Institute, 'The Newcomers' <http://www.screenonline.org.uk/tv/id/1401049/>, accessed 12 August 2015.

Buckingham, J.S., *National evils and practical remedies* (London, 1849).

Buder, S., *Visionaries and planners: the garden city and the modern community* (New York, 1990).

Built Environment Advisory and Management Service, *Broadwater (Marymead) conservation appraisal 2009* (Stevenage, 2009).

Built Environment Advisory and Management Service, *A review of Stevenage Conservation Areas* (Stevenage, 2005).

Bull, D.A., 'New town and town expansion schemes: part I: an assessment of recent government planning reports', *Town Planning Review*, 38/2 (1967), pp. 103–14.

Bull, D.A., 'New town and town expansion schemes: part II: urban form and structure', *Town Planning Review*, 38/3 (1967), pp. 165–86.

Bull, E., 'Fitting in with the locals' <http://www.talkingnewtowns.org.uk/content/towns/hemel-hempstead/eileen-bull/fitting-locals>, accessed 19 August 2015.

Bunker, R., 'The early years', in A. Hutchings and R. Bunker (eds), *With conscious purpose: a history of town planning in South Australia* (Adelaide, 1986), pp. 7–20.

Burge, L., 'Stevenage obesity levels are on the rise', *The Comet*, 19 January 2011.

Burnett, J., *A social history of housing 1815–1985* (London, 1986).

Butt, R.V.J., *The directory of railway stations* (Yeovil, 1995).

Butterfield, R.J., 'The Shredded Wheat factory at Welwyn Garden City', abridged version reproduced in D. Goodman (ed.), *The European cities and technology reader* (London, 1999), pp. 125–38.

CABE (Council for Architecture and the Built Environment), *What home buyers want: attitudes and decision making among consumers* (London, 2005) <http://webarchive.nationalarchives.gov.uk/20110118095356/http://www.cabe.org.uk/files/what-home-buyers-want.pdf>, accessed 11 March 2015.

Campbell, J., 'Marymead Shopping Centre c1960' <http://www.ourstevenage.org.uk/page_id__99.aspx?path=0p164p61p>, accessed 17 August 2015.

Carney, C., 'A Profile of Thetford' <http://www.keystonetrust.org.uk/wp-content/uploads/2015/05/thetfordprofile.pdf>, accessed 12 August 2015.

2011 Census: KS201EW Ethnic group, local authorities in England and Wales, <http://www.ons.gov.uk>, accessed 25 November 2015.

Cherry, G.E., *Birmingham: a study in geography, history and planning* (Chichester, 1994).

Cherry, G.E., 'The place of Neville Chamberlain in British town planning', in G.E. Cherry (ed.), *Shaping an urban world* (London, 1980), pp. 161–79.

Cherry, G.E. and Penny, P., *Holford: a study in architecture, planning and civic design* (London, 1986).

City of Liverpool Post-War Re-development Advisory (Special) Committee, *Town planning exhibition* (Liverpool, 1947).

Clapson, M., *Anglo-American crossroads: urban planning and research in Britain, 1940–2010* (London, 2013).

Clapson, M., *Invincible green suburbs; brave new towns: social change and urban dispersal in postwar Britain* (Manchester, 1998).

Clapson, M., 'The rise and fall of Monica Felton, British town planner and peace activist, 1930s to 1950s', *Planning Perspectives*, 30/2 (2015), pp. 211–29.

Clapson, M., *A social history of Milton Keynes: middle England/Edge City* (London, 2004).

Clapson, M., Dobbin, M. and Waterman, P., *The best laid plans: Milton Keynes since 1967* (Luton, 1998).

Clarke, A.M., 'The Welwyn Garden City Light Railway', *Industrial Railway Record*, 62/October (1975) <www.welwyngarden-heritage.org/archive/>, accessed 18 August 2014.

Claxton, E., 'The cycle and pedestrian ways of Stevenage', in H. Rees and C. Rees (eds), *The history makers: the story of the early days of Stevenage new town* (Stevenage, 1991).

Claxton, E., *The hidden Stevenage: the creation of the substructure of Britain's first new town* (Lewes, 1992).

Clements, G., 'Matchstick trees and builders' rubble' <http://www.ourstevenage.org.uk/page_id__4.aspx?path=0p3p>, accessed 17 August 2015.

Clements, G., 'More great memories of Stevenage from the Good Friends Group' <http://www.ourstevenage.org.uk/page_id__342.aspx?path=0p3p>, accessed 17 August 2015.

Cobern, J., Irving, D. and Martindale, C., *Hatfield and its people: new town housing, 1948–2008*, part 10, <http://www.ourhatfield.org.uk/page_id__222.aspx?path=0p106p114p ?>, accessed 25 November 2015].

Cochrane, P. 'Cochrane family memories: As it was in the 30s – thro young eyes' <http://www.ourwelwyngardencity.org.uk/page_id__443.aspx?path=0p3p>, accessed 20 August 2015.

Colin Buchanan and Partners, *Llantrisant – prospects for urban growth* (London, 1969).

Collings, T. (ed.), *Stevenage: images of the first new town 1946–1986* (Stevenage, 1987).

Collison, P., *The Cutteslowe Walls: A study in social class* (London, 1963).

Cook, I.R., Ward, S.V. and Ward, K., 'A springtime journey to the Soviet Union: postwar planning and policy mobilities through the Iron Curtain', *International Journal of Urban and Regional Research*, 38/3 (2014), pp. 805–22.

Cotter, M., *Memories of Michael Cotter* (Stevenage, 1986).

Cotter, M., 'Stevenage Oral Interview Heritage Project, Tape No. A014/2', Interview by K. Cotter, 10 April 1986.

Cousins, M., 'Early residents (viii)', in H. Rees and C. Rees (eds), *The history makers: the story of the early days of Stevenage new town* (Stevenage, 1991), pp. 112–14.

Cresswell Film Unit/Stevenage Development Corporation, *Rationalised building – the Mowlem System* [Film] (Stevenage, 1964).

Cullingworth, J.B., *Environmental planning 1939–1969: vol. III new towns policy* (London, 1979).

Cullingworth, J.B., *Environmental planning 1939–1969: vol. IV land values, compensation and betterment* (London, 1980).

Cullingworth, J.B., *Housing needs and planning policy* (London, 1960).

Culpin, E.G., *The garden city movement up-to-date* (London, 1913).

Culpin, E.G. *The garden city movement up-to-date*, 2nd edn (London, 1914).

Cupers, K., *The social project: housing in postwar France* (Minneapolis, MN, 2014).

Dale, O.J., *Urban planning in Singapore: the transformation of a city* (Oxford, 1999).

Daunton, M.J., 'Introduction', in M.J. Daunton (ed.), *Councillors and tenants: local authority housing in English cities, 1919–1939* (Leicester, 1984).

Davenport-Hines, R., 'Lever, William Hesketh, first Viscount Leverhulme (1851–1925)', *Oxford dictionary of national biography* (Oxford, 2004); online edn January 2011 <http://www.oxforddnb.com.oxfordbrookes.idm.oclc.org/view/article/34506>, accessed 24 September 2014.

Day, M.G., 'The contribution of Sir Raymond Unwin (1863–1940) and R. Barry Parker (1867–1947) to the development of site planning theory and practice, c1890–1918', in A. Sutcliffe (ed.), *British town planning: the formative years* (Leicester, 1981), pp. 156–99.

Day, R., 'GALLERY: Campaigners rally at Letchworth march to save world's first garden city', *The Comet*, 2 November 2015.

DCLG (Department for Communities and Local Government), *Ebbsfleet Development Corporation: analysis of consultation responses and next steps* (London, 2014).

DCLG (Department for Communities and Local Government), *Eco-towns prospectus* (London, 2007).

DCLG (Department for Communities and Local Government), *Household projections, 2008 to 2033, England*, Housing Statistical Release (London, 2010).

DCLG (Department for Communities and Local Government), *Locally-led garden cities* (London, 2014).

The de Havilland Aeronautical Technical School Association (De Mercado, R.), *Hatfield aerodrome from the air* (Stockport, c.2010), reproduced at <http://www.dhaetsa.org.uk/dhaets/documents/101457_hatfield_aerodrome_from_the_air_v2.pdf>, accessed 25 November 2015.

De Soissons, L., *Report of the Welwyn Garden City Development Corporation upon the outline plan* (Welwyn Garden City, 1949).

De Soissons, L., Purdom, C.B. and Kenyon, A.W., *Site planning in practice at Welwyn Garden City* (London, 1927).

De Soissons, M., *Telford: the making of Shropshire's new town* (Shrewsbury, 1991).

De Soissons, M., *Telford: the making of Shropshire's new town* (Totnes, 1995).

De Soissons, M., *Welwyn Garden City: a town designed for healthy living* (Cambridge, 1988).

Deakin, D. (ed.), *Wythenshawe: the story of a garden city* (Chichester, 1989) <http://www.wythenshawe.btck.co.uk>, accessed 15 October 2014.

DEFRA (Department for Environment, Food and Rural Affairs), *Statistical digest of rural England 2012* (London, 2012).

Dent, J.M., *The memoirs of J.M. Dent* (London, 1928).

Department of Economic Affairs, *The West Midlands: a regional study* (London, 1965).

Department of Planning Oxford Brookes University, for Department for Communities and Local Government, *Transferable lessons from the new towns* (London, 2006) <http://www.

futurecommunities.net/files/images/Transferable_lessons_from_new_towns_0.pdf>, accessed 19 March 2015.

Domhardt, K.S., 'The garden city idea in the CIAM discourse on urbanism: a path to comprehensive planning', *Planning Perspectives*, 27/2 (2012), pp. 173–97.

Dominiczak, P., 'Bicester announced as new garden city', *The Telegraph*, 1 December 2014.

Donnelly, M., 'Plans for 3,600 Stevenage homes withdrawn after 12-year wrangle', *Planning Resource*, 15 August 2013 <http://www.planningresource.co.uk/article/1207535/plans-3600-stevenage-homes-withdrawn-12-year-wrangle>, accessed 14 August 2015.

Donner, C. (dir.), *Here We Go Round the Mulberry Bush* (1968).

Drackford, G., 'Early residents (vi)', in H. Rees and C. Rees (eds), *The history makers: the story of the early days of Stevenage new town* (Stevenage, 1991), pp. 93–102.

Dunning, J.H., *Economic planning and town expansion: a case study of Basingstoke* (Southampton, 1963).

Edwards, A.T., 'A further criticism of the garden city movement', *Town Planning Review*, 4 (1913), p. 318.

Edwards, A.T., *Good and bad manners in architecture: an essay on the social aspects of civic design* (London, 1945 [orig. 1924]).

Elliott, H. and Sanderson, J. (edited by M. Maddren), *Letchworth Recollections* (Baldock, 1995).

Field, D., 'New town and town expansion schemes: part III: five new towns planned for populations of 80,000 to 100,000', *Town Planning Review*, 39/3 (1968), pp. 196–216.

Filler, R., 'Dinah Sheridan' <http://www.ourwelwyngardencity.org.uk/page_id__490. aspx?path=0p3p>, accessed 29 September 2014.

Filler, R., *A history of Welwyn Garden City* (Chichester, 1986).

Finnegan, R., 'Council housing in Leeds, 1919–39: social policy and urban change', in M.J. Daunton (ed.), *Councillors and tenants: local authority housing in English cities, 1919–1939* (Leicester, 1984), pp. 134–5.

First Garden City Ltd, *The best location in England for manufacturers is the new industrial town of Letchworth (Garden City)* (Letchworth, c.1908).

First Garden City Ltd, *First garden city estate – why manufacturers move to garden city* (Letchworth, c.1909).

First Garden City Ltd, *Guide to garden city* (London, 1906).

First Garden City Ltd, *Letchworth – a town in the country: a description of its advantages* (Letchworth, c.1929).

First Garden City Ltd, *Letchworth as a manufacturing centre* (Letchworth, 1908).

First Garden City Ltd, *Letchworth: where town and country meet* (Letchworth, 1934).

First Garden City Ltd, *Where shall I live? Guide to Letchworth (Garden City) and catalogue of urban cottages and rural homesteads exhibition* (Letchworth, 1907).

Fishman, R., *Urban utopias in the twentieth century: Ebenezer Howard, Frank Lloyd Wright and Le Corbusier* (New York, 1977), pp. 23–88.

Fogarty, M.P., *Plan your own industries: a study of local and regional development organizations* (Oxford, 1947).

Forshaw, J.H. and Abercrombie, P., *County of London plan* (London, 1943).

Forster, E.M., 'The challenge of our time', *The Listener*, 11 April 1946, as reproduced in E.M. Forster, *Two cheers for democracy* (Harmondsworth, 1965), pp. 64–9.

Forsyth, A., *Reforming suburbia: the planned communities of Irvine, Columbia and the Woodlands* (Berkeley, CA, 2002).

Forsyth, B. (dir.), *Gregory's Girl* (1981).

Fowler, W., 'Early residents (vii)', in H. Rees and C. Rees (eds), *The history makers: the story of the early days of Stevenage new town* (Stevenage, 1991), pp. 103–11.

Garden Cities and Town Planning Association, *Royal Commission on the Geographical Distribution of the Industrial Population: Evidence of the Garden Cities and Town Planning Association* (London, 1938).

Garvin, A., *The American city: what works, what doesn't* (New York, 1996).

Gaudin, J.P., 'The French garden city', in Ward, S.V. (ed.). *The garden city: past, present and future* (London, 1992), pp. 52–68.

Geo Wimpey & Co., *No Fines Concrete* (London, c.1954).

George, H., *Progress and poverty: an inquiry into the cause of industrial depressions and of increase of want with increase of wealth – the remedy* (1879; British edn, 1880 [50th anniversary reprint New York, 1949]).

Gibson, M.S. and Langstaff, M., *An introduction to urban renewal* (London, 1982).

Gill, H., 'End in sight for town council as Letchworth votes for abolition', *The Comet*, 2 November 2012.

Godfrey, V., 'A 1940s Eastside Memory' <http://www.ourwelwyngardencity.org.uk/page_id__347. aspx?path=0p162p137p>, accessed 20 August 2015.

Godfrey, V., 'A difficult journey to WGC in 1939 from Leipzig with help from WGC Quakers' <http://www.ourwelwyngardencity.org.uk/page_id__391.aspx?path=0p162p137p>, accessed 20 August 2015.

Godfrey, V., 'A family arrives in 1924' <http://www.ourwelwyngardencity.org.uk/page_id__417. aspx?path=0p162p137p>, accessed 20 August 2015.

Godfrey, V., 'A move from Sunderland' <http://www.ourwelwyngardencity.org.uk/page_id__433. aspx>, accessed 20 August 2015.

Godfrey, V., 'An east side home' <http://www.ourwelwyngardencity.org.uk/page_id__444. aspx?path=0p2p57p60p>, accessed 20 August 2015.

Godfrey, V., 'East-side and West-side' <http://www.ourwelwyngardencity.org.uk/page_id__392. aspx?path=0p162p137p>, accessed 20 August 2015.

Godfrey, V., 'First impressions of the town in 1931' <http://www.ourwelwyngardencity.org.uk/ page_id__420.aspx?path=0p162p137p>, accessed 20 August 2015.

Godfrey, V., 'From South Shields to WGC' <http://www.ourwelwyngardencity.org.uk/page_id__409. aspx?path=0p162p137p>, accessed 20 August 2015.

Gold, J.R., *The experience of modernism: modern architects and the future city 1928–1953* (London, 1997).

Gold, J.R., 'The making of a megastructure: architectural modernism, town planning and Cumbernauld's central area, 1955–75', *Planning Perspectives*, 21/2 (2006), pp. 109–31.

Gold, J.R. *The practice of modernism: modern architects and the urban transformation, 1954–1972* (London, 2007).

Gold, J.R., 'Revisiting the new town that might have been', in London County Council, *The Planning of a new town: design based on a study for a new town of 100,000 at Hook, Hampshire* (London, 2015 reprint of original 1961), pp. vii–xxviii.

Goodrich, W.F., *Watford: its advantages as an industrial and residential centre* (Watford, c.1908).

Grace's Guide, 'British Tabulating Machine Co' <http://www.gracesguide.co.uk/British_Tabulating_ Machine_Co>, accessed 15 March 2015.

Greater London Regional Planning Committee, *First report* (London, 1929).

Greater London Regional Planning Committee, *Second report* (London, 1933).

Gregory, J. and Gordon, D.L.A., 'Introduction: Gordon Stephenson, planner and civic designer', *Town Planning Review*, 83/3 (2012), pp. 269–78.

Hall, P., *Cities in civilization: culture, technology and urban order* (London, 1998).

Hall, P., *Cities of tomorrow: an intellectual history of planning and urban design in the twentieth century* (Oxford, 1988).

Hall, P. and Tewdwr-Jones, M., *Urban and regional planning*, 5th edn (London, 2011).

Hall, P. and Ward, C., *Sociable cities: the 21st-century reinvention of the garden city* (London, 2014).

Hall, S., '20 million plan to rebuild homes' <http://www.ourwelwyngardencity.org.uk/page_id__538_path__0p162p.aspx>, accessed 28 April 2015.

Hall, T., 'Urban planning in Sweden', in T. Hall (ed.), *Planning and urban growth in the Nordic countries* (London, 1991), pp. 167–246.

Hardy, D., *From garden cities to new towns: campaigning for town and country planning, 1899–1946* (London, 1991).

Hardy, D. and Ward, C., *Arcadia for all: the legacy of a makeshift landscape* (London, 1984).

Harloe, M., *Swindon: a town in transition* (London, 1975).

Harrison, M., *Bournville: model village to garden suburb* (Chichester, 1999).

Harrison, M., 'Thomas Coghlan Horsfall and "the example of Germany"', *Planning Perspectives*, 6/3 (1991), pp. 297–314.

Harrison, P., *Inside the inner city* (Harmondsworth, 1983).

Hastie, S., *Hemel Hempstead: the story of new town development 1947–1997* (Hemel Hempstead, 1997).

Hayes, D. and Hudson, A., *Basildon: the mood of the nation* (London, 2001).

Hebbert, M., 'Frederic Osborn 1885–1978', in G.E. Cherry (ed.), *Pioneers in British planning* (London, 1981), pp. 177–202.

Hebbert, M., 'A Hertfordshire solution to London's problems? Sir Frederic Osborn's axioms reconsidered', in J. Onslow (ed.) *Garden cities and new towns: five lectures* (Hertford, 1990), pp. 38–47.

Hemel Hempstead Development Corporation, *Hemel Hempstead – new town from old* (Hemel Hempstead, 1957).

Hemel Hempstead Development Corporation, *Hemel Hempstead – new town from old* (Hemel Hempstead, 1960).

Heritage Foundation, Letchworth Garden City <http://www.letchworth.com/heritage-foundation>, accessed 18 March 2015.

Heritage Foundation, Letchworth Garden City, 'Our Charitable Commitments' <http://www.letchworth.com/heritage-foundation/our-charitable-commitments>, accessed 17 August 2015.

Hine, R.L., *Relics of an un-common attorney* (London, 1951). .

Holley, S., *Washington: quicker by quango – the history of Washington new town* (Stevenage, 1983).

Home, R., 'A township complete in itself': a planning history of the Becontree/Dagenham estate* (London, 1997).

Homer, A., 'Administration and social change in the post-war British new towns: a case study of Stevenage and Hemel Hempstead 1946–70', PhD thesis (University of Luton, 1999).

Horn, B., 'Memories of Bill Horn, Part Three – reminiscences of Welwyn Garden and area' (recorded 1976 by R. Filler) <http://www.ourwelwyngardencity.org.uk/page_id__143.aspx?path=0p4p29p>, accessed 20 August 2015.

House of Commons, *Transport, local government and the regions committee publications – memoranda*, Session 2001–02, 'Memorandum by Dacorum Borough Council (NT 27)' <http://www.publications.parliament.uk/pa/cm200102/cmselect/cmtlgr/603/603m01.htm>, accessed 9 March 2015.

Howard, E., *Garden cities of tomorrow* (London, 1902).

Howard, E., *To-morrow: a peaceful path to real reform* (London, 1898), pp. 98–9.

Howard, E. *To-morrow: a peaceful path to real reform* (London, 2003 [Original 1898 facsimile edition with commentary by P. Hall, D. Hardy and C. Ward]).

Hubbard, E. and Shippobottom, M. *A guide to Port Sunlight Village* (Liverpool, 1988).

Hughes, M.R. (ed.), *The letters of Lewis Mumford and Frederic J. Osborn: a transatlantic dialogue* (Bath, 1971).

Hull City Council, *Garden Village Conservation Area character statement* (Hull, 1997).

Hunter, A., *A life of Sir John Eldon Gorst: Disraeli's awkward disciple* (London, 2001).

Hyder, J., *The case for land nationalisation* (London, 1913).

Hyndman, H.M. (ed.), *The nationalization of land in 1775 and 1882 being a lecture deliver(ed.) at Newcastle/Tyne by Thomas Spence 1775* (London, 1882).

Inauguration of the Welwyn Chamber of Commerce (1929) <www.ourwelwyngardencity.org.uk/page_id__230_path__0p82p.aspx>, accessed 21 August 2014.

Inman, P., 'UK house prices hit new record as London average breaks £500,000', *The Guardian*, 16 September 2014 <http://www.theguardian.com/business/2014/sep/16/house-prices-record-bubble-interest-rates-uk>, accessed 11 March 2015.

Irvine Development Corporation, *Irvine new town 1966–1996* (Irvine, 1995).

Jackson, A.A., *Semi-detached London: suburban development, life and transport* (2nd edn, Didcot, 1991).

Jackson, A.A., *Semi-detached London: suburban development, life and transport, 1900–1939* (London, 1973).

James, M., 'John Sutton Nettlefold, liberalism and the early town planning movement', *Journal of Liberal History*, 75 (2012), pp. 30–37, <http://www.liberalhistory.org.uk/wp-content/uploads/2014/10/75_James_Nettlefold_Liberalism_and_Town_Planning.pdf>, accessed 1 September 2015.

Jellicoe, G.A., *The report accompanying a plan for Hemel Hempstead new town* (3 June 1947), National Archives NA HLG 91/63.

Jennings, M., 'Molly Jennings Part 1: Welwyn Garden City's first resident (reminiscences written down by R. Filler 1969–76)' <http://www.ourwelwyngardencity.org.uk/page_id__90.aspx?path=0p3p62p>, accessed 20 August 2015.

Jennings, M., 'Molly Jennings Part 4: Welwyn Garden City's first resident' (recorded 1969 by R. Filler) <http://www.ourwelwyngardencity.org.uk/page_id__93.aspx?path=0p3p62p>, accessed 20 August 2015.

Jevons, R. and Madge, J., *Housing estates: a study of Bristol Corporation policy and practice between the wars* (Bristol, 1946).

Johnson, A., *This Boy* (London, 2014).

Jones, G., 'Foreign multi-nationals and British industry before 1945', *Economic History Review*, 2nd series, 41/3 (1988), pp. 429–53.

Knudsen, T., 'International influences and professional rivalry in early Danish planning', *Planning Perspectives*, 3/3 (1988), pp. 297–310.

Kotkin, S., *Magnetic mountain: Stalinism as a civilization* (Berkeley, CA, 1997).

Kropotkin, P., *Fields, factories and workshops* (London, 1974 [orig. 1899]).

Larsson, B. and Thomassen, T., 'Urban planning in Denmark', in T. Hall (ed.), *Planning and urban growth in the Nordic countries* (London, 1991), pp. 6–59.

Lebow, K., *Unfinished utopia: Nowa Huta, Stalinism and Polish society 1949–56* (Ithaca, NY, 2013).

legislation.gov.uk, 'Letchworth Garden City Heritage Foundation Act 1995' <http://www.legislation.gov.uk/ukla/1995/2/enacted>, accessed 18 March 2015.

Lennon, C., 'Tighter planning rules for student homes in Hatfield', *Welwyn Hatfield Times 24*, 10 January 2012 <http://www.whtimes.co.uk/news/tighter_planning_rules_for_student_homes_in_hatfield_1_1172812,> accessed 2 May 2014.

Letchworth Garden City Heritage Foundation, *Scheme of Management*, 2004 <http://www.letchworth.com/sites/default/files/attachments/scheme_of_management.pdf>, accessed 3 March 2015.

Lewis, J. and Ames, D., 'A model for investment and governance', *Town and Country Planning*, 81/9 (2012), pp. 389–92.

Liberal Land Enquiry Committee, *The land, vol. 2: urban* (London, 1914).

Ling, A. and Associates, *Runcorn new town. Master plan* (Runcorn, 1966).

Liverpool Housing Committee, *City of Liverpool housing* (Liverpool, 1937).

Llewellyn-Davies, Weeks and Partners, *Washington new town master plan and report* (Washington, 1966).

London County Council, *London housing* (London, 1937).

Luhman, A., 'The builders (ii)', in H. Rees and C. Rees (eds), *The history makers: the story of the early days of Stevenage new town* (Stevenage, 1991), pp. 27–8.

Luton New Industries Committee, *Luton as an industrial centre* (Luton, 1900).

Luton New Industries Committee, *Luton as an industrial centre* (Luton, 1905).

M'Gonigle, G.C.M. and Kirby, J., *Poverty and public health* (London, 1936).

McClelland, W.G., *Washington, over and out: the story of Washington new town, 1983–1988* (Stevenage, 1988).

MacFadyen, D., *Sir Ebenezer Howard and the town planning movement* (Manchester, 1933).

MacFadyen, D., *Sir Ebenezer Howard and the town planning movement* (Manchester, 1970 [orig. 1933]).

McKay, D.H. and Cox, A.W., *The politics of urban change* (Beckenham, 1979).

MacKeith, M., *The history and conservation of shopping arcades* (London, 1986).

MacLeod, M., 'Early residents (iii)', in H. Rees and C. Rees (eds), *The history makers: the story of the early days of Stevenage new town* (Stevenage, 1991), pp. 77–82.

McSheffrey, G., *Planning Derry: planning and politics in Northern Ireland* (Liverpool, 2000).

Manzoni, H.J., *The production of 50,000 municipal houses* (Birmingham, 1939).

Marley Committee, *Garden cities and satellite towns: report of the departmental committee* (London, 1935).

Marshall, A., 'The housing of the London poor: where to house them', *Contemporary Review*, 45 (1884), pp. 224–31.

Mattson, H., 'Where motorways meet: architecture and corporatism in Sweden 1968', in M. Swenarton, T. Avermaete, and D. Van Den Heuvel (eds), *Architecture and the welfare state* (London, 2015), pp. 154–75.

May, R., 'Planned city Stalinstadt: a manifesto of the early German Democratic Republic', *Planning Perspectives*, 18/1 (2003), pp. 47–78.

Merrett, S., *State housing in Britain* (London, 1979).

Mill, J.S., *Principles of political economy with some of their applications to social philosophy* (London, 1909 [orig. 1848]).

Miller, M., *C.M. Crickmer 1879–1971* (Letchworth, 1999).

Miller, M., *Letchworth: the first garden city* (Chichester, 1989).

Miller, M., *Letchworth: the first garden city*, 2nd edn (Chichester, 2002).

Miller, M., *Raymond Unwin: garden cities and town planning* (Leicester, 1992).

Miller, M., *Robert Bennett 1878–1956 and Benjamin Wilson Bidwell, 1877–1944* (Letchworth, 1999).

Miller, M. and Gray, A.S., *Hampstead Garden Suburb* (Chichester, 1992).

Ministry of Housing and Local Government, *The South East study 1961–1981* (London, 1964).

Mitchell, J.R. and Stebenne, D., *New city upon a hill: a history of Columbia, Maryland* (Charleston, SC, 2007).

Model, G., 'Setting up a new business in Hatfield' <http://www.talkingnewtowns.org.uk/content/category/towns/hatfield/mr-g-e-model>, accessed 19 August 2015.

Mohr, C., 'The new Frankfurt housing construction and the city 1925–1930', in C. Quiring, W. Voigt, P. Schmal and E. Herrel (eds), *Ernst May 1886–1970* (Munich, 2011), pp. 50–67.

Morison, I., 'The corridor city: planning for growth in the 1960s', in S. Hamnett and R. Freestone (eds), *The Australian metropolis: a planning history* (London, 2000), pp. 113–30.

Mortimer, S., 'The Oval Shops. 1969' <http://www.ourstevenage.org.uk/page_id__131.aspx?path=0p2p33p>, accessed 17 August 2015.

Moss, J.A., 'New and expanded towns: a survey of the demographic characteristics of newcomers', *Town Planning Review*, 39/2 (1968), pp. 117–39.

Mullan, B., *Stevenage Ltd: aspects of the planning and politics of Stevenage new town 1945–1978* (London, 1980).

Naslas, M., *The concept of the town in the writings of William Morris*, paper presented at the History of Planning Group Meeting, University of Birmingham, March 1977.

Nathaniel Lichfield and Partners for Letchworth Garden City Heritage Foundation, *Economic assessment of growth options final report* (London, 2013).

Nettlefold, J.S., *Practical housing*, 2nd edn (London, 1910).

Nettlefold, J.S., *Practical town planning* (London, 1914).

Newsome, W.B., *French urban planning 1940–1968: the construction and deconstruction of an authoritarian system* (New York, 2009).

Nicoson, W., 'The United States: the battle for title VII', in M. Apgar (ed.), *New perspectives on community development* (London, 1976), pp. 38–58.

North Hertfordshire District Council, *Letchworth Conservation Area, Letchworth Garden City: North Hertfordshire District Council*, 2001 <http://www.north-herts.gov.uk/letchworth_conservation_area_appraisal.pdf>, accessed 4 March 2015.

Now the War is Over: A Home of Your Own (BBC, 1985).

Nuttgens P., 'Criticism: Cumbernauld town centre', *Architectural Review*, 141/850 (1967), p. 444.

Ogilvy, A.A., 'Employment expansion and the development of new town hinterlands 1961–66', *Town Planning Review*, 42/2 (1971), pp. 113–29.

Ogilvy, A.A., 'The self-contained new town: employment and population', *Town Planning Review*, 39/1 (1968), pp. 38–54.

Olsen, J., *Better lives, better places: a biography of James Rouse* (Washington DC, 2003).

Olssen, E., 'Mr Wakefield and New Zealand as an experiment in post-enlightenment experimental practice', *New Zealand Journal of History*, 31/2 (1997), pp. 197–218.

Orlans, H., *Stevenage: a sociological study of a new town* (London, 1952).

Ortolano, G., 'Planning the urban future in 1960s Britain', *The Historical Journal*, 54/2 (2011), pp. 477–507.

Orwell, G., *Homage to Catalonia* (Harmondsworth, 1962 [orig. 1938]).

Orwell, G., *The road to Wigan pier* (Harmondsworth, 1962 [orig. 1937]).

Osborn, F.J., *Genesis of Welwyn Garden City: some Jubilee memories* (London, 1970).

Osborn, F.J., 'Preface', in E. Howard, *Garden cities of to-morrow* (London, 1965), pp. 9–28.

Osborn, F.J. 'Sir Ebenezer Howard: the evolution of his ideas', *Town Planning Review*, 21 (1950), pp. 221–35.

Osborn, F.J. and Whittick, A., *The new towns: the answer to megalopolis* (London, 1969).

Osborn, F.J. and Whittick, A., *New towns: their origins, achievements and progress* (London, 1977).

Owen, A.D.K., 'The social consequences of industrial transference', *Sociological Review*, 29 (1937), pp. 331–54.

Page, R., 'Expectations of a new home, Letter dated October 5th 1922' <http://www.ourwelwyngardencity.org.uk/page_id__218.aspx?path=0p3p109p>, accessed 20 August 2015.

Page, R., 'Quaker social night: preparing refreshments – 16th December 1923' <http://www.ourwelwyngardencity.org.uk/page_id__229.aspx?path=0p3p109p>, accessed 20 August 2015.

Parker, J., 'How to get a house', in A. Burke and M. Corbett with the Boomtime Group, *Voices of Hatfield from the '50s and '60s* (Stroud, 2011), p. 17.

Parsons, D.W., *The political economy of British regional policy* (Beckenham, 1986).

Pattison, G., 'Planning for decline: the "D" village policy of county Durham', *Planning Perspectives*, 19/3 (2004), pp. 311–32.

Patton, K., 'The foundations of Peterlee new town', in M. Bulmer (ed.), *Mining and social change: Durham county in the twentieth century* (Beckenham, 1978), pp. 218–33.

Payne, J., *Co-operation and conflict in the garden city: the Letchworth rent strike of 1915* (Hitchin, 1982).

Pearsall, H.D., 'The building of workmen's cottages in garden city', in C.B. Purdom, *The garden city: a study in the development of a modern town* (London, 1913), pp. 261–71.

Pearson, L., *The architectural and social history of co-operative living* (London, 1988).

Peel, M., *Good times, hard times: the past and the future in Elizabeth* (Melbourne, 1995).

Pendlebury, J.R., 'The urbanism of Thomas Sharp', *Planning Perspectives*, 24/1 (2009), pp. 2–27.

Philipson, G., *Aycliffe and Peterlee new towns 1946–1988: swords into ploughshares and farewell squalor* (Cambridge, 1988).

Pitfield, D.E., 'The quest for an effective regional policy, 1934–37', *Regional Studies*, 12 (1978), pp. 429–43.

Planning Exchange, *New Town Record*, DVD (Glasgow, 1995). Now available from <http://www.idoxgroup.com/knowledge-services/idox-information-service/the-new-towns-record>.

Plinston, H., *A tale of one city: the story of Letchworth's fight for independence* (Letchworth, 1981).

Powers, A., 'Obituary: Viscount Esher', *The Independent*, 13 July 2004.

Price, T., '"Southern Victory" to hit Old Town', *Hemel Hempstead: the new town years 1947–1997* [special series], *The Gazette*, 13 (1997).

Purdom, C.B., *The building of satellite towns* (London, 1925).

Purdom, C.B., *The building of satellite towns*, 2nd edn (London, 1949).

Purdom, C.B., *The garden city: a study in the development of a modern town* (London, 1913).

Purdom, C.B., *The Letchworth achievement* (London, 1963).

Purdom, C.B., *Life over again* (London, 1951).

Read, D., *Edwardian England 1901–15: society and politics* (London, 1972).

Rees, C., 'The first neighbourhoods', in H. Rees and C. Rees (eds), *The history makers: the story of the early days of Stevenage new town* (Stevenage, 1991), p. 55.

Rees, C., [unpaginated illustrative section], in H. Rees and C. Rees (eds), *The history makers: the story of the early days of Stevenage new town* (Stevenage, 1991), pp. 104–5.

Rees, H., 'The Valley 1961 and Road 9 1966', in H. Rees, and C. Rees (eds), *The history makers: the story of the early days of Stevenage new town* (Stevenage, 1991), pp. 126–9.

Rees, H. and Rees, C. (eds), *The history makers: the story of the early days of Stevenage new town* (Stevenage, 1991).

Regeneris Consulting, *Hertfordshire strategic employment sites study* (London/Hertford, 2011).

Reid, A., *Brentham: a history of the pioneer garden suburb 1901–2001* (Ealing, 2000).

Reiss, C., *R.L. Reiss: a memoir by Celia Reiss* (privately published, 1966).

Reith Committee, *Final report of the new towns committee* (Cmd 6876) (London, 1946).

Reith Committee, *Interim report of the new towns committee* (Cmd 6759) (London, 1946).

Reith Committee, *Second interim report of the new towns committee* (Cmd 6794) (London, 1946).

Richardson, B.W., *Hygeia or the city of health* (London, 1876 [reprinted New York, 1985]).

Richardson, H.W. and Aldcroft, D.H., *Building in the British economy between the wars* (London, 1968).

Riden, P., *Rebuilding a valley: a history of Cwmbran Development Corporation* (Cwmbran, 1988).

Rook, T., *Welwyn Garden City past* (Chichester, 2001).

Rowntree, B.S., *Poverty: a study of town life* (London, 1901).

Royal Commission on the Distribution of the Industrial Population, *Report* (Cmd 6153) (London, 1940).

Royal Commission on the Geographical Distribution of the Industrial Population, *Minutes of evidence taken before the Royal Commission on the Geographical Distribution of the Industrial Population: twentieth day*, Thursday 5 May 1938, Memorandum of Evidence Submitted by First Garden City of Letchworth.

Rubenstein, J.M., *The French new towns* (Baltimore, 1978).

Sakamoto, K., 'The theory of the Japanese garden city: its acceptance and development 1906–1942', in T. Saiki, R. Freestone and M. van Rooijen (eds), *New garden city in the 21st century?* (Kobe, 2002), pp. 75–97.

Schaffer, F., *The new town story* (London, 1970).

Scholtz, G.P., *Ebenezer Howard in Nebraska*, paper delivered to the Association of Collegiate Schools of Planning/Association of European Schools of Planning Joint Congress, Oxford Polytechnic, 8–12 July 1991.

Schubert, D., 'Theodor Fritsch and the German (völkische) version of the garden city: the garden city invented two years before Ebenezer Howard', *Planning Perspectives*, 19/1 (2004), pp. 3–35.

Scott Committee, *Report of the committee on land utilisation in rural areas* (Cmd 6378) (London, 1942).

Scott, P., *The triumph of the south: a regional economic history of early twentieth century Britain* (Aldershot, 2007).

Seeley, I.H., *Planned expansion of country towns* (London, 1974).

Sharp, D., *The Kenney papers: a guide*, typescript (Norwich, 2004) <https://www.uea.ac.uk/polopoly_fs/1.76986!the%20kenney%20papers.pdf>, accessed 24 February 2015.

Sharp, T., *Town and countryside: some aspects of urban and rural development* (Oxford, 1932).

Sharp, T., *Town planning* (Harmondsworth, 1940).

Sheail, J., *Rural conservation in interwar Britain* (Oxford, 1981).

Simpson, M., 'Thomas Adams 1971–1940', in G.E. Cherry (ed.), *Pioneers in British planning*, (London, 1981), pp. 19–45.

Simpson, M., *Thomas Adams and the modern town planning movement: Britain, Canada and the United States, 1900–1940* (London, 1985).

Skilleter, K.J., 'The role of public utility societies in early British town planning and housing reform, 1901–36', *Planning Perspectives*, 8/2 (1993), pp. 125–65.

Smith, J., 'Days Mead to Bishops Rise', in A. Burke and M. Corbett with the Boomtime Group, *Voices of Hatfield from the '50s and '60s* (Stroud, 2011), p. 23.

Smith, L., *Garden cities, standard note: SN/SC/6867*. Last updated 31 December 2014 <http://www.google.co.uk/url?sa=tandrct=jandq=andesrc=sandsource=webandcd=5andved=0CDkQFjAEandurl=http%3A%2F%2Fwww.parliament.uk%2Fbriefing-papers%2Fsn06867.pdfandei=hdMCVfryIfC07Qayk4H4Cwandusg=AFQjCNESGeKdh38JINUSR5V8cLosn8rYmAandsig2=anP8rs79TJJiDrGpcGGWSgandbvm=bv.88198703,d.ZGU>, accessed 13 March 2015.

Socialist Unity, '1945 Labour Party Manifesto' <http://socialistunity.com/1945-labour-manifesto/>, accessed 11 November 2014.

Sorensen, A., *The making of urban Japan: cities and planning from Edo to the twenty-first century* (London, 2002).

Spencer, H., *Social statics: or the conditions essential to human happiness specified, and the first of them developed* (Charleston, 2009 [London, 1851]).

Spens, M., 'Obituary: Lionel Brett (4th Viscount Esher)', *The Studio*, 28 August 2004.

Stannage, T., *Lakeside city: the dreaming of Joondalup* (Nedlands, 1996).

Stein, C.S., *Toward new towns for America* (Liverpool, 1951).

Stepanov, V.K., 'Union of Soviet Socialist Republics', in A. Whittick (ed.), *Encyclopaedia of urban planning* (Huntingdon, NY, 1980), p. 1146.

Stephenson, G. and DeMarco, C., *On a human scale: a life in city design* (Perth, 1992).

Stern, R.A.M., Fishman, D. and Tilove, J., *Paradise planned: the garden suburb and the modern city* (New York, 2013), pp. 241–4.

Stevenage Borough Council, 'History of Fairlands Valley Park' <http://www.stevenage.gov.uk/about-stevenage/fairlands-valley-park/28583/>, accessed 27 August 2015.

Stevenage Borough Council, 'Recent improvements' <http://www.stevenage.gov.uk/about-stevenage/fairlands-valley-park/28585/>, accessed 27 August 2015.

Stevenage Borough Council, *Town square conservation appraisal 2010* (Stevenage, 2010).

Stevenage Development Corporation, *Principles proposed for the planning and development of the town centre*, 8 September 1950, HALS, CNT/ST/17/1/14.

Stevenage Development Corporation, *Stevenage master plan 1966 summarised report* (Stevenage, c.1967).

Stokes, E.G., *Basingstoke – expanding town* (Southampton, 1980).

Störtkuhl, B., 'Ernst May and the Schlesische Heimstätte', in C. Quiring, W. Voigt, P. Schmal and E. Herrel (eds), *Ernst May 1886–1970* (Munich, 2011), pp. 32–49.

Strauss, E.F.H., 'Some 1940s memories of Welwyn Garden City' <http://www.ourwelwyngardencity. org.uk/page/some_1940s_memories_of_welwyn_garden_city?path=0p3p>, accessed 20 August 2015.

Sultzbach, T., 'Early residents (i)', in H. Rees and C. Rees (eds), *The history makers: the story of the early days of Stevenage new town* (Stevenage, 1991), pp. 69–74.

Sutcliffe, A., 'Britain's first town planning act: a review of the 1909 achievement', *Town Planning Review*, 59/3 (1988), pp. 289–303.

Swenarton, M., *Artisans and architects: the Ruskinian tradition in architectural thought* (London, 1988).

Taber, U., 'What the people of Hemel Hempstead thought of the new arrivals' <http://www. talkingnewtowns.org.uk/content/towns/hemel-hempstead/una-taber/people-hemel-thought-new-town>, accessed 19 August 2015.

Talking New Towns, 'Hemel Hempstead' <http://www.talkingnewtowns.org.uk/content/category/ towns/hemel-hempstead> accessed 21 October 2015.

Talking New Towns, 'Leonard Vincent' <http://www.talkingnewtowns.org.uk/content/category/ towns/stevenage/leonard-vincent>, accessed 17 August 2015.

Talking New Towns, 'Mrs Galliers is frontline news' <http://www.talkingnewtowns.org.uk/content/ topics/building-communities/mrs-galliers-frontline-news>, accessed 19 August 2015.

Tarn, J.N., *Five per cent philanthropy: an account of housing in urban areas between 1840 and 1914* (Cambridge, 1973).

Taylor, J., 'Cumbernauld: the conception, development, and realisation of a post-war British new town', PhD thesis (University of Edinburgh, 2010).

Taylor, N., 'The mystery of Lord Marley: Nicole Taylor on the trail of an English peer in Stalin's Jewish Autonomous Region', *The Jewish Quarterly*, 198 (2005) <http://www.jewishquarterly. org/issuearchive/article8d4f.html?article id=113>, accessed 21 July 2011.

Taylor, S., 'Sharon Taylor about playing by Aston Brook' <http://www.talkingnewtowns.org.uk/ content/towns/stevenage/sharon-taylor/sharon-taylor-playing-aston-brook>, accessed 19 August 2015.

Tennenbaum, R. (ed.), *Creating a new city: Columbia, Maryland* (Columbia, MD, 1996).

The Galleria, Hatfield <http://www.landsecurities.com/retail-portfolio/retail-property-portfolio/the-galleria>, accessed 19 August 2015.

The Glasgow Story, 'Knightswood Housing' <http://www.theglasgowstory.com/image.php?inum=T GSA00787&t=1&urltp=story.php?id=TGSEA10>, accessed 20 October 2015.

The Irish Network Stevenage (edited by T. Barnes), *From the Emerald Isle to the green belt of Stevenage: an oral history of Irish settlers in Stevenage* (Stevenage, 2013).

'The New Townsmen' [E. Howard, F.J. Osborn, C.B. Purdom, W.G. Taylor], *New towns after the war, an argument for garden cities* (London, 1918).

Thetford's Great Heritage, 'Town expansion and migration' <http://www.thetfordsgreat.org/eras. aspx?age-of--empire>, accessed 20 March 2015.

Thompson, Anthony (dir.), *A home of your own* (Data Films for HHDC, 1951).

Tokyo Metropolitan Government, *A hundred years of Tokyo city planning* (Tokyo, 1994).

Town and Country Planning Association, *New towns and garden cities – lessons for tomorrow. Stage 1: an introduction to the UK's new towns and garden cities, appendix the new towns: five minute fact sheets* (London, 2014).

Tudor Walters Committee, *Report of the committee to consider questions of building construction in connection with the provision of dwellings for the working classes in England and Wales, and Scotland* (Cd 9191) (London, 1918).

Tyrwhitt, J., *Life and work in Welwyn Garden City* (1939) <http://cashewnut.me.uk/WGCbooks/>, accessed 26 August 2014.

Udell, F., 'The builders (i)', in H. Rees and C. Rees (eds), *The history makers: the story of the early days of Stevenage new town* (Stevenage, 1991), pp. 19–20.

University of Hertfordshire, 'History of the University of Hertfordshire' <http://www.herts.ac.uk/about-us/history>, accessed 2 May 2014.

University of Hertfordshire, *The University of Hertfordshire: sixty years of innovation* (Hatfield, 2012).

University of Hertfordshire, *Travel plan update* (Hatfield, 2010).

University of Liverpool Social Science Department, *Population problems of the new estates with special reference to Norris Green* (Liverpool, 1939).

Unwin, R., *Nothing gained by overcrowding! How the garden city type of development may benefit both owner and occupier* (London, 1912).

URBED, *Uxcester garden city: submission for the 2014 Wolfson Economics Prize* (London, 2014).

Uthwatt Committee, *Final report of the Expert Committee on Compensation and Betterment* (Cmd 6386) (London, 1942).

Uthwatt Committee, *Interim report of the Expert Committee on Compensation and Betterment* (Cmd 6291) (London, 1941).

Vadelorge, L., *Retour sur les villes nouvelles: Une histoire urbaine du XXe siècle* (Paris, 2014).

Van der Wal, C., *In praise of common sense: planning the ordinary. A physical planning history of the new towns in the Ijsselmeerpolders* (Rotterdam, 1997).

Van Hoogstraten, D., 'Paris 1965 Schéma Directeur d'Aménagement et d'Urbanisme de la Région de Paris', in K. Bosma and H. Hellinga (eds), *Mastering the city: north-European city planning 1900–2000*, vol. II (Rotterdam, 1997), pp. 324–9.

Vann, J., 'Cooler up the hill', in A. Burke and M. Corbett with the Boomtime Group, *Voices of Hatfield from the '50s and '60s* (Stroud, 2011), p. 21.

Vincent, L., 'Leonard Vincent about building issues: which kind of buildings and which techniques?' <http://www.talkingnewtowns.org.uk/content/topics/developing-a-new-town/7075-leonard-vincent-about-building-issues-which-kind-of-buildings-and-which-techniques>, accessed 17 August 2015.

Vincent, L., 'Leonard Vincent about Stevenage pedestrianised town centre' <http://www.talkingnewtowns.org.uk/content/topics/developing-a-new-town/leonard-vincent-about-stevenage-pedestrianised-town-centre>, accessed 19 August 2015.

Vincent, L., 'Leonard Vincent about traffic, residential areas and cycleways in Stevenage', <http://www.talkingnewtowns.org.uk/content/topics/developing-a-new-town/leonard-vincent-traffic-residential-areas>, accessed 18 August 2015.

Vollerin, A., *Histoire de l'Architecture et de l'Urbanisme à Lyon au XXe Siècle* (Lyon, 1999).

Von Hertzen, H. and Speiregen, P.D., *Building a new town: Finland's new garden city – Tapiola*, revised edn (Cambridge, MA, 1973).

Waddilove, L., *One man's vision* (London, 1954).

Wakefield, E.G., *The art of colonisation* (London, 1849).

Walker, D., *The architecture and planning of Milton Keynes* (London, 1982).

Wall, C., Clarke, L., McGuire, C. and Brockmann, M., *Building a community – construction workers in Stevenage 1950–1970* (London, 2011).

Wallace, A.R., *Land nationalisation: its necessity and its aims, being a comparison of the system of landlord and tenant with that of occupying ownership in their influence on the well-being of the people* (London, 1892).

Wannop, U., 'New towns', in B. Cullingworth (ed.), *British planning: 50 years of urban and regional policy* (London, 1999).

Ward, S.V., 'Consortium Developments Ltd and the failure of new country towns in Mrs Thatcher's Britain', *Planning Perspectives*, 20/3 (2005), pp. 329–59.

Ward, S.V., 'Ebenezer Howard: his life and times', in K.C. Parsons and D. Schuyler (eds), *From garden city to green city: the legacy of Ebenezer Howard* (Baltimore, 2002), pp. 14–37.

Ward, S.V., *The geography of interwar Britain: the state and uneven development* (London, 1988).

Ward, S.V., 'Gordon Stephenson and the "galaxy of talent": planning for post-war reconstruction in Britain 1942–1947', *Town Planning Review*, 83/2 (2012), pp. 279–96.

Ward, S.V., 'Introduction', in E.G. Culpin, *The garden city movement up-to-date* (London, 2015 [reprint edition of 1914 original]).

Ward, S.V., 'New garden cities and the lessons of the past', *Town and Country Planning*, 81/9 (2012), pp. 381–4.

Ward, S.V., *Planning and urban change* (London, 2004).

Ward, S.V., *Planning the twentieth-century city: the advanced capitalist world* (Chichester, 2002).

Ward, S.V., 'Public–private partnerships', in J.B. Cullingworth (ed.), *British planning: 50 years of urban and regional policy* (London, 1999), pp. 232–49.

Ward, S.V., *Selling places: the marketing and promotion of towns and cities 1850–2000* (London, 1998).

Ward, S.V., 'Soviet Communism and the British planning movement: rational learning or Utopian imagining?' *Planning Perspectives*, 27/4 (2012), pp. 499–524.

Ward, S.V., 'Thomas Sharp as a figure in the British planning movement', *Planning Perspectives*, 23/4 (2008), pp. 523–33.

Ward, S.V., 'What did the Germans ever do for us? A century of British learning about and imagining modern town planning', *Planning Perspectives*, 25/2 (2010), pp. 117–40.

Watanabe, S.J., 'The Japanese garden city', in S.V. Ward (ed.), *The garden city: past, present and future* (London, 1992), pp. 69–87.

Waterson, T. and S., 'Thoughts on the new arrivals' <http://www.talkingnewtowns.org.uk/content/topics/attitudes/like-idea-others-moving-hemel-hempstead>, accessed 19 August 2015.

Webber, M.A., 'Planning in an environment of change: part I: beyond the Industrial Age', *Town Planning Review*, 39/3 (1968), pp. 179–95.

Weight, R., 'Silkin, Lewis, first Baron Silkin (1889–1972)', *Oxford dictionary of national biography* (Oxford, 2004); online edn <http://www.oxforddnb.com/view/article/31684>, accessed 6 December 2010.

Weightman, G. and Humphries, S., *The making of modern London 1914–1939* (London, 1984).

Wells, H.W., 'A chartered surveyor looks at Soviet Russia', *The Chartered Surveyor*, 91/7 (1959), pp. 374–81.

Welwyn Garden City Development Corporation, *Welwyn Garden City new town* (Welwyn Garden City, 1961).

Welwyn Garden City Ltd, *The book of Welwyn* (Welwyn Garden City, n.d. *c.*1937).

Welwyn Garden City Ltd, *A selection of admirable detached houses to let and for sale in Sherrards Park, Welwyn Garden City* (Welwyn Garden City, n.d. *c.*1937).

Welwyn Hatfield Borough Council, *Welwyn Garden City Conservation Area appraisal* (Welwyn Garden City, 2007).

Welwyn Hatfield District Council and St Albans City and District Council, *Hatfield Aerodrome: Supplementary Planning Guidance* (Welwyn Garden City, 1999).

White Paper, *Central Scotland: a programme for development and growth* (Cmnd 2288) (London, 1963).

Whittick, A., *F.J.O. – practical idealist: a biography of Sir Frederic Osborn* (London, 1987).

Williams-Ellis, C. (ed.), *Britain and the beast* (London, 1937).

Willis, M., 'Sociological aspects of urban structure: comparison of residential groupings proposed in planning new towns', *Town Planning Review*, 39/4 (1969), pp. 296–306.

Willmott, P., *The evolution of a community: a study of Dagenham after forty years* (London, 1963).

Wills, E., *Livingston: the making of a Scottish new town* (Maidenhead, 1996).

Wilson, H. and Womersley, L., *Skelmersdale new town planning proposals. Report on basic plan*

(Skelmersdale, 1964).

Wrench, J., Brar, H. and Martin, P., *Invisible minorities: racism in new towns and new contexts* (Coventry, 1993).

Wright, K., 'The day I may have met Barbara Cartland!' <http://www.talkingnewtowns.org.uk/content/topics/work/ken-wright-day-may-met-barbara-cartland>, accessed 19 September 2015.

Yelling, J. 'Planning and the land question', *Planning History*, 16/1 (1994), pp. 4–9.

Young, D.F., 'Mitchell, (James) Leslie (1901–1935)', *Oxford dictionary of national biography* (Oxford, 2004); online edn May 2008 <http://www.oxforddnb.com.oxfordbrookes.idm.oclc.org/view/article/38328>, accessed 29 September 2014.

Young, T., *Becontree and Dagenham: a report made for the Pilgrim Trust* (London, 1934).

Welwyn Public Utility Society 107, 109
Welwyn Restaurants Ltd 95–6
Welwyn Rural District Council 90–1, 106–7
Welwyn Stores Ltd 96–7, 123–4, 260
Welwyn Times 96
Welwyn Trades Council 120
Whitehill-Borden, Hampshire 355
Williams, Aneurin 26
Williams, Shirley, 212
Williams-Ellis, Clough 192–4, 196, 270
Willian 37, 66
Wilson, Hugh 298, 303
Wimpey 199, 206, 250, 254–5, 277, 348
Wolfson, Lord 356
Women's Social and Political Union 70
Woodhall, Welwyn Garden City 110, 121–2, 124
Woodhall Farm, Hemel Hempstead 255
Woodlands, Texas, The 328
Wright, Henry 213
Wythenshawe, Manchester 160–5, 306

Zetetical Society 6, 18
Zoetermeer, Netherlands 323

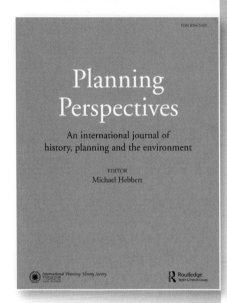